Dr Roy Eskapa lives in
therapy practice.

ROY ESKAPA PhD

Bizarre Sex

·PARRALLEL·

This edition published 1995 for
Parrallel Books
Units 13–17 Avonbridge Industrial Estate
Atlantic Road
Avonmouth, Bristol BS11 9QD
by Diamond Books
77–85 Fulham Palace Road
Hammersmith, London W6 8JB

Published by Grafton Books 1989
First published in Great Britain by
Quartet Books Ltd 1987

ISBN 0 261 66709 2

Set in Baskerville
Printed in Great Britain

To my parents,
Raymond and Shirley Eskapa

Acknowledgements

I would like to thank all those who encouraged me to go ahead with this book. I must acknowledge Ray Anderson, Shawn Johnston, Richard Laws and Sy Zelen for their professional guidance while I was a graduate student at the California School of Professional Psychology, Los Angeles; Les Squier and Allen Neuringer for their 'positive reinforcement' and considered introduction to psychology while I was at Reed College in Oregon.

I deeply acknowledge the positive influence of Arnold Lazarus for his inspiration, clinical genius, fundamental humanity and uplifting sense of humour. I appreciate beyond words the love and constant emotional backing of the following families: Eskapa, Beck, Grosse and Kaye. I would also like to acknowledge Sam Rosen, Lorette Scheiner, Dr M. Panos, Steve Herman, and especially my wife Lisa Kaye.

Finally I would like to acknowledge extracts from the following publications: G. Talese, *Thy Neighbour's Wife*, Collins, 1980; C. Allen, *The Sexual Perversions and Abnormalities*, Oxford University Press, 2nd edn, 1949; E. J. Haeberle, *The Sex Atlas*, Sheldon Press, 1983; J. Bennett, *Sex Signs*, Pan Books, 1981; T. O'Carroll, *Paedophilia: The Radical Case*, Peter Owen, 1980; B. Masters, *Killing for Company*, Jonathan Cape, 1985; J. Cassidy and A. Stewart-Park, *We're Here: Conversations with Lesbian Women*, Quartet Books, 1977; N. Friday, *My Secret Garden*, Virago, Quartet Books, 1975; J. Johnston, 'The Myth of the Myth of the Vaginal

Orgasm', in M. Evans, *The Woman Question*, Fontana Books, 1982; N. Friday, *Men in Love*, Century Hutchinson, 1980; B. Toner, *The Facts of Rape*, Arrow Books, an imprint of Century Hutchinson, 1977; S. Brownmiller, *Against Our Will: Men, Women and Rape*, Simon and Schuster, New York, 1975; A. Phillips and J. Rakusen (eds), *Our Bodies, Ourselves*, Simon and Schuster, New York, 1971; R. Tannahill, *Sex in History*, Hamish Hamilton, 1980; C. D. Tollison and H. E. Adams, *Sexual Disorders*, Gardner Press, New York, 1979; E. Schoenfeld, *Jealousy*, Pinnacle Books, New York, 1979; C. S. Ford and F. A. Beach, *Patterns of Sexual Behaviour*, Harper and Row, New York, 1951; J. Rechy, *City of Night*, Granada, 1965; H. Greenwald and R. Greenwald, *The Sex-Life Letters*, J. P. Tarcher, Los Angeles; A. B. Gerber, *The Book of Sex Lists*, W. H. Allen, 1982; M. Stern and A. Stern, *Sex in the Soviet Union*, W. H. Allen, 1981.

Contents

Preface

In addition to an arduous academic curriculum, most American doctoral programmes in psychology require that students rotate each year through a variety of clinical settings to familiarize themselves with a wide range of patients. In my case, we were often at the mercy of a lottery system when it came to the choice of an internship; a poor lottery number meant fewer good clinics and mental facilities from which to choose. The lottery system did not operate during the first year, and most of us were assigned to work in a child-guidance clinic in the Los Angeles area. I spent my first year in graduate school working with severely disturbed children – victims of indescribable child abuse, brain damage and psychotic disorders.

During the second year, I was fortunate enough to draw a good lottery number and had the choice of several excellent hospitals and clinics to work in. I took an internship in a community mental health agency, where I worked with adults suffering depressions, phobias and schizophrenia, and facilitated an inspiring group for blind old people. I drew a mediocre lottery number in the third year, but still managed to secure an excellent internship treating disturbed families and doing marital and group therapy. Until this point I had been exposed to ordinary mental suffering – patients who had not broken the law.

I was not at all happy about drawing a poor lottery number at the final stage of the doctoral programme. After all, I had begun research for a dissertation on the phobic patients I had worked with before, and would no longer have as much access to them. In the spring of 1981, I reluctantly set out for an interview to intern at a small outpatient clinic without knowing anything about its clientele. I was dismayed.

The clinic serviced an entirely different group of patients, *social undesirables* who had unmistakably run foul of the law. Most of them were especially hated by society because they were *sex offenders*, dreaded felons who had broken their social contracts by sexually molesting innocent children, exposing themselves in public, raping, and even murdering others for their own sexual kicks. I could see now why there were so few takers among my fellow students – no one, however dedicated and compassionate, really wanted to work with the scum of the earth.

I arrived for the interview and was given a warm welcome: 'Hello, Roy! Good to see you again.' I recognized my interviewer instantly. He already had his PhD in social psychology and had recently completed one year as a doctoral retainee in applied psychology at our graduate school. He had stood out in class, not just because he was highly articulate, but because he had not permitted his almost total blindness to hinder him.

'We cannot offer you much of a stipend. In fact, I'm pretty sure we cannot offer you anything in the way of money. We're non-profit. But we can offer you the most incredible population to work with.'

It transpired that he was not understating anything.

My interviewer proceeded to explain that, while the practice dealt mainly with sex offenders, a group I knew little about, it also took on adolescents with criminal records. He did not beat about the bush.

'This is our new sex booth. It was built by a patient in exchange for treatment. Have a look. You'll see how private it is. The strain gauge should be about here.'

He fumbled around, but soon found the strain gauge, a

rubber device filled with mercury which, when slipped over the penis, measures erection levels if connected to a machine called a plethysmograph. He went on to explain the workings of the strange machine.

'The technician sits outside the booth and is able to show the patient slides and videotapes of sexually explicit matter. Erection levels to various materials – rape scenes, child molestation, consenting adult sex, and many other forms of human sexual behaviour – are recorded and *compared* with each other. It is far more powerful than simply psychological testing, which, of course, we still use. This is about as close to *hard science* as psychology will ever come. And when we testify in court we can objectively tell the judges that we have improved the validity and reliability of our court reports. At least, so far as sex offenders go.' The whole thing sounded bizarre. His detached objectivity struck me as macabre. People came to this clinic because they had fallen sexually in love with children and acted on these impulses. They came because they had exposed themselves in public for the purpose of offending others. They came because they derived sexual satisfaction out of cruelty to others. They came because they were 'flashers', 'sexual perverts', 'deviants' and felons. And *I* was supposed to treat *them*?

My initial feelings were a mixture of horror and intrigue. I felt both challenged and fascinated. I was heartened to hear that I could expect positive results to be forthcoming in some cases, because many sex offenders, impelled by the social stigma of being labelled Mentally Disordered Sex Offenders (MDSOs) by the state, and by the public realization of their deviance, *wanted to change*. At least, according to my interviewer. Still, I was nauseated by the gravity of some of the crimes. Some patients had raped, some had murdered, children – and *they* would be coming, under armed guard, for pre-trial psychological assessments at the request of their defence counsel. Others would be out on bail, and if they progressed well in treatment might receive a more favourable sentence at trial. I was assured that a sizeable percentage of patients were self-referred, people who had offended but had not yet been caught.

I was also impressed by the idea of working in forensic psychology, the sheer interface of psychology and the law, and the fact that my patients would not be confined to sex offenders. I would work with everything from a brilliant young computer hacker guilty of wirefraud to shoplifters, and I would have the opportunity to work on court reports, do group therapy and individual psychotherapy, and develop behaviour therapy strategies to assess and modify undesirable sexual behaviours. I was equally fascinated to know that several women attended the clinic because they were sex offenders.

'If you can guarantee now that you will show up the first week in September, I'll reserve an internship for you right now. We'd really like to have you on board, and I'm sure we could use your previous experience with behaviour and group therapy.'

Just then, the senior psychologist came into the room. We were introduced and he quickly explained that there would be wide scope to conduct original dissertation research through the clinic itself, because there was an excellent liaison between the clinic and a major state psychiatric hospital. I thanked him very much and explained that I was already working on a dissertation with agoraphobics. But I accepted the post, not only because I did not want the alternative, a huge bureaucratic and inefficient psychiatric hospital system, but because these two psychologists appeared enthusiastic, dedicated and knowledgeable. I intuitively knew that I would learn a great deal from them.

I had no inkling that I was destined to become so

involved with this bizarre group of patients and to change the topic of my PhD dissertation from phobias to paedophilia (child molesting). I had even less warning that I would become so intrigued, puzzled and horrified by these aspects of human sexuality to realize that I would want to learn more about the history, politics and psychology of human sexuality. I certainly had no idea, at the time when I joined the clinic, that I would contemplate writing a work called *Bizarre Sex* a few years later.

WHAT IS 'BIZARRE SEX'?

Friends and acquaintances were quizzical as they asked, 'What's bizarre sex? Isn't it purely subjective? How can you judge what bizarre sex is?'

'You're entirely correct,' I would answer. 'Of course it's subjective. I'm writing about practices, attitudes and beliefs about sex which *I* consider bizarre, unusual, outlandish, extreme, monstrous, whimsical and unbelievable. The millions of African and Islamic women who undergo ritual circumcision, the surgical removal of their clitorides and vaginal labia without anaesthesia, might think *me* bizarre for considering *their* ritual bizarre.'

It is perfectly true that so-called primitive peoples might think me bizarre because I find their beliefs and superstitions about genitalia and menstrual blood bizarre. Even though I have always opposed oppression, militant feminists may see me as another manifestation of outlandish chauvinism for citing their beliefs and practices as bizarre. Rapists who enjoy rape, and sadists who conduct sexual killings for pleasure, might consider me 'abnormal' for finding their practices bizarre and cruel. And the same might be said of exhibitionists, polygamists, voyeurs, incest offenders, child molesters and acrotomophiliacs, coprophagics and pantagamists. I make no apology for being subjective simply because I am as biased against oppression as I am against bigotry.

I have taken a stand against the oppression of homosexuals and people who choose different sexual lifestyles. I am biased in favour of women's rights. I have been as clear about my opposition to Freudian psychoanalysis as I have about infanticide. In some cases, I simply state the facts that comprise sex where it merges into the bizarre.

Most readers will find the contents of this book a mixture of the bizarre and serious; of the humorous and absurd; of the horrible and unspeakably grotesque. Its subject matter is wide. It deals with matters ranging from the white slave trade to gurus who advocate ultimate orgasm as a means of reaching God and obtaining spiritual enlightenment. It describes sordid sexual crimes during war and peace, political groups who advocate the legalization of child molestation, women who commit rape, strange historical attitudes towards menstruation, birth control, virginity, sexual positions and prostitution. It focuses on sado-masochism, battered husbands, pornography and weird, oppressive sex laws.

Bizarre Sex covers the absurd and the obscene, the sublime and the ridiculous. For instance, it includes several interesting case histories ranging from a drunk Russian militiaman who directed traffic with his penis to Dennis Nilsen who was sentenced after murdering fifteen young men for sexual delight. It highlights the pornography industry, and even the blatant sexual cruelty in the Bible. Homosexuality and gender identity are discussed – not because they are bizarre in themselves, but because they constitute an oppressed group.

The research for *Bizarre Sex* took me along countless labyrinthine and dark passages of human behaviour. I discovered aspects of human conduct I had never even contemplated, and although this book is not for the squeamish, it may be that some readers will conclude that what they had considered to be banal is, in fact, bizarre.

PART ONE
Sexual Fascism

Introduction

This chapter focuses on sexual slavery, sexism, birth control, chastity, virginity and abstinence, and prostitution. At first these may seem like an unconnected, somewhat odd conglomeration of topics to link together. After all, what does the ownership of women have in common with their virginity? What possible connection could there be between the sale of one's body for sexual purposes and abstinence? What does the reverse sexism of militant feminists have in common with infanticide or with those who oppose abortion? These areas are linked precisely because they represent oppressively cruel beliefs and practices in the course of human sexual affairs.

The term **sexual fascism** covers the ways in which sexual conduct has been, and still is, dictated by those in power. It is well established that totalitarianism, secular or religious, corrupts mercilessly. Sexual fascism is another form of totalitarianism, and it stretches across a wide spectrum of human affairs. It involves everything from outright greed to religious dogma and the absolute subjugation and control of others. Since enough material exists to make a book out of each section, it has been necessary to be selective and to choose only those points which highlight each area.

The second part of this chapter, looking at other aspects of sexual fascism, will focus primarily on ways in which the body is stigmatized among various cultures. Genitalia may, for example, be permanently mutilated through circumcision and immense guilt be induced over the biological processes of masturbation and menstruation. Certain beliefs about sexual positions and the shape and size of genitalia can also portray an oppressive stigmatization of the body. Once again, it has been essential to be selective with the points chosen.

1

The Chains of Culture

1 SEXUAL SLAVERY

'White slavery was to a large extent a fiction of lady novelists
... But in America, San Francisco's Chinese women had
been slaves, in every sense, since the 1850s, while towards
the end of the century procurers began to entice women into
the country from Poland, Ireland, Puerto Rico and Cuba
and use their dependence to force them into prostitution. By
1900 it was big business, with an estimated 50,000 procurers
and ponces making a living from it.' – Reay Tannahill (1980)

Slavery and **sexual slavery** are probably as ancient as
thought. The two things are intrinsically bound together,
slavery traditionally implying the total subjugation of
another person's will and the right to use their body as one
would a work-animal, pet or toy object. Slaves were traded
or acquired via conquest, and any children they bore were
born into slavery. The Greek poet, Homer, was one of the
first to record that most slaves were women – the wives and
daughters of soldiers killed in battle.

Sexual slavery or 'white slavery' ranges from highly
organized trafficking of a few thousand Indian girls for use
in Middle Eastern harems to the kidnapping and sexual
enslavement of hitch-hikers in California. Sexual slavery
includes the simple pimp, who may have only two prostitutes working for him, the importation of oriental girls into
the United States to work as domestics, and, in many parts
of Africa, the sale of brides.

In an extensive study on sexual slavery, Kathleen Barry

(1979) described a slave auction in 1970 on the island of Zanzibar, off the coast of East Africa. Slave auctions were *officially* sanctioned until the revolution in 1964, when the island became an independent nation. This particular slave auction was reported by a businessman who was developing a factory on the island: 'There were about 30 or 40 men and women milling around the way cattle do. They didn't look well fed. There was no obvious bidding ... The purchasers were of Middle Eastern extraction, most of them Arabs.' This businessman passed his initiation test. By remaining silent, he proved to the ruling business class that he could be trusted. Many of the girls had been abducted while on vacation; they seemed to be drugged and had not been given any change of clothing. Prices ranged up to $10,000 – inexpensive compared to the price for an average race-horse. Over 80 per cent of the girls were destined for Middle Eastern harems.

In 1970, Vice-President Karume of Zanzibar sanctioned the forced marriage of four Indian girls to high-ranking government officials. The girls were dragged at gunpoint from their homes, in full view of their parents, and brought before the Revolutionary Council. The London-based Anti-Slavery Society, still active today, reported that all efforts to have the girls released proved futile. Fortunately, in 1973, three of the girls managed to escape their captors and gave evidence about their torture and abuse while in captivity. The plight of Nasreen Hussein, the one girl who remained in captivity, was taken to the United Nations Human Rights Commission. Despite the efforts of Nasreen's father, of Colonel Patrick Montgomery of the Anti-Slavery Society, and of the United Nations itself, Nasreen has never been traced. In 1976, she managed to get a letter to her family saying that she wanted her freedom despite the Attorney General of Zanzibar's contention that she was happily married. President Julius Nyerere of Tanzania, although in a position of influence, deliberately made no attempt to secure Nasreen's release. Zanzibar refused Nasreen's parents a visa to visit their daughter despite an appeal by Amnesty International. As Kathleen Barry points out, the United Nations effectively sanctioned Julius Nyerere's stand on the issue by *not* condemning it: 'Diplomacy at this level is reduced to a conspiratorial brotherhood.' Of the 23,000 complaints of human rights violations presented to the United Nations in 1973, only eight were taken up, Nasreen Hussein's being one of them.

Although INTERPOL suppresses the information it has on the slave trafficking of humans, it did finally release some data in 1974. The information was supplied by countries which had answered a questionnaire about the rates of prosecution and conviction for slave trafficking. The figures, however, represented only a minute fraction of the extent of this practice. The following official INTERPOL figures are summarized from Barry (1979), a comprehensive, well-researched and original book. These figures by no means present the complete picture since the reporting countries do not give the full details, even where they are signatories to the Convention for the Suppression of the Traffic in Persons and of the Exploitation or the Prostitution of Others.

Argentina: Recorded four instances of traffic in women brought before its courts. Sixteen of the thirty-one individuals involved were women.

France: Seventy-five incidents of traffic in women came before the courts between 1965 and March 1973. 'Disguised traffic', or ostensibly hiring women in foreign countries to work in France under false pretext, involved about 1,000 women. Well over a hundred people were implicated.

Hong Kong: Eighteen people were convicted for traffic in women betwwen 1965 and 1971. Most of the women were 'recruited' from Thailand and the Philippines to work as prostitutes.

Luxemburg: Twenty-five instances reported involving the trafficking of 286 women between 1965 and 1973, with thirty-eight persons implicated. Because of a lack of evidence, forty-seven other cases were dropped.

Mexico: Five people were prosecuted for trading in women between 1969 and 1972.

Nepal: Forty-one recorded cases of traffic in women between 1965 and 1972.

Spain: Eighteen reported cases since 1965, with forty-four persons involved. The women originated from Australia, Liberia, Japan, Morocco, Mexico and the Middle East.

United States: Reported eight cases where prosecutions were made against individuals who hired foreigners for 'immoral purposes'.

An Indian reporter for the *Indian Express* described in 1981 how he purchased a woman: 'Yesterday I bought a short-statured skinny woman . . . for 2,300 rupees [$200], about half the price of a head of cattle!' Similar forms of slavery continue unabated in Mali, Afghanistan, Algeria (where girls are sold for as little as $50), Chad, Colombia (where the entire Andoke Indian tribe was reported as being in debt bondage to one rubber plantation owner), Honduras, Guinea, Guatemala, Ivory Coast and Thailand (where girls aged ten to fourteen fetch $50 to $100 a head, with $500 for a certified virgin).

According to the United Nations, an Ache Indian can be purchased in Paraguay for a lump sum of $2. The sex slaves in Paraguay are procured from the countryside and are usually sold by poverty-stricken parents who are told that the child will be given work in the city. Most of these children end up working for brothels and 90 per cent of them are aged between fifteen and eighteen.

Another opportunity afforded to Europeans is that of purchasing wives in Thailand. Men who respond to advertisements offering 'sex-marriage tours' are often – deservedly – taken for a ride: their $2,000 or $3,000 are handed over and the 'merchandise' never materializes. In Hong Kong, in 1975, over a hundred filed complaints with the police after buying Thai brides, sometimes paying $1,000, the brides having disappeared after the marriage ceremony.

In Europe and America, it is not uncommon for pimps to sell their stock. The women they control are usually initially intimidated into being prostitutes through threats of being beaten up, sexually abused or blackmailed. The pimp is highly adept at offering initial love and sympathy to young girls who have run away from abusive homes. These vulnerable girls are then subjected to the 'hot-cold' treatment, which involves the pimp alternating between showing affection and deliberate mistreatment. This often has the effect of setting the stage for a powerful psychological bonding in which the girl 'identifies with her aggressor', sometimes to the point of falling pathologically 'in love' with him.

Identification with the aggressor frequently happens in war-time, where one person gains total power over the life of another. Some of the clearest examples of this occurred in Nazi Germany. Jews, gipsies and other 'undesirables' enslaved in concentration camps were at the perpetual mercy of their captors, who demanded, among other things, the sexual obedience of the inmates. Besides being efficient and productive at murder, the Nazis also excelled at the sexual use of enslaved children, both boys and girls, who were often tortured to death in 'sexual play'. In *The Scourge of the Swastika*, Lord Russell of Liverpool (1954) illustrates this aspect of German tyranny. Even though there was an injunction against the rape of Jewish women by soldiers of the Third Reich – on the grounds of 'race defilement' and 'racial purity' – no directive existed banning the sexual torture of Jewish and gipsy women and children, who were the legal property of the Third Reich. Officers and camp guards could 'get around the problem' of breaking race laws so long as they murdered them. In this way, they could ensure that no racially inferior offspring were produced. In the concentration and extermination camps, sexual torture involved such medical 'experimentation' as impregnating women and later 'surgically' opening them up without anaesthetic simply to see how the foetus was 'getting on'. *Children were also made to have sex with their captors before being genitally mutilated and gassed to death, and mothers and fathers were sometimes made to watch.*

Since the ancient Babylonians, countless nations have used sexual slaves, and the Germans were by no means the sole exploiters of sexual slaves during the Second World War. For instance, it is remarkable that, after its defeat, the government of Japan appealed to the country's prostitutes to make themselves available as 'comfort girls' to 'sex-starved' American soldiers. The State Minister without Portfolio, Konoe Fumimaro, offered 50 million yen to help to pay these women, who were seen as 'protectors' of the 40 million 'respectable' Japanese women. Remembering their own plunder and rape in the Chinese town of Nanking, perhaps the Japanese thought that rape during war was normal, a right of victors.

One of the more insidious forms of sexual slavery occurs

in prisons. In American prisons, the younger, weaker and less aggressive inmate will tend to 'become the property' of a more dominant male, who will 'rent' him out to other prisoners for favours. The sexual intercourse in this social setting, between prostitute, pimp and other inmates, usually takes the form of homosexual rape. For maximum profit, the victim may have to undergo a gang rape so that 'customers' may be serviced as rapidly as possible.

Mikhail and August Stern (1981) report that, in Soviet penal camps for women, 'There are the *zavoditeli*, the "ringleaders", the equivalent of the kingpins and active homosexuals in the men's camps, and the *skobniki*, the "scrapers", who masturbate their companions. Most often they make a career of it and earn considerable sums in that way.' The main difference between men's and women's prisons seems to be that, among females, there does not appear to be much sexual slavery; the women become prostitutes to each other more out of 'choice' than coercion. Soviet prisons are similar to American ones in that the owned male (pederast) 'is chosen by force from the beginning by the active homosexual, and becomes his slave, both sexually and in the performance of everyday tasks' (Stern and Stern, 1981).

2 SEXISM

Sexism, a term generally referring to the sexual oppression of women, occurs almost everywhere in every society. It has been fought by feminists for decades, but, ironically, it has also come to embrace the attitudes of certain radical feminists who, by virtue of their extreme dogmatic and zealous beliefs, are guilty of precisely the same type of prejudice which they so ardently oppose.

SEXISM IN JUDAEO-CHRISTIAN TRADITION

In Judaeo-Christian tradition, sexism starts with creation – with Adam and Eve. It was Eve who gave way to temptation and then corrupted Adam:

> And when the woman saw that the tree was good food, and it was pleasant to the eyes, and a tree to be desired to make one wise, she took the fruit thereof, and did eat, and gave also unto her husband with her and he did eat. And the eyes of both of them were opened, and they knew they were naked; and they sewed the fig leaves together, and made themselves aprons. [Genesis 3:6–7]

Since pre-biblical times, Eve and her sisters have suffered immeasurably.

When they pray each morning, religious Jewish men thank God for having created them as men. Religious Jewish women, who are not permitted to be seen by the men during prayer, thank God for 'making me according to Thy will'. When praying in synagogue, Orthodox Jews keep the women behind a certain so that the men are not tempted to watch them and so take their minds off God. And even as Catholic women cannot become priests, neither can Orthodox Jewish women become rabbis. The physical separation is carried to extremes among certain sects. For instance, some Orthodox Jews who work in the diamond district in New York City travel to work on a bus in which the men and women are separated by a curtain down the middle. Yet sexism in Judaism pales by comparison with its existence in several other cultures.

SEXISM IN CHINESE TRADITION

The Imperial Chinese, who would have agreed with Christian ideals of what constituted a good wife, bound the feet of aristocratic female infants because small feet were considered beautiful. This had the effect of crippling adult women while also making them totally *dependent on the males*. But, as Andrea Dworkin (1976) says, poor women had their feet bound less severely because they were still required to work: 'But the woman who was the wife of a rich man was immobilized; her feet were reduced to stumps so that she was utterly useless, except as a fuck and a breeder. The degree of her uselessness signified the degree of his wealth.'

Lady Pan Chao, who died in A.D. 166, was one of the first Chinese historians. It was unusual for women to be literate in those times, and her literacy placed her in a sort of honorary 'masculine' position. Therefore she advocated the sedate, servile and supine qualities of women, who should be 'chaste and orderly', concerned with

spinning and weaving, to shun jest and laughter, to be neat in preparing food and wine for the guests . . . She must not listen to lewd talk, nor look at unseemly things; inside the house she should not look slovenly, or outside the house be extravagantly made up; she should not mix with crowds, nor spy through windows. [Quoted in Tannahill, 1980]

In a nation of 'foot fetishists', women could hardly be expected to have any say in public affairs. The Confucians disapproved of physical contact between husband and wife or female slaves to the extent where women had to hand objects to their men on bamboo trays. Ideas of contamination were extreme enough to require the sexes to hang their clothes on different hooks and to use different well water. Like the Hindus in India, women defined themselves through their husbands. However, unlike Hindu women, who mounted the funeral pyre in the act of *suttee* (throwing themselves into the flames to join the deceased husband), the Chinese widow was simply known as 'one who is waiting for death' (Tannahill, 1980).

SEXISM IN ENGLISH SOCIETY

Eighteenth-century England seems to have become a nation of patriarchal 'corset fetishists'. According to Laurence Stone (1979), young women were at this time prized for their narrow waists, pallid complexion and mild manners. Wealthy girls were sent to finishing schools, where they were taught such virtues as proper posture, walking, table manners, and were given purges and enemas 'to maintain a fashionably pallid complexion'. The girls were underfed and corseted, often to the most bizarre excess. William Law, who wrote a handbook on the upbringing of children (reprinted ten times between 1729 and 1772), reported a case of a mother who placed her daughters in such tight corsets that one of them died. The autopsy revealed that 'her ribs had grown into her liver, and that her other entrails were much hurt by being crushed together with her stays, which her mother had ordered to be twitched so straight that it often brought tears into her eyes whilst the maid was dressing her'. The object of such physical restraints was, much like orthodontic practices today, to make the girl more alluring to potential husbands. Children who stooped were required to wear irons in addition to corsets. Stone quotes Lucy Aikin, who wrote:

There were back-boards, iron collars, stocks for the feet, and a frightful kind of neck-swing in which we were suspended every morning, whilst one of the teachers was lacing our stays, all which contrivances were intended and imagined to improve the figure and the air. Nothing was thought so awkward and vulgar as anything approaching to a stoop. 'Hold up your head, Miss', was the constant cry. I wonder any of us kept our health.

SEXISM IN ISLAMIC TRADITION

As recently as 1983, female students in Iran were instructed by Ayatollah Khomeini that, in addition to not being seen, they should also not be heard. Iranian classrooms are divided by curtains so that members of each sex cannot see each other. Women may ask questions only by handwritten note, whereas men are permitted to engage the instructor in discussion. Students are taught that women are 'both weak and dangerous' and tempters of men, and are to be controlled for their own good.

Male control over Iranian women is enshrined in law. For instance, a woman requires her husband's written permission to leave the country. Furthermore, children remain the property of the man. In one case, an American woman married to an Iranian returned to Iran with her young daughter, ostensibly on a three-week visit. When her husband became physically abusive and declared that he would not allow her to return to the United States, she sought help from the Swiss Embassy. The Swiss declined any help since a child was involved. Despondent, the woman returned with her child to her husband. He proceeded to lock her up in a room at home and kept her away from their daughter for several months. The husband finally relented enough to allow his wife to see her child. However, he refused to allow her to leave. She then met people who helped with an escape on the condition that she send them $10,000 on her arrival in America. After a treacherous journey over mountains in sub-zero temperatures, mother and daughter managed to escape to Turkey. The three-week vacation had turned into a year's incarceration in fundamentalist Iran.

A woman's first duty in Islam is to provide her husband with a son. She must not be a sexual being. She is not allowed to have a clitoris. She must always walk behind her husband. She must wear a black veil or *chador* so that her face cannot be seen; for, as it is written in the Koran (Sura XXIV: 31), 'Tell the believing women to lower their gaze and be modest, and to draw their veils over their bosoms . . .' It is usually *the woman's responsibility if she is raped*. In 1977, in Saudi Arabia, after a German woman was raped by two men, the judge ordered her to be publicly flogged 'as an accomplice to immorality' (Laffin, 1979). And even as it endorses slavery, so Koranic law permits men to *own* up to four wives. It is very easy, moreover, for a man to get a divorce. All he has to do is to say, 'I divorce thee' the prescribed number of times and he will no longer be married. According to Janssen-Jurreit (1982), a number of Arab societies require a mother who wants to nurse the child of another woman to ask her husband for permission since *he legally owns her milk*. An old Arabic saying explains that 'the straightest woman is as twisted as a sickle' (Bryant, 1982).

SEXISM, SCIENCE AND PSYCHIATRY

Post-Darwinian science was able to show that the average woman had a 'smaller' brain than the average man, this fact being taken to indicate that women were academically and physically inferior to men. Small wonder if few women became great mathematicians, musicians, composers, artists, writers or athletes. Of course, little was made of the countervailing fact that women's brains are *proportionally heavier* than men's brains by 6 per cent in relation to overall body size (Jones, 1980). In 1984, Paul Albrecht informed an audience of German anthropologists at Breslau that, since females are more 'hirsute', have more powerful inner incisors, and different dorsal vertebrae, they come biologically closer to the ape.

Since its inception, the psychiatric profession has tended to emphasize the inferiority of women. Husbands began 'putting their wives away' as early as the mid-sixteenth century. In France, the first lunatic asylum, the Salpêtrière, had, by the seventeenth century, special wards to house prostitutes, pregnant and poor women. Freud thought up the idea of 'castration anxiety' and 'penis envy' to explain a long list of mental disorders. Essentially, Freud said that women could not consciously accept the fact that they felt castrated and that they 'have the hope of someday obtaining a penis in spite of everything . . .' Freud believed that women subscribe to different morals, have 'weaker social interests', and are generally inferior to men. Freud also thought that well-adjusted women, those who had resolved their penis-envy conflicts from early childhood, would accept a passive, inferior social position. Furthermore, lesbianism was explained by suggesting that women who continued unconsciously to desire a penis would become lesbians. And those seductive women, the *femmes fatales* who set out to conquer men only to reject them later, are described by Freudians as having a deep-seated hatred for men, a desire to castrate those who *do* have external genitalia; the rejection is a form of unconscious revenge against men. For his part, Carl Jung wrote that women who take up 'a masculine calling, studying and working in a man's way, [are] doing something not wholly in agreement with, if not directly injurious to, [their] feminine nature'.

CONJUGAL CORPORAL PUNISHMENT

In such traditional South African tribes as the Sotho, Xhosa and Zulu, wife-beating was the norm. In urban areas, the practice is less common for fear of legal reprisals, but, as in most parts of the world, men are prone to beat their wives after drinking. In north-western Brazil, the Yanomamos blow darts into a wife's buttocks or burn her with a hot piece of wood if she has failed to prepare a meal. A husband's right to administer corporal punishment existed in Europe until the end of the nineteenth century, and legal wife-beating occurred, for example, in England,

France and Germany. It was reported in 1853 that an Englishman could beat his wife for disobedience as long as he did not mutilate her, the penalty for mutilation being £5 sterling. In a five-volume document on Bavarian provincial law, published between 1757 and 1768, a legal scholar, Baron Wigulaus Xaverius Kreitmayr, stated that 'the right to corporal punishment with words as well as deeds is also an *effectus potestatis maritalis* and is founded partially in *Jure Divino* itself' (Janssen-Jurreit, 1982). Wife-beating was recognized in Germanic village law, which decreed that a husband's *Munt* or guardianship over his wife included the right to administer corporal punishment.

Corporal punishment is enshrined in Islamic law. The Koran permits corporal punishment of a woman so long as it does not damage her health. Corporal punishment was incorporated in the legislation of many Islamic countries when they became independent, and it is only in the last twenty or thirty years that wife-beating has been illegal in the 'developed countries'. This does not seem so surprising in the light of the fact that very few countries worldwide have as yet outlawed the beating of children. (Sweden, as one of the exceptions, has outlawed beating children, even if they are your own, but at the moment of writing, corporal punishment is still entirely legal in schools in 'civilized' England; a matter which currently rests before the European Court of Human Rights.) Prime Minister Sato of Japan, a Nobel Prize winner, is on record as having stated that he is proud to have beaten his wife on several occasions. The history of battered women is universal, tragic and unabating.

SEXISM IN DEVELOPED COUNTRIES

There is one Swiss canton where women are still denied the right to vote. The men, supported by many women, consistently vote against women's suffrage. Married women in

France were only very recently allowed to maintain their own private current accounts; they could not operate a bank account without the consent of their husbands.

Women do not have the same status in law as men in many societies. This is so even in the United States, where, for many reasons, both positive and negative, the Equal Rights Amendment (a legal amendment simply stating that men and women are equal) has never been ratified. In most countries, the average income for most women is still less than that for most men, even where they do the same work. According to United Nations figures, women perform two thirds of the world's work for 10 per cent of the world's wages and own a mere 1 per cent of the world's property.

REVERSE SEXISM OF MILITANT FEMINISTS

Some feminists are positively sexist. Jill Johnston (1982) shows herself, in *Lesbian Nation: the Feminist Solution*, to be among those who epitomize reverse discrimination. Her tone is bizarre and pedantic, while her revolutionary crusade against men and the thrust of her attack all smack of fascism:

> The man retains the prime organ of invasion. Sexual congress between man and woman is an invasion of the woman, the woman doesn't get anything up to participate in this congress, and although a woman may be conditioned to believe that she enjoys this invasion and may in fact grow to like it if her male partner makes rare sacrifices of consideration in technical know-how, she remains the passive receptive hopeful half of a situation that was unequal from the start. The fate that woman has to resign herself to is the knowledge of this biological inequity.

She continues with such statements as:

> Feminism at heart is a massive complaint. Lesbianism is the solution ... Until all women are lesbians there will be no true

political revolution . . . Feminists who still sleep with the man are delivering their most vital energies to the oppressor . . . Feminists could begin by realizing that not only do they not need a penis to achieve their supreme satisfaction, but they could do better without one since the timing involving the essential stimulation of the outer tissues prior to and/or concomitant with penetration requires a penis that can be erect for entry at a more or less precise moment in the progress toward climax.

The Leeds Revolutionary Feminist Group (see Evans, 1982) expresses a viewpoint which embodies some of the most vehement and absolute hatred of men combined with disgust and revulsion. The group asks women to regain 'equality' by avoiding all sexual contact with men. Instead, women should have sex with each other. Jill Johnston (1974) writes that the 'lesbian woman is not equipped to oppress her own kind'. Furthermore, the group indicates that, by virtue of being a lesbian, the newly liberated woman 'doesn't need any artificial substitute for the instrument of oppression [presumably the penis] to give herself that pleasure'. The Leeds Revolutionary Feminist Group believe that: 'Penetration is a symbolic act of oppression because it is the oppressor [man] who enters the body of the oppressed.'

To liberated women who say that they feel that their boyfriends are not penetrating them but rather that it is the other way about and they are enveloping the penis with their vaginas, the Leeds Revolutionary Feminists simply say: 'A rose is a rose and so is penetration', any act of penetration being tantamount to 'rape'. Women should, in their view, give up sexual intercourse with men even though they may like 'fucking'. Women who do not wish to give up 'fucking' (and that is all they can do, since it is inconceivable that men might even make *love* to women) are not really taking their sexual politics seriously. Women are advised to become lesbians also on the grounds that they

will then know that they are 'not directly servicing men'
and can live 'without the strain of a glaring contradiction
... uniting the personal and the political, loving and
putting [their] energies into those [they] are fighting alongside rather than those [they] are fighting against'. Finally,
women should use only the sperm of male homosexuals to
reproduce the species. If the resulting baby is male, it is to
be given up for adoption.

Extreme reverse sexism can take on tones that are more
sordid, perverse and bizarre than these. In 1967, Valerie
Solanas (1983) wrote the *SCUM Manifesto* and distributed
copies on the streets of New York City, SCUM being the
acronym for Society to Cut Up Men. When the Matriarchy
Study Group in London re-released the *SCUM Manifesto* in
1983, they reported that Ms Solanas had followed through
with her manifesto by shooting Andy Warhol. He survived
the attempt on his life, while Ms Solanas was sent for
psychiatric evaluation to Elmhurst Hospital in New York.
Since then nothing has been heard of her. Here are some of
her graphic sentiments about men.

To be male is to be deficient, emotionally limited; maleness is
a deficiency disease and males are emotional cripples ...

The [male] is a half dead, unresponsive lump, incapable of
giving or receiving pleasure or happiness; consequently, he is at
best an utter bore, an inoffensive blob, since only those capable of
absorption in others can be charming ...

... obsessed with screwing; he'll swim a river of snot, wade
nostril-deep through a mile of vomit, if he thinks there'll be a
friendly pussy awaiting him ...

... women don't have penis envy; men have pussy envy ...

... Every man deep down, knows he's a worthless piece of
shit ...

Once SCUM has gained ultimate control over the United States, it intends, according to the manifesto, to help men by conducting 'Turd Sessions' at which every male present will make a speech beginning with the sentence: 'I am a turd, a lowly, abject turd', and then proceed to list all the ways in which he is. His reward for doing this will be the opportunity after the session to fraternize for a whole solid hour with the SCUM members present.

SCUM will keep on destroying, looting, fucking-up and killing until the money-work system no longer exists and automation is completely instituted . . .

After the elimination of money there will be no further need to kill men; they will be stripped of the only power they have over psychologically independent females . . .

The Matriarchy Study Group affirms that, if Valerie Solanas cannot be found, the royalties accumulated from her book 'will be used to promote her ideas'. The cover of the reissued *SCUM Manifesto* is fittingly decorated with razor blades, and all this in 1983.

SEXISM: ADULTERY, FORNICATION AND BIGAMY

Roman and Jewish law initially decreed that adultery could only occur if the woman involved was married. It did not matter whether the man was married or single. Early settlers in New England treated men and women equally in terms of punishment for 'fornication' (pre-marital sex) and 'adultery' (extra-marital sex). Jones's (1981) research shows that men and women found guilty of adultery were both 'stripped to the waist and whipped in public an equal number of lashes, or both were fined or sent to the gallows'. She cites an incident in 1643 in which James Britton confessed to having sexual relations with eighteen-year-old

Mary Latham. Since both had 'sinned', both were executed. Lesser punishments for 'fornicating' with someone other than a spouse could incur time spent pilloried or in the stocks. Some offenders were lashed to a cart and publicly whipped as it was drawn through the town's streets. Other cases resulted in burning at the stake and forced drowning in Virginia . . .

There were no statutes in England to make adultery a criminal offence, adultery being seen as largely a matter for the Church to deal with. However, cuckolds could file civil suits against disloyal wives. It was the Commonwealth Act of 1650 which made adultery a capital crime in the colonies and probably explains why people should have been put to death for adultery in the early American colonies (Freeman, 1979). Yet it is also worth noting that, in 1959, the then Archbishop of Canterbury wanted to see adultery defined as a criminal offence. Happily, since 1970, people in England can no longer sue for damages on account of adultery.

As recently as the late 1970s, adulterous cohabitation could have resulted in a 'misdemeanour' in California. In other words if you were married and left your spouse to 'live with' your lover, you could in theory be fined. If you continued to 'break the law' by living with your lover, you could in theory have earned yourself time in the county jail.

In the more conservative state of Arizona, adultery remains technically punishable by up to three years in prison, whereas, in Rhode Island, an offender would only receive a $10 fine. According to Freeman (1979), it is still true that, in France, only married women can be found guilty of adultery. Unless a husband agrees to forgive the wife and accepts her back, she can be given up to two years in prison! While a husband may also be guilty of an offence if he keeps a woman at home, he cannot be sent to prison. The Council of the Howard League for Penal Reform

(1985) has recorded that adultery was a criminal offence until 1978 in Italy, and until 1981 in Greece.

The Howard League also drew the conclusion that Saudi Arabian justice requires the flogging of both adulterous parties and then their stoning to death. In January 1978, the papers reported the notorious Saudi Arabian case involving Princess Misha, who was publicly stoned to death for committing adultery. Laffin (1979) describes Princess Misha as an 'accomplished dancer, vivacious and fun-loving'. Since she had been forced to marry an older cousin, who subsequently abandoned her, she started to have an affair with a young Saudi, whom she would meet in London 'despite the strict security imposed by her grandfather, Prince Muhamad Bin Abdul'. The decision to stone Misha to death and behead her lover has been staunchly defended by Saudi Arabian judges. The judges obviously believed that the woman in such cases is more culpable than the man: whereas the princess was stoned and so endured a painful and drawn-out death, the male adulterer was accorded the mercy of a swift beheading. The Chief Justice of the Saudi Appeals Court stated, before the United Nations, that such measures were necessary 'for such a horrible crime that makes men start to doubt if they are the natural fathers of their children'. His sentiments are valid in accordance with Islamic law, the Koran (Sunnah 26A, Sura 24, Verse 2) asserting:

> The woman and the man
> Guilty of adultery or fornication
> Flog each of them
> With a hundred stripes
> Let not compassion move you
> In their case, in a matter
> Prescribed by God, if he believes
> In God and the Last Day
> And let a party

Of the Believers
Witness their punishment

Amnesty International reports the execution for adultery of an unidentified woman in the Iranian town of Mehdi-shahr, near Semran, on 17 June 1979. The most incredible aspect, for a Westerner, is that the woman's execution was carried out by her mother, father and brother. The woman was unmarried and therefore, if she was indeed 'guilty' of fornication, the offence should have carried a penalty of '100 stripes' according to Islamic law. Therefore the death penalty must have been optional.

LOVE ACROSS THE COLOUR LINE

South Africa was, until the reform of 1985, the only country in the world where sexual relationships, cohabitation and marriage – in other words, love – between 'white persons' and 'coloured persons' remained absolutely illegal. Yet similar anti-miscegenation sex laws had existed in the United States long before the South African authorities ever thought up the incredible Prohibition of Mixed Mar-riages Act (1949) and the lurid Immorality Act (1957). Indeed, the United States Supreme Court only declared anti-miscegenation laws unconstitutional as late as 1967. These laws existed in many Southern States and were designed to prevent black men from having sexual relations with white women rather than stopping white men from having sex with black women, a reflection of deep-seated racism and male chauvinism.

The wording of Section 16 of the South African Immor-ality Act is worth close attention, since it forbids 'any white female person' or 'any white male person' to have sex with a person who is not white. The law was intended to 'protect' white purity. It did not set out to hinder the many other 'non-white' groups from engaging in marriage or sexual intercourse across the 'colour line':

Sexual offences between white persons and coloured persons –
(1) (a) Any *white female* person who –
(i) has or attempts to have unlawful carnal intercourse with a *coloured male* person; or
(ii) commits or attempts to commit with a *coloured male* person any immoral or indecent act; or
(iii) entices, solicits or importunes any *coloured male* person to have unlawful carnal intercourse with her; or
(iv) entices, solicits or importunes any *coloured male* person to the commission of any immoral or indecent act; and
   (b) any *coloured female* person who –
(i) has or attempts to have unlawful carnal intercourse with a *white male* person; or
(ii) commits or attempts to commit with a *white male* person any immoral or indecent act; or
(iii) entices, solicits or importunes any *white male* person to have unlawful carnal intercourse with her; or
(iv) entices, solicits or importunes any *white male* person to the commission of any immoral or indecent act, shall be guilty of an offence.
(2) (a) Any *white male* person who –
(i) has or attempts to have unlawful carnal intercourse with a *coloured female* person; or
(ii) commits or attempts to commit with a *coloured female* person any immoral or indecent act; or
(iii) entices, solicits or importunes any *coloured female* person to have unlawful carnal intercourse with him; or
(iv) entices, solicits or importunes any *coloured female* person to the commission of any immoral or indecent act; and
   (b) any *coloured male* person who –
(i) has or attempts to have unlawful carnal intercourse with a *white female* person; or
(ii) commits or attempts to commit with a *white female* person any immoral or indecent act; or
(iii) entices, solicits or importunes any *white female* person to have unlawful carnal intercourse with him; or
(iv) entices, solicits or importunes any *white female* person to the commission of any immoral or indecent act, shall be guilty of an offence.

[Republic of South Africa, Immorality Act, No. 23 of 1957, Section 1b. Author's emphases]

3 CHASTITY, VIRGINITY AND ABSTINENCE

RELIGIOUS TRADITIONS

The virgin is highly valued in Judaeo-Christian, Islamic and Eastern religion, as well as in more primitive religious beliefs. In the first century A.D. St Paul considered marriage as an inferior state: 'Flee fornication. Every sin that a man doeth is without the body; but he that committeth fornication sinneth against his own body. What? Know ye not that your body is the temple of the Holy Ghost which is in you, which ye have of God, and ye are not your own?' (1 Corinthians 6: 18–19). It is also 'good for a man not to touch a woman. Nevertheless, to avoid fornication, let every man have his own wife, and let every woman have her own husband' (1 Corinthians 7: 1–2).

The early Christian fathers Tertullian, Jerome and Augustine propagated the idea that the individual needed to lead a celibate life in order to attain the state of grace originally experienced by Adam and Eve in the Garden of Eden. Augustine's influence had major impact or future generations, the Church fathers accepting without question his decree that sexual intercourse was, by its nature, synonymous with sin. Following Augustinian logic to its ultimate conclusion, it became clear that, if everyone were to attempt to become spiritually enlightened (which could only happen if all were celibate), the world would become devoid of humans. The fallacy was resolved by the rationalization that sex was in the end necessary to 'people heaven'.

Sex was considered by the Catholic Church to be sinful because both Christ and his mother were believed to be virgins throughout their lives. Carnal appetites ought therefore to be curtailed to imitate this 'purity'. As Germaine Greer (1984) points out, 'Virgins could expect to be placed higher in heaven than spouses who lived in perfect married chastity.' In a 'trial of chastity', an individual was required to demonstrate self-control in the face of temptation, and two Christian ascetics, St Swithin and St Brendan, reputedly entered such a contest. After St Swithin had been sleeping with two attractive virgins without giving in to his 'desires', Brendan castigated him for this behaviour. Swithin then challenged Brendan to prove he could do the same. Brendan accepted the challenge and 'succeeded', but, not surprisingly, was unable to fall asleep, and so went home disconcerted.

In the eleventh century, Robert of Arbrissel established nunneries where he forced himself to sleep with nuns without having any sexual contact with them. Deliberately placing such temptations before oneself may seem as perverse as it is masochistic.

In contrast to Catholics and Christian fundamentalists, Jewish tradition seldom praises celibacy. References to marriage stress, however, that married couples should have sexual intercourse *after* marriage, and only when the woman is not menstruating. While sexual intercourse is required, it is only in order to procreate. The 'act' usually took place on the eve of the Sabbath, and then, among certain highly Orthodox persons, only through a hole or tear in the sheet. In Jewish tradition, one could only legitimately remain chaste if one were to devote one's life to the study of the Torah (the body of Jewish law and teachings), and the concept of chaste monks and nuns is anathema to the religion. However, virginity prior to marriage is considered not only virtuous but also required.

PROVING VIRGINITY

Since the advent of Christianity *began* with Mary's *immaculate* conception, it is not surprising that the Church has always been concerned with chastity, the virginity of women in particular. Labelle (1986) found a 1251 account in which the Bishop of Lincoln went around the English countryside visiting nunneries and convents under his dominion to ensure virginity. The author of the account described the bishop as having 'resorted to an expedient which I am ashamed to describe. He had their breasts squeezed, employing that method to ascertain whether they had preserved their virginity.' In one case, it was recorded in 1338 that a young girl was burned to death for failing a similar test.

While Orthodox Jews value virginity prior to marriage, they do not emphasize proving it, unlike those cultures where the bride's virginity had to be validated the morning after the honeymoon. The assumption here was that, provided the hymen was intact, once the bride was deflowered, she would bleed on to the sheets which could then be publicly displayed. This remained a practice even in the traditional Greek neighbourhoods in the United States, when the bride's mother-in-law would arrive at the newlyweds' home the 'morning after' to collect the blood-stained sheets, which she would then hang outside the window (Bryant, 1982). In Egypt, the bride's virginity is vouched for either by a *daya* (traditional midwife) or by the bridegroom. The virgin is 'devirginized' either by the *daya* or by the husband, who uses a handkerchief wrapped round his finger. Often the bride's mother and mother-in-law are present in the room at the time, and the blood-stained handkerchief is then handed over to the bride's brothers, who put it on display for the guests waiting outside. And, in Algeria, if some unfortunate young girl cannot prove her virginity, she is liable to be killed by her brothers and her father.

ABSTINENCE

The Dani of Irian Jaya in Indonesia appear to be the most chaste group known among the world's peoples (Greer, 1984). The anthropologist, Karl Heider, studied the sexual behaviour of the group and discovered that:

> The Dani abstain from sexual intercourse for four to six years after giving birth; there are no significant explanations for this practice; there are no punishments if the practice is not upheld; individuals do not seem to have an alternative sexual outlet; the practice does not appear to produce anxiety or unhappiness.

The most interesting fact about the Dani is that their low level of 'libido' cannot be explained by any supernatural, legal or other beliefs. Even married couples, who get married on pig festivals held only every four to six years, sleep apart from one another. The low level of sexual activity was accounted for by Heider in terms of social learning: the Dani are simply not exposed to erotic stimuli between mother and child during infancy. Another possible explanation for their chaste lifestyle is that the Dani lived in a highly hospitable environment where they were geographically protected from marauding attackers and the diseases they spread. The Dani did not have to be coitally competitive to survive.

In some societies, not only is the adult male responsible for fertilizing women, but he is also enjoined to fertilize 'mother earth', ironically by practising abstinence. For example, the Western Abelam in New Guinea practise sexual abstinence for the six months when their yam crops are growing. These people believe that remaining *chaste* while their crops grow *magically* produces a better crop, wealth in that society being based on the number of yams a man can grow.

Abstinence has become fashionable in some parts of the United States for less magical reasons. During the late 1970s and early 1980s in California, certain individuals were growing disenchanted with the sexual freedom fought for during the sexual revolution of the 1960s. The **singles scene** in American life can be a cold, alienating and lonely experience, and many heterosexual and homosexual singles find themselves desperately craving anything which vaguely resembles real affection and touch. Pervasive contraception, fast abortion and liberal ideology set the stage for promiscuity – even in the face of the herpes and AIDS scares.

It had thus for many single Americans become the norm to go out during the evening and wake up in the bed of a total stranger. In a frantic attempt to find 'tender loving care', some began to question the socio-sexual mores of the time and came to opt for a celibate though not anti-social lifestyle. Some are simply happy with **cuddling**, an activity stressing physical closeness without sexual play and sexual intercourse. The need for touch is fulfilled without the physical risk of venereal diseases. However, there is no accurate statistic on the prevalence of cuddling in America.

[I suspect that cuddling is not common either in the United States or Europe. In an informal survey of over a hundred single males in England and California, I found that only eight (less than 10 per cent) believed it possible to sleep in the same bed as an attractive woman (on the first night) without making sexual advances towards her. Statements like, 'I would be crazy not to', 'I don't believe it's possible', 'The girl would think I'm not much of a man', were common. It is still the case that sleeping in the same bed is synonymous with sex.]

---

4 BIRTH CONTROL

CONTRACEPTION AND ABORTION

The ancient Egyptians, unlike those early and tribal societies which believed childbirth to be a supernatural phenomenon, did associate seminal fluid with childbirth. Egyptian women attempted to prevent sperm from reaching the uterus by soaking it up with a sponge or other absorbent material after the male's ejaculation. Other methods were designed to obstruct seminal fluid from reaching the cervix, using devices similar to modern diaphragms.

The *Kahun Papyrus* advised women to use a variety of techniques. One method involved crocodile excrement being mixed with an unspecified paste and then inserted into the vagina, much like a modern tampon. The Egyptians also soaked lint pads with acacia tips and honey. The physicians of the period may not have known anything about sperm mobility, but they did use compounds which diminished sperm speed. They were logical in their advocacy of oily and gluey substances as well as of acidic compounds which kill sperm. Elephant dung was probably one of the first effective spermicides, it being acidic, and acidic environments being lethal to sperm.

The Greeks were equally as innovative. Aristotle saw the 'logic' of the state regulation of pederasty as an effective form of birth control. Ahead of his times, he was also one of the first recorded advocates of contraception as a means of population control, and believed that there should be a legal limit on the size of a family. The contraceptive he proposed was composed of olive oil mixed with cedar oil, lead linament and a fragrance. Interestingly enough, scientific tests show that olive oil does exert a degree of contraceptive action.

The ancients were also aware of abortion, the Assyrians considering it a capital offence. Assyrian law prescribed that the guilty woman be impaled on a stake and not permitted burial. Even where a woman died as the result of an abortion, her body was *not* buried. Instead, her corpse was to be publicly impaled. Proscriptions against abortion were instituted not so much because of the death of an unborn foetus but because of the possibility that a male child might be lost.

Abortion has been considered illegal and punishable in most societies. Many women in the world today are forbidden, by their governments, to have an abortion. The Catholic Church has not altered its stance on abortion since 1869, when Pope Pius IX proclaimed that the soul enters the body at the moment of conception; which means, in other words, that an eight-celled body of blastocyst is technically a person. Germaine Greer (1984) points to the irony behind this belief. Catholic women who lose their blastocysts when menstruating are *not* told by the Church that a human life may just have terminated:

It may seem very complicated to keep a jug of holy water beside the lavatory bowl to baptise sanitary napkins with, but it is no more elaborate than many of the rituals which believing people all over the world practise several times every day of their lives. It would certainly dramatize the fact that Catholics take life before birth very seriously. The fact that they do not carry out rituals of this kind suggests that in fact they do not really believe what they maintain in polemic

– especially since some Catholic priests will baptize still-born babies so they can go to heaven.

Catholics believe abortion to be murder. And the same notion is law in fundamentalist Islamic countries. One of the more tragic facts about abortion in Third World and Islamic countries is therefore that back-alley abortions are performed by the untrained in contaminated conditions and so result in countless deaths. In a macabre way, this acts as a form of population control, since there are then fewer women to spawn children.

Jewish tradition appears to be more humane where abortion is concerned. While Orthodox Judaism rejects almost all forms of contraception, Jewish law permits abortion to save the life of the mother. Some rabbis have accepted the Pill because the 'seed' (seminal fluid) is not 'spilled' as it would be with a condom. The concept of birth control runs counter to Jewish life, because the biblical command, 'Be fruitful and multiply', is taken literally. It is the man's *duty* to have sex with his wife whenever possible, and he must not deny her sex for longer than two weeks. In the past, Jewish girls of eleven and twelve have been required to use a 'contraceptive sponge', it being thought that a second fertilization might occur and that this would harm the already developing foetus. Other methods involved the woman jumping up and down after sex to discharge the sperm – a highly ineffective form of birth control. In the third century, Rabbi Yohanan described a brew – the 'cup of roots' composed of liquid alum, andrian gum, and garden crocus mixed with wine, to be taken by the woman as either a contraceptive or an anti-VD potion. (Men were forbidden to take it.)

INFANTICIDE

The most outrageous and ugly form of population control is infanticide – the killing of new-born children. In certain instances it appears that, for some tribes, infanticide has served to help survival, the anthropologists Frazer and Whitmarsh observing, for example, that nineteenth-century aborigines actually ate every tenth baby. The anthropologists suggested that this infanticide/cannibalism served to check numbers so that the territory occupied could continue to support material needs. Until recently, some groups in Polynesia murdered two thirds of their new-borns, while the nomadic Jagars of South-West Africa killed their infants to 'free up' the women whenever they moved. The Jagars would make up for their lost children by forcibly adopting adolescents from other tribes.

The British commenced legislation against female infanticide in India in 1795. Sir William Sleeman recorded that, in the mid-nineteenth century, a Rajput landlord spoke of female infanticide as customary: 'a family commonly destroys the daughter as soon as born, when the father is away from home and has given no special orders [to keep her alive] . . ., taking it to be his wish as a matter of course'. In India, female infanticide remains rampant because of the belief that a man is not 'rich' unless he has male heirs. Ironically, the *more male children* he has, the *more* his lands are divided and therefore the *less* productive they become, with the result that his offspring grow poorer. Methods of killing babies vary within India. The Bedees kill baby girls by placing opium on the mother's nipples – especially when no male child has been born. In Gujarat, baby girls are buried alive (Janssen-Jurreit, 1982).

Low ratios of females to males in Islamic societies have been attributed, respectively, to the existence of female infanticide, to the low status of women (making it not worth counting them in any census) and to the enslavement of women in **harems**. As it is written in the Koran: 'If an Arab hears that a daughter has been born to him, sorrow colours his face black. It is questionable whether he will keep the daughter born to him to his dishonour or whether he should bury her quickly in the earth.' Pakistan, an Islamic country, has a suspicious shortage of women. In 1972, there were only 885 women to every 1,000 men.

As recently as 1983, authorities in the People's Republic

of China were forced to decree that those who killed female infants would suffer heavy punishment. The practice has to this day never been eradicated. In Japan, where baby boys are valued more highly than girls, the government has funded research into the development of a drug to help parents pre-select the sex of an unborn child.

ABORTION AND THE LAW

The practice of deliberate removal of a foetus from the uterus prior to its full development as a viable human being is extensive. About 55 million babies were aborted world-wide in 1985. According to Beserra, Jewel and Matthews (1973), there were about 136,000 legal abortions in the United States in 1972, and about 75,000 criminal abortions are performed there annually. These authors also claim that, contrary to popular misconception, abortion has not always been illegal in the United States. The first American anti-abortion law was passed in 1803 in Connecticut, abortion then only being permitted in most states to save the mother's life.

Ann Jones (1981) writes that, in early eighteenth-century New England, women found guilty of murder would be spared execution if pregnant. Mere pregnancy did not suffice – the foetus had to have 'quickened', quickening being the 'point at which church authorities recognized it as a living being which it would be sinful to destroy'. Somehow it was thought that it took forty days for *female* embryos to 'quicken', but eighty to ninety days for *males* to develop into full-fledged human beings who would be murdered if the mother was hanged. As Jones points out, the killing of a foetus through the execution of the mother before it had 'quickened' was legal – even in the eyes of the Catholic Church. Consequently, after Bathsheba Spooner murdered her husband in 1778, and was sentenced to death by a Massachusetts court, she claimed she was pregnant and that her foetus had 'quickened'. Despite her pleas to save the life of the unborn child, the duly appointed panel of male midwives and matrons determined she was lying and Spooner was 'lawfully' hanged. Her last request was to have her body cut open and the foetus examined. The authorities complied, and the autopsy revealed that her foetus was indeed a five-months boy. This resulted in what Jones terms a 'public trauma' of immense proportions. It took fifty years before any other jury convicted another woman of murder, by which time execution was not mandatory because courts could impose a custodial sentence. The legal status of abortion did not change much during the next 189 years until California and Colorado broached changes in abortion statutes.

California stood in the vanguard of states which liberalized abortion. In 1967, abortion was liberalized in California under the Therapeutic Abortion Act. With permission of a hospital medical committee, the Act permitted abortion only to protect the physical and mental health of the mother, or if the pregnancy resulted from rape or incest.

5 PROSTITUTION

In *Sex in History*, Reay Tannahill (1980) has traced the history of prostitution. Contrary to popular myth, prostitution is *not* the 'oldest profession'. Shamans or witchdoctors preceded prostitutes by thousands of years, and when shamans became ordained priests, many temples became 'sanctuaries' for prostitutes. Even during the Middle Ages, the magnificent city of Avignon in southern France, once the seat of the Papacy, housed a Church brothel where 'employees' spent some of their time praying, doing penance and performing chores. The rest of the time the

prostitutes served their clientele. In accordance with prevailing social trends, the brothel was open to Christians
only. Jews and heathens were specifically barred from
entering. Pope Julius II approved of the brothel in Avignon,
and in the sixteenth century had one set up in the Vatican.

Thousands of years before Pope Julius, prostitution was
not considered unusual or bizarre. In Sumeria and Babylon
(*c.* 1750 B.C.), harlots were not stigmatized. On the contrary, it is thought that some were seen as sacred prostitutes
who linked the fertility deity with the worshipper. A by-
product of this was an increase in revenue for the temple
concerned. The prostitutes were sacred in so far as they
were in the service of the temple. In Babylon, they were
classified into three types: (a) the *harimtu*, who were semi-
secular – anyone could take one, and they were equivalent
to the street-walkers of today; (b) the *qadishtu*, who were
sacred – more expensive and reserved for priests and
important citizens; and (c) the *ishtaritu*, who were especially
sacred – reserved for the goddess Ishtar, probably much as
Catholic nuns are reserved for Christ. The more sacred the
prostitute, the better her accommodation in the temple
complex.

About a thousand years after Hammurabi's Babylon, the
Greek historian Herodotus (fifth century B.C.) recorded that
each woman citizen was required *by law* to go to the temple
at least once in her life to

> give herself to a strange men . . . She is not allowed to go home
> until a man has thrown a silver coin into her lap and taken her
> outside to lie with him . . . The woman has no privilege of choice
> – she must go with the first man who throws the money. When
> she has lain with him, her duty to the goddess is discharged and
> she may go home.

Presumably, the money went to finance the temple.
Herodotus recorded that the more attractive women were

able to return home more quickly than the ugly ones, who often had to wait for days to be taken.

The ancient Jews paid no religious homage to prostitution. As Proverbs (29:3) proclaims: 'He that keepeth company with harlots spendeth his substance [semen].' In condemning the people for the sins of Jerusalem, Ezekiel says that, 'She [Jerusalem] did not give up her harlotry which she had practised since her days in Egypt for in her youth men had laid with her and handled her virgin bosom and poured out their lust upon her . . .' In an almost pornographic tone, not untypical of biblical writings, she (Jerusalem) was also accused of doting 'upon her paramours . . . whose members [penises] were like those of asses, and whose issue [ejaculate] was like that of horses'. While the ancient Hebrews were religiously prohibited from becoming prostitutes or sleeping with prostitutes, some were forced to prostitute themselves when widowed or rejected by their husbands, in order to survive.

By the third century B.C., the Athenians had become wealthier as a result of successful colonialism, and therefore had more money to spend on sex. Tannahill writes that statues of women, previously veiled, now appeared nude, and prostitution became big business. One even used a water clock to time her clients' visits. The most expensive courtesans were known as *hetaerae*, the *hetaerae* being accorded a superior status to married women. Their privileges meant that they could eat at the same table as the men, were permitted to read and write, could conduct financial business with men and speak in public. In other words, there were very positive rewards for being a prostitute; and these were conveniently arranged by the Athenian men, who were highly adept at satisfying their own carnal desires.

At about the same time as it was being cultivated in Athens, prostitution was in full force in China. Prior to the Han period, troupes of dancing girls were reserved for the

wealthy who visited palatial brothels. Entire companies of
prostitutes were used as diplomatic or political bribes
between princely states. In the Han period, the Emperor
Wu sanctioned bands of call girls specifically to service
soldiers in his army – in much the same way as the
Americans did in Vietnam. The economics of the girl-as-
merchandise was based on her beauty and knowledge. An
up-and-coming young male would consider investing in the
purchase of a high-class prostitute on account of her vast
knowledge, gleaned during working hours, of business and
government gossip. Tannahill suggests that 'it was not
uncommon for a former regular client to maintain a fatherly
interest in her [the concubine] and to extend that interest
to her husband'.

The Chinese brothel girl underwent an extensive training
in cuisine, religious protocol and skills of professional
entertainment. Businessmen turned to prostitutes, not only
for sexual services, but also to impress their colleagues and
spy on competitors. It is thought that the origin of 'red
light' districts, so common today, is Chinese and arrived in
the United States with the Chinese immigration during the
Californian Gold Rush, there having been in China special
wine bars, some directly under government control, to
service functionaries and bureaucrats, which could be
identified by bamboo lamps covered in red silk that hung
on the front door. But these were only mediocre, middle-
class whore-houses. The elegant tea houses were more
expensive and offered only the finest in wines, food, music
and garments. Interestingly, the sexual aspect of the business seems to have been the least emphasized. Rather
clients came to have their boyish whims catered for – to be
pampered and babied.

By 1290, there were many more women than men in
China. This meant that males could acquire extra wives
from the poorer classes, and, naturally, the prettier peasant

girls went to the wealthiest merchants. New concubines were put through an initiation ceremony designed to prevent jealousy among the other wives. A man was advised to focus his attention on the old wives first. This meant that he should have intercourse with the old wives with the new one looking on for at least five nights. When he did take the new concubine, the man was advised to ensure that his principal wife and concubines be present to witness the act. This was guaranteed to ensure political and emotional peace in the household.

By the end of the nineteenth century, prostitution and brothels had proliferated in Europe and America. In Washington, 'ladies of the night' stayed in town as long as Congress was in session. In New Orleans, mothers negotiated with suitors over the use of daughters. The interested party was given access to the daughter, often as young as fifteen or sixteen years, in exchange for a small house, clothing, jewellery and other bribes. In fact, prostitution was so rife in New Orleans that an official called Story arranged for a special zone, Storyville, to be allocated to commercial sex.

In France and Belgium, legal regulations prevented women from leaving brothels once they had signed on. New York offered more brothels than London, but San Francisco took the cake with its 'cow yards' where, at the turn of the century, there stood 'a bright new barracks of 450 rooms which owners had carefully stocked with nymphomaniacs, on the sound principle that a happy worker was a good worker. They wanted to call it the Hotel Nymphomania but were refused permission' (Tannahill, 1980). It was finally called the Nymphia, but was closed in 1903 under Father Caraher's crusade against sin. London preceded Hollywood's lewd *Hollywood Press* with a publication by Harris which registered the names, faces, vital statistics and specialities of the Covent Garden ladies who visited his tavern in Drury Lane. New Orleans would not be outdone, however. There one could purchase guides by the name of *Blue Book, or Gentleman's Guide to New Orleans*, and *The Green Book*.

Although hardly a new scourge, venereal disease spread rampantly and, by the end of the eighteenth century, was virulent. The medical professions were largely ignorant about the epidemiology and biology of gonorrhoea and syphilis, which they considered to be the same illnesses, and certainly had little idea about curing them. Prostitutes were more likely to spread gonorrhoea because they could go symptom-free for weeks whereas men could experience a painful discharge from the urethra and have difficulty urinating. In Vienna during the 1830s and 1840s, public hospitals annually admitted between 6,000 and 7,000 prostitutes suffering from venereal disease. In 1856, London hospitals admitted over 30,000 cases, and in Paris most prostitutes sent to prison had the 'clap'. Whole armies became infected – the Garde Impériale lost 20,000 duty days in only three months during 1865. It was estimated that, in Copenhagen, one in three citizens had contracted some form of venereal disease. Venereal disease cultured equally well in the United States.

Thus was the stage set in Britain for the insalubrious Contagious Diseases Acts of 1864, 1866 and 1869. These were intended to control the spread of venereal disease in the armed forces by removing infected women from circulation in naval and garrison towns, and empowered police to stop *any woman* on the street and require her to submit to a vaginal inspection. It was therefore possible for an officer of the law to insist on a pelvic examination being carried out on any woman whom he suspected might have venereal disease. Both brothel owners and respectable women condemned these laws. The former, no doubt, because they interfered with business; the latter because it was an intrusive outrage on the bodies of innocent girls. Josephine Butler, secretary of the Ladies' National Association, was among those who successfully campaigned against these laws, which were suspended in 1883. It had, after all, been a male parliament which passed the Acts.

Parliament needed to replace the Contagious Diseases Acts with something, and so instigated the insidious and cruel Criminal Law Amendment Act of 1885. The Act was designed to 'protect women and girls', outlaw brothels and procuring, and prevent homosexual prostitutes from soliciting for business. One upshot of the law was that even private mutually consenting homosexual activity became illegal. The writer, Oscar Wilde, spent time in prison after being successfully prosecuted under this law.

During the First World War, the United States Department of War coped with the problem of venereal infection by issuing soldiers and sailors with condoms to reduce the rate of disease. In 1914, it was estimated that about half the armed forces had contracted some form of venereal disease, but, by about 1919, only one in seventeen had the problem – still an enormous number, since the armed forces were about five million strong. The Germans, for their part, were meticulously efficient in their control of prostitution. The High Command initially decreed that no brothels should be allowed to operate behind the battle lines, but they soon saw how morale diminished without a steady supply of women for its young warriors. In light of the need for improved efficiency, military brothels were therefore organized. These were set up in large tents which advanced or retreated with the army. Private soldiers and NCOs had access to 'red light' tents, while officers went to 'blue light' tents. Medical safety measures were carried out with Germanic efficiency: a sergeant from the Medical Corps was stationed to check health certificates and pay slips, to record the names of new customers, conduct cursory medical examinations, dispense medication and collect payment on behalf of the girls.

PROSTITUTION TODAY

Prostitution flourishes today, from Bangkok to Buenos Aires, from London to New York's infamous 42nd Street. Los Angeles boasts its Sunset Boulevard, where scantily clad ladies hang around the automatic money dispensing machine outside the Bank of America. Just as one can pick up a street-walker at any time of the day, so one can, in the profoundly American tradition, order home delivery twenty-four hours a day – and pay for the service by credit card! Thousands of women advertise in, for example, the *Hollywood Press*, under the pretext of coming in to give a massage or to provide 'escort services' – some charging $200 an hour.

Near by, on Santa Monica Boulevard in Los Angeles, there are hundreds of male prostitutes, mostly under the legal age of eighteen. The boys are usually runaways who were sexually abused as children and had to make it on the streets. Many are prosecuted and sent to reformatories or prisons which serve only to encourage their behaviour. Many are murdered, and many of these murders are never brought to court because no one reports the boys missing. In many American cities, instant sex, both homosexual and heterosexual, is as available as instant coffee. But America has still not shaken off its puritanical sexual manacles. The Swiss, at least in the Canton of Geneva, have managed to deal with certain social pressures connected with the demand for prostitutes. In Geneva, while prostitutes may not have brothels, they may walk the streets – a privilege which costs them tax and the inconvenience of having to undergo regular medical check-ups.

Europeans meanwhile remain fascinated with the 'exotic

East'. Bangkok is big business. As one traveller wrote home:

> The first night we arrived we went to a super massage parlour called Darling. A ritsy joint beautifully appointed, you are greeted at the door by a smart bow-tied doorman and then you take your pick of the services offered. Downstairs at ground-floor level is where you just take 'regular' massage; about 40–50 girls sit behind a glass screen (one-way glass) and you choose the number they (the girls) display in their dresses. We stripped on this floor and took the elevator to the third floor where the girls offer 'body massages'; in other words they massage you with their nude bodies after a little titillation in the bath. All good fun and scrupulously clean. My lady was really quite sophisticated and spoke good English and had a beautiful body. The next night J's friends took us to the bars at Patpong Road. This was too much – most of the bars have large raised areas usually surrounded by the bar itself where the girls in packs take turns to dance nude. Again they are all numbered and anyone can take his choice for the night. As the evening wore on, and we moved from bar to bar, the girls got naughtier until they were performing with each other on stage. Patpong Road is really quite racy and wild but another evening after a super joint we all went to a much more laid-back area called 'Soi Cowboy' where the bars are less go-go and people seemed less hasty. That night I ended up with a lovely girlie with a super figure in my hotel room. Anyway, there is a hellava lot going on in Bangkok – not just sex – although it is a big, big industry. Everyone around takes it all quite naturally and in such a matter of fact way.

2

The Subjugation of the Body

---

6 CIRCUMCISION

'Tribal societies still use extreme methods to ensure chastity. Some modern Nubian women willingly submit to a surgical operation when their husbands have to be away for any length of time. It involves infibulation (sewing up) as a shield against penetration; the operation can be reversed when the husband returns' – Reay Tannahill (1980)

Circumcision represents a primitive form of permanent mutilation, in which, in males, the prepuce or foreskin of the penis is surgically removed without anaeathetic. In females, the practice involves removal of the clitoris and even of the labia majora, the outer lips of the vagina.

MALE CIRCUMCISION

Male circumcision dates back to prehistoric periods, having been practised by groups as diverse as ancient Egyptians and contemporary Americans. In Hebrew mythology, Abraham, father of the Israelites, is said to have had a vision which resulted in his *self-circumcision* at the age of ninety-nine. Genesis (17: 10–11) proclaims: 'Every man child among you shall be circumcised. And ye shall circumcise the flesh of your foreskin; and it shall be a token of the covenant betwixt me and you.' The origin of the Jewish practice is this covenant between Jew and God which guaranteed that circumcised males would not be sent to hell (*Gehinnom*), because Abraham sits at the Gates of Hell to prevent 'minor' sinners from entering. However, if a man has led an especially sinful life, Abraham is supposed to take the foreskin of children who died prior to circumcision and place it on the sinner, who is then sent down to *Gehinnom*. This symbolic undoing of circumcision banishes the individual from the tribe. Not surprisingly, the myth makes no mention of what happens to Jewish women sinners when they reach the gates of hell. Unlike the Islamic tradition, Jews have tended not to practise circumcision on their female infants (Szasz, 1980).

Male circumcision has been the cause of social unrest and martyrdom in the past. Under the Greek Antiochus Epiphanes, the conquered Jews were forbidden to circumcise their male infants (164–168 B.C.). The *Encyclopaedia Judaica* reports the murder of two women for circumcising their sons. They 'were led round the city with their babes bound to their breasts and then cast headlong from the wall'. Later the Roman emperor, Hadrian, also forbade male circumcision by Jews, who, as slaves to the Romans, carried the practice to various parts of the empire. The outlawing of circumcision, among other sanctions, contributed to the successful Jewish rebellion by Bar Kokhba against the Romans in A.D. 132.

Not all Jews resisted foreign customs and laws (Tannahill, 1980). For instance, Jewish athletes in pre-Christian Greece underwent a form of plastic surgery to 'repair' the circumcised penis so they could participate nude in the athletic stadium. The practice also occurred, just after the advent of Christianity, among Jews who wanted to prove that they accepted the new faith. Submitting to a painful mutilation for the second time literally severed ties with the old religion and bound them to Christianity. Such practice would be interpreted by many anthropologists as reflecting a tribal initiation rite which promotes allegiance to the group. The shared pain is seen as increasing the individual's bonding to the community, while the mutilation represents an indelible badge that the person belongs to a particular tribe.

In the United States, about 1,325,000 neo-natal circumcisions are performed each year. The practice gives cause for alarm, since it results in about 230 deaths each year as a result of accident or infection. Urologists and paediatricians generally favour circumcision on hygienic grounds, since smegma, an accumulation of dead skin and dirt, can build up in the foreskin with resultant infection (Diamond, 1984). The practice is less frequent in Great Britain and Europe, where private medicine is less popular. No wonder that opponents of male circumcision suggest that doctors who perform the 'operation' do so out of financial incentive – over $150 million is spent each year in the United States on male circumcision. Opponents of circumcision also say there is no evidence that circumcision reduces the incidence of penile cancer, although advocates of circumcision are correct when they suggest that women who have sexual intercourse with circumcised males are less likely to get cancer of the cervix.

While the civilized world considers circumcision at puberty, with or without anaesthetic, to be barbaric, it still accepts the surgical removal of a newborn's foreskin *without an anaesthetic*. Contrary to popular myth, newborn infants do feel pain, as is evidenced by their screams during the ritual.

FEMALE CIRCUMCISION

Female circumcision varies in extent and covers an array of ritual mutilations to female genitalia. The least extreme form of mutilation is 'simple' **clitoridectomy**, or the removal of the tip of the clitoris. More severe forms of female circumcision involve **infibulation**, in which the clitoris, labia minora (inner lips of the vagina), and most of the labia majora (outer lips of the vagina) are cut out. In some cases, the labia are sewn together with thread or kept in place with thorns until healing occurs. The object here is to produce as small an opening to the vagina as possible.

Female circumcision is practised in the name of religion, for improved sexual attractiveness and to curb the 'natural promiscuity' of women. The ritual is performed on every inhabited continent, and it has been estimated that there are 40 million circumcised women in Africa alone. The procedure is endorsed by the Koran and, consequently, throughout much of the Islamic world. President Jomo Kenyatta of Kenya defended female circumcision in a 1938 paper, when he wrote that no Kikuyu tribe member should even consider marriage to an uncircumcised woman.

INFIBULATION

Infibulation is practised primarily in Somalia. The ritual is typically performed on an eight- to ten-year-old child by her mother while female relatives stand guard outside the ceremonial circumcision hut. The child sits on a chair as her legs are prised apart by several women. The mother separates the labia and fastens them aside with acacia thorns, leaving the clitoris totally exposed. Typically, a kitchen knife is used to remove the clitoris. Cutting goes down to the bone so that surrounding parts of the labia can be taken out. The child screams and comes close to biting off her tongue out of sheer pain. To prevent this, hot pepper is placed on the tongue every time it sticks out. The pepper ensures a rapid return of the tongue to the mouth. When the torturous operation is over, the mother closes both sides of the vulva with the acacia tree thorns.

Once again, the object is to produce as *small an opening as possible* so that only urine and menstrual blood can flow through. A woman's sexual value is, in part, based on the smallness of this opening. Side-effects of the surgery include infections of the urethra and cervix, and womb cysts form profusely. In one particularly sordid case, a husband had been using his fourteen-year-old wife's urethra because he thought it was her vagina. The urethra was 'two fingers wide', and a plastic one had to be fitted by doctors in a hospital in Khartoum, Sudan.

In Egypt, the surgical removal of the clitoris is performed without anaesthesia or sterile implements on the majority of girls between the ages of eight and ten. The ceremony is not confined to Moslems, and also occurs among Christian Copts. A 1965 study by Karim and Ammar concluded that, of 331 circumcised women, 30 per cent had first-degree circumcision (a small portion of the clitoris removed), 50 per cent had second-degree circumcision (removal of the entire clitoris and labia majora). Female circumcision is performed because traditional Islam demands it. Women say they want to get rid of 'something disfiguring, hideous and disgusting', and to prevent girls from touching themselves and becoming sexually aroused. Circumcision of women is also believed to prevent impotence in men whose health will suffer if they have intercourse with uncircumcised women. Present laws in Egypt forbid infibulation, or the removal of two thirds or more of the labia minora and clitoris.

Female circumcision is so rife that the World Health Organization convened a conference at Khartoum, with the help of the Sudanese government, in an attempt to curb the practice. It was reported that millions of girls had had their external genitalia removed, sewn up or infibulated, the 'surgical instruments' used including pieces of broken glass bottles, flakes of flint, razor blades and acacia tree thorns. Islamic religious authorities base the doctrine of female circumcision on a story about the Prophet Mohammed, who advised Um Attiya, a nurse performing sexual surgery on a little girl, to 'reduce but not to destroy' the girl's genitalia (Laffin, 1979).

Islamic societies are by no means the only groups to practise radical female circumcision. Among the Nandi, a Hamatic tribe in Kenya, mutilation of female genitalia is performed along with a 'test for virginity'. Before circumcision, the girls, aged about ten years old, must sleep together with boys in a special hut. They are beaten if they refuse. No sex is permitted when the children sleep together, and the girls are checked the day after to see that they are still virgins. If a girl is found not to be a virgin, she is speared to death, but girls found to be virgins are given gifts of cattle. The actual circumcision rite involves older women placing nettles on the clitoris, while the boys tease and insult the girls. If a girl screams, she is said to be a non-virgin – in which case, her dishonoured family members kill themselves and/or the child. The actual surgical removal of the clitoris is performed in the full view of other tribal members and involves the removal of the swollen, often infected, clitoris by the older women. Girls are secluded from the rest of the tribe between the ages of six months and three years, during which time old women care for them. Nandi males may not touch or communicate with children until the children are at least ten years old. The Nandi believe that, if the clitoris is not excised, it will grow offshoots.

Among the Australian aborigines, female circumcision is performed in tandem with group rape (Janssen-Jurreit, 1982). 'The operation is performed by clan brothers on a girl as soon as she reaches puberty.' A stone knife is used to make an incision from the vagina to the clitoris, thereby cutting the perineum. The young girl is then forced to have sexual intercourse with all those who participate in the ritual. 'Clitoris-free women' are considered to be more sexually desirable and pure.

The Dogon, who inhabit the interior of Mali, West Africa, have a cosmological explanation for female circumcision. According to their mythology, the god Amma created the world by having sexual intercourse with his wife. Unfortunately, Amma bumped into his wife's clitoris, the 'termite mound in the earth'. Amma was angry and tore out the 'termite mound', which resulted in his wife's circumcision. Thus the Dogon imitate their venerable god.

One group in Sierra Leone performs mass clitoridectomy. The initiation rite, witnessed by the whole tribe, is carried out at the full moon. The object here is to render the girl sexless and to prevent her from seducing men. After 'surgery', the girls are locked in huts until a man asks their fathers to permit marriage. All the clitorides are collected at the mass ritual and are buried in the river bank.

FEMALE CIRCUMCISION IN WESTERN COUNTRIES

Female circumcision is performed in Western countries, it being reported as recently as 1983 that clitoridectomies were being carried out by surgeons in London's prestigious Harley Street (ITN News). These surgeons provided the service to wealthy Saudi Arabian businessmen who had brought wives, children and concubines with them to England. The extent of the procedure is unknown, since it is performed in total secrecy. Doctors at the London Hospital, a National Health Service hospital, claimed that they performed clitoridectomies on the daughters of immigrants because, if they refused, the mothers would perform the operations themselves, in the absence of sterile conditions. When interviewed by television reporters, one such mother was highly indignant that the British government should concern itself with what she saw as her cultural heritage and religious freedom. A member of the House of Lords, Lord Kennet, is currently attempting to prohibit female circumcision in England.

There are some women in America who have elected to undergo a form of circumcision after being told by an expert that such an operation would enhance their ability to experience orgasm. The procedure is known as **clitoridopexy** and is therefore not a clitoridectomy. The surgery is alleged to increase the intensity of orgasm in women in addition to increasing the rate at which women can reach orgasm. Thomas Szasz (1980) cites a case report in *Medical World News* (17 April 1978) in which a Dr James C. Burt exhibited his 'stunning 31-year-old blonde wife Joan as demonstrable proof of his claim that reconstructing the vagina to make the clitoris more accessible to direct penile stimulation enables a woman to have more frequent and intense orgasms. Once only "randomly vaginally orgasmic", Mrs Burt describes the operation as a "complete success".' Over the past twelve years, Dr Burt has performed the operation in all stages of its evolution . . . on some 4,000 women.

7 MASTURBATION

THE DARK SIDE

There are certain primitive societies which actively encourage masturbation. For example, among North American Indian groups, the Hopi, Alor, Navaho and Kaingang allow for parents to manipulate a child's genitals as a method of pacification and comfort. Although genital self-stimulation occurs almost universally in infants and children in human society, attitudes towards masturbation vary among cultures and have changed during the course of history.

Genesis (38:7–11) describes how Onan 'spilt his seed on the ground' and was subsequently slain. Onan died because he had broken the law of levirate which required a man to provide his deceased brother's wife with children. In medieval times, Jewish elders declared masturbation to be a heinous crime. According to the strictest Orthodox rules, men should not even touch their penises; even while urinating, a man was required to direct his penis by lifting the scrotum. Women were allowed to examine their own genitals, but only to detect how close they were to their periods. Modern Judaism, however, is far more liberal and views masturbation as normal behaviour when practised in moderation.

During the era of the Ch'ing at the end of the seventeenth century in China, masturbation was frowned upon for men but not for women. The Chinese believed that the female life essence, the *yin*, was limitless, but that the male essence, the *yang*, existed in limited supply and therefore should not be wasted. Chinese priests believed that wet dreams or nocturnal emissions were caused by a succubus or spirit in the form of a beautiful woman come to steal the man's *yang* by seducing him in his dreams.

The social control of masturbation occurs in some folk groups for 'practical reasons'. The Masai of East Africa, for example, require that teenage males cease masturbation and other sexual activity, the young men then being required to direct their lives towards being warriors and tending cattle. The Masai accomplish this by performing an elaborate and painful circumcision rite of passage, in which the penis is so profoundly mutilated that it can take years to heal. Any sexual play or activity prior to full healing would prove painfully impossible.

In South Africa, the Zulus of the late nineteenth century

encouraged heterosexual masturbation among children. Once male warriors reached sexual maturity, however, they were required to be totally celibate until marriage. A breach of celibacy resulted in the slicing off of the genitals with a witchdoctor's knife, and the penalty for rape was having a sharp stake hammered up the rectum. Zulu warriors or *impis* would occasionally be rewarded for their service to the tribe when the chief would order a 'day of ceremonial masturbation' or *ukHlobonga*. The *ukHlobonga* day afforded the warriors hours of 'free masturbation' carried out by the unmarried women.

While the Zulus permitted masturbation among their children, nineteenth-century Europeans became concerned that their children should stop masturbating at all costs. In Germany, in 1786, S. G. Vogel had published *Unterricht für Eltern*, in which he proclaimed, much like the Masai, that masturbation could be prevented by infibulating the foreskin of the penis with a ring of silver wire. Other male chastity devices included small cages which fitted around the male genitalia and could be locked in place by a boy's parents. In England, J. L. Multon's book, *Spermatorrhoea* (1887), which had been through twelve editions, advocated a contraption which would trigger off an electric bell should the sleeper develop an erection and so be in danger of having a nocturnal emission. Penile rings with teeth or spikes provided cheaper alternatives in warning devices. (We know today, of course, that all healthy males have erections during sleep. This may, in part, be a form of 'biological survival' to ensure that the penis does not atrophy when an individual is not having regular sexual intercourse.)

In 1897, in the United States, Michael McCormic patented an anti-masturbation device or male chastity belt to enable parents to prevent their sons playing with themselves. As in Europe, masturbation was, in puritanical

America, believed by the clergy and medical profession to cause insanity, bad breath, pimples and a variety of other ailments. Some anxious men purchased these chastity belts to prevent themselves from masturbating. Essentially, the devices caused pain if the man had an erection. Between 1856 and 1932, thirty-three patents were issued by the United States Patent Office for masturbation locks and other anti-masturbation contraptions. Some inventors patented shoulder braces which incorporated chains and handcuffs to prevent hands from getting to the genitals.

A few seventeenth-century medical texts were indirectly in favour of masturbation (Stone, 1979), the idea being to practise masturbation in 'moderation' so as to 'balance the humours' by getting rid of unwanted fluids: 'blood by blood-letting; and semen by ejaculation'. As Stone records:

> Both bachelors and widows were, therefore, advised by doctors in the seventeenth century to follow a regime of moderate sexual activity. This being the case, the medical profession can hardly have disapproved of occasional pre-marital adolescent masturbation. But the youth still experienced guilt over masturbation, which they knew little about.

In 1753, the pious young James Boswell discovered that he was indulging in 'this fatal practice' when he was thirteen, because he used to reach sexual climax when climbing trees. Boswell wrote in his diary:

> In climbing trees, pleasure. Returned often, climbed, felt, allowed myself to fall from high trees in ecstasy. My youthful desires became strong. I was horrified because of the fear that I would sin and be damned.

He even contemplated self-castration, but changed his mind: 'I thought what I was doing was a venial sin, whereas fornication was horrible.'

Boswell's horrific experience in the eighteenth century of

his own sexuality was influenced by such medical theologians as the thirteenth-century churchman Thomas Aquinas, who proclaimed that any form of sexual intercourse other than that in the 'missionary position' or 'the right way' was evil. According to Aquinas, a masturbator was, by definition, a sinner who would certainly be doomed to purgatory or hell. By the eighteenth century, medical opinion had began to replace theological decree. These new priests proved no less dogmatic and myopic than their predecessors.

The medical commentator, Tissot, was among the first to start a masturbation phobia for both doctors and the public with his treatise *L'Onanisme: dissertation sur les maladies produites par la masturbation* (*Onanism: Diseases Produced by Masturbation*) (See Bryant, 1982). Among the medical myths were that masturbation would produce an early death, 'spinal tuberculosis, general paralysis, generate malformed offspring, impotence (if a man), sterility (if a woman), and epilepsy ultimately leading to insanity'. The climate was perfect for the rise of 'masturbation clinics' in the nineteenth century, to help parents cope with the 'problem' of children who masturbated persistently. The offending child was prescribed aluminium mitts and chastity belts to prevent the behaviour and, consequently, the epilepsy, sterility, insanity and myriad other medical disorders that the experts predicted could follow.

Treatments involved 'spermatorrhoea bandages' and 'spermatorrhoea rings', which, when wrapped tightly around the penis, would prevent erection. Some of these, as mentioned earlier, had spikes to prick the penis if erection occurred. Other devices included electric alarms to awaken the culprit or his parents. By far the most insidious, noxious and severe treatment for excessive masturbation was surgical cauterization of the prostate gland, the severing of nerve pathways leading to the penis and, in females, the excision of the clitoris or even removal of the ovaries. Not surprisingly, these torturous treatments led to persistent pain, impotence, frigidity, infection and sometimes death as a result of post-operative complications.

The Victorians and early twentieth-century professionals promoted the belief that masturbating parents produce weak, immoral and lazy children; that symptoms of masturbation in children could be easily recognized in the form of ennui, laziness, disobedience and 'moral insanity'; and that masturbation was harder on the nervous system than normal sexual intercourse. Moreover, masturbation was supposed to prevent the body's ability to break down nitrogenous waste. It was thought that this resulted in the excessive loss of the biochemical 'spermin' – which do not even exist. Masturbation was also thought to impair the individual's ability to have 'normal' heterosexual relationships, because masturbators lose interest in 'normal' sex since it could cause loss of sensitivity in the sex organs.

Victorian sexual morality persists in twentieth-century Russia, where the Soviet authorities and public consider all forms of masturbation, in adults and children alike, to be a pathological illness. Official views insist that children are born sexually neuter and masturbation is considered 'a stigma of moral dissoluteness and at the same time a survival of, or something introduced from, bourgeois society'. The exiled Soviet psychiatrists, Mikhail and August Stern (1981), describe the epitome of sexism in a male patient who, when he discovered that his wife had masturbated as a child, filed for divorce. The patient declared that he was entitled to masturbate, since he was a man, but that it was despicable for a woman to do so.

Official figures for masturbation are absurdly distorted by the Soviets, who claim that only 8 per cent of girls and 20 per cent of boys masturbate. According to the Sterns, the true figures correspond more to those in Western countries: between 85 to 95 per cent of males and 75 to 85 per cent of females have experimented with masturbation prior to marriage. Repressive attitudes to masturbation and sex in the Soviet Union are not without their consequences. One bizarre case involved the fifteen-year-old daughter of a Vinnitsa judge, who tore her hymen while masturbating, causing herself to bleed severely. Having spent the evening with friends, and confided in one, she went home, when her mother noticed some blood on her leg. After an examination, her mother discovered she had lost her virginity. The frightened girl produced a list of the names of boys at the party – a list which was enough to send one boy to a penal camp for eight years for the rape of a minor! According to the Sterns, when the boy returned from the penal camp he was, hardly surprisingly, impotent.

Another extraordinary and graphic consequence of sexual repression is cited in the same work:

If the practise of masturbation is protracted, if it is repressed, or at least if its perpetrator is seriously inhibited, it tends to assume extravagant forms. A girl was brought to a Leningrad clinic in an ambulance. Her vagina was seriously injured by glass splinters. The doctors began to question her as to the origin of these splinters, which extended to the neck of the uterus, but her only reply was to beg them to tell her whether she was going to die. In fact she had used a cylinder-shaped Czech light bulb as a kind of artificial phallus. During one masturbation session the bulb had cracked and it broke while she was using it. Fortunately, the bulb was not switched on at the time, for the girl also had the habit of turning it on to warm it and to increase her feelings of pleasure.

The Sterns go on to describe an incredible, if not inventive, incident, involving a Vinnitsa schoolgirl who read about the experiments of the British scientist, James Olds. Olds's experiments were concerned with implanting electrodes in the 'pleasure centres' of rats' brains. The

animals could then stimulate themselves to orgasmic
ecstasy by pressing a lever which set off an electric impulse.
They enjoyed the sensation so much that they self-
stimulated by pressing the bar up to 7,000 times in an
hour, totally exhausting themselves. The Vinnitsa schoolgirl, Sveta, connected up an electric circuit to her clitoris
while her parents were away on vacation. On their return,
Sveta proudly showed her parents her modification of
Olds's experiment. The parents were stunned, having
noticed that she had lost over 15 pounds in bodyweight.
The girl had found the sensations so pleasurable that she
had left no time to eat. Her parents referred her for
treatment, which proved uncomplicated, except for getting
Sveta to regain the lost weight. But the case has a happy
ending, with Sveta being selected to enter the mathematics
and physics academy for gifted children at Novosibirsk.

Other cases in the Soviet Union have proved less benign.
Although sado-masochism is discussed later, the example
of the 'sadistic masturbator' is worth describing here. This
bizarre incident involved a fourteen-year-old boy who
would catch stray cats and, while petting them, begin to
literally crucify the animals to the wall with nails. He would
ritually stab a cat in its heart and begin to masturbate the
instant after it died. Then he would wash the knife and use
it for a bookmark.

The book he was reading at the time was *The Three Musketeers*
[the Sterns conclude]. There was an entire cemetery of cats
behind the shed: nearly thirty animals. In the shed itself there
was a pool of dried blood and, beside it on a bench, Dumas's
novel, with the knife between its pages.

Electronic and sophisticated mechanical devices to
enhance masturbation are a phenomenon of twentieth-
century technology. It may seem ironic therefore that our

century should have begun with such an emphasis on anti-masturbation aids. The Sterns claim that such privileged Soviets as the wives of diplomats take vibrators and artificial phalluses back into their country from abroad. These artificial penises can fetch inordinately high prices on the black market.

THE BRIGHTER SIDE

Whereas doctors were in the eighteenth, nineteenth and early twentieth centuries developing techniques to counter masturbation in both adults and children, thier counterparts from the 1960s onwards have been promoting masturbation as an effective treatment for 'pre-orgasmic' women (who used to be termed 'frigid') and for men suffering from erectile failure or impotence. Since the advent of such sex manuals as *The Joy of Sex* and *The Sensuous Woman*, surveys like *The Hite Report* or *My Secret Garden*, and the lifting of obscenity regulations in Western countries, pornographic magazines, films, and sex aids have become exceedingly popular. It is now not all that uncommon for thirteen- and fourteen-year-old girls to own battery-operated vibrators (Dodson, 1974). Their ownership is certainly common for adult women in many Western countries, the machines being advertised in legitimate mail-order catalogues as electric or battery-operated massagers to 'sooth away tension' and 'reduce strain after a long day'.

Some feminists have acclaimed the mechanical aid to masturbation since they view it as liberation from an unhealthy dependence on males (Dodson, 1974). Other feminists deplore the use of electric vibrators, feeling that women can become dependent on a device which provides an even more powerfully erotic sensation than hands, mouths, tongues or penises. I was told by a twenty-six-year-old American woman that she had thrown 'my vibrator under a truck three years ago because it felt too good.

The damn thing was coming between me and my boyfriend who, for all his prowess, couldn't match my vibrator!' Some sex therapists are opposed to the use of the vibrator for similar reasons. Instead, when treating 'pre-orgasmic' women, they suggest that the woman masturbate using her own hands, or have her partner masturbate her. Nevertheless, there is a sizeable constituency in the feminist camp who support masturbation in women as a means of giving up dependency on men.

Betty Dodson, a pioneer in the field of female masturbation, suggests that women should enter into an intense love affair with themselves and recommends women to set up dates with themselves for the precise purpose of masturbation. There is no question but that the vibrator, like the computer, is here to stay. After all, it has been described by one author as the 'last sexual frontier for many people'; while, in a *Redbook* article, Claire Safran (1976) claimed that a woman could manage to have '50 consecutive orgasms using the machine' in the course of an hour.

A bizarre variation on the electric vibrator is the potential of washing machines! The average washing machine emits rhythmic vibrations conducive to female masturbation, and American advertisers are alleged to have taken advantage of the fact that women can use the vibration of revolving washing machines to enhance masturbation. Hence one advertisement which depicted a washer dressed like a man wearing a tie. Ironically, some 'self-help' feminist manuals have even described the sexual potential of the washing machine. It is hard to help but think that the idea of the bored housewife turning to her washer for orgasmic relief reflects unparalleled sexism.

Unsurprisingly, masturbatory devices for men are also on the market. These are often advertised in sex-orientated publications and can be purchased at local sex shops or by mail order. Magazines like *Mayfair* or *Club* are among the dozens in which artificial vaginas, 'suckulators' and 'love dolls' are advertised. Suckulators are shaped like a woman's mouth and are equipped with a suction bulb to help male masturbation. The advertisements suggest that the purchaser make his 'dreams come true' with patented electric sucking machines replete with 'moving and massaging' parts. One machine was even claimed to be able to draw off the 'spent sperm' and therefore to be 'less messy'.

'Love dolls' are one of the more unusual devices available for male masturbation. These are life-sized female dolls constructed of vinyl or plastic and usually designed to resemble 'model-shaped' adolescent females. They usually come with synthetic pubic hair, female odours (chemically produced), exaggerated breasts and very snug vaginas. More expensive versions can include a voice feature in which prerecorded tape mechanisms whisper 'love-talk' at the right moment. The more expensive, *de luxe* models are also equipped with electronic vaginas and 'deep throats' which will vibrate and suck with the help of a built-in air pump. Manufacturers advertise Scandinavian and Greek versions. Greek models feature extra-large breasts and an anal passage for anal sex. Dolls constructed out of foam can be manipulated and bent to any desired position. Others are created to imitate prostitutes and given names like 'Susie Slut' or 'Tanya Tart'. Clothing, at extra cost, of course, is also available. One *Forum Magazine* reader submitted the following appreciation:

I recently acquired the most wonderful mate for my bed partner and I'm sure your male readers will be most interested to hear about her. She is 5'5" with the most beautiful shaped legs, perfect bust, and little waist and a bottom that is perfection itself. We have the most wonderful intercourse together in any position I happen to fancy; sometimes lovingly, with her legs wrapped around my waist, we make love face to face, sometimes I climb in top of her from the back, leaning over a low table. At times I feel like tying her spreadeagled to the bedpost for deep-entry or whipping her and dressing her up in exquisitely designed bondage outfits. Whatever I feel like doing, she never protests. She never nags me if I stay out all night, get drunk, or bring home another woman. And she never talks to me of marriage. In fact, she never talks at all; you see she's made of rubber! Soft and velvety to the touch and sweet and clean to smell, she comes all the way from Japan.

It has been pointed out that the practice of making love to a plastic doll carries features of necrophilia (a sexual dysfunction in which the individual's primary sexual gratification comes from having sex with dead persons, male or female). The love doll caters to men with low self-esteem, and is clearly an exploitation of a market in which certain males need to objectify and control women. Some consider the existence of such items as obscene and therefore that they should be made illegal. Dildos (artificial penises) and artificial vaginas (including love dolls) are in fact illegal in Georgia in the United States (Bryant, 1982).

Real – and living – love dolls are also available. All the consumer needs to do is visit a massage parlour. Massage parlours are most common in North America, but they also exist in various European countries. In America, they are considered an institution and are usually situated on main roads where they can easily be spotted. They are advertised in newspapers and magazines, and sport flashing neon signs. Massage parlours are to sex what McDonald's is to food: fast. Since they are legal in many zones, going to one removes the male guilt associated with seeing a regular prostitute and therefore technically avoids adultery. Massage parlours invariably cater to heterosexual men. The object is rapid orgasm via a 'hand job' – hence the term 'handwhore' – and can take as little as five minutes, although twenty minutes is average. The masseuse is not considered as lowly as the regular prostitute, since she only uses her hands. Studies show that the average customer is white, married, an out-of-towner, approximately thirty-five years old, employed in a lower-to-middle-class job and someone who might 'go to church on Sundays' (Simpson and Schill, 1977).

The phenomenon of paid masturbation in the form of massage parlours is summed up extremely well by Bryant (1982), who writes: 'In the service oriented society of today, the consumer simply lies there, wrapped in erotic reverie and totally indulges his narcissistic hedonism while seemingly sensual females minister anatomically to his sexual appetites.' Massage parlours are used by millions, account for millions of dollars in turnover, employ tens of thousands of women and usually take credit cards.

Gay Talese, author of *Thy Neighbour's Wife*, described his experience with massage parlours in New York City in the third person:

> In his parochial school, the nuns had advised him [Talese] and his classmates that they should sleep each night on their backs with their arms crossed on their chests, hands on opposite shoulders – a presumably holy posture that, not incidentally, made masturbation impossible. Talese had been a sophomore in college before he masturbated . . .

But it was not until much later that he experienced massage parlours for himself. The following is typical:

> After entering a parlour, he could smell her [the masseuse's] perfume, feel his palms perspire, see his penis rising. He closed his eyes and heard the sighs of other men in the adjoining rooms, and he also heard the street noise from Lexington Avenue, the honking of cars, the grinding of buses pulling away from the curb, and he thought of Bloomingdale's and Alexandra's across the street, and the crowds of customers and saleswomen who at this moment were leaning over counters buying and selling . . .
> 'Do you want anything special?' she asked.
> He opened his eyes. He saw her looking at his penis.

'Can we have sex?' he asked. She shook her head.
'I don't do that. I don't do French either. I only give locals.'
'*Locals?*'
'Hand jobs,' she explained.
'Okay,' he said, 'I'll have a local.'
'That will be extra.'
'How *much* extra?'
'Fifteen dollars.'

The masseuse, Talese explains, did an expert job. Using powder, she masturbated him to the point of ejaculation and demonstrated her professionalism by knowing exactly when to get out the tissues. For Talese, the experience proved far more gratifying than solitary masturbation, and he claims that visiting massage parlours is not totally devoid of warmth or fun. Other men disagree and say the experience made them feel small because they were paying for a quick sexual release, and that they had no respect for the masseuse, who viewed the client as a bit of business.

COMPASSIONATE MASTURBATION

Consider nurses who perform masturbation on very sick non-mobile patients who have gone without sexual release for long periods. One American nurse who performed this enormously compassionate service told me, 'You know, you might think me weird or crazy, but I have often masturbated my male patients. It seems to calm them and they sleep better, especially the older men. I usually do this for men who cannot do it for themselves. It is a sort of charity . . .' A resident at a London hospital told me that he had heard of such practices, but 'only around the geriatric wards'. He said that some nurses considered the practice 'outrageous', but that others felt it 'natural'. 'In any event,' he said, 'no one really talks about it. It's taboo, but as far as I know, no nurses have been fired for masturbating their patients, but then, who would catch them?' Interestingly, some geriatric health workers suggest to their patients that they masturbate. This often proves a difficult task for older persons who have maintained a lifelong belief that touching oneself is as wicked as the Catholic Church claims it to be.

8 MENSTRUATION

PRIMITIVE BELIEF AND CUSTOM

There is nothing bizarre about menstruation, the monthly cycle when post-pubescent and pre-menopausal women shed the blood-enriched lining of the uterus, if an ovum has not been fertilized. What *is* bizarre are the numerous beliefs and attitudes associated with the monthly flow of blood through female genitalia. The entire process has, traditionally, been fraught with contamination.

Many primitive peoples did not link sexual intercourse with pregnancy and birth. Some still do not. Menstrual blood was viewed as magical, as having a life of its own, and often as something to be feared. For this reason, shamans and priests considered menstrual blood to be a source of supernatural power. In the majority of cultures, menstruating women were, and often still are, labelled 'unclean'. The Babylonians were among the first to record the use of a sanitary towel or 'blood bandage' (in Sumerian, *tug.nig.dara.ush.a*), and thought that a menstruating woman would contaminate everything she touched. If a menstruating woman should touch a sack of grain, it would be promptly destroyed.

In ancient Egypt, and among the Hebrews, women were obliged to take ritual cleansing baths at the end of menstruation. If a man touched a menstruating woman, or even her bed, he, too, would be contaminated for seven days.

Ancient and modern Orthodox Jews practise ritual purification of unclean women at the end of menstruation. The women are sent to a cleansing bath or *mikveh* (in Hebrew, literally a 'collection of waters') which, according to the Torah, ritually purifies a person who has become unclean through contact with the dead (Numbers 19) or by way of unclean flux from the body (Leviticus 15).

Sexual relations with an unclean woman were seen as being so vile that, according to one Talmudic source, a child born of the couple was considered illegitimate – a *mamzer*. Archaeological discoveries of *mikvoth* (plural of *mikveh*) from the Second Temple period (400 B.C.) confirm that these ritual baths have been in existence for thousands of years.

Contemporary *mikvoth* exist in modern cities and comply with biblical law, which stipulates how much of the woman must be immersed, what kind of water is to be used, and so forth. The ritual cleansing occurs in the presence of the rabbi. The modern *mikveh* is a small, tiled, heated pool filled with water high enough to reach the chest of the average-sized woman, and the water must be natural, from a spring or rain. An Orthodox Jewish woman attends the *mikveh* exactly twelve days after her period begins, and she checks to see that she is no longer bleeding at the time of 'purification'. After being bathed and entering the water, the woman recites the following blessing, 'Blessed art Thou, Lord Our God, King of the Universe, Who Sanctifies Us By His Commandments and Commands Us to Observe the Ceremony of Immersion.' Subsequently, the woman immerses herself in the water two more times, and she can then resume sexual intercourse.

Contamination beliefs are not confined to the ancient Egyptians and Hebrews. In the Chinese province of Tsinhai, people refer to *tsang*, which involves an array of religious contamination taboos. Among these is the regulation that a girl must not allow her menstrual blood to touch the earth. To do so would mean she had offended the earth spirit and would be punished by being condemned to hell. To prevent her menstrual blood falling on the earth, the girl had to fasten her trousers to her ankles. Men blamed misfortune on the *tsang* or contaminating female essence.

The medieval Church was obsessively afraid of menstruation, primarily because it was imbued with superstition (Taylor, 1953). The Church fathers believed that anything sexual would contaminate. For this reason, couples had to abstain from sexual intercourse for three nights after marriage, the so-called 'Tobias nights', and after having had sex, they would not be allowed to enter a church for thirty days. Even then, the couple should do forty days' penance and make an offering. It was especially sinful for a menstruating woman to enter a church. Should she do so, she was required to perform a lengthy penance. It is worth pointing out that the medieval Church forbade sexual intercourse with a menstruating woman, even as it did between a Christian and a Jew, which was equivalent to bestiality and hence very serious in the Church's eyes (Taylor, 1953).

MODERN PERSPECTIVES

Although contemporary attitudes towards menstruation have improved, it is still common practice among some Jewish and Mediterranean societies for a mother to slap the face of a girl when she reports her first menstrual flow. The young girl usually has no prior knowledge of menstruation and has come to her mother in a state of fear. One rationalization for this practice is that slapping the child's face will bring blood back to her pale cheeks.

Kupfermann (1979) underscored the curious tendency to

treat menstruation with secrecy and shame even in the enlightened 1970s and 1980s. Most men remain reluctant to perform cunnilingus (mouth contact with the vulva) during a woman's period, not so much on account of the 'foul odour', but because of the engrained stigma connected with a 'polluting body'. Menstruation continues to be thought of as a cause of insomnia, kleptomania, irritability and mental illness.

Some feminists would rather do without menstruation. Germaine Greer (1970) asks,

> Why should women not resent an inconvenience which causes tension before, after and during; unpleasantness, odour, staining; which takes up anything from a seventh to a fifth of her adult life until the menopause . . . We would rather do without it.

Other feminists are more razor-tongued. In an article entitled 'If Men Could Menstruate', Gloria Steinem (1983) fantasizes that, if men suddenly had the ability to menstruate, or if they were the only sex who could menstruate, then the status of menstruation would be elevated. Steinem seems to think that 'men would brag about how long and how much' they menstruated, and young boys 'would talk about it as the envied beginnings of manhood'. Men would also try to convince women that sex was better 'at that time of the month', and intellectual men would argue that women could not understand mathematics, time or space because they would not be connected with moon cycles. Steinem's sense of irony may, indeed, be well placed in the light of the fact that many Americans, and, to a lesser extent Europeans, remain uncomfortable with television advertisements for feminine hygiene.

9 SEXUAL POSITIONS AND GENITALIA

POSITIONS DICTATED

Since the roots of many socially prescribed sexual codes are in religion, it is hardly surprising that Judaeo-Christian theology should have its share of peculiar required sexual behaviours in marriage. According to the pioneers in American sex research, Kinsey, Pomeroy and Martin (1948), married Catholics used to confess the sin of having sexual intercourse in a position other than with partners face to face, and the woman supine under the man. Preferred sexual positions vary between different people. During the periods of colonialization, Christians became concerned, not only with spreading the Gospel, but also with teaching 'savages and heathens' about holy matrimony and 'correct' sexual practices. Thus the Trobriand Islanders in the South Pacific were taught the 'missionary position' – using drawings on blackboards – which they thought not only absurd but also incredibly funny.

The early Catholic missionaries took a particular interest in the sexual activities of South and Central American Indians, and during confessions specifically asked the natives whether they had sexual intercourse with animals, mothers, brothers, fathers or sisters. The priests judged the sexual posture of rear entry to be immoral since this imitated the sexual posture of animals. The Indians were duly informed that they had been punished by God in the form of Spanish Conquistadores because of their sexual vices. They were also warned not to 'entice your flesh with your own hands' (masturbate), 'sleep mixed up like pigs' (have orgies), or 'sin with another man or with a boy or with a beast'. Breaking these codes would, they were told, certainly condemn them to an everlasting after-life in hell's fires.

In the post-war United States, sexual intercourse in marriage tended to be conservative. People considered rear entry, oral-genital contact and anal sex all to be dirty, despicable and depraved. Pre-sexual revolution America presents a picture of the woman supine performing a not-so-vital marital chore in the briefest time possible. 'Unnatural sexual demands' – such as asking a spouse to perform oral sex – provided grounds for divorce, and, in some cases, for prosecution by the state (Bryant, 1982).

It is enlightening to describe one from among the many incredible legal cases concerning American sexual and marital morality. This case is sensational, not only because it took place as late as 1969, but also since it illustrates how the authorities were able to invade the privacy of a Virginian married couple. The husband and wife invited a third party, a man, into their bedroom, where, with the mutual consent of all parties, the women performed fellatio (oral sex) on both men. The only problem was that photographs were taken and subsequently found by the couple's daughter, who took them to school, where teachers discovered the girl showing off the snapshots to friends. The police and the department of welfare were summoned immediately, a warrant to search the couple's home was obtained and a search revealed dozens of photographs of the couple engaged in 'unnatural' sexual acts with their male friend. The couple was then charged under Virginia's 'infamous crimes against nature' or sodomy laws.

In most American states, as well as in England, the phrase 'crimes against nature' refers to sodomy or buggery, a term coined under English common law in 1533 under Henry VIII. Since the case in modern Virginia involved oral sex (stimulation of the genitals using mouth and tongue) with a third party, the Virginian courts judged the couple's right to privacy defence to be invalid. According to Koplin (1977), the marital right to privacy ceased to protect the husband and wife the moment they performed sodomy *in the presence of a third party*! Furthermore, the wife was subjected to a separate trial, since it was she who had performed the 'unnatural sex act' on the other man. She was found guilty of sodomy and sentenced to the maximum term of three years in the state penitentiary. The court said that, 'by permitting an onlooker into the marital bedroom, the [couple] would have no reasonable expectation of privacy and, therefore, no constitutional protection'.

The fact that a case of this type could occur as late as 1969, and that 'unnatural sex laws' persist in both England and America, attests to the continuing powerful influence of nineteenth-century theology, which would condemn rear entry on the grounds that it imitates animal copulation and perhaps because the male is then no longer in the dominant and presumably natural mode. As Stone (1979) observes, an additional reason for the theological belief that the woman-on-top or rear-entry position is considered unnatural may be that the male's semen would after ejaculation have to fight gravity to reach the cervix (womb) and the chance of pregnancy therefore be reduced.

OBSESSIONS WITH GENITAL SIZE

Penis size is, for many males, their main sexual hang-up. 'Am I big enough?' 'Am I bigger than your last lover?' 'Am I fatter?' 'What's the average length?' 'Is height related to penis length?' All these questions are frequent worries for those men who need constant confirmation of their sexual prowess, which they often confuse with phallic length. Yet the ancient Sanskrit writers in India were equally fascinated with the sizes and shapes of genitals.

The *Kama Sutra* advocates that, if a man seeks to increase

the size of his penis or *lingam*, he should begin by rubbing it with the bristles of certain insects that live in trees – hardly a comfortable practice. On the following ten nights, he should rub his *lingam* with oil, and then with the insect bristles again. From this point, he should sleep in a bed with a hole in it to allow his penis to hang down. Not surprisingly, the penis would then become swollen, the swelling being called *suka* and said to last for life.

The *Kama Sutra* or *Aphorisms on Love* by Vatsyanyana is an ancient Sanskrit treatise in seven parts, Part Two being devoted to perfecting sexual union. Men and women are divided into three groups each. According to the size of his *lingam*, a man may be: (a) a hare man; (b) a bull man; or (c) a horse man. A woman is classified according to the depth of her *yoni* and may be: (a) a female deer; (b) a mare; or (c) a cow elephant. The following is the table of 'equal unions':

Men	Women
Hare	Deer
Bull	Mare
Horse	Elephant

And here is the table of 'unequal unions';

Men	Women
Hare	Mare
Hare	Elephant
Bull	Deer
Bull	Elephant
Horse	Deer
Horse	Mare

While equal unions are considered the best, certain unequal unions are still regarded as 'high unions'. Essentially, if the man is greater in size than the female, the union is a 'high one'. If the woman is larger in size, then the union is considered a 'low one'. An example of the lowest union would be an elephant woman with a hare man. Degree of passion or desire is categorized in a similar manner: men and women are either small, middling or intense. Interestingly, semen is not distinguished from 'female semen', which refers to the amount of lubrication in the vagina during normal sexual arousal.

The Indians were among the first to develop the artificial penis or *apadravyas*, to help a man with a small penis satisfy a *Hastini* or elephant woman, one with a very deep vagina. The *apadravyas* was put around the *lingam* to increase its length and thickness so that it would fit the large *yoni*. An *apadravyas* may be made of gold, silver, copper, iron, ivory, bull's horn, special woods, tin or lead (a poison), to be 'soft, cool and provocative of sexual vigour'. Traditionally, when these substances were not available, objects such as tubes made from wood or apple or the bottle gourd plant could be tried. Perhaps one of the more unusual suggestions was that of self-mutilation − piercing a hole in the penis so that it could house a small *apadravyas*. Disinfection of the wound involved standing in a river all night long to allow the blood to flow and then washing with a mixture of liquorice and honey.

Penis size seems to be a universal concern. No group seems traceable where penis smallness has been associated with high status. It seems that primitive and modern peoples alike all place high value on a longer, bigger and, presumably, more powerful phallus. For example, there is the 'penis sheath', a body adornment, often elaborate, colourful and long, which is worn over the penis to exaggerate its length. In some African tribes these are worn at the time of pubescent circumcision, and pubescent boys wearing penis sheaths are to be seen in many parts of Africa today. In New Guinea, a penis sheath is worn by the chief of a highland tribe as a symbol of status, power and respect (Morris, 1977). In Europe, in the fifteenth and sixteenth centuries, the codpiece became a notable feature of male apparel for the very same reasons.

EUNUCHS AND CASTRATI

Not all groups appreciate their testicles. The early Christians, who believed that sexual desire was sinful and would draw them away from God, practised 'auto-castration' as a form of holiness and purification. In the New Testament, Matthew (19:12) quotes Jesus as extolling the virtuous men who made themselves 'eunuchs for the kingdom of heaven's sake'. Among methods to induce auto-castration was the application of a tight ring above the scrotum to block the blood supply to the testes (as shepherds still do today when castrating male lambs). However, the usual method involved cutting off the testes, sometimes the whole penis, with an unsterilized knife. The absence of testes produces a lack of male hormones and consequently a total reduction of libido when castration is carried out before pubescence. A degree of lidibo may persist in some men who are castrated in maturity, even though they are made infertile.

The practice of castrating males to make them eunuchs dates back thousands of years to the Assyrian, ancient Chinese, Egyptian, Greek, Roman and Inca civilizations. In India, the practice still continues among eunuch cults who are alleged to kidnap pubescent boys and castrate them before inducting them into the community (Diamond, 1984; Lapierre, 1985). It was only in 1878, during the reign of Pope Leo XIII, that the Catholic authorities banned the procedure among choir boys. In Islamic cultures, boys were castrated prior to puberty and used to protect women in harems and female slaves from being impregnated by outsiders. Slave owners were confident that eunuchs would not be sexually attracted to their property.

Eighteenth-century music lovers were well aware that the voices of boys with undescended testicles retained a high-pitched tonality. This voice was known as the *castrato*, and it was not uncommon for gifted boys to undergo deliberate castration. Mozart, Gluck and Handel are among the composers who wrote sections of choral works or operas especially for *castrati*. Some eunuchs eventually developed powerful soprano or contralto voices.

PART TWO

Sex, Violence and Aggression

Introduction

The relationship between violence and sexual behaviour ranges from the expression of territoriality to bizarre mass murders, gang rape and women who rape men. It includes lovers' quarrels, wife-beating, sado-masochism, bondage and violent pornography. Since sex with violence is usually associated with *sadism* and *masochism*, it seems fitting to begin with these.

'The revolt against society explains partly, but not altogether, the increase in violence and sex crime. The psychology of sexual perversion must also be taken into account. Increased sexual activity has always been associated with the final stages of a decadent civilization. Why should this be so? One of the most obvious is proposed by Tolstoy in *The Kreutzer Sonata*. Intense sexual activity, he argues, is associated with people who have nothing to do' – Colin Wilson and Patricia Pitman, *Encyclopaedia of Murder* (1984).

'TYCOON HANGED

'Düsseldorf: Millionaire industrialist Dieter Engelbrecht, 46, hanged himself in his prison cell 24 hours after he was jailed for keeping a teenage sex slave' – *Daily Mail*, 30 January 1985.

'GOLF-CLUB WOMAN ROUTS SEX PEST

'A woman fought off a sex pest who attacked her while she was out walking her dog. After he struck her on the back of her head with a tree branch and threatened her with a chisel, she began wielding a golf club she was carrying and he fled. The woman, 44, had gone prepared following a series of attacks on women at Sheepleas, near Horsley, Surrey. Police are hunting a man they call the "bizarre beast" because of strange clothes he wears when he strikes. They include a gas mask, black floral dress and heavy brown boots' – *Daily Mail*, 25 January 1985.

10 SADISM AND MASOCHISM

SADISM

The term **sadism** is derived from the name of Donatien-Alphonse-François de Sade (1740–1814), who came to be known as the Marquis de Sade. The Marquis is infamous for his writings and activities concerning the sexual humiliation and abuse of women and children. He was born into an aristocratic French family and was among the first of the *avante-garde* pornographers to glorify sexual cruelty.

De Sade celebrated the idea that it was valid to seek pleasure through the infliction of pain on another person. Degradation, torture and bizarre sexual activities were the themes of his novels, *Justine* and *Juliette*, and he seems to have made several attempts in his life to act out his fantasies. Baudelaire, Flaubert and Dostoevsky are among those who have admired his writings for their literary attributes. Themes in de Sade's stories include the degradation of religion (defecation on crucifixes), sexual killings, child molestation, sodomy and the whipping of women and children. One of de Sade's sexual fantasies involved suspending women from the ceiling and flagellating them while his servant masturbated him. Although the Marquis de Sade was on one occasion sentenced to death for attempting to poison a young prostitute with the dubious aphrodisiac Spanish fly, he managed to escape to Savoy and was executed only in effigy.

In psychology, **sadism** refers to sexual gratification by inflicting mental or physical pain on another, and sadism may occur in both consenting and non-consenting situations. Although rape is clearly sadistic, and is sometimes a component in murder, it is dealt with later in this text (pages 142–82) since it is a syndrome which differs considerably from simple sadism.

Sadistic behaviour takes many forms. For example, a convicted shoe fetishist who had stolen women's shoes, then cut them up, also found great pleasure in destroying photographs of women owned by other prisoners. In another case, a man broke into a woman's home, rendered her unconscious with chloroform and, without making any apparent sexual overtures, proceeded to brand her thigh with a hot iron (Coleman, 1972).

MASOCHISM

The term 'masochism' comes from the name of Count Leopold von Sacher-Masoch (1835–95), an Austrian writer whose novels focused on the sexual delights to be obtained from the suffering of pain. He himself enjoyed being beaten with studded whips. Masochism has also come to imply gratification through self-denial, humiliation and suffering in general.

Leopold was told tales of bloody terror by his wet-nurse, Handscha, and by his police-chief father, besides being exposed to terrifying German fairy-tales during childhood. He had developed a taste for punishment long before obtaining his doctorate in law, and became the *slave* to several mistresses besides marrying twice. He signed a contract with one mistress, an extract from which reads: 'Herr Leopold von Sacher-Masoch gives his word of honour to Frau Pistor to become her slave and to comply unreservedly . . . Frau Pistor, on her side, promises to wear furs

. . . when she is in a cruel mood' (Hendrickson, 1982). Sacher-Masoch's best-known novel is *Venus in Furs*, which portrays a man who finds sexual fulfilment in birch rods and studded whips, and by being betrayed by the women he loved.

In clinical terms, **masochism** refers to sexual gratification through being subjected to mental or physical pain. People are diagnosed as masochists if they prefer pain above other forms of erotic activity. Kinsey *et al.* (1953) concluded that masochistic desires occurred to some degree in over 25 per cent of the thousands of males and females they interviewed, although they included in their terms of reference for this type of erotic pleasure mild pain such as erotic biting. In a report by Hunt (1974), 10 per cent of single women and 6 per cent of single men confirmed that they were sexually aroused by pain. Hunt also found that men are more likely to inflict pain than women, the pain inflicted being most usually the result of biting, but also involving slapping, scratching and pinching. Sadism and masochism are inter-related — hence the term **sado-masochism** (S & M).

11 SADISTIC SEX MURDERS

During the 1890s, Herman Webster Mudgett courted over two hundred women and, having promised to marry them and persuaded them to sign over their property to him, proceeded to murder them. Mudgett, initially loving and tender, would, as soon as a woman was won over, kill her and dissect her body. Mudgett does not hold the world record for mass murder, but he may well hold the American record for the sadistic sexual killing of women.

George William Rae, also known as 'the Boston Strangler', raped and murdered so many women that he could not recall the exact number. Rae claimed to have committed several rape murders during the course of a single day. In his frenzy, he would sometimes bite into a victim's breasts and stomach.

In the mid 1960s in England, as disciples of the Marquis de Sade, Ian Brady and Myra Hindley sexually tortured children to death. The children's screams were tape recorded so that the sadists could listen to the tapes and become sexually aroused later on.

In 1946, William Heirens, a seventeen-year-old student at the University of Chicago, kidnapped and strangled six-year-old Suzanne Degnan. Before killing the child, Heirens sexually molested her and, once she was dead, dissected her body. He also committed burglaries and attacked two women, leaving one dead. Heirens claimed that his *alter ego*, George, was responsible for his actions, and psychiatrists testified that he was a psychotic with a split personality.

Caryl Chessman, who wrote a bestseller about his experience on death row in California, was sentenced to die in the gas chamber for kidnapping, robbery and forcing young women to engage with him in unnatural sex acts. One seventeen-year-old woman, who was forced to have intercourse with him, was later confined to a mental hospital suffering from schizophrenia. Chessman's style involved driving around lovers' lanes in Los Angeles with a flashing red light on top of his car, causing his victims to believe he was a policeman. Chessman's book inspired several groups and individuals to demonstrate and appeal against his death sentence.

A savage and sadistic mass murder was committed in 1966 by Richard Speck, who forcibly entered the nurses' residence at South Chicago Community Hospital and, at gunpoint, bound and gagged nine nursing students. Speck proceeded to stab some, to strangle others, and to stab and strangle the rest. Evidence revealed that at least one nurse was sexually molested. It took him several hours to complete his work, at the end of which eight nurses lay dead. Speck could not recall having committed the crimes. He was intoxicated with alcohol and drugs on the night of the murders and could give no reason for why he had murdered the nurses. Although psychiatrists did not testify that he was insane, they found that Speck had syphilis, a low IQ and a history of hating women. His criminal record revealed that he had served time in jail for attacking women and for committing fraud and robbery. A psychiatrist explained Speck's behaviour by describing him as brain damaged, immature and puritanical, and as having an 'unconscious hostility to females because of a Madonna-prostitute complex'. He may have been seeking revenge against women in general after his wife left him.

Wilson and Pitman (1984) discuss the bizarre sexual sadist, Peter Kürsten, born in 1883 in Köln-Mulheim, Germany. Kürsten was forty-seven when he was finally arrested for a wide range of lust murders – a well-groomed, modest man, much liked by his fellow workers. He had been brought up in a disturbed family, his father being an alcoholic who was jailed for having intercourse with his daughter. Peter had also witnessed his father raping his mother on several occasions. The young boy's first sexual encounters were with dogs; a dog-catcher, who lived in the Kürsten home, taught him how to masturbate the animals.

When he was nine years old, Peter killed two boys by pushing them into the Rhine. His first full sexual experience was with a sheep, but when the poor animal would not stay still, Peter stabbed it and had an orgasm as soon as he saw the gushing blood. The young sexual sadist was launched on his macabre career.

During time served in prison for robbery, arson and attacking girls and women, he would masturbate to fantasies of killing women. He told Dr Berg, the psychiatrist who eventually investigated his case, that he would arrange to get himself put into solitary confinement so he could spend the hours masturbating to these fantasies. Using the logic of a criminal psychopath, Peter believed that he could exert revenge on society by killing innocent women.

His first sexual murder was committed in May 1913, when he killed thirteen-year-old Christine Klein as she slept. He 'strangled her, cut her throat with a penknife, and penetrated her sexual organs with his fingers', then dropped his blood-stained handkerchief next to her body. By a strange twist of fate, Christine's father, Peter Klein, had the same initials as Peter, and was tried for the murder of his daughter! Mr Klein was released for lack of evidence, but when he died during the First World War, was still suspected of having been the murderer.

Soon after this first killing, Peter used a hatchet on a strange woman and became aroused at the sight of her blood. Since the power and spectacle of fire also aroused him, he set light to a hay wagon. It was at this time that he was jailed for eight years for arson and the attempted strangulation of two women.

After his release, he married a woman who had herself spent five years in prison for shooting her fiancé when he refused to marry her. Peter identified with the injustice of her situation and was able to develop a normal attachment to her which lasted for the remainder of his life. But his wife could not satisfy his lust for real blood, and so, in 1925, he began 'Düsseldorf's reign of terror'.

At his eventual trial, Peter proudly used his photographic memory to reveal every deed. He had attempted to strangle four women and set seven major fires between 1925 and 1928. In February 1929, he stabbed a Frau Kuhn twenty-four times as she walked home at night. In the same month, he killed a drunk mechanic named Scheer by stabbing him twenty times. In March, he stabbed eight-year-old Rose

Öhlinger thirteen times, molested her sexually, then tried to burn her body with paraffin. Detectives could not fathom out this pattern of sexually killing men, women and children with equal enthusiasm, and eventually pressured a mental defective called Stausberg into confessing to the killings.

Peter claimed that, in August 1929, he strangled a girl called 'Anni', but could not prove it. Indeed, it is possible that some of his fantasies were masturbated to so often that he ceased to be able to distinguish them from reality. During the same month, he did, in truth, cut the throats of five-year-old Gertrude Hamacher and fourteen-year-old Louise Lenzen. The naked bodies of children and women continued to be discovered all around Düsseldorf until the end of 1929. Yet when police stepped up their search, the murders stopped, although the non-fatal stabbings continued.

Peter finally confessed the crimes to his wife, but she would not believe him. She was desperately afraid of dying a lonely, penniless widow. He took her out for a dinner, which she could not finish, ate the rest and arranged to give himself up to the police, who, despite 2,650 clues and 900,000 denunciations (one in fifty Germans informed on their fellows!), had been unable to solve the case. Peter showed no remorse. He described to Dr Berg how he casually went out with a pair of scissors, found a girl, invited her for some beer, then took her to Grafenberg woods where he slowly strangled her: 'She struggled violently, and screamed. I threw her down the ravine that runs down to the Wolf's Glen and went away.'

One of the more lurid aspects of the accounts given by Peter Kürsten is the way his sexual preoccupations combined necrophilia with sadism. After he killed one girl in the woods, he proceeded to rape her dead body anally and vaginally, autopsy showing leaves and earth in her anus. After burying her in a shallow grave, he returned with the

—

intention of crucifying her to two trees and leaving the body to be discovered by passers-by. When the body proved too heavy for this plan, he settled for returning to the grave to masturbate over the corpse.

Peter Kürsten was executed on 2 July 1931. His last meal consisted of Wienerschnitzel, fried potatoes and wine, and he asked for a second helping. Wilson and Pitman write:

> He told Berg that his one hope was that he would hear the sound of his own blood running into the basket, which would give him intense pleasure. He also admitted to wanting to strangle Berg's stenographer because of her slim, white throat. He was guillotined, and seemed cheerful and unconcerned at the last.

Forcible sadistic sexual acts are not always heterosexual. Sadistic killings and mass murders also occur within homosexual circumstances. In 1973, *Newsweek* magazine reported an outlandish case concerning the murder of at least twenty-seven teenaged males. The ringleader of the killings, Dean Allen Corrl, a thirty-three-year-old single man who lived in Houston, Texas, befriended Elmer Henly, seventeen, and David Brooks, eighteen. Corrl paid Henly and Brooks $200 for each boy they could lure to his residence, and thus Henly and Brooks went out seeking young hitch-hikers, who they invited home with the promise of glue-sniffing parties. When the unsuspecting boys arrived, Corrl would drug them. They would awaken to find themselves in a torture chamber, stripped naked and handcuffed to a wooden board. The torture chamber was filled with implements which Corrl used on the victims, sometimes taking days to savour his 'catch' as he sexually abused and slowly tortured a boy to death. If the victim did not die as a result of the sexual torture, Corrl would either strangle him or shoot him with a pistol. The acts would undoubtedly have continued if Corrl had not attempted to kill Henly and Brooks. Instead, Henly shot Corrl with the pistol and then confessed the story to the Houston Police Department. Police were led to mass grave sites. In all, twenty-seven bodies were dug up, but it was likely the figure was greater, because many of the boys were runaways who would not have been recorded as missing.

Allen (1979) gives an account of the incredible case of 'infantosexual sadism' committed by Gilles de Rais, a former companion to Joan of Arc. Over five hundred years before the Corll murders, Gilles de Rais was executed in 1440 for killing 200 young boys. Furthermore, he seems to have been influenced by the sado-masochistic 'kiddy-porn' of the day, child pornography being even then over a thousand years old. He told at his trial how he imitated the cruel pornography of Roman Caesars:

'I do not know why but I, myself, out of my own head without the advice of anyone, conceived the idea of acting thus, solely for the pleasure and delectation of lust; in fact I found incomparable pleasure in it, doubtless at the instigation of the devil. This diabolical idea came to me eight years ago; that was the very year in which my relative the lord of Suze died. Now being by chance in the library of his castle, I found a Latin book on the lives and customs of the Roman Caesars by the learned historian called Suetonius; the said book was ornamented by pictures, very well painted, in which were seen the manner of these pagan emperors, and I read in this fine history how Tiberius, Caracalla and other Caesars sported with children and took singular pleasure in martyring them. Upon which I desired to imitate the said Caesars and the same evening I began to do so following the pictures in the book . . . For a time I confided my case to no one; but later I took the mystery to several persons, among others to Henriet and Pontou, whom I trained for this sport. The said individuals aided in the mystery and took charge of finding children for my needs. The children killed at Chantoce were thrown into a vat at the foot of a tower, from which I had taken them out on a certain night and put into a box to be transferred to Machecoul and at Nantes in the Suze mansion, they were burned in my room except for a few handsome heads I kept as relics. Now I cannot say exactly how many were thus burned and killed but they were certainly to the number of six score per year.'

Returning to our own times, police recently found in Wilseyville, California, a secret underground hideout which was used by Charles Ng, twenty-four, and Leonard Lake, thirty-nine, to torture sexually more than twenty-five persons to death. Most victims were women, but they also included men and babies. The pair were also survivalists, people who go into seclusion and build shelters to protect themselves against the impending nuclear holocaust. They made videotapes of young women strapped to easy chairs and recorded the women's pleas. Some women begged for the lives of their babies, but were told they would have to become sex slaves or else would be killed. They were placed in leg irons, tortured with vices, whips, muzzles and other instruments. The torture chamber even had a one-way mirror so an observer could watch the proceedings. Police found badly decomposed bodies and the body of a headless woman. They also collected ten large bags of fractured bones from bodies which had been burned on the pair's property. Leonard Lake committed suicide by swallowing a cyanide capsule on being arrested in April 1985, and Charles Ng was finally apprehended.

12 MUTUALLY CONSENTED SADO-MASOCHISM: FLAGELLATION

When two individuals agree to engage in sexually sadistic games, one is the dominant sadist, the other the servile masochist. There is an enormous market for paraphernalia devoted to sado-masochistic gadgetry. Sex shops sell whips, chains, ligatures, racks, canes and other assorted objects used for torture. In England, there is even a society called Motivation, dedicated to sado-masochism.

One of London's night clubs reserves Monday nights for

> anyone into rubber, leather, bondage or latex . . . [the] clientele are of all ages and sexes, looks and sizes, corseted, chained, bound or spiked in a variety of shiny, slippery garments. There's a girl up against the far bar; she wears a nippleless white rubber bra and a short, flared miniskirt, and chats happily to her friend. At her feet kneels a man wearing jeans, sweatshirt and unzipped leather rapist mask; his head is up her skirt. Behind him stands a young woman dressed in black rubber, complete with thigh-high boots. She is alternately teasing and cracking a riding crop across his buttocks. [*Time Out*, 24–30 January 1985]

The incidence of consenting sado-masochistic practices in society is probably higher than it was when Kinsey *et al.* (1953) reported that 3 per cent of females and 1 per cent of males surveyed admitted erotic interest in stories involving 'erotic pain'. After all, individuals can purchase the 'equipment' by mail order and through advertisements in magazines while the indications are that sales of sado-masochistic paraphernalia are on the increase. The British sex researcher, Alex Comfort (1972), advocated in *The Joy of Sex* the use of 'light spanking' of a sexual partner to enhance sexual pleasure. He even suggested the use of 'canoe birch' or 'grey birch' to produce 'a genuinely decadent European sensation'. He warned, however, against the use of 'bamboo', because 'it cuts like a knife', and admonished, 'Don't play this game [spanking] with strangers, ever. Lovers have enough feedback not to let the most violent play go sour. And never mix purely erotic beating with real anger or bad-temper – it could be dangerous. A game is a game is a game.'

One problem with making consenting sado-masochistic sexual practices socially acceptable is that some people, to say the least, do get carried away. Tollison and Adams (1979) quote from a case on their files:

> I don't know what got into him. It started out as a game. I trusted him and thought he was just playing. He wanted to tie me down to the bed during sex. I thought it might be kinda fun so I agreed. I had no idea what could happen. He seemed content at first but after a while he started talking mean to me and slapping me on the face and breasts. I was getting scared and begged him to untie me. He went to the dresser and got a hairbrush and shoved it up my vagina over and over again. I screamed and thought he was going to kill me . . . I nearly passed out from pain.

Those who wish to take their sado-masochistic sexual preferences out of the bedroom can do so by going, for example, to clubs like Hell Fire in New York or Skin Two in London. Games include 'slaves and masters', a more sophisticated and elaborate version of the 'doctors and patients' played by many children. Slaves are recognizable by their collars attached to leashes. Slaves are usually male, though a few are female. Male slaves are, as a rule, naked except for a small rubber jockstrap and chains around the waist. The slave wears lots of hooks which render him ready for binding and *discipline*. The female dominants can be identified by their high spiked-heel shoes or boots and the riding crops and whips they carry. Their general appearance is severe, menacing and designed to 'show who is boss'.

Those adherents who cannot afford their own dungeons can rent one for £15 an hour at the British headquarters of the sado-masochism (S & M) society, Motivation, which also sells the necessary racks, whipping benches, whips, enema kits and sundry articles associated with S & M. Lindsay Shapiro (1985) claims that, 'Bank managers, professors, pensioners and housewives are all into this back-room scene, which is evenly spread across the age groups.'

She believes that the younger participants see S & M activity as a game, it being the older age groups who are more likely 'to be found hanging bat-like from their living room rafters on a Saturday night, covered in rubber and gasping through a gas mask'. After interviewing a couple involved with S & M, Shapiro reported that, 'Wendy's the mistress and John's the slave – he looks at her before answering most of my questions, and it's obvious who's in control.' Wendy stated that she and her husband were not 'into it [S & M] heavily. Some of the people here [at Skin Two] are into really nasty things. I've been here and seen blood drawn. I'd be careful if I were you.' Many of the submissives are men who hold dominant positions in the 'work arena'.

It hardly seems surprising that the practice of seeking out a prostitute to punish, humiliate and denigrate should be so popular in Europe and America when children are still routinely punished by being placed over the lap of an adult to have their buttocks spanked. The result is an engorgement of blood to sexually sensitive areas which, in young children – including the young Jean-Jacques Rousseau, as he recorded – acts as a sexual stimulant as the child's genitals rub against the adult's knees. Meanwhile, many teachers in British schools continue to exercise what they view as their right: the administration of corporal punishment. This often involves the child bending over and receiving *ritualistically* several strokes of the cane on his or her buttocks; or, for lesser offences, a rap over the hands with a ruler or other stern object. No critic can avoid entertaining the notion that such teachers may well derive a perverse sexual pleasure from the practice.

A company in the South of England still issues a catalogue which lists various paddles, canes and other instruments devised for the corporal punishment of children. Parents and teachers may purchase these articles by mail order. Small wonder that the demand for S & M 'adult magazines' should continue so strong in Britain that thousands of copies of *Roué, Spanking Letters* and *Justice* are sold each month. Such magazines are dedicated to the deification, glorification and promotion of corporal punishment specifically to create sexual arousal. Their material includes stories and pictures of schoolgirls being caned on the naked buttocks by cruel teachers, and so advocates the corporal punishment of children in the cause of fantasy.

Any cursory glance at the advertisements in Los Angeles' *Hollywood Press* will yield several offers from dominant prostitutes who can, for many men, satisfy their masochistic desires. Here is only one example:

> Slaves required: Dare to call your Mistress Samantha and you will receive the most severe discipline and punishment. I will teach you how to submit to my every whim. You will lick my feet and do exactly as I tell you, Slave.

Shapiro (1985) interviewed one dominatrix who called herself 'Madame Astra' and expressed contempt for those prostitutes in the Earl's Court district of London 'who'll have you in and out of bondage in half an hour, with a token whack and total lack of satisfaction'. Astra is not discomforted by any aspects of her clients' demands and regales Shapiro with her esoteric knowledge: 'There are certain people who like torture – genital torture – but that's mainly men, only a few women. At Club Doma in The Hague, I once witnessed a woman suspended spreadeagled from the ceiling, while a dom lady whipped her between the legs with a cat o'nine tails. But that's unusual.' Astra explains that her men like to be 'testicle trained', for which she has special equipment. Furthermore, the range of her devices includes 'ball stretchers', in connection with which she calmly states that 'balls' are 'much tougher than they seem to be. It's just the male castration complex.'

Astra claims that the men simply want to 'grovel'. One rather bizarre client, who visits her three times a year, only 'wants ... to be totally encased in rubber, blindfolded, gagged, trussed up on the floor, and just left alone quietly, while I rustle around in a mack'. Most clients do not want sexual intercourse, but 'something that goes beyond the boundaries. Caning is very popular – Europeans call it the "English syndrome". In Germany they like heavier stuff, extreme rubber, watersports.'

Theresa Berkley preceded Madame Astra by over 150 years in offering elaborate flagellation services, for which she developed in 1828 a device called the Berkley Horse or Chevalet. This contraption was essentially an adjustable ladder to which the client could be tied, 'so that his face projected through one space and his genitals through another. The "governess" stood behind and administered the whip to back or buttocks, according to taste, while a scantily dressed girl sat in front and massaged his bollocks' (Tannahill, 1980). The invention was said to have made more than £10,000 over the course of eight years, which was at the time a considerable sum of money.

Flagellation seems to have been popular enough in the nineteenth century to justify the publication of manuals like *The Romance of Chastisement; or revelations of school. By an expert & c.* Prostitutes who catered to these tastes were encouraged by brothel owners to have a flagellation manual at the ready so that a customer could choose, from a series of sketches, the exact form of punishment desired. Theresa Berkley believed the 'tools of the trade' to be very important to her work. She stored her rods in water

so that they should be green and supple. She had a dozen tapering whip thongs, a dozen cat-o'nine-tails studded with needle points, various kinds of thin supple switches, leather straps as thick as traces, currycombs and oxhide straps studded with nails, which had become tough and hard from constant use, also holly and gorse and a prickly evergreen called 'butcher's bush'. During the summer, glass and Chinese vases were kept filled with green nettles. ['Pisanus Fraxi', cited by Tannahill, 1980]

Much attention was paid to the attire of nineteenth-century dominatrixes. It was felt that they should not appear entirely naked, but should be partially clothed in furs, sensuous undergarments, a nun's habit or all-white silk outfits.

13 SEX, TERRITORIALITY AND AGGRESSION

Humans can be as savage as any animal when guarding their territory. Men and women are capable of extremely violent behaviour when they discover an intruder on their property. Both sexes experience an emotion, labelled as 'jealousy', when they perceive another person poaching on their property, this ranging from seeing another person making a pass at a sexual partner to finding the partner in the throes of a passionate love affair. Perhaps out of a sense of honour, or partly because self-worth is defined on the basis of the love and approval of a *single* lover, people will in certain circumstances assault or even murder total strangers as readily as those closest to them. *Violence in the family accounts for the majority of murders committed, and sexual jealousy for a significant proportion of all murders.*

Some individuals are more possessive of their mates than others. While this often happens among insecure individuals with poor self-esteem and feelings of inferiority, it can also occur among the most apparently well-adjusted individuals, who may suddenly behave irrationally when sexually jealous. In their study *Open Marriage*, a husband-and-wife team, the O'Neils, proposed that it was possible for married couples to have one or more sexual partners outside the marriage. Yet many experiments in open marriage have led to sexual jealousy and ended in failure (for the Oneida and Sandstone ventures, see pages 401–9). According to the humanist psychologist, Carl Rogers, experiments of this kind have led to suicide. In prisons, violence and murder are often associated with homosexual jealousy (Bryant, 1982). However, most people associate sexual jealousy with the *crime passionel*, which is still, in some European and American states, regarded as justifiable homicide.

Germaine Greer (1984) has noted that the public is sometimes outraged by what it views as harsh sentences meted out for this type of crime. She cites the case in which Louis Castalas, a police inspector in the French city of Orléans, was given seven years for the fatal shooting of Paul Laurent in February 1980. Catalas had fought for the French Resistance during the Second World War, been caught by the Germans and sent to Buchenwald. Torture at Buchenwald had left him sterile, and this, he claimed, was the reason why his first two wives divorced him. However, his third wife finally bore him a child, a child he adored and thought to be his 'own blood'. When Castalas discovered that his seven-year-old son, Hervé, was in fact the 'son' of Paul Laurent, he deliberately shot Laurent to death with three witnesses present.

According to Greer, the light sentence 'represents the survival of archaic concepts of shame and the vindication of honour'. She explains that Castalas might have been jealous of Laurent for psychobiological reasons; Laurent had stolen Castalas's claim to 'biological immortality'. Castalas did not harm his wife because, in his mind, the matter was one for men. *The wife did not even enter the picture.* Since women are seen as 'sex objects and vessels of posterity', they cannot compete with men in the arena of honour.

In the public gallery of the court, Castalas's supporters shouted that he should be let go free, and that he should not be stripped of his decorations for heroism during the war.

Some societies attempt to regulate the level of sexual tension associated with courtship by prearranging marriage; sometimes even prior to birth. (In parts of India, marriages are often arranged by the couples' families, who pay a *gataka* for astrological advice.) Chaperones are still popular in many Islamic and Catholic countries. In more liberal Western countries, however, courtship is left to the individuals concerned. Sociological studies indicate that, in these more free societies, males tend to employ coercion and even violence in their attempts to have sexual intercourse with females.

Studies of courting behaviour on American campuses indicate that over one half of the women students report that they have been exposed to offensive sexual overtures by men. About five per cent claim that they experienced sexual violence during intercourse with men.

MARITAL VIOLENCE

In the United States, the FBI estimates that at least a million cases of wife-beating occur each year. Non-scientific estimates put the figure as high as 28 million (Jones, 1981). Further, Jones cites a study which concluded that wives who are beaten are found to control their husbands; they tended to be 'aggressive, efficient, masculine, and sexually frigid'. By contrast, husbands who engaged in wife-beating were 'shy, sexually ineffectual, reasonably hard-working "mother's boys" with a tendency to drink excessively'. Roles would reverse and the husband beat up his wife after becoming intoxicated. The researchers thought that, by beating up his wife, the husband was symbolically attempting to regain his masculinity. Fights could also occur as a direct consequence of the wife refusing her husband's sexual advances. The study also suggested that, by beating his wife, a husband served the masochistic needs of her 'guilt arising from the intense hostility expressed in her controlling and castrating behaviour'. Controlling and castrating behaviour is manifested in the wife's withdrawing of affection and sex and indulgence in sexual affairs with other men. It would appear that, in some cases at least, immature and 'helpless' husbands react to adversity by turning to violence – a violence which sometimes ends in the tragic murder of a loved one.

Women also commit marital violence under certain conditions. Although they are seven times more likely to be acting in self-defence, almost as many murders of spouses are committed by women as by men (Jones, 1981). Jones describes the case of Francine Hughes, who came home from college one evening in March 1977, to her home in Dansville, Michigan, and attempted to serve her unemployed husband, James, a frozen dinner. He resented Francine's attempts to further her education and believed she should stay at home preparing decent meals. James proceeded to punish her by beating her and forcing her to destroy her academic papers. He also threatened to kill her. The couple's daughter, Christy, called the police, who, used to the violence in the family, did not arrest James. He promptly fell asleep in the bedroom. Francine then poured an inflammable liquid around the room in which he was sleeping, and set it alight.

James died in the fire and Francine immediately gave herself up to the authorities. Michigan feminists took up the case, which they viewed as a genuine example of self-defence. People were becoming more aware of the helpless and hopeless situation in which many women found themselves. Battered women had nowhere to turn. They had no money of their own and relatives were often unsupportive, while the police maintained a 'hands off' strategy. A committee for Francine's legal defence was established and, as a result of the prevailing social climate, charges against her were reduced to manslaughter and second-degree murder. She was sentenced to five years' probation.

BATTERED HUSBANDS

After an American study by Suzanne Steinmetz (1978) stated that husbands suffered more battery at the hands of their wives than was previously thought, the husband-beating topic became an issue for national attention. *Time* magazine, newspapers and television all hopped on the bandwagon and forced the whole thing out of proportion. Statistics became thoroughly distorted (Jones, 1981). Steinmetz had claimed that a quarter of a million American men were beaten up by their wives annually, while Langley and Levy in Jones (1981; p.283) argued that 20 per cent of American men were the actual victims of marital battery.

Anne Jones believes the issue of husband-beating to be a hoax, since no shelters have been established for battered men. However, in this she neglects the fact that, in different ways, men may also be victims of discrimination. It would, after all, take a very brave man to admit that his wife was beating him up. He would be the laughing stock of the local police department, his friends and family. What police officer would take such a complaint seriously? What jury would believe him?

SEXUAL JEALOUSY

Sexual jealousy colours behaviour, emotion, physical sensations, dream life, thought and friendships. People can became physically ill when they become sexually jealous. Eugene Schoenfeld (1979) detailed several occurrences of sordid human emotion and behaviour connected with sexual jealousy in his comprehensive book, aptly entitled *Jealousy*. He presents the case of one young woman, who quite accurately wrote:

Jealousy is a painful disease. It nags at your head. It makes you dream terrible things, and makes you think of things unbeliev-able. When I get jealous I go off into an unknown world of hate. I think of sickening things to do to people. My heart beats fast and blood seems to rush to my head. My face burns with heat. I can't hold my temper, though I try very hard to hold it in. I went through stages where I hated my boyfriend so much I could kill him. I'm not really sure, but I feel my mind would be at ease if he were dead. I feel that I could accept this fact. But seeing him with other women and trying to keep cool is something unbelievable to bear. This pain is lingering on and on, and it lives within me at all times. To me it is a disease, and I wish I knew what to do about it.

Hardly a week goes by without some sordid sexual jealousy affair being turned up by the press. For instance, in England, a middle-aged man was rejected by his wife. On discovering that his wife had taken a new lover, the man attached a detonator and explosives to his own body and proceeded to track down the other man. On finding the hated culprit, the husband detonated the explosives. Miraculously, both men survived the initial explosion. On seeing that the other man was still alive, the jilted husband beat him to death with the battery box he had used to detonate the device. He told police, 'My only regret is that I too am not dead.'

In another instance, a sexually jealous woman attempted suicide by jumping from the balcony of her sixth-floor flat. She indulged in what some would call theatrical behaviour because she was convinced that her husband was being unfaithful. The irony of the story was that the woman jumped out of the building just as her husband was arriving home. She fell on top of him, with the result that she lived and he died.

A Texas man attempted to ram his ex-wife's car with his pick-up truck. He was so upset that he totally lost control of his senses and his truck eventually ended up in a neighbour's swimming pool, having traversed an intersection, thirty feet of fencing and the neighbour's backyard. Fortunately, no one had been in his path.

In the summer of 1976, Edward Alloway, a thirty-seven-year-old custodian of California State University at Fullerton, and considered a decent sort of person, was under a jealous delusion that all the males around him were enjoying sexual intercourse with his estranged wife. Impelled by this overwhelming sexual jealousy, Edward took a .22 calibre rifle into the campus library's Instructional Media Center, where eyewitnesses heard him say, 'I'm going to kill all those sons of bitches for fucking my wife.' Seven university employees lay dead when Edward Alloway left the building. Minutes later, and much calmer, he was arrested in Anaheim, California, while trying to speak with his wife, a woman described by co-workers as a 'sweet, trusting, naïve woman-child'.

Penises are sometimes the target for revenge. On 10 October 1977, a drunk twenty-four-year-old labourer and his eighteen-year-old half-brother broke into the home of a twenty-year-old student who was having an affair with the labourer's estranged wife. The young brother pointed a gun at the student's room-mate while his older brother rendered the student unconscious. He then bound the student's hands and feet and proceeded to sever his penis with a butcher's knife. Fortunately, a team of surgeons managed to re-attach the penis. The labourer received a sentence of life plus forty-five years. According to Schoenfeld (1979), maliciously 'severed penises were successfully reattached in 1976 at Nare Medical University in Japan and Massachusetts General Hospital in Boston, and at a Trenton, New Jersey hospital in 1977'.

Pathological sexual jealousy has led to bizarre and sadistic torture murders. In 1962, a San Francisco anaesthetist was convicted of murdering his wife. The doctor was convinced that his wife was being unfaithful. He tortured her to death by slowly dropping concentrated nitric acid on the most sensitive parts of her body. His wife lay in a state of indescribably acute pain before dying thirty-four days later. The doctor is now a free man. He was paroled after serving twelve years and works with a Seventh-Day Adventist medical team in Taiwan.

But these are extreme cases and sexual jealousy more usually has its humorous side. Sexually jealous wives and the 'other women' who are their rivals have been known to play nasty tricks on each other. In a book aptly called *Woman Versus Woman*, Shirley Eskapa (1984) illustrates dozens of instances where women employed bizarre tactics when going to war with each other over the same man. In one case, Mavis, a married woman, discovered that her husband Ian was having an affair with a woman who had a young child of her own. Mavis wanted Ian to know what life would be like with a young infant, so she offered to take care of a 'borrowed' baby and filled the house with all things infantile. Their home became littered with baby toys, baby food, 'and that sweet smell of baby urine and baby crap. I made sure of all of that. These days you can get disposable nappies, but Ian didn't know that, and if he had asked I would have told him that Priscilla was allergic to man-made fibres.' Ian soon thought twice about leaving his wife for the other woman.

One leading American criminal attorney, Percy Foreman, has said he prefers all-male juries when defending women on murder charges. He believes that women are always hardest on each other, and has asserted: 'Man's inhumanity to man is exceeded only by woman's inhumanity to woman' (Jones, 1981). Perhaps Foreman is stretching his point a little far.

Nevertheless, women, like men, are prone to vengeance during and after love affairs. Eskapa (1984) records how one wife resorted to using liquid paraffin, a powerful laxative, in the dressing of a salad she was serving to her opponent. A mistress who realized she had lost the 'battle of love', maliciously pierced a hole in her opponent's diaphragm. A rejected and vengeful woman went to her ex-lover's London home while he was away and dialled the number for the time in New York City. She left the receiver off the hook until he returned, days later. His telephone bill ran into thousands of pounds. In the throes of battle, a mistress, attempting to prove to the wife that she was having an affair with her husband, actually mailed the wife her husband's underpants by recorded delivery.

Jean Harris, the headmistress of an elite girls' school in Virginia, who was convicted in January 1981 of murdering her lover, Dr Tarnover, famous for his book *The Scarsdale Diet*, had one of Dr Tarnover's other lovers brought to her attention in the most bizarre circumstances. Dr Tarnover's other mistress wanted to show Jean Harris that she was sleeping with him in the room where Jean Harris kept her clothing, while also seeming to have had a pathological need to spite Jean Harris. And so she smeared her own faeces on a beautiful unused négligé which Jean Harris had left wrapped in tissue paper. After doing this, she neatly replaced the garment in its box for Jean Harris to find.

14 SADO-MASOCHISTIC PORNOGRAPHY

Derived from ancient Greek, *pornography* literally means the writing of harlots. The term was probably derived from the signposts outside ancient Greek brothels (Hendrickson, 1982). Pornographic writing consists of erotica and exotica. **Erotica** is the portrayal of 'normal' love-making between heterosexuals, while **exotica** encompasses the spectrum of other sexual experience. There is nothing new about erotica or exotica. Passages of both can be found in the Old Testament and in the plays of Aristophanes. One of the earliest pornographic pieces of European literature is Boccaccio's *Decameron* (1348–53).

'The pornography industry accounts for more business than the record and film industries combined' (Dworkin, 1981). Travellers from countries where sexually explicit materials are banned are often astounded by the pervasiveness and variety of pornographic representations in the West. While many Westerners may hardly notice copies of *Penthouse* prominently displayed in thousands of newsagents, the foreigner is sometimes horrified. Visitors may similarly be amazed by the literature and paraphernalia on show in the 'sex boutiques', as their senses are literally assailed by double-sized, vibrating, electronic, artificial penises (dildos); by life-size blow-up 'love dolls'; by videotapes in which the camera zooms in on every body orifice and all shapes and sizes of genitalia; by whips, chains and other torture devices for sexual 'pleasure'. And, of course, by sado-masochistic films.

Although they stand millennia apart ideologically speaking, militant feminists, religious fundamentalists and moral crusaders share one wish in common: they abhor pornography and would like to see its total demise. Religious fundamentalists, such as Jerry Fallwell who is staunchly supported by President Reagan, lobby for the banning of pornography because it leads the sinful into further temptation by the devil. Moral crusaders, including the anti-homosexual activist, Anita Bryant, despise exotica because it produces depravity and enhances 'unnatural' sexual conduct. Mary Whitehouse, the British moral crusader, caught national attention when she publicly opposed the distribution of 'video nasties', which brought rape, sexual beatings and sado-masochism on to the television screens of private homes where parents were not preventing their children from viewing them. She alleged that children could become disturbed by exposure to such films, and advocated that their makers and distributors be outlawed and punished. Militant feminists, like Andrea Dworkin (1981), Kathleen Barry (1979) and Ruth Christenson, oppose pornography on the grounds that men exploit women through its media.

Women, they say, are not only exploited but are also dehumanized, debased and denigrated in pornographic films. Both men and women are seduced by the large sums of money offered to actors in 'pornflicks'. The films show women having sexual intercourse with each other, participating in sordid sado-masochistic orgies, being urinated on, defecated on, whipped, having hot wax poured into open wounds, having sex with children and animals, giving and receiving sexually arousing enemas, with multiple variations on all these themes. Homosexual pornography mimics the same themes of kinky dominance and submission. Creators of pornography are especially adept at conveying the impression that the victims enjoy their painful sexual adventures. Sado-masochism is undoubtedly a dominant component in pornography, and if pornography accounts for billions of dollars' worth of hard currencies, sado-masochism accounts in its own right for a mega industry.

The ultimate form of sado-masochistic pornography is the 'snuff film', in which, according to the FBI, the central actor is actually murdered in the course of a sexual encounter. The sexual encounter usually involves rape and the severe mutilation of the victim's body. Such films are reportedly shot in Third World countries, where officials are bribed into ignorance and loved ones frightened into silence. According to a police officer in the Los Angeles Police Department, films showing sexual encounters between children and adults fetch thousands of dollars apiece on the black market once they reach their destination.

There is a great deal of continuing controversy over the connection between pornography and sexual crimes. The United States Commission on Obscenity and Pornography during the Johnson Administration came out in favour of liberalizing pornography because it could find no causal or correlational link between the availability of pornography and sexually related crimes. The commission reported that sex offenders were in fact less exposed to pornography during adolescence than were members of a control group of non-sex offenders (see Table 1).

Barry (1979) justifiably points out that the data in the table remain problematic since a majority of rapists in the population go free. This meant that only a select few, perhaps a special type of rapist, was interviewed by the commission. Yet, despite Barry's objections, the data were sufficiently convincing to suggest that no significant correlation existed between the incidence of sex crime and exposure to pornography during adolescence.

If no correlation exists between sexually related crimes and prior exposure to pornography, then the following question arises: do violent sex crimes actually diminish with the liberalization of pornography? It all seems to

TABLE 1. Exposure of males to pornography (photographic depictions of coitus) during adolescence.

	Percentage of Group Exposed
GENERAL POPULATION (Controls)	
White Adults	85
Black Adults	74
SEX OFFENDERS	
Female target child-molester	56
Male target child-molester	35
Rapists	62

SOURCE: *The Report of the Commission on Obscenity and Pornography*, Part 3, Chapter II, 'The Impact of Erotica', Figure 10 (cited in Barry, 1979).

depend on who is fiddling with the sociological data. The US Commission on Obscenity and Pornography concluded that the incidence of rape had gone down in Denmark since the legalization of pornography. By contrast Danish Police records showed that the incidence of rape had increased since the legalization of all forms of pornography. Table 2 illustrates this problem.

One militant feminist and anti-pornography activist who took her beliefs very seriously was Ruth Christenson. She caused a sensation when, on 10 July 1984, she walked into Shinder's bookstore in downtown Minneapolis, poured a bottle of inflammable fluid over her head and body and proceeded to set herself on fire. Tom Dolan, a shop assistant, managed to put out the fire by rolling Ruth in rubberized carpets, but although her life was saved, Ruth was badly burned. Before her protest, she had sent copies of a letter to both Mayor Frazer and Mr Hoyt, a City Council member. The letter began, 'Please read this entire

TABLE 2. Denmark: comparison of rapes reported.

Year	Number of Copenhagen rapes	
	Police (1) Records	Commission (2) Research
1959	32	30
1960	21	20
1961	25	24
1962	29	21
1963	22	18
1964	20	16
1965*	24	21
1966	34	28
1967	23	18
1968†	28	23
1969	27	19
1970	31	—

* Year pornography was first legalized.
† Year pornography escalated to massive sales of hard-core pornography.

SOURCES: (a) Kutchinsky, 'The Effect of Easy Availability of Pornography on the Incidence of Sex Crime: The Danish Experience', *Journal of Social Issues*, 1973; (b) Richard Ben-Venista, 'Pornography and Sex Crime: The Danish Experience', US Commission on Obscenity and Pornography, *Technical Report*, VII; cited in Barry (1979).

letter!' and stated, 'Society has never and will never recognize me but as a piece of meat . . . Sexism has shattered my life . . . Because of this, I have chosen to take my life and destroy the persons who have destroyed me.' In addition, Ruth called for the death sentence for 'all pimps, rapists, wife-beaters of women' (Weiss, 1984).

Militant feminists would probably condemn numerous 'sociological surveys' currently on the market as blatant pornography. Many of these surveys are compilations of hundreds of bizarre sexual fantasies contributed by the public. It is unsurprising that they should have become bestsellers. Being presented as 'major scientific studies' makes them more socially acceptable on the average book-shelf than 'real hardcore porn'.

Religious fundamentalists (Fallwell and Swaggart), and even some liberals, have endorsed the 1986 United States Commission on Pornography under Attorney General Edwin Meese. Ironically, the report has been described as pornographic in its own right (freely available from the US Government Printing Office in Washington, DC) and claims a causal link between pornography and violence. The committee conducted no original research of its own and based much of its interpretation on questionable, outdated studies. While there is evidence that depictions of violence are sometimes correlated to a change in attitude and belief on the part of some observers, it becomes increasingly clear that a causal link between violence and pornography has not yet been proved. In other words, it is safe to say that, while watching sexually violent videotapes will not cause people to go out and rape, those who do watch rape scenes on so-called 'video nasties' may come to view women and children as sexual objects. The psycho-social effects on children of showing pornography and violent pornography will only become apparent after many years. Since there are so many social variables, it is practically impossible to isolate a single cause for the increase in violent sexual crime in the United States.

FROM NANCY FRIDAY TO THE STORY OF O

Among the more well-known surveys of sexual fantasies are *Men in Love: Men's Sexual Fantasies* and *My Secret Garden: Women's Sexual Fantasies*, both by Nancy Friday (1980; 1975); *The Cosmo Report* by L. Wolfe (1982); and *The Sex-Life Letters* by Greenwald and Greenwald (1984). Although some of these surveys include bizarre sexual fantasies, the authors do not view themselves as pornographers; rather do they see their publications as advancing knowledge about human sexuality. The authors who compiled these surveys consider them to be sociologically and psychologically relevant, and far from being 'obscene' publications.

Men in Love consists of over 200,000 words of allegedly genuine sexual fantasies, these being categorized under more than twenty headings, such as 'Oral Sex'; 'Anal Sex'; 'Starry-Eyed Oedipus'; 'Water Sports'; 'Voyeurs and Exhibitionists'; 'Animals'; 'Breast and Vagina Envy'; 'Sado-masochism: The Chains of Love'; 'Virgins'; 'Women with Women'; 'Sharing the Woman with Another Man'. In the section on sado-masochistic fantasies, Friday includes the contribution of a 'Dr Lewis Brown' (names are changed to protect the identity of contributors). Dr Brown writes that he finds masochism a 'real turn-on', especially humiliation – *as long as it stays a fantasy*. 'I have had a "dominant massage" and found it to be only painful.' Dr Brown says that he has not had homosexual experiences. However, in his fantasy he imagines his wife as the lover of a friend, Frank, who rapes him anally and beats him up. In the fantasy, his wife, Sharon, is sexually aroused by the sight of the 'raw animal sensuality of the beating'. Tied up by Sharon and Frank, Dr Brown proceeds in his imagination:

After fucking her multiple times, he [Frank] seems even more sexually vigorous than before starting. His penis is immense. He notices that I am moving about a bit more, so he stops fucking her and he stands me up and punches me a few more times, until I go limp and helpless again. Then he turns me over, mounts me and fucks my asshole. Even though I'm thoroughly beaten, I still have to scream in agony – but both Frank and Sharon notice that while he is in me I, in turn, develop my own huge erection . . .

Frank gets sterile towels and instruments (we are both physicians) and starts washing my scrotum and penis with alcohol. For some reason, my courage seems to have returned, and I tell him his plan is fantastic; that he'll never get away with it; that I shall report him and they'll toss him in prison.

Now he is silent as I continue to berate him . . . he just keeps washing and preparing me. He puts gloves on, but no mask. He then seats himself in front of my balls and instructs Sharon to hold my penis up so it won't get in his way.

For the first time the full impact of what is really about to happen comes crashing down on me – and I totally panic! I plead; I cry; I scream; I threaten; I try to squirm and thrash, but am tied too securely.

Frank just smiles and, holding a scalpel and forceps, says: 'I'm going to castrate you without any anaesthesia, Lewis, because I want you to feel everything – especially that moment when you lose your last ball.' Throughout the operation I continue to scream, cry and beg pitifully, but to no avail.

The surgery begins with Frank grasping the left side of the base of my scrotum with a toothed forceps – I feel white pain! He then slices in with his scalpel – I'm nauseated. He directs Sharon to hold my penis up just a bit more. She is watching the surgery with intent fascination. When the incision is large enough, he reaches in and pulls out my left testicle. He loops two sutures across its stalk and cuts between them, freeing the ball. He shows it to me – I babble incoherently. Sharon, however, notices that I am becoming erect. Frank drops my ball in a bottle of formaldehyde – with a loud plunk! Smiling, he next slices the front and continues around to the right side of the base of my scrotum, letting it fall back in front of my asshole. Working slowly, he throws two sutures over the stalk of my right testicle. Then he holds it up and, placing the scalpel where I can see, he says, 'Okay, Lewis, this is it!' and with me watching he completes my emasculation. That ball also gets dropped in a jar as well as the scrotum.

The moment of emasculation is very powerful and very primitive. The inevitable, the ultimate, result of the struggle of two savage males competing for one female. The finale is total, as one savage completely defeats the other and takes his strength – his maleness – the ultimate in domination – the ultimate in defeat and humiliation . . .

As the fantasy closes, Frank is inside of Sharon and she is amazed at the size of my erection. Frank, beaming with self-satisfaction, says: 'Yes, but it's his last!'

'Eliot', who signs himself 'The Master Rod', contributes the following sadistic fantasy to the same book:

I often fantasize about punishing Barbara Walters, Luciana Avedon (of the Camay commercials), Anne Francis, Elizabeth Montgomery, Bernadette Peters – and Nancy Friday . . . Though I must admit Barbra Wawa is my favourite, let me state the complete fantasy in this way: Nancy Friday reads this letter and feels a pang of impulse she never felt before; it becomes an obsession; her husband can't satisfy it; he's just the old husby, not the Demon Lover. (Most of my women are married, and not unhappily.) The impulse haunts her. At last she writes and makes an appointment.

At my studio, she is sent to the bathroom to change; then she walks into the studio wearing only a garter belt, stockings, and shoes; tingling all over with self-consciousness; she is required to parade up and down before a fully clothed man this way. Now totally aroused, she is tied over a bar; her stomach rests on the bar, her wrists and ankles are tied together; she is in a calisthenic exercise position of one bending over and touching her toes without bending her knees; and she cannot move. I then attach a pair of moderate-strength nipple clamps to her nipples; they hurt just enough to give pleasure.

Going around the other side, I anoint her vulva, from anus to clitoris, with 'orgy butter' (no kidding, there is such stuff in the sex boutiques). This is very soothing, and our Nancy is now aflame with desire, all caution and inhibition gone, she is now totally spontaneous; which of course is the whole idea, not only of my exercise, but of lust, even of sex itself . . . While she watches, I take a cat out of the drawer; now the big moment is coming! She attains a new level of apprehension She is required to say, 'I've been a bad girl, so please whip me.' I caress her back with the whip; it is an indescribable sensuous sensation. Then, as described above, I whip poor Nancy mercilessly (well, not really), and soon she begins to cry out – not with pain but a series of soul-wracking orgasms . . . After this, she must kiss the hand that whipped her and say 'Thank you for punishing me,' and she promises to forward to me all letters from masochistic females; she makes an appointment to return next week . . .

Mona contributed a perverse sado-masochistic fantasy to *My Secret Garden*, one that supports the idea that sexual arousal to pain and punishment can become a conditioned response. It also shows how violence begets violence. The children Mona enjoys punishing may be a 'projection' of her own 'inner child', so frequently humiliated and sexually beaten by a nun during puberty. It is well documented that puberty is a particularly vulnerable period in the development of sexual identity:

I hope you will keep my name confidential as I have never told anybody this before. From what I've read, I think that I am a sadist. I may be a masochist as well, as I very often daydream about being tortured.

I developed sexually at about twelve, and as I was very wild and disobedient growing up, my parents decided to send me to a strict convent school. A strap was always used. The head nun, Sister Rosario, would take an offender – which was very often me – up to the front of the class, tell her to bend down and touch her toes, and then, having lifted up her tunic, she would hit her across the buttocks.

During a holiday I met a lovely boy whom I fell in love with. I made him promise not to write to me while I was in the convent because I could get expelled for it. One evening after class, Sister Rosario said she wanted to see me in her room. She told me she had intercepted a letter from a boy written to me and that she had no alternative but to expel me. I pleaded on my knees to her not to expel me, and eventually she said that she would not but she would have to deal severely with me and that I was to tell nobody. I gladly agreed to this, but I can tell you that if I had my choice again I would not. She told me to take off all my clothes, which I very embarrassingly did. I was nearly thirteen at this stage and I was fairly well developed. I had to kneel down in front of her while she asked numerous questions which shocked and embarrassed me, for instance:

'What is your bust measurement?'

'Do you masturbate?'

'What colour is the hair between your legs?'

'What do you call it?'

She wanted to know exactly what I did with the boy and what he did. She then made me lie across a chair and gave me about twenty lashes with the leather across the buttocks. I then had to lie on my back and open my legs. She gave me six in between the legs.

After this I had to come to her room regularly and she would make me strip and would beat me with the leather each time.

She would always ask me about masturbating. I tell you all this because after two weeks I definitely got a certain pleasurable sensation from the beating. It was during this time that I first started to masturbate. I still do it regularly.

Now I am a teacher and I get my pleasure from administering the punishment. The boys I teach are between ten and fourteen. I regularly take one to my room where I administer the whip and cane, having ordered him to strip naked. I enjoy punishing him but I enjoy it most when I see him getting an erection. I wear provocative clothes and I enjoy embarrassing him when he gets the erection.

I have never punished a girl, mainly because I never had the opportunity to do so . . . but I often daydream about it. I imagine her being strapped to a bed with only pants and a bra on. I then order one of my boy pupils to strip her and to torture her. The tortures I normally dream about are pulling the hairs from her pubic region one at a time, inserting needles into her breasts, burning her with hot candle grease, whipping her, caning her, while at the same time making her admit filthy thoughts, masturbation, etc.

I also dream about having intercourse with one of my pupils. Some of my thoughts and indeed my actions are very diverse and queer, and I find it hard to put on paper. I have never before told anyone about these things. Sometimes I feel frustrated and I would like to know if my practices are very unusual. I would be elated if you could give me some information on what other girls think. It would make me feel easier to know that others like me exist.

P.S. I find it difficult to get the type of whips that I would like here in Ireland, so I would be grateful if you could help me. [Letter]

These long quotes, selected from hundreds similar, may be thought to cater more for the pornography market than for students of social change. In this sense, Nancy Friday may be seen as capitalizing on the voyeurism in our society.

Story of O by Pauline Réage (1970; original edition 1954) is one of the most popular sado-masochistic works of literature. It has been reprinted many times, continues to sell and has even been made into a film. Although we do not really know anything about the true identity of its author, the reader is told it was written by a woman. The book has been hailed as a work of art by Susan Sontag because it is written in beautiful language, is replete with symbolism, repetition of themes and allegory, and because it focuses on the individual's search for meaning in life.

'Meaning' for the main character of O is found in her complete 'obedience' to her lover, René, and her 'master', Sir Stephen. O willingly submits to the sadistic sexual whims of her tormentors. She is whipped with a riding crop, has a special ring pierced through her labia, is the victim of anal rape, all this being suffered to win the unattainable love of her torturers. In one instance, René 'caressed her hair, ran the tip of his finger gently along her eyebrows, gently kissed her lips. He gazed at her and, aloud, said that he loved her.' In keeping with this kind of pornography, O has, a moment before, been whipped by men she could not see:

It was explained to her that as long as she was in this château it would always be this way: she would see the faces of those who violated and bullied her, but never at night, and in this way she would never know which ones were responsible for the worst of her sufferings. When she was whipped the same would hold true, except when it was desired that she see herself being whipped, as happened to be the case the first time: no blindfold but the men in masks in order to be unidentifiable . . . Her hands were still pinioned behind her back. She was shown the riding-crop, black, long and slender, made of fine bamboo sheathed in leather, an article such as one finds in the display-windows of expensive saddlemakers' shops; the leather whip – the one she'd seen tucked in the first man's belt – was long, with six lashes each ending in a knot; there was a third whip whose numerous light cords were several times knotted and stiff, quite as if soaked in water, and they actually had been soaked in water, as O was able to verify when they stroked her belly with those cords and, opening her thighs, exposing her hidden parts, let the damp, cold ends trail against the tender membranes.

O was bound to the wall, made to perform her toilet publicly, gagged and tied up while she slept, forced to wear a device designed to stretch her anus, whipped over hassocks until she eventually loses her own identity. O's meaning in life came to be defined through obedience to Sir Stephen, so much so that she fully identified with him and defined herself through him. O 'identified with her aggressors', in much the same way that many concentration camp victims did with theirs. Whippings are described in a cool and aloof language. O is chained to a post:

The chain, although unyielding, for, after all, it was a chain, was nevertheless slack enough to allow her leeway. Owing to her excessive writhing, her belly and the front of her thighs received almost as heavy a share as her rear. They left off for a moment, deeming it better to tie her flat up against the post by means of a rope passed around her waist; the rope being cinched tight, her head necessarily angled to one side of the post and her flanks jutted to the other, thereby placing her rump in a prominent position. From then on, every deliberately aimed blow dealt her struck home.

The similarity between the concern for the mechanics of O's punishment in *Story of O* and Nazi preoccupations with how efficiently Jews could be disposed of is striking. In a profoundly detached manner, Réage savours the detail of sexually sadistic acts – in much the same way as Himmler does with the problem of 'corpse production'. Both sanctify dehumanization, degradation and negation of others. Both mix cruelty with tenderness. Himmler could be, at one minute, 'moved to tears' at the sight of innocent Aryan children; at the next, concerning himself with the difficult logistics of 'corpse per hour disposal'. The notorious Nazi German doctor, Josef Mengele, used young twins in his 'medical experiments' on young girls, to whom, on the odd occasion, he would kindly offer chocolates as they suffered seething pain. Likewise, in Réage's 'artistic' pornography,

René is perversely loving and tender about the total control and punishment of his beloved O's body.

---

15 THEORIES OF SADISM AND MASOCHISM

PSYCHOANALYSIS

Psychoanalytic theorists propose an explanation for **sadism** similar to the one they put forward for exhibitionism. In essence, sadists 'unconsciously' attempt to diminish their victims by rendering them powerless. The sadist is attempting to relieve neurotic *anxiety*, which he has come to associate with sexual feelings. In psychoanalysis, the anxiety is viewed as being produced by a fear that, if the sadist fails to act on his sexual impulses, someone else will hurt him first (Fenischel, 1945). The sadist does exactly what he unconsciously thinks the victim will want to do to him, and by so doing he escapes having to fear the victim. As the sadist acts out, he feels powerful, and this power serves as a defence against his fear.

Many psychoanalysts would say that sadists are 'fixated' or 'stuck' at an early psychosexual stage of development. Sadists are seen as being stuck in the past. Because of this, they *relive* over and over unresolved conflicts experienced when growing up. The sadist may deal with conflicts arising out of, for example, punishment as a child, by projecting his internal feelings on to his victim. Instead of thinking, 'I am sexually afraid of him or her,' the sadist will say, 'He or she is afraid of me.' The sadist then attempts to prove these feelings correct by inflicting punishment. He or she is stuck in what Freud called the 'pregenital phase' of 'sadistic-anal eroticism'. Sadism is also said to result from an externalization of death instincts and the sexualization of orifices and organs (Allen, 1979). Children develop 'oral sadism' as they grow teeth and nails. Later on, this sexual energy is supposedly displaced to the anus and excretory functions.

Another psychoanalytic approach claims that hate is a primal reaction against the very small infant's narcissistic pleasure requirements. In other words, if the baby is frustrated by the mother because she has not fed him, he will experience hate for her. Presumably, then, sadists become 'fixated' on very early frustrations which make them hate the person they eventually choose as a love or sex object.

The psychoanalytic explanation for **masochism** is much the same as it is for sadism, except that, somehow, the 'instinctual' destructiveness is 'turned inwards'. In *Civilization and Its Discontents*, Freud (1930) explained:

> In sadism, long since known to us as a component instinct of sexuality, we should have before us a particularly strong alloy [of this kind] between trends of love and the destructive instinct; while its counterpart, masochism, would be a union between destructiveness directed inwards and sexuality – a union which makes what is otherwise an imperceptible trend into a conspicuous and tangible one . . . I know that in sadism and masochism we have always seen before us manifestations of the destructive instinct (directed outwards and inwards), strongly alloyed with eroticism; but I can no longer understand how we can have overlooked the ubiquity of non-erotic aggressivity and destructiveness and can have failed to give it its due place in our interpretation of life.

PROBLEMS WITH PSYCHOANALYSIS

Psychoanalytic theory is speculative and unscientific. The main problem is that it does not help with the treatment (education) of the sexually deviant. It provides fascinating, interesting and elaborate explanations for why someone is behaving in a certain manner, but cannot specify what treatment is best for whom, how and under what conditions the person would be treated best. For example, Freud interpreted a newly wed woman's dream as a 'reaction to the loss of her virginity'. The woman was supposed to have 'a wish to castrate her husband and to keep his penis for herself'.

Lacking much solid evidence, some psychoanalysts believe that the sadist specifically wants to hurt his mother's breasts. He subsequently transfers this hate on to other women. If the sadist is homosexual, the process (conveniently) differs: 'The buttocks are equated with the breast and so pain is inflicted on the buttocks' (Allen, 1979). Psychoanalytic tradition therefore beats about the bush, constantly injecting this interpretation and that fascinating insight. Many patients come off the psychoanalytic merry-go-round psychologically dizzier than they were years before when they first got on. Many Americans pay $5,000 (over £3,500) a year to ride on this emotional roller-coaster, and many claim that they benefit a great deal. However, a few patients referred for treatment after three, four or even five years of 'being in analysis' look as though they have just emerged from the most terrifying ghost-train ride in Disneyland.

THE ROLE OF LEARNING

Under this heading, sadism is considered to be **learned behaviour**. Sadistic sexual behaviour is acquired when sexual arousal and orgasm come to be associated with the physical abuse of another person, or even an animal. A member of a sado-masochistic club stated, in interview, that he was sexually aroused by both giving and receiving what he called 'light whippings in which no one really gets seriously hurt'. Without knowing it, the young man seemed to have an excellent grasp of behavioural psychology. He explained his sado-masochistic sexual urges by saying that he had been to a school where corporal punishment was used to control the students and to get them to do their homework. He first noticed becoming sexually aroused at the age of twelve when a woman teacher used to cane boys in front of the class. The sexual arousal occurred because he was so frightened that he would rub his legs together whenever the teacher beat someone. Later, he would go home and masturbate to fantasies of caning the naked teacher and other boys and girls, and receiving corporal punishment in return. Although he described himself as 'otherwise a normally straight guy' who had been able to form a lasting relationship with a girl, he continued to masturbate to these fantasies. Eventually, he found 'incredible release' in the sado-masochistic clubs.

In terms of the psychologist Albert Bandura's (1969) social learning theory, the young man had learned sado-masochism through **direct experience** with corporal punishment and by **modelling** the behaviour of his teacher – at first in masturbatory fantasy and later by acting it out in the sado-masochistic club. He **reinforced** this behaviour by mentally reconstructing and habitually masturbating to images of the ritualized, sanctioned pain he had **observed** being administered in the classroom. Ironically, receiving and administering 'punishment' became a 'reward' or powerful **reinforcer** as a prelude to orgasm. The clinical evidence for the development of both masochistic and sadistic sexual preferences is overwhelmingly supported by prior exposure to pain and humiliation as the individual matures. Contrary to psychoanalytic dogma, sexual preferences can be acquired in adults with no prior sado-masochistic experience when they are 'taught' sado-masochism by a sexual partner.

The psychological experiments of Stanley Milgram (1974) demonstrated that subjects can be taught to induce pain deliberately in others. In an experiment by Geen and

Pigg (1970), subjects were deceived into thinking that, if they delivered electric shocks to other subjects, they would be helping them to learn a task. It was found that subjects who were rewarded with verbal praise were far more likely to deliver intense shocks to their 'students' than subjects not so rewarded.

Sadists act out their behaviours, in fantasy, reality or both, because they have **learned** or been **conditioned** to do so; they have come to associate inflicting physical or emotional pain with pleasure, a reward. The nature of the reward can range from orgasm to the acquisition of social status, and therefore to the illusion of higher self-esteem. The histories of guards in German concentration camps as well as of sadistic officers in police organizations around the world is telling. Previously 'powerless' persons with low self-esteem suddenly find themselves feeling more socially important, powerful and happy when they become free to exert total domination over the bodies of others. Sadists find the subjugation and humiliation of fellow beings highly reinforcing.

2

A Perspective On Rape

INTRODUCTION

The term **rape** comes from the Latin *rapere*, which means 'to seize'. Forceful, non-consenting sexual 'seizure' is observed in many species, including rodents and apes, especially in captivity, but it occurs in all human cultures (Fisher, 1982). Statutory rape has been broadly described as 'sexual activity with a person other than one's spouse (legally) under conditions of force, threat of violence, or trickery, or with a person not competent to give consent . . . a drugged, drunk, mentally unsound, unconscious person under the age of 18' in the United States; in England, the lower age of consent of sixteen applies (Tollison and Adams, 1979). Rape is universal, and almost all societies proscribe it as an outrageous felony. Until recently, rape was a capital crime in most parts of North America.

Rape victims are not restricted by socio-economic class, age, sex, marital status, race, religion, occupation or other demographic factors. Most rapes involve sexual attacks by men on women, and adult men are the major protagonists. One rape hotline in America estimated that rape occurs every three minutes, or about 150,000 times a year – approximately three times the official figure. It is usually reckoned that between 10 and 25 per cent of rapes go unreported by their victims. A recent survey conducted in 1985 by the Greater London Council recorded that one in six women out of a total sample of 1,200 had been sexually assaulted by males. The number of *reported* rapes in the United States, representing the *official* figure for 1973, was 51,000 rapes.

Like rats under certain laboratory conditions, groups of men will sometimes 'gang rape' single, defenceless women and girls. Spouses are raped. Male and female children are raped. Babies are raped. Physically handicapped persons are raped. Anaesthetized patients are raped. Mothers, fathers, brothers and sisters are raped. Adolescents rape one another as well as old persons and younger children. Male and female prisoners rape each other. During wars, soldiers have been known to rape entire communities. Contrary to the thesis of Susan Brownmiller (1975), who spread the myths that 'all men keep all women in a state of fear' and that rapists are 'exclusively male', women have also been arrested for sexual assault (McCarty, 1980). No individual is immune to rape. Necrophiliacs rape corpses. Humans rape animals. Animals only rape humans in mythology.

16 RAPE IN HISTORY

In an overview of the history of rape, Susan Brownmiller described how, over 4,000 years ago, the Code of Hammurabi gave women low status in Babylonian law. A woman either belonged to her father or was the property of her husband, who purchased her from her father. *If a woman were raped, she was liable to the same punishment as the rapist; victim and attacker were thrown bound hand and foot into the Tigris or Euphrates rivers.* The woman's husband had the right to try and free her immediately after she was hurled into the waters, and the king could pardon either criminal if he chose.

In Hebraic law, women were valued for their virginity. A father could place a price on what Brownmiller describes as 'title to his daughter's unruptured hymen, a piece of property he wholly owned and controlled'. If a virgin was raped inside the city walls, she would be stoned to death along with her rapist, it being argued that, had she resisted, someone would have heard her cries and saved her. If the girl was raped beyond hearing range – outside the city walls – the rapist could compensate the father with fifty pieces of silver, the normal cost of a bride. Rapists were executed by stoning if they defiled a married woman, whose dishonoured husband would sell her at a financial loss, the raped wife having become a 'tainted', devalued article.

The Assyrians endorsed the ancient 'an eye for an eye' dictum of the region. According to Brownmiller, 'under the *lex talionis*, the father of a raped virgin was permitted to seize the wife of the rapist and violate her in turn'. Women were therefore victimized for being raped, not because of the humiliation they had personally suffered but because of the sexual dishonour on their households.

Retribution for sexual dishonour features prominently in the Old Testament. The Book of Judges (19–21) recounts a bizarre story about a Levite traveller and his concubine who found themselves in the home of an old man in Benjamite territory. A group of rampant Benjamites decided to rape the Levite. The old man protected the Levite saying: 'Behold, here is my daughter, a maiden, and his concubine; them I will bring out now, and humble ye them, and do with them what seemeth good unto you: but unto this man do not do so vile a thing' (Judges 19:20). The Benjamite men agreed to rape the concubine, but not the old man's virgin daughter. The concubine was 'abused . . . all the night until the morning: and when the day began to spring, they let her go' (v. 25) but the rape killed her.

The Levite then dissected his dead concubine into 'twelve pieces' and 'sent her into all the coasts of Israel' (v. 29) to be rid of her raped, contaminated, abominable body. The other Israelite tribes then attacked the Benjamites, and although the Benjamites killed 22,000 members of the assembled tribes, they were finally overwhelmed. Since few Benjamite women and children survived, the Elders of the Israelites arranged the kidnapping of four hundred young virgins among the inhabitants of Jabesh-Gilead who had 'known no man by lying with any male' (21:12) to increase the number of Benjamites once they had paid the penalty. The story concludes (v. 25) by saying: 'In those days there was no king in Israel: every man did that which was right in his own eyes.' Ironically, the people avenged rape by killing off the entire female population of the transgressing tribe, and then sanctioned the kidnap and rape of virgins from a non-Israelite tribe.

Brownmiller alludes to the biblical equivalent of 'Hell hath no fury like a woman scorned' in the Old Testament story of Joseph. Joseph was the favourite Israelite slave of the Egyptian, Potiphar. Potiphar's wife found Joseph's sex appeal so enticing that she attempted to seduce him. When Joseph rejected her, she cried 'Rape!' Joseph was thrown into prison, his release coming to depend on a successful interpretation of Potiphar's dreams.

The penalties for rape in the Dark Ages and medieval times proved no less barbaric than they had in biblical ages. Toner (1977) presents some interesting though highly speculative archaeological evidence for the special ways in which raped or unchaste women were buried in pagan times, garnered when two burial sites were uncovered at the Kingsworthy digs in Hampshire. Two of the bodies found had been buried face down, forensic archaeological interpretation indicating that the skeletons once belonged to two human females, aged respectively about twenty and fourteen years. The bodies had been buried naked, and injuries occurred prior to death:

The bones of the younger girl suggested she was lying fully extended with her head turned to the left. Her wrists were crossed together under her waist and her feet were together, which indicated that she may have been tied. It looked as if she had been buried naked. Examination of her bones revealed a small cavity just above the left knee which was consistent with a dagger wound. On the right thigh bone, at a point where the major muscles from the pelvis join the thigh, was a bony projection. This was almost certainly produced by the tearing of these muscles which caused bleeding followed by clotting of the blood and ossification of the clot.

Such findings provoked this observation:

Tearing of these tendons, which is very uncommon in young persons of this age, is almost invariably due to violent separation of the thighs while trying to resist this and bring them tightly together. In a 16-year-old girl the effort to draw her thighs together and perhaps cross her legs whilst a powerful man was forcing them apart could easily produce the injury we find here.
Both injuries could be typical of a brutal rape which was strongly resisted. A dagger prodding her thigh would have encouraged the girl to draw up her legs to make the rape easier for her attacker or attackers.

While the above is highly speculative, it is not inconceivable, considering the regularity with which raped women or women convicted of adultery were drowned in mire during pagan times. Further archaeological evidence is derived from a peat bog at Windeby in Domland, Germany, where the remains of a fourteen-year-old girl were found. The girl had been buried naked, blindfolded, and with a halter around her neck. She was sunk into the muddy bog with the aid of weights attached to her body. Bodies found in bogs may often be relatively well preserved, even down to the materials they are wearing.
By the time of King Alfred (871–99), penalties for sex offenders were comparatively sophisticated. Essentially, the

more 'valuable' the raped woman, the harsher the penalty. Anyone who raped the slave of a peasant had to pay sixty shillings but a slave who raped a slave was castrated. Rape of a minor incurred the same penalty as rape of an adult. Toner (1977) suggests that, if the penalty for rape of a slave by a slave resulted in castration, then rape of a freewoman by a slave would probably incur the death penalty.

Henry of Bratton, a thirteenth-century historian, recorded punishments from the days of Alfred's successor, the tenth-century King Athelstan. A man who raped a high-class virgin was not merely deprived of his life and genitalia, but 'even his horse shall to his ignominy be put to shame upon its scrotum and tail, which shall be cut off as close as possible to the buttocks', the same punishment applying to the rapist's dog. If the rapist owned a hawk, its beak, claws and tail were to be cut off.

Under Edward I (1044–66), the penalty for rape was reduced to two years' imprisonment plus a fine. By 1285, however, the second statute of Westminster was firmly decreeing:

> . . . if henceforth a man ravishes a wife, maiden or other woman, without her consent beforehand or afterwards, he shall have judgement of life and member; likewise if a man forcibly ravishes a wife, maiden or other woman, even if she consents afterwards, he shall have judgement at the King's suit, and the King shall have suit.

Rape laws were not concerned with the honour of the individual women, but were enacted 'to protect the property interests of the family'. Rape laws could be evoked to prevent the daughter or suitor from getting married. By the end of the fourteenth century, a statute from the reign of Richard II decreed:

> . . . if a woman afterwards assent to the ravisher, both shall lose their inheritance, dower or joint estate after the death of

husband or ancestor and the next in blood shall enter; and he or the husband shall have an appeal.

The next four hundred years saw little change in English laws on rape. By the late seventeenth century, the law focused on details of proving penetration (even without *emissio seminis*), the age of the rapist, aiding and abetting rape, a husband's inviolable immunity from a rape prosecution and the process of trial. Although rape was a capital offence, of 678 executions carried out in London between 1749 and 1771, only two were for rape.

17 THEORIES OF RAPE

No one really understands why some certain people commit rape. Rape has, however, been attributed to various biological and psychological factors.

BIOLOGICAL FACTORS

One group of researchers (Baker, Telfer and Richardson, 1970) has implicated genetic factors in anti-social personality disorders (absence of conscience or guilt), suggesting that distinctive chromosome patterns are detectable in aggressive offenders. There is, however, no clear-cut evidence for genetic factors as a determinant of rape.

Neuroanatomical and **neurophysiological** components have also been implicated. It is known that brain pathology is often associated with alterations in personality, and Rada (1978) pointed out that brain pathology has been linked with abnormal sexual behaviour. Some researchers even suggest that rape can be predicted by abnormal electroencephalograms (EEGs), or 'brain wave' patterns. One psychologist who runs an EEG research laboratory at a large British psychiatric hospital claims he can differentiate violent rapists on the basis of abnormal EEG brainwave patterns. It has to be said at this point, however, that there is no firm evidence to connect abnormal EEG patterns and violent sexual behaviour.

Endocrinological or **hormonal** studies, on the other hand, indicate that higher levels of the male hormones or androgens are often more prominent among sexually violent individuals than those which exist in non-violent individuals. Rada, Laws and Kellner (1967) found that plasma testosterone levels were significantly higher in very violent rapists than they were in child molesters or normal males. More research is needed in this area because, if high testosterone levels are an important factor, then violent rapists could benefit from treatment by drugs which block the production of testosterone.

PSYCHOLOGICAL THEORIES

PSYCHOANALYTIC THEORY

Predictably, psychoanalytic theory connects, in the development of his deviant behaviour, the rapist's relationship with his mother. During childhood, the rapist supposedly struggles with his mother, whom he loves and hates simultaneously. Subsequently the rapist 'unconsciously' projects his love and hate for his mother on to other women. In an attempt to get even with the internalized hated part of his mother, he displaces his aggression on to his victims, hurting and humiliating them in place of his 'bad mother'. Although some rapists have been known to rape their mothers, these are a tiny minority, for the rapist's moral code, such as it is, prevents him from breaking the incest taboo. It is not unusual for rapists to maintain a close relationship with their mothers even as they commit multiple rapes. In England, for example, the rapist who came to be known as 'The Fox' committed some of the most heinous multiple bondage-fetish rapes over a period of months in 1984 yet still found time dutifully to visit his mother.

Several psychoanalysts propose a 'hatred for the mother's breasts' as responsible. For instance, a child who damages a prize cabbage by poking it in the middle is viewed as attempting to hurt his mother's nipples (Rosen, 1979). While this could conceivably be true in some cases, it seems tantamount to sorcery to suggest that rapists generally seek to damage their hated mother's breasts and so mutilate the breasts of victims as a substitute.

SOCIAL LEARNING THEORY

Extraneous and high-sounding psychoanalytic theory need not be invoked to explain the development of rape. In terms of Albert Bandura's (1977) social learning theory, people are seen to acquire sexually aggressive behaviour in part by observation.

People who grow up in families where violence is used to solve problems learn that violence solves problems. While parents, siblings and other relatives may not be criminally violent, they set the example for any impressionable youngster. The child copies his father, who, frustrated at not being immediately gratified, says: 'I'll fuck that bitch up next time I catch her double-crossing me'; or, 'Women are users. All they want is your cash. I'd never let one screw me over.' The child is rewarded with approval and develops an aggressive disposition towards others. He sees that the answer to frustration is violence and comes to believe what he sees. Furthermore, when children are subjected to corporal punishment, they learn that violence is the norm. In other words, they learn the language of violence: that you can get what you want if you hit someone else, especially someone less strong. Later in life, when the individual has failed to develop the appropriate social skills, he uses violence to get what he desires. It is especially interesting to note that research shows that almost every violent prisoner investigated turns out to have been subjected to severe corporal punishment during childhood.

If, according to social learning theory, people learn by observation, then it is highly probable that violent pornography could set some horrific examples. While there is no conclusive *causal* link between violent pornography and violent sexual crimes, there certainly are *correlations* between violent representations and violent acts. Sexually violent pornography can easily lead some to consider sexual violence as more acceptable. Indeed, several criminal cases in the past have been connected with the offender first watching sexually violent films and then performing the act on a live person. The infamous British 'Fox' rapist claimed to have begun his career of rape after watching pornographic films featuring sexual violence. Most insidiously, violent pornography often portrays women looking sexually fulfilled after having been raped. Homosexual pornography and child-molestation pornography in films and magazines is governed by similar mechanisms. For example, dozens of bondage and S & M magazines depict outlandishly degrading scenes of women, and in some cases of men and children, being raped, whipped, bound and tortured. In one film, *The Punishment of Anne*, the protagonist has the thorns on the stem of a rose flower inserted into her vagina; she is bound, gagged, whipped and made to experience the most incredible humiliations – the likes of which were cited to convict war criminals at the Nuremberg trials after the Second World War. Many social learning theorists would agree that such violent pornography provides a rich fertilizer for masturbation fantasies by setting up the powerful conditioning association of rape resulting in orgasm.

18 THE RAPISTS

THE HETEROSEXUAL RAPIST

The vast majority of rapes are heterosexual. They involve males forcing women to submit to sexual intercourse. Most victims are complete strangers to the attacker.

PATTERNS OF HETEROSEXUAL RAPE

Tollison and Adams (1979) list four categories of rapist as elucidated by Cohen *et al.* (1971). The classifications are: (a) the **aggressive-aim** rapist, (b) the **sexual-aim** rapist, (c) the **sex-aggressive-fusion** rapist and (d) the **impulse** rapist.

Aggressive-aim rapists are alleged to be motivated specifically by a wish to humiliate, hurt and 'dirty' the victim. The point is that sex *per se* is not the issue. Sex is merely used as a means to denigrate women. Such a personality will often mutilate the 'female' parts of the woman's body. Angry at women and the world, he may slash his victim's breasts and insert bottles into her vagina. His sexual history is one of hatred for women.

The sexual-aim rapist desires sex. He is acting out masturbatory fantasies. Although coercive, less force is used. He is best described as a 'romantic rapist', one who fantasizes that his victim will fall in love with him after his display of sexual prowess. He may also have the audacity to ask his victim, after the encounter, whether she has had an orgasm.

The sex-aggressive-fusion rapist is a sexual sadist aroused by seeing the woman in pain. Her suffering will cause him to have an erection. Her pain is his pleasure. His history often shows 'psychopathic' tendencies, including inability to develop lasting relationships, an absence of conscience, remorselessness, and poor impulse control. Unlike many other classifications of rapist the sex-aggressive-fusion rapist is liable to suffer a paranoid type of psychosis. The impulse rapist who commits a robbery, and if a woman just happens to be present, he will also 'steal' her body in the process. I have met rapists who speak of 'snatching a little pussy, that's all. For that they give you fifteen or twenty-five years.'

There is some debate, in the State of California, surrounding whether the man who takes a woman out on a date and employs 'some force' in the process of petting should be classified as a rapist. The woman may not want to 'go all the way', in which case she is called a 'cock tease'. The frustrated man may then be forceful, even if he does not penetrate the woman. He may sometimes assault her sexually to the point where he could be prosecuted for rape – if, for example, he puts his hand in her vagina.

MEETING HETEROSEXUAL RAPISTS

When I was doing doctoral research at a state hospital, I was dismayed to find that some of the rapists I met were 'likeable'. Like any other human beings, they joked and told me about their families. I felt chilled by what they had done, but could still acknowledge their basic humanity. Here is how Tony went about his crime:

TONY: A tall well-built blond, blue-eyed young man, aged twenty-seven. His eyes were deep-set, and full of expression. He appeared to take a genuine interest in me and what I was doing at the State Hospital.

'I lived with my parents abroad. My Dad worked for a US company and was making lotsa bread. He was tough on us boys. Real strict. He had this fast car, a Maserati, but never allowed us in it. I went to the American School and made a few good friends. My Dad didn't want us to get into trouble with girls and so we had an early curfew. There had been a case of a man in his company losing his job because his son got a supervisor's daughter pregnant.

'Anyway, I never got into any trouble until I got back to the States. My parents still can't believe what happened. I was the favourite, if any of us were. Well, I came back to go to community college because my Dad said that he'd had it tough and so why shouldn't I. He put himself through school. And it had done him no harm.

'I was working and going to school. Life was real different back in the States. I didn't know anyone, and what's more I got real lonely. I don't know how it happened . . .

'I have raped three women in total. One I followed from the supermarket and went right into her apartment before she could close the door. I told her that I'd use a knife if she yelled. I didn't even have a knife on me. I'm not that kinda guy. Then she pleaded with me, said I could take anything. I told her all I wanted was to make love. After I finished I saw the hurt in her eyes, she just turned her face away, and said softly, "Get out. Now you are through then go, just leave me alone," she sobbed and I felt terrible.

'But I succeeded in putting it out of my mind. Until the next time. The next time I went to the movies alone I followed a girl home. She resisted, yelled and screamed. So I hit her and told her I had a gun. She shut up. I raped once more, about a month later.

'Then I read about rape in the local paper. I read about how girls' lives change, how they can't stand their boyfriends, how sometimes it breaks up families' cause the husband blames her or she just hates all men.

'The next day I went and turned myself in. I confessed. The officers at the station didn't believe me. They thought I was some kinda crank or weirdo! But the girls were contacted and identified me. I suppose I was. Now I know I could have gone and gotten professional help from someone and remained outside of this hospital. My parents got a great lawyer, but I got fifteen years with a possibility of early parole. They think I'm quite amenable to treatment.'

Not all rapists are like Tony. Others clearly do not care that they have been found 'unamenable' to treatment and are quite happy to be sent back to prison to complete their sentences. Some are not sure that they will never rape again. Some become transparent to the clinician. For example, I once sat in on an interview in which a man was being considered for early parole. While undergoing a behaviour modification programme, the man had shown 'very high' readings in response to stimuli (audiotapes) of rape sequences on a penile plethysmograph, an instrument which measures erection in response to videotapes of rape scenes. Now he was trying to impress the interviewer with his readiness for parole, but while he was very enthusiastic, he was in fact merely parroting the jargon which he constantly heard from the psychiatric technicians around the hospital: 'I can now relate to women as real human beings. I can see them as a person in their own right. They have feelings too. I realize the gravity of my crime, but feel ready to get out on parole, especially as I am doing well in the behaviour modification programme.'

THE HOMOSEXUAL RAPIST

Rape occurs among homosexuals even as it does among heterosexuals, although the incidence is lower. It is a type of rape which usually occurs in prisons, but it does also happen among homosexuals in open society, and can, indeed, happen to non-homosexual men. One member of a group therapy session admitted to having raped several hitch-hikers on a single occasion. He had driven around in his van, holding out the offer of a lift to unsuspecting hitch-hikers. Once a victim was inside the vehicle, he drew a gun and handcuffed him to the inside of the van. He drove on, picked up another victim and did the same. As soon as the vehicle was 'full', he drove to a remote area and raped each victim anally.

Homosexual rape between male prisoners is common in

prisons around the world. Rape also occurs among female prisoners, but to a lesser extent. Prison life is a question of survival of the strongest. Physically weak or 'unprotected' prisoners find themselves forced into 'prostitution'. Sometimes they are protected by a larger brute, who offers his services in return for sex. New arrivals are particularly at risk wherever they go. Shower rooms are said to be especially unsafe areas. Among men, the sexual rape requires victims to submit to anal penetration and fellatio by and on the victim. Women prisoners will force their victims to engage in mutual masturbation and/or cunnilingus. Sometimes phallic objects are inserted into the vagina or anus.

In Soviet prison camps, homosexuals are called **pederasts** (Stern and Stern, 1981). A prisoner need not be 'gay' in reality to be labelled a pederast. Most pederasts are not truly homosexual. They are inmates who have been anally raped by a more dominant prisoner. Pederasts become 'untouchables' and special sleeping, eating and washing areas are arranged for them. Anyone who is touched by a pederast becomes contaminated – catches the 'disease', so to speak. Contamination can result from simply accepting a cigarette from a pederast. The degraded prisoner is then known as *opustivshiesya*. Pederasts are given women's names and are made into prostitutes, operating out of 'fuckrooms' (*ebalniks*). Pederasts have one distinct advantage in Soviet prisons: if they can get to the food first, no one else will touch it.

There is little reason to believe that the incidence of rape in prisons differs as between the Soviet Union and the United States. Together with South Africa, they share the distinction of having the highest known numbers of prisoners (behind bars, as opposed to bonded labour) *per capita* among the countries in the so-called free world.

WOMEN RAPISTS

In contradiction of Brownmiller (1975), who wrote that rape offenders are 'exclusively male', women are certainly known to rape, not only each other, as in prison, but also men. The incidence of female rape may be relatively low, but it exists.

Among the Colombian Kogi tribe, women are alleged to ambush men for the express purpose of violating them sexually (McCarty, 1981). MacDonald (1971) reports that Vakuta women in Melanesia consider it their 'right' to rape strange males from other villages who wander on to their garden plots.

The man is fair game of the woman for all that sexual violence, obscene cruelty, filthy pollution and rough handling they can do to him. Thus they first pull off and tear up his pubic leaf, the protection of his modesty and, to a native, the symbol of his male dignity. Then, by masturbatory practices and exhibitionism, they try to produce an erection in their victim and, when their maneuvers have brought about the desired results, one of them squats over him and inserts his penis into her vagina. After the first ejaculation he may be treated in the same manner by another woman. Worse things are done by some of the women who will defecate and micturate all over his body, paying special attention to the face, which they pollute as thoroughly as they can. 'A man will vomit, and vomit, and vomit', said a sympathetic informant. Sometimes these furies rub their genitals against his nose and mouth, and use his fingers and toes, in fact, any projecting part of his body, for lascivious purposes.

In a random check of arrest statistics around the world, McCarty (1981) concludes that no women were prosecuted on any rape charge in the years 1962, 1972 or 1977. Indian rape statistics register an insignificant figure of 1.5 per cent of the total arrests for rape. However, Newman (1980) reports that, for unknown reasons, 96 out of the approximately 800 persons arrested in Greece for sexual assaults (12 per cent) were women.

TABLE 3. Females (Males) Arrested For Rape In The United States

	City	Suburban	Rural	Total
1930–74	No female arrests reported			
1975	149 (13,991)	58 (4,949)	23 (2,136)	230 (21,076)
1976	143 (13,755)	42 (4,738)	17 (2,071)	202 (20,564)
1977	167 (15,649)	65 (6,349)	24 (2,614)	256 (24,612)
1978	147 (16,395)	39 (6,337)	17 (2,503)	203 (25,235)

In the United States, rape laws vary between states. Only since about 1977 have rape laws in Texas and New Hampshire been used to deal with female sex offenders. Table 3 shows that only about 1 per cent of those arrested for forcible rape are female. McCarty (1981) quotes FBI statistics, which indicate that over 85 of 256 or one third of all females arrested for rape were under eighteen years old. He also cites reports of rape committed by young women against each other:

Lisa woke up one morning with two girls holding her down and a third climbing on top of her . . .
'. . . this Big Sis that was like a king came on my cot and touched me. She said, "You like this, baby? Well, you better like it because it's a racket and you got to belong or get hurt. You'll get killed if you don't join and the officers won't do nothing."
Two dykes had me against the wall and the third burned me with a cigarette [between the breasts] . . . [My husband] and I talked and I didn't tell him everything what I had done after they burned me, that I let them do whatever they wanted.'

McCarty (1981) quotes a passage from *The Violent Few* (Hamparian et al., 1978) where 'one seventeen-year-old girl was found in a compromising position with a ten-year-old boy and was charged with rape but later found delinquent on a charge of assault'. If the same girl had been found in a compromising situation with a twenty-seven-year-old man in California, *he* could technically have been prosecuted under sex laws applying in that state.

In New York State, twelve females were charged with rape in 1976, twenty-six in 1977 and sixteen in 1978. McCarty correctly points out that these figures could be misleading, the reason being that many women could have been arrested under other sexual offences, like sodomy, incest and the 'other sex offences' category: '... it is possible that more females were taken into custody for sexual assaults than appear in the records'.

The issue of women and sexual offences almost invariably involves a male accomplice. The only instance I have seen where a male accomplice was not involved was a case in which a mother had been having sexual relations with her thirteen-year-old son over a period of two years. By way of illustration, we may look at the following case histories from New York State (McCarty, 1981):

Case No. 1
A. and her husband invited an adult female acquaintance to come to their home for dinner. Shortly after arriving, the friend was tied to a bed and sexually abused for the next 6.5 hours by both of her hosts. A. inserted a large cucumber into the victim's vagina, kicked her, struck her with a cowhide whip, and pushed her vagina into the victim's face with such force that the victim's nose began to bleed. A. and her husband also took photographs and threatened to distribute the pictures unless the victim agreed to work as a prostitute for them.

A. is white, comes from an intact home, and was 25 years old at the time of the offense. She is a high school graduate with experience working as a bookkeeper. A. admitted herself to a psychiatric hospital when she was 19 for a nervous breakdown following her first divorce. She married the man who was her accomplice in this crime a year later, but she has since divorced him; neither marriage produced any children. A. was formerly addicted to both heroin and cocaine. She concedes that she drinks excessively, and a recent psychiatric report concluded that she has a drug dependence. Her only prior arrest was drug related. A.'s latest institutional evaluation describes her as 'polite, respectful of authority, even-tempered, considerate, punctual, neat and clean, and cooperative'. She has also been approved for a furlough, which is an extraordinary accomplishment for a sex offender in New York. It is worth noting that the chief of police in the town where the crime was committed believes that A. would not have become involved in such serious illegal behaviour were it not for the influence of her second husband.

Case No. 2

B. and two male accomplices intervened on behalf of a 14-year-old retarded female classmate who had been involved in a school yard fight. That afternoon, they lured her in to an abandoned apartment building where all three had sexual relations with her. The victim was forced to drink beer prior to being released and was warned to forget what had taken place.

B. comes from an intact Puerto Rican home. Although she was in the tenth grade when arrested, tests administered by the Department of Correctional Services indicate that she reads at the second grade level. B. carved the word 'HELP' on her arm with a razor blade while she was still in grammar school and attempted to commit suicide just one year prior to committing this offence. She also tried to kill herself while in jail awaiting trial. A psychiatrist who examined B. soon afterwards concluded his evaluation with a diagnosis of a 'depressive reaction in an hysterical personality with borderline features'. The most recent appraisal of B.'s institutional behaviour states that 'her adjustment has been good. . . . She has displayed no outstanding psychiatric problems since admission'. B., who had never been arrested before, was 18 years old at the time of her arrest and had herself been raped two years earlier.

Case No. 3

C. suspected her 16-year-old daughter of trying to seduce C.'s boyfriend. As punishment, C. and her boyfriend tied up the daughter and prevented her from leaving the house for a period of 20 days. During this time, C. reportedly punched, kicked and burned her daughter with a cigarette. The daughter also complained that she had been molested sexually. Both C. and her accomplice were charged with sexual abuse but only the accomplice was convicted on that count of the indictment.

C. comes from a broken home and dropped out of school in the twelfth grade. She is white, divorced and has two children in the custody of foster parents. Despite a former heroin addiction, C. had only been arrested on three previous occasions, all of which were drug related. No psychological evaluations have been included in C.'s folder. Assessments of her adjustment to prison have been very favourable, however, and she has never received any disciplinary reports. C. was 40 years old when she attacked her daughter.

Case No. 4

D. and her ex-husband asked an adult female acquaintance to stop by D.'s apartment for a visit. As soon as the victim walked through the door, D. cut her with a knife and ordered her to commit acts of sodomy with D.'s ex-husband. D. took several photographs and threatened to send prints to the victim's family unless she immediately paid them a large sum of money. All three then went to several banks and commercial establishments so that the victim could cash some cheques. The victim told police that D. was primarily responsible for the offense.

D. was 27 years old when she was arrested. She is white, comes from an intact home, and has an eleventh grade education. D. was first committed to a state psychiatric hospital shortly after her tenth birthday. In all, she has been committed on five occasions. D. has nine previous arrests, but all were for property offenses, and only one resulted in incarceration (three months). Psychiatrists believe that D. may be suicidal. More specifically, she has been diagnosed as having a 'passive aggressive dependent personality disorder with manipulative and hypochondriacal features'. A pre-sentence psychiatric report recommended 'intensive insight-oriented psychotherapy at least five times a week while living in a structured situation'. Due to the fact that she was only recently sent to prison, no reports of her institutional adjustment were available at the time of this study.

Case No. 5

E., a 20-year-old prostitute with 48 prior arrests, struck another prostitute on the head with a bottle and robbed her of $500 worth of jewelry. E.'s pimp and two other men who were present at the time of the robbery then decided to rape the victim as well. During the rape, the victim was beaten so badly that she ultimately had to be hospitalized. E. participated in the rape to the extent that she forced the victim to perform oral sex on her.

E. is black, unmarried and a junior high school dropout. Like many prostitutes she comes from a broken home, and has never held any legitimate employment. E. has been incarcerated briefly on eight different occasions, but only one of her many arrests was for an assault. While incarcerated, E.'s disciplinary record has been 'spotty'. She was returned from a minimum security facility for committing a major disciplinary infraction and, in an unrelated action, had 60 days restored to her sentence that had previously been subtracted for good behaviour. A prison psychiatrist diagnosed E. as having an anti-social personality.

Cases No. 6 and No. 7
F., G. and another female accomplice beat a 14-year-old girl who had been visiting them at G's home. G. cut the victim with a pair of scissors and telephoned a slightly retarded male acquaintance to come over as quickly as possible. The record indicated that he raped the victim while G. and her friends held her down, but it is not clear what motivated the assault or if the assailants had been drinking at the time. The third female involved in the attack was sentenced to one year in the County House of Correction.

F. was 17 years old when arrested for this offence. She is single, white and comes from an intact home. F. left school in the seventh grade; her revised Beta IQ score is in the low range of average intelligence. She was arrested twice before for criminal mischief and once for a minor assault. Her probation report states that she attempted to commit suicide when she was 15 years old following her father's death from cancer. Recent MMPI scores indicate that F. has a personality pattern disturbance, paranoid type with anti-social tendencies. Overall, F. has made an 'extremely poor institutional adjustment ... her conduct indicates a need for intensive therapy'.

G. also comes from an intact home. She was 28 years old and separated with four children at the time of the offence. Though unskilled, she does have a high school equivalency diploma. G. admits that she drinks excessively. She attempted to commit suicide once when she was 23 years old and three times during the twelve month period preceding her arrest. She tried again one year after being admitted to prison. Although G. had no prior arrests, she is adjusting well to the institutional routine. Her counselor states that she is 'good in all areas except for social behavior, in which she is very good . . . She is polite, respectful, and even-tempered . . . generally speaking, her conduct has been fine.' G.'s folder does not contain copies of any psychological evaluations.

The Soviet psychiatrists, Stern and Stern (1981), claim that women in the Kuril Islands rape men because they are 'sexually starved':

The most extraordinary cases of rape are undoubtedly those committed by women upon men. This occurs in situations where the women are sexually starved. In the Kuril Islands this kind of thing is common. Fishing-boat captains dare not let their sailors go ashore, for there are thousands of women working in the canneries who have no man for years on end, and the sailors genuinely run the risk of death.

In another strange episode, a former beauty queen, Joyce McKinney, kidnapped a Mormon missionary, Kirk Anderson, and forced him to have sex with her. Ms McKinney 'was accused of knocking him out with chloroform, handcuffing him with fur-lined manacles to a bed in a remote cottage for three days and forcing him to have sex with her. Her companion, Keith May, was also charged with abduction' (*Standard* (London), 19 June 1984). McKinney and May broke bail in England and fled to the United States. The British did not press for extradition, but McKinney, thirty-three, continued to harass Anderson, twenty-nine, at his workplace outside Salt Lake City, Utah. Charged with disturbing the peace and giving false information to the police, McKinney said that 'she would ski down Everest backwards naked with a carnation between my teeth for Anderson'. McKinney claimed that she had used bondage on Anderson to help him work out his sexual hang-ups. When arrested, police discovered a large sum of money on her person and notebooks detailing her victim's daily activities. Maps locating Anderson's residence and photographs of his home were also confiscated.

RAPE VICTIMS

Adults as well as children are invariably traumatized by rape. The physical effects commonly include broken bones, acute neck injuries, and injuries to breasts, vagina and rectum. Apart from these injuries and the high risk of contracting any one of several forms of venereal disease, the emotional after-effects are drastic. Victims often feel too embarrassed and humiliated to speak about the experience, and this is partly the reason why only between 10 and 25 per cent of rapes are reported. Some victims mistakenly believe that they have been responsible for being raped and lapse into long depressions. Like torture victims studied by Amnesty International, rape victims experience anxiety, guilt, self-disgust, humiliation and a general lack of trust of others.

Unfortunately, family members do sometimes blame the victim. A husband may feel personally violated because he sees the rape as a violation of his property. People sometimes react by saying that the victim was probably asking for it, some citing the prevailing moral climate and 'free sex' as the reason for rape: 'Well, she deserved it, didn't she? What with all this free sex life, she shouldn't have gone out alone. The young of today deserve what's coming to them.' Many fail to realize that the incidence of rape has probably always been high. No one heard about rape before, not because it did not occur, but because victims were too reluctant to speak about it. Rape is especially traumatic in young heterosexual males who are homosexually violated. I was told by one such victim that he could never tell his family for fear that they might think him homosexual; nor could he dream of sharing the trauma with his girl friend for fear that she might lose 'respect' for his masculinity.

Very young children often do not understand anything about the violation. They know that something bad happened and become depressed by the reactions of adults around them. It is known for young children to accept responsibility for being raped: 'If I didn't take those sweets from that man, and go with him to the fair, like my Mummy and Daddy said I shouldn't, then he wouldn't have done anything. My Mummy and Daddy are cross with me. I am bad.' Child victims should routinely be seen by a fully qualified child psychologist who specializes in that kind of trauma. The problem is compounded when the child has been sexually violated by a family member, such as a father, uncle or grandfather. (See the section on 'Incest', pages 255–66.)

Many psychologists who specialize in assessing and treating sexually violated children use dolls or mannequins to help to explain exactly what happened. The mannequins can be undressed and are especially designed to display adult and female genitalia. In this way, the child does not have to rely on a limited vocabulary in explaining what happened.

Tollison and Adams (1979) elucidate three reactions to rape: (a) acute reaction; (b) outward adjustment; and (c) integration and resolution.

Acute reaction just after the attack is usually accompanied by shock, disbelief and dismay. The victim is likely to show up at a police station or casualty ward in an agitated, incoherent and emotionally insecure state. The trauma may be so extreme that the victim is taken as being 'psychotic'. However, some victims remain in control and only show signs of acute fear when they try to discuss what happened. Self-blame is frequent: the victim may say that she should not have worn such provocative clothes, or sadly even claim she is being punished by God.

Outward adjustment is characterized by a desire to resume normal life. The victim declares that everything is resolved and that she no longer needs help. She tends to sweep anger and resentment under the rug and to rationalize the rape. The rape may be rationalized by attributing it to such external factors as fate or bad luck. She may also explain the rape in terms of class or racial struggle: rich *versus* poor or black *versus* white.

Integration and resolution is indicated by the victim's desire to talk about the trauma. She experiences a normal 'reactive' depression and may want to work through her anger and resentment. For example, she may find that she has generalized her fear of rape into a fear of all men, whom she has come to resent. Reactive depression as a result of such trauma occurs in most rape victims and can be overcome through the help offered by rape crisis centres, women's support groups and skilled psychotherapists. The sensitive psychotherapist, male or female, is often most qualified to treat rape victims.

REPORTING RAPE

As already mentioned, the rate of rape has since 1960 been increasing in both the United States and the United Kingdom. This trend is not fully understood, although the increase in rape has been correlated with increased use of alcohol and drugs, higher unemployment, greater availability of guns (in the United States), and increased levels of poverty. The increase in the rate of rape may also be explained by its having come to be somewhat more reported. Consciousness-raising groups for women, rape crisis centres and the media have made the reporting of rape more socially acceptable.

Although many victims are now more ready to report rape, it should be stressed that doing so is still not a simple affair. Police will interrogate a rape victim for long periods, often without much sympathy. Victims have been known to drop charges because of the lack of co-operation from the police, and because they do not want to relive the ordeal in court. Some victims report being made to feel as though they were the criminal:

I rang the police and they showed up very casually about ten minutes later. They sauntered in and one of them produced a flick knife when I asked him to untie me. They started saying things like, 'Well, I don't think you have been raped. This was obviously someone you met last night. It got too heavy and you decided to call the police this morning.' They kept suggesting it was a casual affair gone wrong. They said, 'If everything you say happened had happened you would be completely hysterical now. You would have thrown yourself out the window to get away.' They obviously didn't believe me. [Toner, 1977]

SELF-DEFENCE

It has become not uncommon for women living in densely populated urban areas to enlist in martial arts classes. Women are being encouraged to learn how to fight back. In *Our Bodies, Ourselves* (Phillips and Rakusen, 1978), women are advised:

If you're caught by surprise or have nowhere to run, you can fight off an attacker in a number of different ways. He comes at you from the front: you kick his knees (or shins), hard. If he grabs you before you can kick, ram your knees up into his groin. If your arms are free, use them: chop or punch at his head – temple, eyes, right under the ears, mouth, nose. If not you can spit or bite.

Women are also advised to carry a pepper-shaker or deodorant spray – any substance that can be used to cause a burning sensation to the eyes. Other weapons recommended for self-defence include umbrellas, hammers, bottles and special 'scream sprays' to frighten off an attacker.

Many women are raped while out on a 'legitimate' date. Women confronted by a 'rampant' man during a 'date rape' situation have been advised to divert the potential rapist by talking about matters which are incompatible with sexual arousal. For instance, they might effectively say:

'I've got my period.' *Some* men are revolted by the whole concept of menstruation.

'Wait a moment. Stay right there, I just have to go to the toilet. Back in a second.' She need never return.

'I would dearly love to make love, sweetheart. Only thing is, I've got *herpes*!' Even violent rapists might be fended off in face of this dreaded venereal condition. Currently, it might be more effective to say, I am an AIDS carrier and it's terminal. It's transmitted through intimate contact between mucous membranes.'

Take his penis in your hand and say, 'What is this? I've never seen such an ugly, weird-looking one in my life!'

If you can, vomit in his lap!

Try to distract your aggressive date. Tell a joke, tell him you are ravishingly hungry again, tell him that you just got out of a mental hospital . . . do anything to distract his attention. Once you manage to distract him his concentration will diminish, and you may have a chance to get away.

Talk about his family – his wife, children, mother. These topics may be incompatible with his lust.

Talk about money, his overdraft, any business anxiety. Remember, anxiety is incompatible with sexual arousal.

GANG RAPE

Between 40 and 50 per cent of rapes involve group rape, where more than one person sexually assaults a defenceless victim. The phenomenon is supposed to represent a special type of male-bonding, not dissimilar to that applying in any other all-male club. Gang rapes arise in rich and poor neighbourhoods, in parks, homes and university campuses. Gang rape is the ultimate in sexual bullying. Members of a gang-rape 'team' are usually themselves intimidated by a group leader. The pressure to conform is powerful in any group. All it takes is someone who understands how much people need to identify with a group to win acceptance and avoid being made an outsider. Group leaders, constructive and destructive, capitalize on the insecurities of their audience by getting the individual to perform ritualized initiation rites which serve as a 'tattoo' of exclusive membership. In the case of gang rape, many of the weaker participants go along with something against their conscience, just to belong and win the approval of the charismatic leader.

In early 1983, four males raped and tortured a woman over a period of two hours on a games table in Big Dan's Bar, Bedford, Massachusetts. The men did this while onlookers cheered them on, much like crowds encouraging a football team. A few weeks later, seven young males were charged with the kidnap and repeated rape of a seventeen-year-old girl in Charlestown, a suburb of Boston. The rape lasted for seven hours. About the same time, a group of fraternity brothers at the University of Pennsylvania gang raped a young woman as part of their fun.

I interviewed one young woman who, in 1977 at the age of thirteen, was attacked by three adolescents as she walked home from school. The incident occurred in the rather opulent Los Angeles suburb of Woodland Hills. In the girl's words, 'About three houses from my own these Mexican guys jumped out of their truck and grabbed me. I kicked one in the nuts and boy did I pay for that. They drove up to Mulholland Drive and raped me for what seemed like ten years. But it was probably about two hours.' Dismayed, I asked her what she meant. She continued, 'Yeah . . . I mean like rape. You know. They ripped off my pants and all three had a go. I stopped yelling 'cause they had showed me this knife. I never wanted to live so much in my life. All I could think of was my family, and prayed they'd not kill me. I could see my body found weeks later in the canyon. All while they stuck it in front and back. Then they dropped me off up there in the hills and said that if I told they'd get me.' When asked whether she hated men because of the incident, she replied, 'No. But I sure as hell won't be going around in the dark any more. I worry about my younger sister.'

Common to many rape victims is a reluctance to report these crimes. This young woman looked at me as though I was insane when I suggested that, even if she had been raped a few years before, she might still be able to help the police at least to pick up a pattern. Perhaps she could recognize the rapists, perhaps they had done the same thing to others. 'No!' she exclaimed. 'You can't understand.

That's because you're a man. Do you know what I'd have to go through, what the cops would say when I walked into the station? More humiliation. I just wanna forget about the whole damn thing.'

Even pubescent boys rape. Brownmiller (1981) records how she sat in on a trial of two boys, aged thirteen and fifteen, for raping an eleven-year-old girl. The mother of the fifteen-year-old tried to assault her in the corridor of the courtroom, having identified her as a feminist and hence, by implication, someone involved with the boy's ninety-day youth custody sentence. Given this woman's son's history of early gang rape, it is not inconceivable that, by some twist of fate, she might herself become one of his victims. In a first-hand account, Stern and Stern (1981) give an example from Soviet Russia, one of the authors underscoring the point that rapes are committed by ordinary men. All rapes are outrageous, but the following describes a particularly outrageous attack:

Rapes of old women are fairly rare, but not exceptional. Again, in the cases which I have encountered, the rapists are not sadistic maniacs escaped from an asylum, but ordinary citizens. One such case was described to me by the culprit in Kharkov camp. Nine drunken louts had attacked and raped an old woman returning home at nightfall. The man who told the story was almost sober at the time he returned home. A terrifying picture waited for him: his mother was lying in bed, covered in blood.
'What's happened to you?' he cried, horrified.
'I've been raped. I'm dying.'
'Where? Who raped you?'
'My son. You were the last. I recognized you . . .'
The boy fainted with shock at the news.
'When I came to,' he continued, 'my mother was dead. She had hung herself in the room before my very eyes. Life is unbearable for me. Sooner or later, I shall kill myself. There is no place on earth for swine like me.'
The man always ended his confession that way, and these were not empty words: he had already twice tried to kill himself.

MILITARY MASS RAPE

Although rape is endemic to warring armies, it has not invariably been sanctioned in military context. Long before the US Army outlawed it, the Articles of War formulated under Richard II of England in 1385 decreed that soldiers caught raping should be hanged.

Victorious armies are notorious for opportunistic plunder and rape. Throughout history, from the Golden Horde of Genghis Khan to Vietnam and the Pakistani campaign in Bangladesh, victorious soldiers have regarded rape as part of the spoils of war: rape as reward. Rulers like Genghis Khan considered raping the women of fallen communities to be a way of earning the support and motivation of their own soldiers. Besides, there was an inevitable economic benefit: by raping the women of conquered peoples, the enslaved population became socially diluted and broken, yet increased.

The infamous raping of the Sabine women occurred prior to the founding of Rome. The opportunity to rape numerous women was used to entice volunteer crusaders by Byzantine emperor Alexius during the First Crusade. Mass rape was committed in the name of God during the sixteenth-century religious wars waged against the Huguenots in France. In the mid-eighteenth century, when Lord George Sackville crushed a rebellion in the Scottish Highlands for King George, women were sexually mutilated by English soldiers. They were then required to witness the ritual bayonetting of their sons and husbands.

According to Brownmiller (1981), 'Rape of a woman may be as much an act against her husband or father, for the rapist, as it is against the woman's body.' She also observes that acts of rape during war were not recorded in detail until after the First World War. Mass rape occurred frequently during the Polish and Russian pogroms against the Jews, most notably under Hetman Bogdan Chelnitzky in the mid-seventeeth century at the time of the Cossack revolt. In America, mob rape was recorded during the American Revolution, the persecution of Mormons, and when the Ku Klux Klan (KKK) attacked blacks. Ritualized rape of large numbers of women occurred in 1960 in the Congo; and in Uganda under Idi Amin during the 1970s.

It is hardly feasible to give a comprehensive account of every mass rape known, yet it seems worth highlighting the following groups who have excelled in mass rape.

GERMANS DURING THE SECOND WORLD WAR

The US Army recorded 971 convictions for rape during the Second World War. Undoubtedly many more cases must have gone unreported and no official inquiry into Allied atrocities was ever held. The Allies, however, could have proved no match for the servants of the Third Reich, whose forefathers had proved especially adept at raping Belgian women during the First World War. The Nazi Germans take their place among the most sadistic, vicious and cruel mass rapists of all time. (Given social psychological evidence for the powerful influence of 'modelling' behaviour (Bandura, 1977), and ethological studies of 'imprinting' (Lorenz, 1966), it is hardly surprising that, even today, West Germany should have by far the highest level of child abuse in Western Europe; a problem which alarms the West German government.)

Nazi ideology stressed that non-Aryans, and especially Jews, were profoundly weak and feminine. All things feminine were hated, precisely because they were the antithesis of fascism. Feminist writers like Kate Millett and Susan Brownmiller suggest that Jews would therefore logically provide prime targets for rape, degradation and murder in the service of the Super-race. Brownmiller (1975) writes: 'Rape for the Germans, and to a similar extent for the Japanese, played a serious and logical role in the achievement of what they saw as their ultimate objective: the total humiliation and destruction of "inferior peoples" and the establishment of their own master race.'

Russell (1955) recounts one atrocity from the summer of 1944, at a farm near Presles in the South of France, where the SS were searching for two members of the Maquis: 'They were not there, so the SS, deprived of their prey, arrested the farmer and his wife. The Germans shot the husband, raped his wife, then killed her, and after torturing their little son aged three, crucified him on the farmyard gate.'

German troops systematically massacred many inhabitants of Lvov on the Russian front, the object being to intimidate the population. Women were raped, and their mutilated, naked bodies put on display for survivors to see. Breast hatred might be something profoundly Germanic. Reports of the raping of young pregnant women, cutting their throats and bayonetting their breasts were common and documented when war crimes were being recorded.

Rape and fearless acts of mass murder earned the German soldier promotion. Promotion meant more frequent sexual access to captured women and children. In Smolensk, a German commander orchestrated a special brothel for officers, the brothel comprising local women who were forced to give their bodies to German officers. It was a reward for becoming emotionally neutral and detached from the mass shootings and burning of civilians in local churches. It seems an incredible situation. In Smolensk, and all over occupied Europe, German officers would use and abuse the bodies of countless women, *without ever considering the shared humanity between the women and children they were raping and the mothers, wives and daughters they had left at home.*

Under the Nuremberg race laws of 1935, it was illegal for Germans to have sexual relations with Jews. Hitler's doctrine of the 'purity' of Aryan blood also implied that rape, marriage and extra-marital sex were forbidden. Many non-Jewish Germans, male and female, were sent to concentration camps for disregarding these sex laws. Much like the race laws in the American South and Southern Africa, the object was to prevent births of 'mixed marriages', the main difference being that the Germans believed in direct extermination of the unwanted races. German commanders who set up brothels in which Jews and other non-Aryan women could be used to boost troop morale were logically able to reason that, provided they killed the women after raping them, then no births of 'mixed marriages' could occur. The Nuremberg race laws were upheld in other ways. In the Lithuanian town of Kovno, the Germans ordered immediate death for any Jewish woman who became pregnant.

In keeping with a respect for hierarchy, the German army sanctioned two types of brothel: one for officers, the other for the common soldier. The officers got the 'choice' women, while the ordinary private had to make do with 'ordinary' women. The Germans ordered the Jews of the Warsaw ghetto to form a special committee, the *Judenrat*, which was to become responsible for delivering certain quotas of Jews each day into German hands. One of the tasks of the *Judenrat* was to organize a brothel composed of young Jewish girls. The *Judenrat* did not comply, but this did not prevent the Polish Black Police or German army from coming into the ghetto to help themselves to whatever Jewish female they could scavenge.

THE SOVIETS

While the Soviets were meticulous in preparing for the Nuremberg Trials records of atrocities committed by the

Germans, their armies had also, as they marched into Germany, participated enthusiastically in rape. Mass rape of German women by the Soviet army was not documented nearly as well as that committed by the German war machine. However, Stern and Stern (1981) make the following observation:

> . . . one must mention the consequences of the war with Nazi Germany. When the Soviet army moved onto the counter-offensive, the local population suffered very harsh treatment; rape became particularly common, the habitual reaction of soldiers drunk with victory. The same soldier who before the war could recite poems to his beloved, was now capable of raping any woman who came into his hands. There were even extraordinary cases where, for example, Russian female prisoners in German camps were raped by their liberators; according to one of my patients from Kharkov, the Russian soldiers who had captured a small town in Eastern Germany were unable to find a single woman or girl alive (everyone had fled), so they threw themselves upon the still-warm bodies of the victims of the latest shellings.

The above passage corroborates Susan Brownmiller's understanding of what happens to 'ordinary men' as they become drunk with the power of military victory. But it is dangerous to generalize: clearly, not *all* Germans were cruel killers. Hundreds of thousands may have been, but not *all*. The driveway to *Vad Vashem* in Jerusalem, the memorial to Holocaust victims, is lined with pine trees symbolizing those Germans who attempted to save Jews during the war. However, German families were acutely aware of the victorious Russians as they marched into private homes, hospitals and nunneries in Berlin and other German cities. Brownmiller (1981) recounts the following:

> Klaus Kuster, a member of the Hitler Youth, saw three Russians grab a woman on the street and take her into a hallway. He followed. One soldier trained his pistol on Klaus. The second held the screaming woman while the third raped her. Klaus

watched the Russian who had done the raping emerge from the doorway. Tears were streaming down the soldier's face as he wailed, '*Ya bolshoi svinya*' – 'I am a big pig'.

The guilty Russian probably saw himself as 'doing his duty' in avenging the rape of his people by Germans. In this sense, the rape would primarily be a 'crime of aggression' rather than a 'sexual crime'. Although the debate over considering rape as a 'violent crime' and not a 'sexual one' continues to rage, it should not be forgotten that rape is, by definition, a forced sexual act.

THE JAPANESE IN CHINA

From the invasion of China in 1936, Japanese plunder and rape is on a par with that of the Nazi Germans. Like the Germans, the Japanese saw themselves as a 'superior' race, but although they actively used concentration camps, they never developed so sophisticated a system of extermination camps as the Germans achieved. The Allied tribunal held in Tokyo in 1946, however, produced numerous affidavits to attest to atrocities committed by Japanese troops.

There was, for example, the incredible mass rape of the women of the defenceless Chinese city of Nanking in 1936. Brownmiller (1981) cites the testimony of Wong Pan Sze, aged fifteen when the Japanese occupied the city:

At the time the Japanese entered the city on December 13, 1937, I and my father and my sister had already been removed to live in a house on Shanghai Road No. 100 which was in the refugee zone. There were about 500 persons living in that house, and I often saw the Japs come to the house asking and searching for women. On one occasion one woman was raped in the open yard. This happened in the night, and all of us could hear her cry as she was being raped. But when the Japs left we could not find her, they had taken her away with them. Twice I saw the Japs' truck come to the house and round up the women living in the house. These women were taken away by the Japs and none of them returned with the exception of one girl who managed to get back home after having been raped by the Japs, and she told me that all the girls who had been taken in the trucks had been raped many times by the Japs, one after the other. This one girl who managed to get back to the house told me that she had seen one of the girls raped, and after being raped the Jap had stuck weeds into her vagina and the girl died from this treatment. At the time I was about 15 years of age. I hid every time a Jap came near the house and this is why the Japs never caught me.

Japanese troops are reported to have raped 20,000 women in the first month of the occupation of Nanking, a figure comparable with the Pakistani rape of Bangladesh thirty-four years later. Soldiers showed no mercy. They executed anyone, woman or family member, who resisted. The Japanese general in charge of the operation sanctioned the rape of Nanking on the grounds that its inhabitants needed to be 'chastised'. The Japanese War Ministry attempted a cover-up by instructing troop commanders to instruct soldiers that they should either 'pay off' the raped women or 'kill them'. Internees in Japanese concentration camps also recorded instances of rape by guards.

MASS RAPE POST-SECOND WORLD WAR

Mass rape did not end with the war. One of the more infamous post-war instances of large-scale rape took place during the Pakistani invasion of Bangladesh in 1971.

When the Indian subcontinent became independent in 1948, it was split into largely Hindu India and Islamic Pakistan. Pakistan was divided into two sections, East and West. East Pakistan attempted to declare independence from West Pakistan in 1971, with the result that West Pakistan sent troops to quash the rebellion. India, which separated the two areas, used armed force to eject the West

Pakistanis, or Panjabis, from what was to become Bangladesh. It is estimated that between two and three million persons died as a direct result of the war, and that between 200,000 and 300,000 Bengali women were raped by the Panjabis. Bengali women and young schoolgirls were kidnapped and taken to army headquarters, where they were stripped naked to prevent escape. They were also used in the making of pornographic films. Brownmiller (1981) cites this incident:

Khadiga, 13 years old, was interviewed by a photojournalist in Dacca. She was walking to school with four other girls when they were kidnapped by a gang of Pakistani soldiers. All five were put in a military brothel in Mohammedpur and held captive for six months until the end of the war. Khadiga was regularly abused by two men a day; others, she said, had to service seven to ten men daily. At first, Khadiga said, the soldiers tied a gag around her mouth to keep her from screaming. As the months wore on and the captives' spirit was broken, the soldiers devised a simple quid pro quo. They withheld the daily ration of food until the girls had submitted to the full quota.

The suffering did not end with the war. Since Bengalis are devout Moslems, raped women could find no husbands. Bengali men expect that women should live in purdah, and only accept virgins as marriageable. While a few might accept one of the sexually abused women, it would only be if the bribe was sufficiently high. Furthermore, most rape victims suffered from venereal disease, a tell-tale sign which made the victims loathe themselves even more. The rape of Bangladesh destroyed the hopes, aspirations and lives of hundred of thousands of Bengali women.

RAPE AND THE LAW

Historically speaking, rape was considered a crime against *property*, women being the legitimate property of their families. It was therefore the 'proprietors', not the victim, who experienced a 'larceny', since a victim who had been made non-virgin would command a lower bride price than a virgin. The Bible states that a man who rapes a married woman should die, but that if the woman were a virgin, the rapist 'that lay with her shall give unto the damsel's father fifty shekels of silver, and she shall be his wife; because he hath humbled her, he may not put her away all his days' (Deuteronomy 22:29). Rape can still result in the death penalty in countries as ideologically remote from each other as China, the Soviet Union, Iran and South Africa.

Rapists were executed in Great Britain and in the United States well into the twentieth century. In the United States, black men were more liable to receive the death penalty than white men, especially if they had raped a white woman. Predictably, the law was inclined to be lenient where white men had raped black women. Prior to the reintroduction of the death penalty in 1976 in the United States, sentences up to hundreds of years were handed down for 'aggravated' rape, Bryant (1982) recording that one Texas man was given 800 years for raping a schoolgirl. By contrast, certain rapists have been handed down probationary sentences in the same courts, when it was ruled that the woman 'had asked for it'.

The crime and punishment of rape forms a complex issue. Generally, in both the United Kingdom and the United States, even though men rape men in both countries, only women can be 'raped' in terms of the law. I say 'generally', because a California woman was convicted of rape in 1971 after being found guilty of forcing her husband to have sex with another – at gunpoint! In England, a man cannot be prosecuted for rape (*per se*) if he rapes *per anum*; he can only be prosecuted for rape if he rapes *per vaginam* (Howard League for Penal Reform, 1985). However, if he rapes either a man, woman or child *per anum*, he can receive a life sentence for buggery, but not for rape. Ironically, if he has sexual intercourse with a girl aged between thirteen and sixteen, he will receive only two years in prison. For some reason, English courts are more ready to hand down prison sentences for unlawful sex against boys than against girls. If penetration does not occur, a man may be prosecuted for 'indecent assault on a woman' under Section 14 of the Sexual Offences Act 1956. Boys under fourteen, husbands and women may be found guilty of 'aiding and abetting another to commit rape'.

In Californian law, rape is defined by Penal Code 261 as follows:

Rape is an act of sexual intercourse, accomplished with a female not the wife of the perpetrator, under either of the following circumstances:
1. Where she is incapable, through lunacy or other unsoundness of mind, whether temporary or permanent, of giving legal consent;
2. Where she resists, but her resistance is overcome by force or violence;
3. Where she is prevented from resisting by threats of great and immediate bodily harm, accompanied by apparent power of execution, or by any intoxicating narcotic, or anesthetic substance, administered by or with the provity of the accused;
4. Where she is at the time unconscious of the nature of the act, and this is known to the accused;
5. Where she submits under the belief that the person committing the act is her husband, and this belief is induced by any artifice, pretence, or concealment practiced by the accused, with intent to induce such belief.

Unlawful sexual intercourse, or 'statutory rape', is defined by Penal Code 261.5 as 'an act of sexual intercourse accomplished with a female not the wife of the perpetrator where the female is under the age of 18 years'. Under this law, a Californian man of nineteen *could* be sent to prison for having intercourse with his seventeen-year-old consent-ing girlfriend. Hundreds of thousands of Californian men are guilty of this felony, and very few, or none, are sent to jail for it. (If they went and confessed the 'crime' to the public prosecutor, they could be tried.) A nineteen-year-old woman *could* be sent to prison for having sexual intercourse with her seventeen-year-old boyfriend, but she *could not be charged with rape*. Instead, she could be charged and punished for 'child molestation'. Other complexities in Californian law include the punishment of sterilization for raping a *girl* under ten years of age, which would not apply for raping a *boy* under ten years of age . . .

According to the Howard League for Penal Reform (1985), English law is equally perplexing. For instance, a woman who 'indecently assaults' a man could receive up to ten years, while a man who indecently assaults a woman would only get two! A woman who drugs a man in order to have sex with him would go unpunished, but a man who got a woman drunk to have sex with her could receive a severe prison sentence.

PART THREE
Anonymous Sex

19 EXHIBITIONISM

GENERAL CHARACTERISTICS AND THEORIES

There are millions of women in the West who have seen an unsolicited display of male genitalia at least once in their lives. The exhibitionist, or 'flasher', attains sexual arousal and gratification by exposing his penis to a non-consenting stranger. An individual is classified as an 'exhibitionist' if exposing himself is his preferred or primary source of sexual gratification. 'Victims' are usually adult women, but are often young girls or, to a much lesser extent, boys. Three patterns of 'flasher behaviour' emerge (Tollison and Adams, 1979), the first being the simple exhibitionist, who merely exposes his non-erect penis without attempting to communicate with or harm his victim. The second variety is the 'public masturbator', who actively attempts to involve his victim in his sexual fantasy. Finally, there is the more serious offender, who acts out his aggressive fantasies and is sexually gratified when he succeeds in producing expressions of shock in the victim. It should be stressed, however, that an overwhelming majority of exhibitionists represent no threat to physical safety. Nevertheless, law enforcement in both Britain and the United States comes down hard on exhibitionists, despite the fact that they are not usually dangerous.

Police authorities tend to prosecute flashers because they offend moral codes and because they believe that flashers are dangerous, or potentially so. Conviction often results in job loss, divorce, having to register as a 'mentally disordered sex offender' (in California) and a prison sentence. If there is no prior criminal record, the convicted exhibitionist is considered a good candidate for probation, the recidivist rate being only about 10 per cent. Probation usually requires the offender to seek psychotherapy for his 'condition'. Clinical observation suggests that flashers are merely attempting to have vicarious communication with females who, in reality, frighten them. From the examples of several exhibitionists referred to me for treatment, it appears that such men often experience what amounts to a 'phobia' of women, particularly of adult women.

Mental health professionals are often culpable in making gross over-generalizations, seeking to classify their patients into neat categories and, in so doing, performing injustices not only to themselves and their patients but also to their profession at large. This is especially the case when they discuss exhibitionists. Exhibitionists are individuals and may present as more complex cases. For example, while it is true to say that 'most' flashers are not dangerous, a few clearly will be, such as those exhibitionists who engage in paedophilic (child molestation) activities, voyeurism (peeping) or frottage (illicit touching of non-consenting strangers).

The exhibitionist can also be viewed as an 'addict', because his behaviour is compulsive and because, even though he may not often be caught reoffending, he tends to repeat the behaviour and avoid being caught. (A self-help group calling itself 'Exhibitionists Anonymous' has reportedly been formed in England.) Typically, the flasher starts exposing himself at the onset of puberty, receives his first conviction aged thirty, and has less than an average experience of sexual intercourse. He is usually shy, introverted and basically law-abiding in other respects. In the

United States, there is a greater frequency of exhibitionists among white Protestant males than among blacks or Roman Catholics.

Exhibitionists choose public and semi-public places to perform their stunts. Parks, streets, parked cars, college campuses, subways, or any public place which facilitates rapid escape are favoured spots. Arrests are more common in the spring and summer months, since more people are out and about then. On the other hand, the more 'committed' flasher is always willing to brave the elements. Several women reported seeing a man masturbating one night in a public telephone booth in south London during the unusually cold spell ($-7°C$) during January 1985.

Abel *et al.* (1970) claim from their research that exhibitionists referred to them for treatment follow their own particular scenarios when acting out an uncontrollable urge to expose themselves. Typically, the exhibitionist mentally rehearses a previous flashing experience and then selects an appropriate site, choosing a victim before exposing himself and/or masturbating to orgasm. The exposure is usually preceded by a period of emotional frustration involving authority figures.

Certain exhibitionists are excited by the prospect of being arrested. It is possible that, at some non-conscious level, they secretly desire arrest to alleviate the shame and guilt experienced over feelings and behaviour which they believe to be wrong. Since so few cases of exhibitionism are reported to the police, the typical flasher is likely to get away with his neurotic behaviour for years. He will finally be caught, either because he becomes careless, or because he begins to expose himself with increasing regularity in the same place.

There is an abundance of psychological theories about the causes of exhibitionism, some of them involving a good deal of creative guesswork. One theory suggests that, when exhibitionists select young girls as victims, it may be because they symbolically desire to soil virgins. Others suggest that exhibitionists dissociate, and go into a fugue or dream-like state. This would imply a sort of amnesia for what transpired during the exposure, especially when the suspect claims he was merely overcome by an uncontrollable urge to urinate. Most exhibitionists will flee any female who interprets and accepts an exposure as an invitation for a sexual encounter.

In psychoanalytic theory, the exhibitionist is viewed as attempting to deny 'castration anxieties'. Orthodox Freudian psychoanalysts believe that the exhibitionist was, as a young child, afraid his father would castrate him because of a competitive sexual and emotional desire for his mother. The flasher is said to be 'fixated' or stuck at the Oedipal stage of psychosexual development. It is for this reason that he actively, though unconsciously, attempts to shock the female sex. Shocking the female sex serves to affirm that he still has a penis – that his father has not cut it off; and that he is more powerful than females – even if they happen to be six-year-old girls.

Although it is not causal, a more plausible and certainly less complex explanation for exhibitionism is that the offender is fundamentally immature. Immaturity is a significant component in the personal histories of many exhibitionists. Exhibitionists are often like little boys who persist in showing off their penises to the world. The act is a symbolic defiance of authority. Many exhibitionists had mothers who punished masturbation, endorsed puritanical ideas and reinforced the child's feelings of inadequacy. Exhibitionists often claim that they struggle against the urge to expose themselves in much the same way as adolescents will try to fight off the urge to masturbate. They are usually aware that society is opposed to their behaviour and experience intense guilt when they act out, particularly if the act culminates in ejaculation (Tollison and Adams, 1979).

Further evidence for immaturity as a significant personality factor in the make-up of many exhibitionists is that they seldom manage to form lasting sexual relationships or learn how to manage 'normal' stress. They may get married as a result of family pressure, often at a late age, and fail to establish fulfilling relationships. It is stress within the marriage that then often precipitates their behaviour. Since exhibitionists are usually shy, introverted and non-assertive, they are easily frustrated, being unable to voice emotional needs. In other words, an exhibitionist is, if dissatisfied, unlikely to assert himself over a range of issues, including job dissatisfaction or sending back undercooked food at a restaurant, as much as any emotional problem. The frustration is then pathetically dealt with by a symbolic gesture – the public display of genitalia which becomes the exhibitionist's primary sexual outlet.

It goes without saying that many people who are not exhibitionists will masturbate or have sexual intercourse under stressful conditions. Married couples often 'make up' after an intense argument by having sex, which they may then describe as excellent. In more extreme instances, human beings cope with stress by having sexual intercourse with complete strangers – as was sometimes the case with victims travelling to their deaths in Nazi death camps. By way of comparison, under the same circumstances, an exhibitionist would, in theory, compulsively and perpetually expose himself or even masturbate in front of the others, in preference to having sexual intercourse.

Causal explanations for the development of exhibitionism need not be complex. Several flashers report that their first exposures occurred accidentally when urinating or masturbating in a public place. The discovery usually led to feelings of embarrassment and excessive worry. Subsequently, the individual began to ruminate and think about the initial exposure. Simply thinking about showing his genitals in public then led to his becoming sexually aroused, and he would masturbate, replaying the event each time. One exhibitionist, referred by the Probation Department for treatment, reported the following masturbatory fantasy:

I imagine myself going to a college campus. I am usually in an angry mood. I spend quite some time choosing a particular woman's dorm. I enjoy selecting a particular woman. I like to go at night because if a girl is in her room studying she can't see outside too well because of the reflection created by there being more light inside the dorm than outside. I watch her at her desk, or perhaps she is putting on make-up. Then I begin to take out my pecker and play with myself while watching her. As I get more turned on I move closer to her window and use a flash-light [torch] which I point at my pecker. When the student sees me she gets a fright and I love the expression of fear on her face. At this point I come.

The patient had begun to masturbate to these fantasies soon after he was accidentally discovered masturbating by his sister and her friends, who led him to believe they had been spying on his masturbatory activities over several weeks. Although guilty and ashamed, he found that masturbating to fantasies in which he showed off his erect penis and shocked girls or women was very rewarding. In this way, he was conditioning himself to associate sexual arousal with exposure. His masturbatory preference for exhibitionistic fantasy became exclusive to the point where he was unable to gain much pleasure from looking at photographs of nude women. He even sought pornography with exhibitionistic themes. Getting the patient to shift his masturbatory fantasies towards more 'appropriate' or socially acceptable ones proved an important part of his treatment.

AN AGGRESSIVE FLASHER: AN ATYPICAL CASE

The patient, Alberto, was a nineteen-year-old sex offender, referred for group and behaviour therapy by the Probation Department. Alberto denied that he had a history of exhibiting himself. He was charged and found guilty of indecent exposure under Section 314 of the California Penal Code. The probation report indicated that he had become drunk and exposed his penis to a woman delivering mail to his home. The victim reported the incident to the police and claimed that Alberto had been abusive to her on more than one occasion. Furthermore, the victim claimed, without provocation Alberto had screamed at her after unzipping his trousers: 'I'll show you what you need, you whore. I'll fuck you. It's what you need, bitch. Just come inside and I'll give you the best screw you ever had, cunt.' Alberto did not deny the event and showed no remorse. He said that the woman deserved it, because she was 'a bitch, and if it weren't for her I wouldn't be sitting in your office. I don't need a shrink anyways!'

In contrast to the widely held belief that exhibitionists seldom manage to form stable and lasting sexual relationships, Alberto seemed to care for his girlfriend of two years. He was, however, 'more emotionally into her than into having sex with her'. On interview, his girlfriend concurred: 'Alberto is sweet and kind to me. He doesn't want me for my body like lots of others guys do. He was so nice when my parents got divorced. Sure, he sometimes yells at me, but never hits me.'

As treatment progressed, it proved possible to establish rapport and trust. Alberto's troubles seemed to have begun when he was fourteen. He confided he had been masturbating to themes of exposure ever since he was discovered 'jerking off' in the school lavatory. He found, whenever he thought about the incident, he would become sexually aroused. He created fantasies in which he exhibited himself. Alberto masturbated to aggressive fantasies on a daily basis, and there is no doubt that his desire actually to exhibit himself was maintained by them.

THE CASE OF A PASSIVE–AGGRESSIVE FLASHER

The patient, Don, was a sixty-five-year-old docker (long-shoreman) who was referred for treatment by the Department of Paroles. He reported frequent arrests for exposing himself to young girls ever since he was twenty years old. Don had managed to evade arrest for many years, since he had been able to act out his exhibitionistic urges in foreign countries, entering the merchant marine primarily because it enabled him to 'go to countries where people had more worries than chasing a poor old man like me who gets his kicks out of showing my dick in public'. Don preferred countries where 'the ladies got a fright' when seeing his exposed penis. He did not care for India, where people 'just laughed and made me feel small'. He lost his job with the merchant marine after spending time in prison for exposing himself in an American city. He had finally been caught exposing himself to a group of kindergarten children and given a suspended prison sentence of three years.

Don managed to evade being caught for years by select-ing public places from where he could escape easily. He seldom returned to the same place twice, and claimed he never masturbated in public. Furthermore, he stated that he did not even display an erect penis in public, since 'I am diabetic and can't get a hard-on'. Yet while his physician confirmed the diagnosis of *diabetes melitus*, our psychophys-iological examination (conducted in a private 'sex booth' using a penile plethysmograph) revealed that Don obtained on average an 80 per cent erection to an audiotape which presented stories describing exhibitionistic activity.

–

Don lived alone and gave the distinct impression of being lonely. He had no 'real friends' and the group therapy seemed to provide added meaning to his life. He would arrive an hour before sessions were scheduled and sit in the reception room, chatting with anyone present. Don liked to shock people and, metaphorically speaking, seemed to want 'to get a rise' out of others. He would, for example, tell other patients that he had joined a nudist club and would soon go sky-diving in the nude. He said that the nudist club provided him with the opportunity of showing himself off to other members' children. His greatest triumph came when he thought someone had seen him exposing himself. He announced this five minutes before the end of the group therapy session. Although his suspicions proved unfounded, the pronouncement enabled him to shock the supportive members of the therapy group and he succeeded in gaining the attention of the therapist. Don was attempting to prove that he was a 'terminal' case, that he was beyond help and not even the most skilled psychotherapist could make the slightest dent in his disorder. In a sense, he was 'exhibiting himself'.

Several of the exhibitionists in Don's group *competed for the highest profile*. In other words, they were concerned with who could be classified as the most 'perverted' among them. During the scorching summer months in Los Angeles, one arrived at the group therapy session wearing what may best be described as a pair of 'scant bikini' bottoms. He also, however, had the courtesy to wear shoes and socks – on the grounds of 'hygiene'. Another claimed he had exhibited himself moments before arriving, in the hope that the therapist and the group would be devastated at having failed to help him. Don was concerned not to miss out on any of this 'action'. He quietly informed the group of his new discovery: an almost fool-proof method of exhibiting himself.

Don had been renting four garages which he used for storing 'junk' – any discarded object he could find which caught his fancy. For years he had been collecting anything, from old record-players to women's underwear salvaged from dustbins. He was simply unable to part with this useless material and was especially pleased if he actually knew the 'owner' of an object. One day he found in the street a wooden plank which he thought would make an excellent candidate for storage in his recently rented fifth garage. The plank had in it a knothole (a hole in a piece of lumber where a knot has dropped out or been removed), just large enough to place his penis through. Suddenly he realized that the neighbourhood was a 'goldmine' of such knotholes in the form of wooden fences constructed of wooden planks. It occurred to him that he could insert his penis into any one of these knotholes and passers-by, on the other side of the fence, would be able to see his penis but remain unable to identify its owner. Don appeared to be genuinely elated as he related his new-found method. After all, he had been successful in gaining the undivided attention of an amused audience. He seemed to thrive on derisive remarks and ridicule, which, to his unending dismay, were not as a rule forthcoming in the therapeutic group.

It should be stressed that Don was well liked by other members of his therapy group. As time went by he was able to show an active interest in others' problems. He seldom missed a session, and began to be able to 'laugh at himself'. He had grown up in conditions of near poverty, had never known his father, had been bullied in school and always been a 'loner'. During the course of his individual therapy sessions, it emerged that he felt that, if he were to be 'cured' of his exhibitionistic tendencies, he would no longer be allowed to attend group therapy sessions and so would lose his only friends.

Like many exhibitionists, Don initially proved highly resistant to treatment. However, within a year of having completed a course of comprehensive therapy involving individual therapy, group therapy and behaviour therapy (see the Appendix, page 415) specifically designed to modify his masturbatory fantasies, he had not, to the best of our knowledge, reoffended.

THE CASE OF THE DRUNK RUSSIAN MILITIAMAN

Since alcohol intoxication results in a reduction of inhibitions, it is not surprising that an individual with exhibitionistic tendencies should be more inclined to 'express' himself while inebriated. Mikhail and August Stern (1981) describe a bizarre spectacle on their return from a summer holiday in the Soviet Caucasus. To their surprise, the vehicle in front began to zigzag, its driver paying no attention to the Sterns' hooting. The reason for the vehicle's zigzagging was soon explained. Its driver was watching

. . . a militiaman directing traffic at the intersection which we were approaching. His pose was, to say the least, bizarre; he had taken his member out of his trousers and was squeezing it at its base with his right hand. Left, right, stop: the officer was directing the traffic with his penis, which was red as a pepper. The drivers and their passengers were splitting their sides with laughter. If there were no women, the militiaman did not stop the vehicle.

The Sterns suggest that the militiaman may have been using the fact that he was drunk as a release for his real desires.

FEMALE EXHIBITIONISM

While some female prostitutes expose their genitalia in an effort to solicit business, it can hardly be claimed they usually do so for sexual gratification. Certain women are, however, sexually excited by exposing themselves to strangers. Bryant (1982) observes that, 'The drunken female party goer who strips naked and jumps into the host's goldfish pond or swimming pool is sufficiently frequent that many persons have heard of or seen such an occurrence.' Cases of female exhibitionism where the intent is to arouse males have been recorded, but only infrequently.

The Sterns cite the examply of a fifteen-year-old Russian schoolgirl who would travel on the bus to school wearing a short skirt and no underwear, spreading her legs to the other passengers. Unfortunately, she was seen by a friend of her parents, who told them about it. The parents reported the behaviour to the school authorities, taking the view that control of such behaviour was the domain of the state. The school referred the problem to the police, who, in turn, referred it to the courts. A few years later, the girl was exiled for 'parasitism'.

It is hardly a profound observation to say that moral values differ vastly between the Soviet Union and the United States. It is inconceivable that the self-proclaimed sex therapist Amanda Stewart could be tolerated by Russian society as she was by American society. In her book, *Sex Therapist: My Story*, she described 'therapeutic' practices to educate her clients. Her repertoire included a technique in which she would lecture a client while concurrently encouraging him to examine her genitalia with a gynaecological speculum and magnifying glass. As the client examined her thoroughly, she would continue her lecture on female physiology and sexual responses in relation to her anatomy. The technique, though ethically controversial, probably served as a form of sexual desensitization for those clients who suffered from a phobia or irrational fear of female genitalia. Although the service she described might have been helpful to many of her clients, it is also probable that Amanda Stewart was herself engaged in a legitimized form of exhibitionism.

SEXUAL INTERCOURSE IN PUBLIC PLACES

According to Mikhail and August Stern (1981), the Russians do not create any impression of being promiscuous or importunate. These authors do, however, claim that sexual intercourse in public does occur on the overcrowded public transport of many Soviet cities, especially during rush hours. In 1966, 640 citizens of Leningrad wrote to Alexei Kosygin, the president of the council of workers, to complain that rush hours had become 'hours of shame and indignation, a hot-bed of churlishness and coarseness', particularly for women. The Sterns comment:

One may, therefore, witness unexpected scenes in Soviet buses and trams: two students caressing each other's sexual organs, a girl raising her skirt to make it easier for men to slip their hands underneath, or – even rarer – a homosexual in search of adventure. In Leningrad even sexual intercouse may sometimes take place on public transport. The woman installs herself on a kind of platform which exists in Soviet buses, and the man clings to her from behind; it requires great dexterity not to be noticed by the other passengers while he is busy with her. In the course of the operation the woman does not even turn round: everything takes place by tacit accord; the partners recognize each other without knowing each other, and everything happens without anything appearing to happen. But this clandestine meeting has a code which much be respected, limits which must not be transgressed.

The code guarantees anonymity, for the couple must never strike up a conversation after the sexual contact. The Sterns also report the case of a patient from Vinnitsa who claimed that, when he attempted to strike up a conversation with a woman who had one minute previously held his penis in her hand on a public transport vehicle, she accused him of immorality.

Sexual relations between males in public lavatories or the balconies of cinemas is known colloquially in the United States as 'tea-room' sex, in England as 'cottaging'. One of the myths concerning this behaviour is that it is exclusive to homosexual males. The activity also occurs among married men, including 'pillars of society', who might be characterized as ambisexual. The sexual 'transaction' remains essentially, though not invariably, anonymous. When it is conducted anonymously, names are not exchanged. Often the individuals do not even see each other's face. The sexual activity usually involves fellatio to achieve rapid orgasm.

Some psychologists view the participants as highly alienated and lonely. Others consider this kind of impersonal sex to be an attempt to avoid commitment, a way of obtaining kicks or instant sex. Tea-room sex or cottaging is, to sex, what McDonald's (TM) is to fast food. One difference is that, although illegal, it is free. And, it needs to be stressed, this type of sexual behaviour remains highly illegal even if it does occur between mutually consenting adult men. Socially and legally speaking, it is considered an affront to human decency, which is why police authorities in both England and America will go to great lengths to 'entrap' men who engage in it. Law enforcement officers will often stake out a notorious public lavatory and entrap an unsuspecting man by offering to have a 'quickie' with him. One patient referred to me by the Probation Department for 'treatment', after having been arrested and prosecuted in California, recounted his ordeal:

I have been going to public toilets for the purpose of having sex ever since I was a teenager. Anyway when I moved out to California from New York I didn't know that things were so tight out here. I just continued. I located what I thought was a favourable place and went there about three or four times. One day I was standing at the urinal and a good looking guy was having a leak at the next urinal. He glanced at me and I noticed that he had an erection. He then made the right gestures, sort of asking me to get it on with him. I nodded affirmatively. At that point he zipped up his pants and took out a pair of handcuffs. I couldn't believe it when he read me my rights. I didn't think that anyone really bothered with us. The worst thing was that it was a Friday and I had to spend the entire week-end in the county jail, where I was almost raped. Then I got 'lost in processing' because they said that the computer was down. I can't believe that they sentenced me to five years' probation. My job takes me out of state and I can't leave without each time applying for permission. I am afraid of losing my job.

Furthermore, under Californian law, this patient was required to register as a 'mentally disordered sex offender'. This meant that, if he were stopped for a routine check by the California Highway Patrol and they entered his driver's licence number into their computer, the officer would not be able to distinguish him from a rapist, child molester or exhibitionist. He could conceivably then be harassed, being held for a period of time while he was 'checked out' further. It needs to be stressed that the patient was in all other respects a law-abiding citizen. Contrary to the popular conception about the inability of homosexuals to maintain lasting relationships, this man had been living with a man whom he viewed as his spouse.

The incidence of anonymous sex in public conveniences has probably dropped since the fatal sexually transmitted disease, Acquired Immune Deficiency Syndrome (AIDS), came to be associated with promiscuity. Many homosexuals report that the level of promiscuity in 'gay baths' has been drastically reduced since the AIDS scare began. It will be interesting to see whether the statistics for this type of arrest eventually show a reduction. Above all, it seems ironic that, in the United States, police officers will go to great lengths to arrest and molest gay men who choose to have sexual relations in public restrooms while generally ignoring the gay baths.

Gay baths are a good example of sexual intercourse in semi-public conditions. They are popular, since they offer protection from the law (being private clubs) and provide a relatively easy way to meet others with the express purpose of sexual contact. The baths have sauna or steam rooms, shower rooms, television facilities and a generally comfortable environment. Some men who frequent them claim to have had thousands of partners over the course of the year. It seems hardly surprising that such a level of promiscuity should have led to the spread of venereally disseminated diseases ranging from gonorrhoea to syphilis and even AIDS.

20 VOYEURISM

GENERAL CHARACTERISTICS

Voyeurism, scoptophilia or mixoscopia is a condition in which the individual experiences a compulsive urge secretly to observe nudity and/or sexual activity in others. The diagnosis of voyeurism is made when the secret observation of a naked person becomes the focal point of an individual's sexuality.

Voyeuristic behaviour is far more common in males than it is in females. McCary (1973) estimates that it occurs at a male-to-female ratio of 9:1. While some women proudly admit to being avid crotch watchers of clothed men, few are genuine real 'peeping toms'.

Not all voyeuristic behaviour comes under the heading of a sexual deviation. Gawking at females is a perennial

pastime. Beauty contests flourish, 'men only' magazines
sell by the million, topless bars and burlesque shows make
fortunes. American cheerleaders are almost as popular as
the team they are supporting, and women tourists in Italy
are often stunned by the overt manner in which the males
there whistle at them and undress them with their eyes.
Men holidaying at beach resorts often cry that they are
about to have major heart attacks when feasting their eyes
on the scantily clad nubile bodies of their fellow women
sun-worshippers, yet continue to watch, look and salivate.
The Miss Nude America contest retains an enormous
following and sales of soft-porn videos continue to rise.

Peeping becomes a sexual deviation only when it is
preferred to sexual intercourse, when the 'victims' do not
know when they are being observed and when the voyeur
risks arrest for his activity (Tollison and Adams, 1979).
The voyeur will perch himself on dangerously high ledges
so as to watch a couple making love or simply to glimpse
someone's genitals as they undress. It is possible that some
voyeurs, like some exhibitionists, find the element of danger
sexually arousing. Few real voyeurs find nudist colonies
and beaches stimulating; they are too 'safe' and the viewing
is not 'forbidden'. The avid voyeur is happiest clutching a
pair of powerful binoculars while positioning himself on the
roof of a skyscraper in order to peer into an apartment half
a mile away. Some voyeurs are especially excited by
observing another person urinating or defecating. Others
are satisfied to see up a woman's dress as she climbs a
staircase. A few even find pleasure in watching animals
copulate. The predilection can also be purchased. Peep-
holes are often installed in brothels in America so that
prostitutes having sexual intercourse with their clients may
be surreptitiously viewed. The charge for peeping is lower
than that for real sex. Many voyeurs prefer this type of
sexual gratification, and it eliminates the risk of being

caught peering into someone's private home. The brothel owners meanwhile 'kill two birds with one stone.'

Although most convicted voyeurs are male, it is probable that female voyeurs go largely undetected. It would be naïve to assume that women, because they are women, have no voyeuristic tendencies. After all, the magazine *Playgirl* features a centrefold of a nude male and has a wide circulation. Contrary to the general assumption, women are aroused by sexually explicit materials in the form of pictures, films and actual nude men and/or women. It should come as no shock to realize that, even as many men are breast or leg watchers, so are many women 'crotch-watchers'. The fact that so few women are prosecuted for voyeurism may be due to prevailing sexist attitudes in the population at large. After all, who would think women capable of such despicable, unladylike behaviour? Several authors (Bryant, 1982; Tollison and Adams, 1979) have observed that, if a man goes out for a walk in his neighbourhood and stops to look through a window at a woman undressing, he might well be prosecuted for voyeurism. On the other hand, if a woman stops to peer under reverse circumstances, it is far more likely that the man will be arrested for exhibitionism.

The typical profile of a voyeur is that he receives his first conviction aged, on average, 23–28 years. Over 60 per cent of voyeurs are unmarried, a quarter are married, the remainder either widowed, single or divorced. Few suffer from any major mental disturbance and it is rare for a voyeur to be intoxicated at the time of arrest. In an overview of the literature, Smith (1976) finds peepers to be, in comparison with the 'normal male population', less likely to have had wet dreams and less likely to have grown up in an all-female home; more likely to have entertained sadistic masturbatory fantasies and more likely to have experienced anxiety over masturbation. Peepers are more introverted in that they are less likely to be gamblers, alcoholics or married. It appears, moreover, that voyeurs are late developers when it comes to sexual intercourse. The one demographic factor that seems to differentiate them from the greater run of the population is that they do tend to be youngest children in families (Gebhard *et al.*, 1965).

Voyeurs are more interested in observing nude strangers than persons known to them. They are aroused by the forbidden, by the fact that the victim is unaware of their viewing presence. Many tend to lose interest in a particular victim after a period of watching, simply because the novelty wears off. They then move on to seek new haunts.

THE DANGEROUS VOYEUR

The general view that peeping toms are never dangerous is a fallacy. Most voyeurs are benign, but a small percentage of them do go on to commit rape, burglary and assault. Voyeurs tend to hide in the shadows, and may attack when apprehended. The kind of voyeur who breaks into someone's home to satisfy his curiosity is most likely to be dangerous, but some voyeurs will be content with stealing an article belonging to the victim – usually a pair of knickers or a brassière. Others may attempt or threaten rape. In these cases, the distinction between a voyeur and rapist often becomes clouded. Tollison and Adams (1979) argue, from their clinical experience, that voyeurs who end up committing rape are rapists first and voyeurs second. The records of many rapists certainly indicate that they began their 'careers' as voyeurs.

Victims of voyeurism are usually angered by the surreptitious invasion of privacy. They often feel raped. One victim described it as leaving her feeling the same way she had felt when she came home to find her house burgled. She said that she had seen the man at her local supermarket on more than one occasion, become afraid to shop there afterwards and was contemplating a move away from the 'pervert'. But another victim described how, when she became aware of a local peeping tom, she put on a show for him. She undressed slowly, caressed her body in a sensual manner and ran to the window, calling his name. The man fled swiftly and never returned.

THEORIES OF VOYEURISM

Psychoanalytic theory holds that normal sexual development in humans proceeds through the 'oral', 'anal' and 'phallic' stages before the adult develops a full-blown 'genital' sexuality. Each of these phases is associated with pleasure. The infant, and later the older child, finds fondling, kissing, exhibiting and looking all sexually pleasurable. In the case of a perversion, the individual becomes fixated or stuck on a particular activity which he or she finds particularly pleasurable. The voyeur is thought to be stuck on 'looking', and is thought to be fixated at the genital phase of sexual development.

Among the reasons for such a fixation suggested by orthodox analysts is the proverbial 'unresolved Oedipus complex', the voyeur having an unconscious need to have sexual intercourse with his mother. His ego, however, experiences the desire as anti-social and likely to provoke punishment. Since, in psychoanalytic theory, women represent the individual's mother, the voyeur confuses other women with his mother. He unconsciously comes to fear that, if he has actual sexual intercourse with a woman, he will be castrated. There are psychoanalysts who will tell you, in all seriousness, that the voyeur is afraid of the vagina because he 'unconsciously' confuses it with a mouth; and, of course, mouths are filled with teeth. Thus the voyeur prefers peeping to actual sexual intercourse, because he imagines that teeth in the woman's vagina will bite off his penis. In this way, he can avoid actual genital contact and obtain some form of sexual gratification without risking the loss of his precious organ. It is, in other words, the same fear of castration which is postulated as an explanation for exhibitionism and other perversions. Another psychoanalytic theory explaining the psychological development of a voyeur is that the voyeur harbours an unconscious desire to prove that women do not own penises, and that his penis belongs to him exclusively – precisely because he is male.

Psychoanalytic theory can be adopted to explain any form of human behaviour in much the same way as religious explanations. Many psychoanalysts believe that little boys want to have sexual intercourse with their mothers and, as adults, often get into sexual trouble with these desires. It sounds reminiscent of the Christian belief that we are all born in 'original sin' because of Adam and Eve's fiasco with the Tree of Knowledge in the Garden of Eden. The point is significant since psychoanalysts will, as a notable psychologist once commented, make their patients fit into their theories and treatments rather than designing the treatment to the individual's requirements.

Psychodynamic explanations for the development of voyeurism which sound more reasonable are to be found in the work of Alfred Adler. Adler was initially a disciple of Freud, and an honoured member of Freud's 'inner circle' until banished for advancing his own ideas. In Adlerian terms, the voyeur is seen as having an **inferiority complex** – poor self-esteem. Low self-esteem results in a lack of confidence and shyness in relating to women. Peeping is seen as a substitute for making sexual advances. In this way, the voyeur satisfies some of his sexual needs while avoiding the possibility of rejection. He prevents his already low self-esteem from descending to even lower depths. In

Adlerian terms, the voyeur is said to be compensating for his feelings of inferiority in relation to women. Peeping satisfies his neurotic need for power and superiority over the women he watches. However, the voyeur must continue to repeat his behaviour, since the superiority he gains from watching anonymously wears off. The voyeur is caught in a vicious cycle – he is addicted to peeping.

Another realistic way of understanding voyeurism is through the eyes of the behavioural psychologist. Most people engage in many forms of sexual behaviour, ranging from kissing, fondling and genital stimulation, to looking at the nude body as part of normal sexual arousal leading to sexual intercourse. The voyeur, however, is behaviourally deficient in these areas. He derives his primary sexual gratification from watching his 'sex object' without permission. Even though the voyeur may masturbate regularly, or even have occasional sexual intercourse, he is labelled a voyeur because the act or fantasy of secretly watching is his preferred sexual turn-on.

Elaborate theories involving 'castration anxiety' and 'unresolved Oedipal complexes' need not be invoked to explain the psychological formation of the voyeur. It is possible that the voyeur learns to become a peeper simply by accident. For instance, it is common for young boys and girls to spy secretly on each other while getting changed. As a child or adolescent, the voyeur may have gone along with a group of friends to spy on girls getting undressed in the school locker-room. He may then experience the event as a great 'turn-on', continue to think about it and include it as part of his masturbatory fantasies. Continued and exclusive masturbation to these fantasies serves to strengthen the association of peeping and sexual arousal. The more he imagines himself spying on naked women, and the more he fantasizes about it during masturbation, the more he is likely to want to repeat the experience in reality. Voyeurism will then become a pattern of sexual preference.

Other factors predisposing or increasing the risk of an individual becoming a voyeur involve a life history which reinforces a fear or phobia of adult women, a learned deficit in heterosocial and heterosexual skills, and a puritanical upbringing in which nakedness is seen as sinful. After all, as every parent knows, as soon as a child is told that something is forbidden he or she will experience temptation to taste the forbidden fruit. The voyeur may be hooked on tasting the forbidden fruit in the form of peeping, an activity he may have learned as a child while secretly spying on his naked parents, siblings or friends. In this case, the peeping tom is immature, stuck on a childish fantasy.

THE CASE OF THE BENIGN VOYEUR

Bill was a twenty-eight-year-old telephone engineer. He had referred himself for treatment because he was afraid that his voyeuristic behaviour was getting out of hand and that he would soon be caught if nothing was done about it. His job took him inside many homes, and required that he climb telephone poles to install new lines. This enabled him to get regular peeps at naked women, women getting undressed and couples making love. Furthermore, because he had begun to spend extra time watching the victims, he was regularly late for the next assignment and his supervisor had complained that he was not performing to standard.

Bill began, moreover, to dress up in his telephone company gear and climb poles outside working hours. He usually chose a home which stood relatively distant from others and parked his car near by to make a quick escape if spotted. He was able to spot homes with 'good potential' during his working hours. For instance, if he knew that several female college students were sharing a house, he also knew his chances for a good peeping session would be improved. He also noticed what kind of curtains or blinds were used to 'protect' the homes he visited during the day. He possessed an incredible amount of patience and could spend hours perched up a tree or pole while waiting for something to happen.

One of his favourite scenes was to watch others having sexual intercourse. He said that he couldn't get over having seen a lesbian couple making love. The scene was so powerful a turn-on that he kept spying on them. He went unnoticed on four occasions, but the fifth time one of the women spotted him and came out of the house hurling insults. Bill realized that he was bound to be caught sooner or later. Furthermore, he felt very guilty about his behaviour. He was in an abject state, saying: 'I don't know what I'm going to do. I must be sick. Please help me, doc. Is there any hope for me?'

Bill's sexual history revealed that he had begun to peep as a ten-year-old. He used to climb trees with his neighbourhood chums to watch girls and women getting dressed and undressed. He knew nothing about masturbation and certainly would never ask his puritanical parents about it. He did, however, find that he experienced pleasure when rubbing his penis against a tree trunk while watching nude girls and women. He continued to spy on girls even after his friends had outgrown the activity, and began to weave his experiences into his masturbatory fantasies. These always involved the theme of Bill 'as observer' and never included scenes of himself 'as participant'. In other words, he did not see himself participating in a sexual interaction. Sex was something to watch, not to do. He did not date girls as he grew up, and although he was not a virgin, he preferred peeping to sexual intercourse. He did enjoy looking at a woman's naked body, but preferred it if she was unaware of his presence.

Bill's treatment focused on encouraging him to obtain sexual gratification through active participation. He was instructed to alter his masturbatory fantasies to include scenes in which he was an active participant. In addition, he attended a group therapy session in which he discoverd that he was not alone in the world, that others had similar problems, and this provided added hope that he could change. Bill was initially placed in individual psychotherapy to help him gain 'insight' and perspective into his lifestyle. Most significant was his participation in a programme of behaviour therapy which entailed a thorough psychophysiological assessment of his sexual arousal patterns in the sexual behaviour laboratory. (See the section on Psychological and Medical Treatments in the Appendix, pages 425–42.)

THE CASE OF THE DANGEROUS PSYCHOPATHIC VOYEUR

As mentioned above, not all voyeurs are harmless, benign individuals who should be viewed as poor pathetic souls. A colleague recounted a case in which voyeurism was associated with aggressive behaviour. It involved a forty-two-year-old man currently incarcerated in a psychiatric prison.

The man had a history of peeping since the age of thirteen, when he spied on his sisters while they were washing. He also enjoyed secretly watching both males and females while they urinated or defecated. As a boy, he had been banned from visiting several of his friends' homes for spying on their mothers and sisters as they bathed. The school authorities had suspended him on more than one occasion, not only for smoking, but also for spying on the girls' toilets. He was finally expelled from High School for attempting to peep into the female teachers' lavatory.

His sexual history revealed that he had been accused of

possessing pornography as a child. He also admitted to theft as a child. He had stolen from stores, from his friends and parents. He took articles of clothing, including underwear and ladies' dresses, which were essentially of no value to him except for the purpose of masturbation.

When he reached adolescence, he began to drink. Intoxication made him 'braver', and he found himself actually breaking into homes to spy on people making love. He even had the courage to spend almost one entire night in the closet of a married couple's bedroom without being caught. It was an achievement of which he remained very proud. However, he was caught eventually and began a life swinging in and out of youth custody.

He had served two relatively short prison sentences before his present long-term sentence. The short sentences were for breaking and entering, disorderly conduct and theft. The current long-term sentence was for attempted murder when he attacked a single woman into whose apartment he had broken after she left for work. He spent the whole day there, helping himself to food and drink. Just before she arrived home, he hid himself under the bed. On discovering the intruder, the woman shrieked and frightened her uninvited guest. He reacted by attacking her, placing his hands over her mouth to try and stop her screaming. He also struck her, seriously injuring her. Fortunately, a neighbour came to the woman's rescue, and managed to subdue the offender, who was, surprisingly, unarmed.

VOYEURISM IN A LIGHTER CONTEXT

Legend has it that the term 'peeping tom' derives from the Saxon story in which Lady Godiva, the kind wife of a landlord, rode naked through the streets of Coventry. Lady Godiva performed this rather 'heroic' act so that her husband would not levy such a harsh tax on his subjects. In return for her bravery, the townspeople voluntarily closed their curtains – all except for a salacious fellow, Tom the tailor, who did peep at the naked lady. Tom was supposedly blinded by a supernatural power; or, more likely, by the townspeople themselves. Poor Tom the tailor paid a heavy price for his curiosity.

As children, human beings are naturally curious. As they grow, they continue to look, leer and be genuinely interested in novelty. Millions may be accused of being 'normal' peeping toms, because millions of people buy and read the results of sex surveys. The market for private sexual fantasies is enormous, and the publications print detailed exhibitionistic fantasies of individuals, who, it is alleged, send them in for publication. Their fantasies involve masturbation, oral sex, anal sex, semen, sado-masochistic desires, fetishism, animals, transvestism and deformities – to name only a few. The surveys, while making scientific claims, have pornographic qualities and attest to the voyeuristic inclinations of millions of people. Apart from having a natural curiosity satisfied, many people feel less alone, perverted or guilty about their own sexual preferences when they read that others have similar inclinations.

SEXUAL EXPOSURE, VOYEURISM AND THE LAW

Prohibitions against exposing genitalia have been enforced by most societies for thousands of years. Some societies, such as the Bushmen of Southern Africa, barely regulate the exposure of genitalia and female breasts. Others, like Islamic groups, require the covering of the *entire* female body while in public. Indeed, according to Amnesty International (1980), nude sunbathing in Iran has incurred sentences of up to forty lashes.

One of the earliest myths describes how people lost their

innocence when the first man, Adam, was beguiled by the first woman, Eve, who was in turn tempted to taste from the forbidden Tree of Knowledge by the serpent. Adam and Eve were punished by God, who forced them out of paradise. According to religious fundamentalists, we are the inheritors of their crimes.

In Britain, indecent exposure or exhibitionism is prosecuted under the Vagrancy Act, 1824, and is punishable by a fine and/or imprisonment. The law is primarily aimed against a 'man who wilfully, openly and obscenely exposes his person [penis] with the intent to insult a female'. Voyeurism, or 'peeping tomism', is similarly proscribed by the Vagrancy Act. But wandering around central London naked would be considered so bizarre that prosecution would follow under the Mental Health Act.

Predictably, Californian law is specific about exactly what body parts may not be exposed, and by whom. For instance, adult men are allowed to expose their breasts in public, and many do. Adult women are not allowed to expose their breasts in public. On the other hand, prior to the period of breast development during puberty, girls who publicly expose their breasts are not liable to prosecution. The criterion for 'indecent exposure' is exposing 'post-pubertal male and female genitals, and buttocks, and the females' breasts'.

The law is stringent on these matters. Until 1972, a second conviction for indecent exposure in California could have secured a sentence of five years to life. It would seem that Americans are, as a group, offended by the exposure of the male penis in particular. Indeed, visitors to America from countries where urination in public is the norm have been arrested and imprisoned for using the pavement as a urinal. One such case involved two South Africans who were arrested in Florida for indecent exposure for urinating in the street after leaving a bar.

Had those visitors been in California after 1972, they would probably not have been prosecuted for indecent exposure, for nudity without sexual intent, accidental nudity or nudity in secluded places is no longer considered indecent exposure under Penal Code 314. Moreover, the right to privacy and self-determination allows certain municipalities to permit topless bars and even nude apartment complexes in which the occupants, including their children, use swimming pool facilities and hot tubs together regardless of race, colour, age or creed. There are, currently, several such nude apartment complexes in the Southern California area.

Even though few exhibitionists are dangerous offenders, they are still liable to 'not less than one year' in the Californian State Prison System, when they will be typed as 'sex offenders' – and therefore become the target in prison for severe persecution by other prisoners. In prison society, murderers are accorded higher status than voyeurs and flashers.

PART FOUR

Sex between Adults and Children

1
Paedophilia

---

21 CHILD MOLESTATION AND EXPLOITATION

GENERAL CHARACTERISTICS AND OTHER CULTURES

In 1769, the explorer Captain Cook recorded in his *Account of a Voyage Around the World* how he had observed 'the rites of Venus' performed on a little girl of eleven or twelve by a 'nearly six feet high' South Pacific islander. The performance was held in public and was, according to Cook, something the little girl 'did not seem much to stand in need of'. Captain Cook was influenced in his viewpoint by Judaeo-Christian culture, which values virginity and has always frowned on sexual play between children, exacting harsh punishments on adults who have sexual relations with children. Had Captain Cook been an ancient Greek explorer in the South Pacific, he would have been revolted not by the age of the child but by its sex. The ancient Greeks considered males to be 'sexually superior' beings. Young boys were 'taught' about sex by their academic tutors; it was part of the tutor's duty.

In a few cultures, adults 'pacify' young infants by actively stimulating an infant's genitalia. For example according to O'Carroll (1980), in Mexico 'mothers and grandmothers often lick their babies' genitals to soothe them to sleep'. Furthermore, not all cultures prohibit sexual play between children. It is sanctioned, for instance, among the Trobrianders of New Guinea and the Nama Hottentots. The Nama Hottentots of Southern Africa, the Hopi of North America and the Sirionos of South America also encourage sexual relationships between adults and children. In *Patterns of Sexual Behaviour*, Ford and Beach (1951) describe several cultures where child–child and adult–child sexual behaviour is sanctioned:

Adults in a large number of societies take a completely tolerant and permissive attitude towards sex expression in childhood. Under such conditions, youngsters engage in a certain amount of sexual play in public ... Handling the genitals of others of the same or opposite sex occurs frequently under conditions of free sex play. Additional forms of sexual activity on the part of young children sometimes include oral-genital contacts and attempted copulation with a sex partner ...

In a few permissive societies, adults participate actively in the sexual stimulation of infants and young children. Hopi and Siriono parents masturbate their youngsters frequently. And in these societies self-masturbation passes practically unnoticed during early childhood, adults taking a tolerant and permissive attitude toward all sexual behaviour at least until the age of puberty. Among the Kazak, adults who are playing with small children, especially boys, excite the young one's genitals by rubbing and playing with them. In this society autogenital stimulation on the part of young children is accepted as a normal practice. Mothers in Alorese society occasionally fondle the genitals of their infant while nursing it. During early childhood Alorese boys masturbate freely and occasionally they imitate intercourse with a little girl. As the children grow older, however, sexual activity is frowned upon and during late childhood such behaviour is forbidden to both boy and girl. Actually, however, they continue their sexual activity, but in secret ...

Among the Pukapukans of Polynesia where parents simply ignore the sexual activities of young children, boys and girls masturbate freely and openly in public. Among the Nama Hottentots no secret is made of autogenital stimulation in early childhood. Young Trobriand children engage in a variety of sexual activities. In the absence of adult control, typical forms of amusement for Trobriand girls and boys include manual stimulation and oral stimulation of the genitals and simulated coitus.

The same authorities write that the Chewa of Africa believe that children should practise sex when young. Otherwise, they believe, the children will not be able to reproduce when adults: 'Older children build little huts some distance from the village, and there, with the complete approval of the parents, boys and girls play at being husband and wife. Such trial matings may extend well into adolescence, with periodic exchanges of partners until marriage occurs.' The Lepcha of the Indian subcontinent hold similar beliefs. They maintain that girls do not develop normally unless they experience sexual intercourse at an early age. Young children begin by masturbating each other, and later on attempt full sexual intercourse: 'By the time they are 11 or 12 years old, most girls regularly engage in full intercourse. Older men occasionally copulate with girls as young as eight years of age. Instead of being regarded as a criminal offence, such behaviour is considered amusing by the Lepcha.'

Among the Siwans of North Africa, adult men who do not 'engage in anal intercourse' with young boys are considered to be abnormal. A further case cited is that of the Aranda aborigines of Australia, where fully initiated but single men commonly 'take a boy of 10 or 12 years old, who lives with him as his wife for several years, until the older man marries'. The Keraki of New Guinea practise sodomy as a part of puberty rites, every pubescent boy being subjected to anal intercourse by the older males. Western attitudes would see this puberty rite as tantamount to ritualized homosexual rape of young boys by older men. Nevertheless, the Keraki firmly believe that sodomizing young boys is healthy, a necessary part of their maturation. They are also under the misconception that boys can become pregnant as a result of sodomy. To prevent conception, the boys undergo a special lime-eating ceremony.

It should be stressed that the groups described, in which sexual behaviour between adults and children is considered 'normal', form a tiny minority of cultures. The technical term for sex between adults and children is **paedophilia**. Translated from the Greek, the word literally means a 'love of children'. While most adults in Judaeo-Christian societies today love children, they also fervently believe that sexual activity between adults and children is immoral, depraved and a sign of pathological immaturity. Hostility towards paedophiles is reflected in prisons, where many paedophiles or 'child molesters', as they have otherwise come to be called, are harassed by other prisoners – many of whom have committed even more heinous crimes.

Paedophiles or child molesters are adults who have had sexual contact with minors. Such sexual contact involves one or more of the following: manipulation of the child's genitals; inducing the child to manipulate the adult's genitals; partial or complete penetration of vaginal and/or anal cavities; or oral sex. Tollison and Adams (1979) suggest that 'any practice utilizing the sexual parts or organs of a child so as to bring the person in contact with the child's body in any sexual manner' could qualify as paedophilia.

On the other hand, legal and psychiatric definitions for paedophilia differ considerably. In most parts of the United States, the legal 'age of consent' for both homosexuals and heterosexuals is eighteen. In Britain, the legal age of consent for heterosexuals is sixteen. In most parts of the United States, regardless of gender, any person over the age of eighteen could be prosecuted and sentenced to years of imprisonment for having sexual relations with a seventeen-year-old. In Britain, any sixteen-year-old can be prosecuted for indecent sexual assault for having sex with a fifteen-year-old. Furthermore, the person's gender is paramount. Under the Sexual Offences Act 1967, the age of consent in England for homosexuals is placed at twenty-one, raising the implication that a twenty-one-year-old homosexual could be prosecuted for having sexual relations with a twenty-year-old partner, even where both parties had consented. In practice, few cases are prosecuted where an age difference is narrow. (See the section on 'Homosexuality', page 297.)

Psychiatric diagnosis of paedophilia differs from legal definitions precisely because it does not make sense to label as deviant, for example, a nineteen-year-old girl for having sex with a fifteen-year-old boy. In the light of this sort of problem, the American Psychiatric Association lays down the following criteria in diagnosing paedophilia (DSM III, 1980):

A. The act or fantasy of engaging in sexual activity with pre-pubertal children as a repeatedly preferred or exclusive method of achieving sexual excitement.

B. If the individual is an adult, and the prepubertal children are at least ten years younger than the individual. If the individual is a late adolescent, no precise age difference is required, and clinical judgement must take into account the age difference as well as the sexual maturity of the child.

INCIDENCE

Paedophilia is widespread and, because it is seldom reported, occurs with far greater frequency than is realized. Although the Kinsey *et al.* (1948) survey is getting on for forty years old, it remains the most comprehensive and extensive investigation of sexual behaviour in the United States. Kinsey and his co-workers found that twice as many girls as boys are paedophilia victims and published the alarming fact that, of American women interviewed, 24 per cent reported that they had as children been sexually approached by an adult male. In this sample, the girls were younger than fourteen, and the males at least five years older than their victims, but not younger than fifteen, when they made their approaches. A 1985 survey in Britain estimated that over a million children could expect to be sexually assaulted before reaching the age of fifteen, but the results of polls vary, between 10 and 20 per cent of British adults claiming to have been sexually approached by an adult in childhood.

In the late 1950s, a majority of Kinsey's informants showed no apparent signs of permanent emotional harm from the experience, but said they had been distressed at the time. The children's upset was interpreted by Kinsey as reflecting a culturally conditioned fear of sex in general, especially where parents actively punished a child's interest in sexuality.

The true incidence of paedophilia is uncertain for several reasons. Children are often told to keep 'what happened a secret' by the adult concerned. When children do tell other adults about such incidents, the report is seldom passed on. Other adults may fail to report an occurrence of child molestation so as to 'protect' the child and, to a large extent, to avoid social stigma. More enlightened adults are aware that the paedophile can often be successfully treated outside prison. Apart from this, charges of child molestation may often be reduced to lesser ones, especially in the United States, once the accused has agreed to plead guilty. All these factors make it impossible to gauge the real incidence of child molestation, but the scale of the problem is underscored in the United States by the number of sex offenders convicted annually: approximately 55,000. Of these convictions, 40 per cent involve victims or sexual partners under the legal age of consent.

MYTHS ABOUT CHILD MOLESTERS

Paedophiles can be heterosexual, homosexual or bisexual in their choice of children. Paedophilic behaviour frequently incorporates voyeurism (peeping at the nude child), exhibitionism (flashing), pornography (taking photographs of nude children) and prostitution (pimping and sexually abusing children's bodies). Less frequently, it involves sadism (spanking the child for sexual pleasure); on very rare occasions, it culminates in rape or child murder. It should be stressed, however, that a vast majority of paedophiles are non-violent.

Before presenting the psychosocial characteristics of paedophiles, it is worth demystifying the issue by listing what paedophiles are not. As Groth (1979) asserts, there are several common myths about paedophilia. From a study of 148 convicted paedophiles at the Connecticut Correctional Institution, eight common myths about child molesters emerged:

Myth 1: that child molesters are 'dirty old men'. Most are under the age of thirty-five, though they range in age from fourteen to seventy-three. Ten per cent of Groth's sample first offended when they were younger than thirteen.

Myth 2: that child molesters are strangers. In the sample, 105 (71 per cent) knew their victims, while only 43 (29 per cent) were total strangers. Incestuous paedophilia occurred in 20 (14 per cent) of these cases where the offender was the victim's father, grandfather or brother. The incidence of incest is probably higher but goes unreported, families being reluctant to report it.

Myth 3: that the child molester is retarded. Paedophiles were found to have no lower levels of intelligence than the general population. In Groth's sample, 80 per cent were in the normal range of the Wechsler Adult Intelligence (IQ) Scale. Only 10 (7 per cent) fell within the defective range, while 8 (6 per cent) obtained superior IQ scores.

Myth 4: that the child molester is a drug addict or alcoholic. Use of drugs and alcohol did not differ in incidence between child molesters and normal males.

Myth 5: that the child molester is basically sexually frustrated. In the sample, 70 (47 per cent) of the child molesters were married. Sexual contact with children did not mean that paedophiles abstained from sexual contact with adults. Most of the child molesters interviewed were motivated primarily by the need for intimacy, and a sense of being admired.

Myth 6: that the child molester is insane. No child molesters in the sample were psychopaths. Only 7 (5 per cent) showed signs of psychosis at the time of their offences.

Myth 7: that child molesters become increasingly violent as they grow older. Only 13 (9 per cent) of the subjects studied had used force when sexually molesting children. More usually, child molesters employ deception and enticement in the sexual seduction of their victims. They are largely non-violent in the commission of a child molestation.

Myth 8: that homosexual paedophiles are more dangerous than heterosexual child molesters. It is a mistake to assume that, if a child molester selects a boy as his victim, he is automatically to be considered homosexual. Furthermore, girls were molested almost twice as often as boys. While 73 (49 per cent) of the sample claimed they were uninterested in sex with adults, 75 (51 per cent) had turned to paedophilic activity when their adult sexual relationships were under stress. Of those who were attracted to both adults and children, most were heterosexual, the remainder being bisexual. Child molesters are more likely to be heterosexual than homosexual.

Paedophilic sex offenders vary in terms of age, education, developmental history and the situation concerning the act of child molestation. Most are males, although several females have been convicted of child molestation, or 'aiding and abetting' sexual offences. Older offenders tend to be or to have been married, are themselves parents and are aged on average forty years. When Revitch and Weiss (1962) studied 836 child molesters in New Jersey, they found that younger offenders preferred adolescent girls aged between twelve and fifteen. Older paedophiles were generally more strongly attracted to less developed children.

Gibson and Klein (1969) report that of eighty-nine murders in Britain between 1957 and 1968, 12 per cent were linked with sexual assaults. The Home Office reported a figure for that period of 20 per cent for murder victims under the age of sixteen. This figure did not take into account victims of those offenders judged to be insane or of 'diminished capacity', or those who committed suicide. In fact, according to the National Society for the Prevention of Cruelty to Children, figures for child sexual abuse continue to rise in the United Kingdom, which saw a spate of sexually related child murders during the summer of 1985.

Some investigators claim that a fair percentage of children involved with adults in sexual activity have been willing participants. Walmsley and White (1979) looked at

incidents of victim 'compliance' on the basis of documen-
tary evidence in which no coercion was used, and found
that 80 per cent of homosexual offences with children were
'consensual', heterosexual offences with 'consenting' children accounting for 33 per cent. Other researchers (Gibbens, 1963; Gebhard *et al.*, 1965) agree that the majority of
paedophiles are not aggressive. Where aggression was
present, it was usually in cases of attacks by children upon
other children not much younger than themselves. Yet,
although West (1981) writes that 'most sexual contacts
between adults and children are seemingly characterized
by affectionate playfulness and willing participation', he is
also positively aware of the other end of the spectrum,
where children have been brutally and sadistically tortured
to death as part of a sexual ritual.

According to an extensive survey of convicted sex
offenders by the Indiana Institute of Sex Research (Gebhard *at al.*, 1965) there was a high incidence of alcoholism
and anti-social lifestyle among those offenders who had
shown violence in sexual attacks on young girls. These data
were, however, based on convicted persons, and so suggest
a general inclination towards violent crime rather than
towards paedophilic offences of a violent nature as such.
Most violent sex offenders are anti-social in a specifically
sexual as opposed to a generalized sense.

TYPES OF CHILD MOLESTERS

Cohen *et al.* (1969) described three types of paedophiles.
The most usual type of offender is known as **immature**,
feels emotionally uncomfortable with adults and is more at
ease with youngsters. During adolescence, he does not
establish normal relationships with his peers. He is likely
to seek employment which gives him access to children. He

befriends the children and may actually 'fall in love' with a child; he is likely to 'court' and then 'seduce' the child.

The **regressed** offender is thought to have developed some degree of 'normal' inter-personal relationship with his peers. While he may have been able to develop some sexual relationships during adolescence, he is, as an adult, unable to cope with stress. He turns to alcohol, which results in 'the breakdown of a relatively stable marital, social and work adjustment. In almost all instances the paedophilic acts are precipitated by some direct confrontation of his sexual inadequacy by an adult female or some threat to his masculine image by a male peer.' This type of paedophile goes for children when he discovers that his wife or girl friend is having an affair with another man. This is especially the pattern in cases of incest. The regressed paedophile is less likely to plan his sexual encounters with children, and more likely to act out of impulse.

The **aggressive** paedophile acts out of aggression. This thankfully far rarer character is the child rapist, a sadist whose 'pleasure' is to penetrate the child's vagina or anus with his penis or some other object. Usually, he is sexually aroused by hurting the child. The aggressive paedophile has no developed conscience, is hostile, and the type most likely to attack a child brutally. Few paedophiles fall into this category.

THE CASE OF AN IMMATURE PAEDOPHILE

Alan, a thirty-three-year-old paedophile who had not yet been caught, came for treatment. He arrived in an extremely depressed state, claiming he had already been in therapy three years but it hadn't helped. He calmly stated: 'I'll commit suicide if you can't help me. My life is not worth living.'

Alan's sexual history revealed that he was still a virgin.

He had, however, made one 'bungled attempt, with a woman while on a rafting trip in South America'. He was terrified of adult women, and of his mother in particular. She was a devout fundamentalist Christian who gave the money Alan earned to her church while living in an old person's home. She was also most adept at inducing guilt in her son, an only child. His father, an army sergeant, had sexually molested him on several occasions between the ages of three and seven before abandoning the family.

Alan grew up both loving and fearing his mother, who taught him that girls were 'bad', that sex was 'dirty', and that the most he could hope for was a woman who would use him for his money. It was clear the mother and son had developed a pathological attachment for one another. The dutiful son visited his old, sick mother weekly.

Alan lived on a small farm as help to a woman who had three children, aged seven, ten and twelve. Alan was 'deeply in love' with the twelve-year-old daughter, but also found that 'play wrestling with the ten-year-old boy gets me so turned on that I think I'll burst sometimes'. He said he liked the woman who owned the farm, but added he would never think of her in a sexual context. As an adolescent, Alan had always masturbated to images of nude children. He still did. Moreover, Alan had few friends and, although he possessed a sense of humour, he claimed to have always been 'an introvert'.

It was apparent that Alan had developed a phobia, not only of adults but of nude female bodies in particular. An assessment of his physiological sexual arousal (see page 420 of the Appendix) showed he was aroused by slides of nude children, both male and female, aged between eight and twelve years. To his delight, he evidenced some arousal to slides of nude adult women (about a 30 per cent erection) and no arousal to slides of adult men. Alan therefore realized that he had deficits in social skills in relation to adults.

He decided that he was definitely heterosexual and stated the wish to become a 'normal heterosexual'. Placed in group therapy, he understood, for the first time, that he was not the only one with such difficulties. After two weeks, his 'level of hope' for success improved by leaps and bounds. He was also placed in individual therapy, in which he 'worked through' ambivalent feelings about his mother and learned skills of assertiveness. In addition, he actively participated in the clinic's behaviour therapy programme to help him overcome his fear of women's bodies. The therapy involved masturbatory training to encourage sexual arousal to adult women. It also involved an aversive conditioning procedure (see page 428 of Appendix) to reduce his arousal to children. Alan attributed the eventual success of his treatment to three factors: the group therapy, where he made 'real friends for the first time ever'; the individual therapy sessions, which 'helped me to sort out troubles with my Mom'; and finally, a series of 'sex lessons' with a sexual surrogate.

Sexual surrogacy remains controversial, but it was decided that Alan would benefit from it because, however much insight he got in individual therapy, however much support he gained from group therapy, it could still take him a long time to break through the final 'barrier'. The surrogate was paid literally to teach Alan about sex in a non-threatening manner. The ten weekly sessions began with body touching, where he was exposed to his greatest fear: touching a clothed woman. He began by touching her hands, feet, arms and legs. The next stages involved his receiving and giving massage in bathing suits. The two then proceeded to massage in complete nudity, and sexual intercourse took place during the tenth and last session.

Alan now knew for certain that he was capable of having

sexual intercourse with an adult woman. It proved to be what he called 'a great revelation', and accelerated his progress in therapy. He became more confident, his self-esteem improved and he made himself look more physically attractive. A year later, he had a girl friend and had moved into an apartment of his own having got a job as a salesman. He no longer felt that he required individual psychotherapy, but continued with the group for 'support'. His physiological measures of sexual arousal showed that, although he was now attracted to slides and videotapes of nude adult women, he was still sexually aroused by children. Therefore he felt that he remained at 'risk', especially when under stress.

THE CASE OF A 'REGRESSED' PAEDOPHILE

Eric, a thirty-two-year-old in training to become a Catholic priest, was referred for treatment and psychological assessment by the local probation department. He was in the process of being tried under Section 288 (Exciting Lust of Child Under Age Fourteen), Section 288.1 (Lewd Act on Child Under Fourteen – Psychological Report Required Before Suspension of Sentence), and Section 288a (Oral Sex Perversion) of Californian state law.

Each summer, Eric would work as a counsellor at a summer camp for children aged between seven and fourteen. And each summer, for three years, Eric would 'teach' young boys about the facts of life:

I didn't really think I was doing a bad thing. Every night I would get the boys ready for bed. It was real hot and they used to sleep without covers. Sometimes they would ask if they could take their pyjamas off 'cause it was boiling hot and humid. My pattern was that I invariably would find a boy who stood out because he was shy. I would climb on to the bed with him when it was dark and he was asleep. I can only describe what happened as a sort of fugue state. I sort of had amnesia for what happened afterwards, though not really. Once on the bed with the kid I would gently touch his penis, stroking it until it became hard. Then I would masturbate him to orgasm. When he ejaculated I would anoint his balls with his sperm. I felt enormous satisfaction because I had initiated him into the world of sex. It's strange because I don't think I'm gay or anything. It all seemed to get worse when my wife divorced me. I just wasn't turned on to her and we fought bitterly. I feel more at home with young boys, aged between ten and thirteen, those who are just beginning to show pubic hair. I felt compelled to initiate them into the wide world of sex. Then of course I got caught when this one kid squealed on me. I feel terribly guilty because I know I could have done him irreparable harm. But lots of boys seemed to like it. They looked up to me. And now I only hope that they don't find out I am a sick common criminal, because I don't see it that way. My intentions were and are good, and it's society that should change these dumb laws.

Eric was given a five-year suspended sentence and required to register as a Mentally Disordered Sex Offender (MDSO) under Californian law. Part of his probationary requirement was that he go for psychiatric treatment while on probation. He was described as having a 'narcissistic personality disorder' by more than one expert witness on his case. Essentially, this meant that he was 'manipulative', unable to establish mature relationships with others and had a 'grandiose' artificial sense of self-importance.

He did not stay at our clinic because he resented the therapist who ran the group. A self-proclaimed expert on psychotherapy, he identified her as a 'Freudian, who would not let me take more charge of the group. After all, I have taken dozens of courses in psychology at college, and in any event I am a counsellor.' Furthermore, he strongly objected to the behavioural strategies which examined his sexual arousal patterns in depth.

Even though he was not 'required' to participate in the behavioural programme, he managed to criticize it as 'ineffective', unethical and theoretically unsound. Eric grasped intellectual concepts easily and read up on the various psychotherapeutic approaches. As a 'regressed' paedophile, he was most eloquent in proving it. For example, when 'confronted' by the experienced 'Freudian' group therapist as to the nature of his offence, he stormed out of the room. He reappeared at the next session, blaming the group for his 'nearly going out last night and getting some boy hustlers into his apartment'.

He left the clinic soon afterwards, after obtaining permission from his probation officer, who sanctioned a move to a more 'humanistic' psychologist. It was my distinct impression that Eric was a 'therapist killer', someone who would flit from therapist to therapist, proving each one unable to help him. A follow-up in this case did indeed reveal that Eric left his 'humanistic' therapist for another therapist after three months. It appeared that he had a very soft probation officer who unwittingly sabotaged therapeutic progress by allowing Eric to switch therapists and thus avoid confronting his problem.

CATHOLIC PRIESTS AND PAEDOPHILIA

It is not that uncommon for the lay person to cast Catholic priests as 'child molesters' and 'sexual perverts' who 'prey on the bodies of innocent kids'. Some have suggested, 'We know why they loved to use corporal punishment as part of their teaching methods ... it's because they're into S & M.' Other stereotypes depict Catholic priests – especially those in charge of young boys – as 'repressed homosexuals'; 'lascivious'; 'lecherous'; and 'impotents craving power over kids'.

While such observations are certainly excessive, if not outright oppressive and prejudiced, they may hold a modicum of truth. For instance, Jonathan Friendly reported on the problem of child sexual abuse among Catholic priests in an article in the *New York Times* (4 May 1986). In essence, the report suggested that although sexual molestation of children by Roman Catholic priests was not ubiquitous in the United States, it was serious enough to cause over 100 priests and representatives of Catholic institutions on the East Coast to convene a special conference on the subject. Apparently, Church fathers are concerned that 40 to 50 of its 44,000 priests have been accused of molesting children over the period between 1984 and 1986.

According to a psychologist, Stephen Montana, who was present at the meeting, the rate of child molestation among Catholic priests is no higher than it is among other groups who care for children. Montana said that the overwhelming majority of convicted priests appear to prefer boy over girl victims. In one case, a parish priest, Gilbert Gauthe, admitted to having 'raped and sodomized at least 37 children'. The priest was sentenced to a twenty-year prison term, was defrocked, and cost his parish's insurance companies $10 million in legal damages. Evidently, the case has provided the impetus for further civil and criminal proceedings against Catholic priests by disenchanted parents.

Mr Mouton, the lawyer who acted for Fr Gauthe, claimed that Church officials should not rely on public prosecutors to permit internal solutions to cases of child molestation. Indeed, many states have enacted legislation which actually *requires* the reporting of child abuse to the authorities; not to do so is punishable under law. Mr Mouton and Father Doyle, a Vatican representative to Washington, advocated that the Church should remove unproven allegations of indecent assault on children from individual priests' personal dossiers. It was felt that this would ensure the protection of innocent priests. Finally, it should be pointed out that the actual number of cases of child molestation committed by priests far exceeds the reported figures. Most cases are quashed and never brought to the attention of the authorities.

THREE CASES OF AGGRESSIVE PAEDOPHILIA: CHILD MURDERERS

Two police deputies brought a young man back to our clinic for a psychodiagnostic assessment. He was hand-cuffed, and his feet were manacled. He had a police record literally three inches thick, his first juvenile offence having been for 'possession of pornography' at the age of thirteen (pornography being illegal at the time). His series of later crimes included assault with a deadly weapon, burglary and a variety of sexual offences concerning young boys and women. Most of his life had been spent in some sort of detention. On this occasion, he had committed the ultimate crime – killing a young boy. He was only recently out of prison on parole, unemployed and living with a girlfriend.

One morning, a young newspaper boy had been making a delivery to his apartment. His girlfriend had left for work, and the boy was invited in. Once inside, he grabbed hold of the boy and tied him to a bed, then proceeding to rape him anally. The boy struggled against the ropes, and the more he struggled the more the rapist hit him. He beat him to try to get him to shut up. Suddenly he grew aware that unless he killed the boy, he was bound to be found out and be sent back to prison.

A witness testified to seeing him leaving the apartment, carrying a large suitcase. In spite of efforts to claim extenuating circumstances, based on a 'deprived child-hood', the court sentenced him to death. He is currently appealing and sits on death row.

Another sordid case of child murder was reported in *The Times* (London: 18 December 1984). The article was head-lined 'Marie Payne Was Victim of a Persistent Child

Molester'. The murderer of four-year-old Marie Payne was Colin Evans, sentenced to thirty years' imprisonment for her brutal sexual killing in Epping Forest. It had taken detectives over a year to track Evans down. Several hours after arresting him, they obtained his confession: 'You will never know what has been going through my mind since that day. When I woke up the next day I could have killed myself. Can't you take me outside and hang me?'

On the day of little Marie Payne's death, Evans had been to see his mother. As she was out, he decided to buy some food and sit in his car while waiting for her. After a short time, Marie passed by the car with her dog. Evans forced her into the car, with the initial idea of taking pornographic photographs. Marie started to cry. He struck her with a piece of wood and killed her.

Evans stripped off her clothing, photographed her body and buried her in a shallow grave, hiding her clothes elsewhere. But it so happened that his camera had malfunctioned, ruining his 'snapshots'. And so, even while volunteers were searching the forest three miles away, Evans was digging up Marie's body, which he proceeded to photograph and mutilate. He reinterred the body and fled. The day after confessing to the crime, he led police to the grave. Forensic analysis showed that the skull had been split.

Evans had a long history of paedophilic offences and attributed his sexual behaviour to a childhood incident. His first conviction had been in 1966, when he was twenty-seven and working as a bus driver. Incredibly, the Central Criminal Court fined him only £10 on each of three charges of sexually assaulting children, having abducted them to a forest near his home in Barking. In 1970, he received ten years on six counts of violent child molestation. One of the victims had been his own daughter. He did not serve the full ten-year term, however. He was released in 1975, having served five years. At the time, he was being treated with drugs to reduce his sexual arousal. The treatment was soon discontinued as a result of its 'side-effects'.

In 1978 (three years later, or two years before his original ten-year sentence would have been up) Evans was convicted of sexually assaulting a nine-year-old spastic girl. He was given three years, but was again freed in 1980. Nine months later, he came before Judge Hilliard of Reading Crown Court, charged with sexually assaulting a twelve-year-old girl. The judge asserted that, although Evans had a 'disgusting' history, he could not take into account the other crimes when sentencing.

In late 1983, about the time that he murdered Marie Payne, Evans was fined £200 by the Reading magistrates. This fine was imposed because Evans wrote to the parents of several children he had molested demanding to be allowed to see them!

The claim of the Berkshire Social Services to have had no record of his criminal activity seems extraordinary. In early 1982, the service had sanctioned his working for the Christian charity, Toc H, where Evans volunteered to work as a childminder to three children for two months. In June 1982, he appeared in court charged with sexually assaulting two of the children. The family for whom he babysat had had no idea of the nature of his criminal record! He was acquitted of three charges only four months before killing four-year-old Marie Payne. It is above all unbelievable that, in a 'civilized' country such as England, where health care is public, Evans should never have received any appropriate treatment.

THE CASE OF THE PROMISCUOUS WOMAN PAEDOPHILE

An overwhelming majority of paedophiles are adolescent and adult males. Isolated incidents involving adult women do, however, occur. One such case was referred by the courts to Tollison and Adams (1979) for a psychiatric assessment.

The woman's history revealed that she was forty-five years old and divorced, and had previously been arrested for abuse of alcohol and narcotics. She had been successfully treated for drug addiction five years before being referred for the psychiatric evaluation. Her sexual history revealed that she had first had sexual intercourse when aged ten with an older boy. At fifteen, she had married a man thirty years her senior. The twelve-year marriage was unsuccessful. Her husband beat her up regularly and she began an affair with an adolescent, who lived in the same apartment building.

After divorcing her husband, she took employment in an establishment known as a hang-out for young drug dealers. The young dealers introduced her to narcotics, and she befriended people twelve to fifteen years younger than herself. The youths were kind to her, made her feel important, and got her hooked on heroin. They also used her for sex. She would sleep with five or six boys a night, their ages ranging between twelve and eighteen years, although eight- or nine-year-olds would sometimes be brought along for sexual favours.

She found the sexual experiences enjoyable: 'unlike older guys, including my husband, they seemed to appreciate me so much and were always concerned that I climaxed too'. At one point, an older man paid her to perform oral sex on a five-year-old boy while he watched. She did, however, also want the local highschool boys to consider her 'a mistress without pay', and they visited her regularly.

After being successfully treated for her drug addiction, she found a factory job. But her sexual preferences had not changed. She had *learned* to find younger boys sexually stimulating. Everything proceeded according to plan until two boys whom she seduced told their parents. Like many male paedophiles, she enticed her victims with promises of rewards of food. In this case, the boys were aged respectively eight and thirteen.

VICTIMS

Kinsey *et al.* (1953) discovered that, out of a total of 1,200 adult women interviewed, 334 (28 per cent) claimed to have had a sexual encounter with an adult prior to puberty. Of these instances, however, only 20 (6 per cent) had been reported as cases to the authorities. Fewer than 7 (2 per cent) accounted for a situation in which a young girl was actually forced into a sexual encounter, and about 26 (8 per cent) collaborated in the act. The rest were exposures to exhibitionists or being sexually fondled.

Heterosexual paedophiles generally choose girls between the ages of six and twelve, while homosexual paedophiles select slightly older boys, aged eleven to fifteen. Most victims know the offender prior to being molested.

Contrary to public expectation, a majority of these women were not, at least in Kinsey's view, emotionally damaged for life. On the other hand, most victims were scared and it seems unlikely that, in the majority of cases, the experience will have proved beneficial. A minority experienced a good deal of fear, reacting hysterically. Some victims had positive reactions and claimed to have actually enjoyed the sex. By contrast, three women claimed that the experience had been aversive enough to carry the memory through into adulthood.

Most of those I interviewed, both formally and informally, evidenced disgust at having been molested. They viewed the offending adult as abusive: at best as a pervert or bully who seeks to use power over children to get sexual pleasures. One college student told me how, when he was eleven, one of his teachers used to 'bunny us, and then threaten us with punishment if we told'. Essentially, 'bunnying' meant that the teacher would fondle the boys' genitals. He would take the unsuspecting boys away on weekend camp and use the opportunity of sleeping in the same dormitory as them to molest them. This teacher had invented a variety of 'strip poker' games.

Another witness remembered how a stranger had once 'grabbed my balls while urinating in a department store toilet' when he was fourteen years old. He felt disgusted at the time – 'invaded', as though he had been robbed and raped. 'You never know what it's like until it happens to you.'

And a young man of twenty-six testified how he had had 'an unfortunate thing for older women, ever since this thirty-six-year-old seduced me when I was fourteen'. He maintained that he was not attracted to women his own age, and that he 'blamed her'. The problem was very real for him, but, by contrast, a friend who heard his complaints was envious: 'If only I'd been so lucky. Boy, you've nothing to bitch about . . . I'd have loved it!' The two then proceeded to indulge in an argument about morality which proved futile.

O'Carroll (1980) narrates a case of 'lesbian paedophilia' recounted by Beth Kelly, a 'radical lesbian feminist'. Beth Kelly's first experience of sexual love was with her great-aunt, Aunt Addie, 'who refused, all her life, to be cowed by convention'. Aunt Addie was a lesbian, and was unusual in that she read books and travelled at a time when it was frowned upon for a woman. Beth and her Aunt Addie were caught in a sexual situation by Beth's disapproving mother.

THE CHILD PORNOGRAPHY–PROSTITUTION CONNECTION

No one knows how many children, some as young as four or five, have to fend for themselves in the slums of many

Third World countries. A traveller recently returned from Indonesia told how he had seen dogs and children for sale, side by side. Losing his 'British stiff upper lip' for a moment, he exclaimed: 'I saw children and dogs for sale. The dogs were in cages, but the children were not. They had been cleaned up for sale, to work, I suppose, in other countries. The dogs were barking, but the children were very quiet. Very quiet . . .' He paused a moment, stared into space and added, 'The dogs were to be eaten. That's the difference.' I could see he had been profoundly disturbed by what he had seen, and my intuition told me two things. First, that my friend was not lying, and secondly, that there was a strong chance the children were being offered, not for slave labour alone, but also for the sexual gratification of their new owners.

On a visit to Cape Town, I noticed several 'street kids' begging for food. These were 'coloured' children – that is, children classified by the South African government as being of 'mixed blood'. They were loitering around a well-known beach-front restaurant, exclusive to 'whites only' under South African law. The management did not, however, seem to mind if a customer ordered food for some of the children, provided they remained in the eating area – *outside*. Then two children aged about eight and ten years who came into the 'outside' area were promptly ejected by a waiter. I could not understand the altercation, since it took place in Afrikaans, but later discovered that these children were known for bothering male customers; they had been known to solicit for sex.

Soon after the incident, a priest came looking for some of the children. In conversation with him I learned a little about child prostitution in that country. He ran a shelter for some of the 'street kids' and was all too aware of how the children used prostitution as an added source of income. He said that the children could make R10 ($5) a turn, 'the kind of money they've never seen before'. When I asked if the police did anything, he laughed at my naïveté: '*Ja*, man,' he grinned. 'They sometimes take the bastards who use these kids up into those hills and give them a good hiding. But otherwise, they don't seem to mind. Now, if these were *white kids*, you be sure, s'trooos Gawd, they'd soon fix up the blarry problem. They should lock those criminals up and chuck away the key for life.' Then he rounded up several of the children, which proved no easy task, put them in his van and vanished into the city. Various children remained behind to play the video games machine.

In the United States, one estimate has it that almost 1 per cent of the total population consists of runaways and 'missing' children. This would mean that over a million American children were runaways. There is even a Runaway Hotline which children can call freephone, the hotline organizers estimating that, additionally, another million children come under the heading of 'missing children'. Most of them are destitute and trying to escape abusive families. Many are never even reported as missing. The problem is so extensive that, early in 1985, a campaign to print the photographs and names of missing children on milk cartons was launched in the United States. Thousands of them survive in practice by making 'easy money' out of prostitution and pornography. (It has been pointed out that a figure of a million missing children in the United States is an exaggeration since a majority of those reported missing to the Runaway Hotline are back home within a week.)

The 'kiddy-porn' business is certainly highly lucrative, and is, like any other business, controlled by the law of supply and demand. In 1983, a forty-three-year-old grandmother pleaded guilty in a Los Angeles court to one count of pornography. She was alleged to have run the largest child-pornography ring in the United States. She easily put up her bail of $1.1 million and was immediately released. The maximum sentence she could have incurred was, in any case, a mere four years in the state penitentiary.

The woman lived in an exclusive Los Angeles neighbourhood, and owned a Rolls-Royce in addition to other glamorous cars. Detectives alleged that she distributed by mail-order 80 per cent of the kiddy-porn available in America, her business being worth an annual turnover of more than $500,000. The business sold such titles as *Child Discipline*, *Naughty Horny Imps*, *Lollitots* and *Children Love*.

On Thursday, 25 October 1984, Erskine McCullough reported in the *Standard* (London) that the FBI was searching for the bodies of six children thought to have been murdered after participating in pornographic film-making. The events proved to be as tragic as they were bizarre.

In the small Mid-West town of Jordan, Minnesota, twenty-two people had been charged with the sexual abuse of about a hundred minors. Psychologists, when asked to interview some of the kiddy-porn 'actors', also known as 'chickens', were horrified to uncover reports that children aged between four and thirteen had been murdered in what may be termed 'kiddy snuff films'. Furthermore, a psychotherapist, Susan Phipps-Yomas, reported that several children had told her how they were forced to witness the murders, this serving as an intimidation tactic, since the murders were committed just after the children had been forced into sex games with adults. Two children who had been made to take part in the killings were led to believe that they would be held equally responsible with the perpetrators.

A policeman searching for bodies stated, 'We are looking for dead bodies of kids', after one child described how a body had been buried in a forest, another in a backyard. The police were also concerned about the mysterious appearances and disappearances of children in Jordan. In the event, the prosecutors had to drop charges against all twenty-two adults 'to protect an investigation of great magnitude'. They did so because, under Minnesota State Law, they would have been forced to expose their evidence to defence lawyers, who would then be placed in an advantageous position.

Since connoisseurs of child pornography have highly specific stimuli films are shot to individual 'tastes'. For instance, persons aroused by male children masturbating one another might very well be indifferent to the idea of an adult male having sex with a six-year-old girl. According to Bryant (1982), films entitled *Young Stud* or *Chicken Supreme* portray young boys masturbating and involved in homosexual encounters; *Children Love* stars young boys and girls having intercourse; and *Young Lolitas* and *Youthful Lust* depict six- to eleven-year-olds engaged in oral sex with adult men and women. I viewed various films confiscated from inmates at a psychiatric prison, one of which showed two adult women putting a vibrator into the vagina of a girl aged about ten. Another showed an adult man having anal sex with a boy of eleven or twelve. None of the children I saw in these films showed the slightest degree of interest in the sex. All appeared unhappy, dejected and confused.

These cases should come as no surprise to the population of Southern California. For example, Bryant (1982) cites data from the Los Angeles Police Department which 'estimated that in 1976, 30,000 children in that city alone were sexually exploited by adults for pornography purposes'. The figure of 30,000 is quite believable. Inhabitants of inner-city Los Angeles will know how sections of Sunset Boulevard, a few blocks south, swarm with young male hustlers. In *City of Night* (1963), a sensitive account of adolescent male prostitution written over twenty years ago by John Rechy, the author describes his life in America. The book opens:

LATER I WOULD THINK OF AMERICA as one vast city of Night stretching gaudily from Times Square to Hollywood Boulevard – jukebox-winking, rock-n-roll moaning America at night fusing its dark cities into the unmistakable shape of loneliness.

Remember Perishing Square and the apathetic palmtrees. Central Park and the frantic shadows. Movie theatres in the angry morning-hours. And wounded Chicago streets . . . Horror movie courtyards in the French Quarter – tawdry Mardi Gras floats with clowns tossing out glass beads, passing dumbly like life itself . . . Remember rock-n-roll sexmusic blasting from jukeboxes leering obscenely, blinking manycoloured along the streets of America strung like a cheap necklace from 42nd Street to Market Street, San Francisco . . .

One-night sex and cigarette smoke and rooms squashed in by loneliness . . .

And I would remember lives lived out darkly in that vast City of Night, from all-night movies to Beverly Hills mansions.

BIZARRE CAMPAIGNS TO LEGALIZE PAEDOPHILIA

In 1962, a group calling itself the René Guyon Society was established in Los Angeles, California, by seven couples who met at a lecture. They took as their slogan: 'Sex by eight, or else it's too late!' (Tollison and Adams, 1979; O'Carroll, 1980). The society named itself after a French Freudian psychologist who believed that social disease was produced by repressed sexuality. Tim O'Hara, a representative of the organization, showed pictures of children having sex with each other and with adults.

Soon afterwards, in San Diego, California, the Childhood Sexuality Circle published the following bizarre and to some degree outrageous manifesto:

CHILD'S SEXUAL BILL OF RIGHTS

Whereas a child's sexuality is just as much a part of his whole person from birth as the blood that flows in his veins, making his sexual rights inherent and inalienable, and

Whereas the United Nations Organization proclaimed a Universal Declaration of Human Rights in 1948, stating everyone is entitled to all the rights and freedoms encompassed in this Declaration without discrimination of any kind, such as race, color, sex, language, religious opinion, national or social origin, birth or other status, and

Whereas a declaration of the Rights of the Child was proclaimed by UNO in 1959, but no mention was made of the sexual needs and rights of children, and

Whereas a child not allowed to express all the instinctive desires nature endowed him with becomes an unhappy, frustrated, anti-social being and potential criminal, and

Whereas it is time the people of the United States and their lawmakers recognize these facts of life and act accordingly.

Therefore, the following inalienable rights are specifically set forth, to be implemented by appropriate legislation on a national and state level, and measures taken for the re-education of the citizenry in every part of the United States, this education to be available to every citizen, whether school child or adult:

1. **Legal protection**. Every child shall be legally protected in his sexual rights regardless of age or status as a legal minor.
2. **Child's right to his own person**. Every child has the right to privacy for his own personal thoughts, ideas, dreams, and exploration of his own body without any kind of adult interference, directly or indirectly expressed.
3. **Sex information**. Every child has the right to accurate sex information and to be protected from sex misinformation as soon as he is able to understand this information in simple terms.
4. **Emotional growth**. Each child has the right to grow mentally, physically, emotionally, and spiritually as a free, uncrippled happy person in security so he will be tolerant and appreciative of other individuals and their sexuality.
5. **Sensual pleasures**. Each child has the right to fully enjoy the sensual pleasure he may feel without shame or guilt.
6. **Learning the art of love**. All children have the right to

learn the art of love beginning at any age he is able to understand, just as he is entitled to learn any other art or skill.

7. **Choice of a sex partner**. Every child has the right to loving relationships, including sexual, with a parent, sibling, or other responsible adult or child, and shall be protected and aided in doing so by being provided with contraceptives and aids to prevent venereal disease.

8. **Protection from sexual suppression**. Each child has the right to be protected from any form of sex suppression at home or in society so that in adulthood he will be capable of living his sex life according to his natural desires and not according to the dictates of tradition.

Ironically, while the above is, in certain respects, laudable, indeed, profoundly humane, the fact remains that its authors promote child molestation. Members of the Childhood Sexuality Circle of America believe that small children are capable of deciding for themselves whether they wish to have sexual intercourse with whomever they may choose. Children, they assert kindly enough, ought, by law, to be provided with contraceptives. In their view, this would help to prevent the contraction of venereal disease.

Yet the manifesto is blatantly self-contradictory. It asks that children be 'protected' from 'any form of sex oppression at home or in society', when if point seven ('Choice of a sex partner') were legally enacted, children would lose all protection under the law. If this came about, we would see a change and a return to sixteenth-century values where children were not 'children' but treated as 'little adults'. It would become very easy for an adult to say, 'Listen, kid, do what I want or you don't get your supper. If you don't like it, go out and get a job.'

Campaigners for the legitimization of paedophilia are not as altruistic as they would like to appear to be. They are poignantly hedonistic, and flagrant in their self-serving lust after undeveloped bodies. It is safe to say that an overwhelming majority of young children would be horrified if asked to drive a car let alone to have sex with an adult. The René Guyon Society meanwhile maintains that young children are anatomically capable of full sexual intercourse with adults.

The campaign to legalize paedophilia is more organized in Britain than it is in the United States. The group which calls itself the Paedophile Information Exchange (PIE) has received a good deal of media coverage since its inception in 1974. One of its members, Tom O'Carroll, states he is a paedophile because he is in favour of 'all consensual sexual acts between children and adults'. PIE and O'Carroll have both faced legal prosecution. The police have raided O'Carroll's house on more than one occasion and confiscated his research materials.

O'Carroll originally took a job as a teacher in a boarding school, but was eventually fired for 'falling in love' with and having an 'affair' with a young boy. He states that when he was himself near completion of secondary school, he found that, 'Girls, especially grown-up ones, held little interest; nor did boys my own age any more, for I remained attracted only to the prepubescent ones, especially each year's new "fuzzers" – the eleven-year-olds in their little grey shorts, who seemed even more appealing. Not just in a sexual way.' He complains that he never found a 'skinny, boyish, flat-breasted' woman, and asks his readers to put themselves in his position: if he could not find women's breasts sexually arousing, then the reader should try to 'get excited about little boys' penises'. O'Carroll claims that he feels 'maternal' towards 'his boys', that he loves them and is capable of modelling adult 'masculine' behaviour for them.

The first question to ask is therefore what will happen to this 'love' as the boy grows older, as his body matures into that of an adult man? Must he then be abandoned because his body is no longer nubile and sexy? While O'Carroll may give us his rationalizations, the answers are hardly complex. He will form no committed relationship with a sexual partner since the partner is undergoing constant anatomical metamorphosis incongruent with his sexual tastes. (Many so-called radicals reject the whole notion of commitment, viewing it as capitalistic. How, they ask, can anyone presuppose ownership of another's body? Tom O'Carroll utilizes such arguments to bolster his own cause.)

The fact remains that O'Carroll is not behaving as a mature adult and therefore can hardly pose as a stable model for young boys. It is well established that boys sent to boarding schools from the age of seven suffer profound deprivation of love and affection. How easy it must therefore be for a school master with O'Carroll's sexual tastes to take advantage of such children. His eleven-year-old 'fuzzers', as he calls them, will be ready to respond to advances in any form, even if they pay for it with their bodies – and futures.

O'Carroll is quick to make the point that the courts are responsible for victimizing the child victims of paedophiles. He describes a case in which parents discovered that their son was 'having sex' with a twenty-six-year-old man, the victim then being subjected to a rectal examination by a doctor. O'Carroll quotes a psychiatrist in the case, who said that, 'If he [the victim] hadn't been buggered by the man, he certainly had been by the doctor.' There may be a grain of truth, albeit a flippant one, in this expert psychiatric opinion. Nevertheless, what O'Carroll conveniently neglects to mention is that, had the adult been able to resist his sexual urges, then both he and the victim would have been spared their subsequent ordeals. Had he acted responsibly towards himself, but more especially towards the child, then he would also have been spared the inevitable assault which he received at the hands of self-righteous fellow prisoners while serving his sentence.

PIE proposes that the 'age of consent' should be dropped

by six years. The organization states that, 'In fixing ten as the age of criminal responsibility the law assumes not only that most children should be held responsible for their actions at this age but also that they can communicate their intent.' It also states that parents ought to be legally prevented from interfering with the choice of sexual partner by any child of ten or over. In its opinion, four-year-olds are fully capable of communicating consent, but where a child is aged between four and nine years, then parents or guardians should be allowed to object!

O'Carroll and PIE take an astoundingly sordid position where babies are concerned: 'a baby may well get a great deal of pleasure from having its genitals tickled'. PIE's proposals would change the law so that a citizen would have 'an available option, *not* to complain about a sexual relationship known to exist between an adult and a baby, providing that citizen has no reason to believe the relationship was a non-consensual one'. Police would not be required to seek prohibition orders, provided that they were 'satisfied that the baby was happy with it'.

In March 1981, O'Carroll was sentenced to two years' imprisonment, following his conviction for conspiracy to corrupt public morals (Crane, 1982). O'Carroll was at the forefront of PIE contact sheets, in which readers were encouraged to help those who advertised their desire to have sex with children. He was also found guilty of soliciting obscene material by post. O'Carroll (1980) presents examples of actual paedophilic 'lonely hearts' advertisements in his book *Paedophilia: The Radical Case*:

Energetic middle-age male sincere and discreet like boys 8–15 years and the various ways in which they dress. Int swimming. Wld lk to hear from others with similar ints.

Male. Interested in public school type boys, 12–16, either in football shorts or corduroy trousers, wd like to meet young male, 20–30, with similar interests. (SW London/Surrey)

Doctor, male. Poet and author, interested photos little girls in white pants and little boys out of white pants. Wd like to hear from male or female with similar interests. All letters answered. Perfect discretion. (Reading, Berks)

Anglican priest, South London, anxious to meet other paeds for friendship and help.

The public dearly loves a scandal, and so Fleet Street has, in Britain, helped to nourish the memory of PIE. The *News of the World* especially and predictably cashed in on the sensational nature of PIE activity.

THEORIES OF PAEDOPHILIA

Little is known about the psychophysiological causes of paedophilia. Some researchers have suggested that alcohol plays an important role; others disagree. It is also claimed that paedophiles are primarily psychopathic, retarded, neurotic and personality disordered. Paedophiles have, in short, been accorded a host of psychiatric labels in addition to the diagnosis of paedophilia. Paedophiles come in a variety of shades, shapes, and sizes. They may be homosexual, heterosexual or bisexual; dangerous or non-dangerous; kind or malicious; white, oriental or black. Nevertheless, 'theories', however inadequate, do exist which attempt to explain why some personalities become paedophilic.

PSYCHOANALYTICAL THEORY

The theories of psychoanalysis focus on the 'weaning process', on 'unresolved Oedipus complexes' and 'castration anxiety', to explain the phenomenon. In *Three Contributions to the Theory of Sex*, Freud (1905) defines a paedophile as 'someone who is cowardly or has become impotent [and] adopts [children] as a substitute, or when an urgent instinct (one which will not allow postponement) cannot at the moment get possession of any more appropriate object'. According to Freud, the most common reason why teachers and child attendants commit paedophilia is that they 'have the best opportunity for it'. He does not consider whether paedophiles may seek these jobs precisely because they are paedophiles. Rather does he see the paedophile as a sexually 'normal' adult who has temporarily veered off course. It is now realized, however, that many paedophiles are exclusively attracted to little children and hence tend to veer off course most of the time.

Freud considered paedophilia to be a manifestation of 'neurosis'. He saw it as a regression to infantile sexuality. As in the case of other sexual perversions, paedophiles are thought to be fixated at a particular stage of infantile sexuality. Freud and his followers would argue that a man who becomes sexually involved with a child does so because he unconsciously fears castration – having his genitals cut off. To cope with his instinctive sexual fears and impulses, he therefore chooses 'safer and developmentally more primitive forms of sexual expression' (Howells, 1979).

The more sophisticated psychoanalytic thought which exists among 'ego-psychologists' (Stoller, 1979) stresses the role of aggression in paedophilia. The paedophile is, in a symbolic way, trying to protect himself from childhood trauma. His sexual fantasies incorporate themes of revenge and malice in which the victim is dehumanized. In other words, something terrible happened to the paedophile while he was growing up from which he could not recover. He is stuck, and uses the child to solve his 'neurotic fixations' in a form of 'conflict resolution'. Essentially, the paedophile himself wanted, as a child, to have 'sexual intercourse' with his mother, but was afraid his father would 'cut it off' if he dared. A paedophile who selects little girls is unconsciously protecting his penis from the father he has always feared. Apart from this, adult women remind him of his mother, someone unconsciously known to him as sexually taboo. Other psychoanalysts would, however, claim that the paedophile molests children when his 'ego' has been hurt. The pained ego reflects low self-esteem, and the pervert responds by bringing into reality the content of his fantasies (Rosen, 1979).

In psychoanalytical theory, paedophiles are seen as dependent, immature individuals who did not grow up for the very reason that they have remained dependent on their mothers. They are narcissistic and 'symbiotically' attached to their mothers, and this is why they are unable to establish fulfilling sexual relationships with people their own age. All of this may, of course, be true in certain cases, but it also needs to be stressed that many people who are similarly dependent do not turn into paedophiles.

SOCIAL LEARNING THEORY

Social learning theory acknowledges the importance of genetic predispositions, but, when it comes to explaining behaviour, stresses the environment. For example, it is possible that, in certain individuals, arousal to physically immature love objects (young physiques, absence of secondary sexual characteristics) was first experienced during 'normal' sociosexual play in childhood. What may then occur is that the individual masturbates to fantasies involving sexually immature bodies and so becomes habituated to these fantasies, reinforcing mental images in which he sees himself engaged in sexual play with a child. The proverbial 'Out of dreams comes reality' applies: the stage is set for paedophilic development, especially when associated with situations which provide the element of opportunity.

Case histories indicate that 'modelling' is also an important factor. Many paedophiles themselves experienced molestation when young and therefore grew up thinking of sexual molestation as just another secret adult activity. The adult who does the molesting sets the example. The implication becomes, 'It's OK for me to get my special kicks. After all, Uncle John did it to me, and I'm none the worse for it.'

There is some evidence that 'female phobia' also plays a significant role in the acquisition of paedophilic behaviour, the phobia being learned as the paedophile grows up. Tollison and Adams (1979) report a case where a paedophile had bullied several boys, aged between seven and ten, into having anal intercourse and fellatio with him. The same man had, however, reported that he found the idea of sex with adult males disgusting, and it was clear he enjoyed the fact that his victims were afraid of him. He had been afraid of dating in high school, and had never made any sexual advances to girls whom he did date. When he married, he had initially been impotent, but soon discovered that, provided he thought of the seven- to ten-year-old boys, he could maintain an erection with his wife.

OTHER POSSIBLE EXPLANATIONS

Learned helplessness may also play a significant role. In the above case, the paedophile's fear of sexual encounters with women was a learned response. He felt powerless, except in relation to young boys. An Adlerian psychologist might suggest that he 'compensated' for his anxiety about women his own age by sexually intimidating the boys. It was an important aspect of the case that he was sexually aroused by expressions of fear on his victim's faces – it gave him a temporary sense of power.

The need for power is often associated with low self-esteem, and several researchers believe that paedophiles fall into this category. The adulation of young children provides the child molester with an artifical sense of self-importance, even of omnipotence. No adults look up to the paedophile in the way that his students do. The paedophile is in control when with children in a way that he is not when in the company of adults. As the self-proclaimed paedophile, O'Carroll (1980), writes:

> I must admit it: letting children do what they want makes me nervous. I'm scared of anarchy. I used to like a reasonable orderly classroom, full of well-behaved children who put their hand up to ask questions one at a time, who paid attention to what I told them and didn't give too much trouble. Even now, if I'm chatting to children who don't know who I am, even if I'm being friendly and relaxed and informal, I tend to give the impression, despite myself, that I'm a school teacher. I don't boss children around, but just in small things – like suggesting that they put their lollipop wrappers in the waste bin – I automatically find myself modelling their behaviour.

2

Incest

---

22 SEX BETWEEN CONSANGUINEOUS RELATIVES

STILLWATER, Minnesota, USA.
'John Rairdon, 39 years old, was convicted Friday of murder in the death of his daughter Sarah Ann, 13, and District Judge Donald Gray set sentencing for March 17. The judge said Mr Rairdon, who had led a publicized search for his daughter, would probably be sentenced to a high-security prison for his own safety. The prosecution said he had molested the girl for years and killed her last year after she rejected him. She disappeared May 20 and her body was found July 16. Mr Rairdon was arrested August 13' – *Associated Press*, February 1986

GENERAL CHARACTERISTICS

Responding to the media interest in a spate of child killings during the summer of 1985, a spokesman for an incest hotline in Britain told reporters that not even babies aged two weeks were exempt from incest. Incest (Latin for 'soiled') is listed in *Roget's Thesaurus* under 'impurity'. The words listed in association with incest include 'unclean', 'vulgar', 'dirty', 'Rabelaisian', 'immoral', 'salacious', 'obscene' and 'licentious'. Incest is thought of most commonly as involving marriage or sexual relations between biologically closely related (consanguineous) persons, as where sex occurs between a parent and child. Although some commentators may define incest as also including step-relatives (as under Californian state law, for example), biology is the true determining factor: incest is not applicable in cases of adoption, step-relatives or relatives by affinity (Gatov, 1973), although the law may prevent marriage in such cases. Incest, strictly speaking, only applies between these biologically related groups:

Parents and children
Brothers and sisters
Grandparents and grandchildren
Aunts and nephews
Uncles and nieces

Laws against incest are a relatively recent matter. Indeed, as Diamond (1984) notes, 'in the West laws against incest are only a twentieth-century phenomenon'. Apart from encouraging Michelangelo to begin the rebuilding of St Peter's, Pope Alexander VI (1431–1503) dealt in the lucrative business of simony – the purchase and sale of religious favours. On one occasion, the Pope sold a nobleman, for 24,000 pieces of silver, the 'right' to commit incest. Having paid the price, the nobleman then believed that he would be free to enter the Kingdom of Heaven and not risk being turned away.

Taylor (1953) suggests that sexual permissiveness is dependent on the relative degrees of matriarchy (high status of women) or patriarchy (high status of men) which apply in a particular culture. While incest is more feared in matriarchal cultures than homosexuality, patriarchal societies, by contrast, tolerate incest more and homosexuality less.

THE INCEST TABOO

Patriarchal societies may be more tolerant of incest, but the behaviour remains close to being a universal taboo. As already mentioned, isolated instances do exist, as among the Hopi, Alorese and Siriono, where parents actively masturbate their children. Yet while there are no universals in human affairs, incest approaches the absolute in socially forbidden conduct. Alongside paedophilia, it is currently thought of as being the 'last taboo' – which may well be the major reason behind social disapproval for an older woman having an affair with a younger man. Adultery, homosexuality and masturbation, and a variety of other sexual behaviours once considered anathema, are now more tolerated, but few conversational topics set off as much indignation as paedophilia and incest.

The incest taboo is purported to regulate several socio-biological functions. The offspring of incestuous parents will, it is argued, inherit biological defects and so be more prone to recessive illness. The defects are thought to occur because of the parents contributing similar defect genes. Thus inbreeding is considered to be a cause of idiocy, sickliness, sterility and general biological weakness because it prevents natural selection taking place. On the other hand, animal experimentation involving inbreeding as well as studies made of the children of incestuous parents fail to lend any support to these beliefs (Bagley, 1968). In any case, the alternative and much neglected side of the 'genetic coin' is the theory that each parent might equally contribute genes to mutually enhance each other's strengths in their offspring.

The taboo may, in fact, have evolved to maintain familiar harmony. Incestuous relations would disrupt the basic authority structures within the nuclear family; would challenge territoriality and place members in destructive competition with one another. Social scientists argue that the incest taboo reduces tension, guilt and social disapproval. The cultural anthropologist, Claude Lévi-Strauss, considered that human beings took the step from 'nature to 'culture' when they forbade sexual relations within the family.

Despite the 'nature to culture' theory, it has been discovered that African baboons avoid incest through a complex breeding system, while, within human societies, the Mbuti pygmies of Central Africa have no term for incest (Diamond, 1984). The ancient rulers of Egypt and Peru showed their divine status by breaking the incest taboo (Tannahill, 1980). Cleopatra, for instance, married two of her brothers to keep the crown 'within the family'. Royalty among the pre-Columbian Incas were positively required to enter into brother–sister marriages. And, Diamond observes, 'among the Vavado Indians incest extends to all members of the mothers' or fathers' own clans, or "linked" clans, effectively ruling out hundreds of people as marriage partners. In the Trobriand Islands a girl who marries her mother's brother is committing incest; in Sri Lanka this relationship would be considered an ideal basis for marriage.' Among the Trobrianders, it would be a greater taboo for a girl to eat a meal with her mother's brother than to go with him into the special 'lovers' house' called a *bukumatula*. Clearly, among certain groups, the expression 'incest is best' is taken to heart.

INCEST IN WESTERN SOCIETY

The Morton Hunt survey on sexual behaviour in the 1970s produced a figure of 15 per cent of respondents admitting to having had some form of sexual contact, ranging between petting and full sexual intercourse, with a relative. If applied to the US population as a whole, this figure would account for well over 20 million individuals, but it's basis is misleading. Most such sexual contact occurred between siblings and cousins. Sexual relations between parents and children are a far rarer occurrence. No more than 0.5 per cent of women interviewed admitted to having had any sexual contact with their fathers. The figure for men admitting to having sexual relations with their mothers came to zero, although it may be felt that even where a male interviewed has had sexual contact with his mother, he will be unlikely to admit it. Over 3.5 per cent of both men and women admitted to having sexual contact with a brother or sister, but the most frequently reported contact with a relative remained that between cousins, over 9 per cent of men admitting to having had sexual contact with a female cousin, and over 3 per cent of women admitting to having had sexual contact with a male cousin.

Sexual explorations between brother and sister or between cousins is therefore the most frequent event under the heading of incest, but is seldom taken seriously – except when brothers and sisters actually marry, intentionally or unintentionally. Sexual relations between fathers and daughters is, on the other hand, taken very seriously by society. Despite the difficulties with establishing accurate figures for incest, the problem between daughters and fathers was shown to be large enough in the United States to justify the creation of a self-help group called Parents United. Although several psychologists have criticized it for taking treatment into its own hands, the group serves a positive function in bringing the problem into the open.

In such cases, punitive measures against the father usually have deleterious effects on the whole family. Once the offender is sent to prison, the family breaks up and experiences financial disaster. Both victim and family become socially stigmatized, often being rejected by their extended families and circles of friends. As the more enlightened law enforcement agencies are aware, it is best for the father to be placed on probation and treated outside prison. Restraining orders can be served on the father, who may be allowed access to his children in the presence of a social worker. By this means, the father is able to continue working and therefore to contribute to the financial support of his family.

Father–daughter incest can occur in any racial or socio-economic group, and 'incestuous families' are usually described as 'immature'. In a review of the literature, Bryant explains that incest may for long periods be tolerated by the entire family to reduce separation anxiety. Fathers seldom use force, go to lengths to rationalize their behaviour and are otherwise concerned for the child's welfare. It is also thought that, in families where love is conditional, some victims learn to be seductive to gain affection. Daughters, however, experience intense guilt as a result of sexual relations with their fathers, and such guilt may often be carried as a heavy burden throughout adulthood. Female victims may later present themselves for psychotherapy, and some have seen fit to file civil suits against their fathers on the grounds of disturbing their trust in other men. The daughters' mothers also experience guilt, and may actually have contributed to the fathers' behaviour.

The literature also indicates that father–son incest is also a more widespread incest than was previously assumed. In these cases, the fathers tend to have a history of alcoholism and anti-social behaviour outside the family. Fathers who sexually molest their sons may, as a group, be more violent than fathers who molest their daughters. They are generally heterosexuals whose wives feel powerless to do anything about the situation. The effects on sons are sometimes strong enough to make the son wish to kill his father. And, of course, there are fathers who sexually abuse both sons and daughters.

Yet society continues to fear mother–son incest even more than it does father–daughter incest. Such cases are rare, but they do exist. In 1979, a nineteen-year-old US marine and his forty-two-year-old mother were charged with incest in the state of Virginia. They had managed to secure a marriage licence and were living together. The marine was also accused and found guilty of unlawful sexual relations with his four- and five-year-old half-sisters. Mother and son were found guilty of illegal marriage and incest, and each was given a five-year suspended sentence and instructed not to see the other for ten years. When mother and son failed to comply with the court order, their sentences were invoked.

Marriage between brother and sister rarely occurs, but cases have been reported. In 1979, Victorio Pittorino married David Goddu. The two were adopted at birth and lived in separate families. Victorio sought out her brother twenty years later and the two soon fell in love and married. When they were brought to trial in New England, charged with incest, the judge ordered them to have psychotherapy and to stop living as husband and wife. The marriage was declared legally void and so there was no need for divorce.

A CASE OF FATHER–DAUGHTER INCEST

Manuel Sánchez was referred for treatment on the instructions of his probation officer. He had been found guilty of incest and of molesting his daughters aged nine and eleven. He worked as a truck driver and owned a restaurant which his wife managed. Abject, depressed, hiding and immensely shamed as a result of the charge and having to submit to treatment 'for nuts', he described the circumstances of his case:

I dunno how it all happened. It just took place over time, about three maybe four years all in all. I love my daughter, please Doc, don't get me wrong [*holding back tears*]. It all started when my wife was having this thing with another man. I wasn't sure of it. I guess I didn't want to see what was happening. He worked for us as the manager of our restaurant and they had an affair. Doesn't make you feel like much of a man does it . . . I worked nights sometimes, long hours, you know on long hauls. We wanted to move up in this world and so I was accepting longer trips outta state to supplement our income.

I trusted her, but inside myself I knew she was up to no good. But I loved her. We was childhood sweethearts. We got married and all went well. So much in love we was. And the business was doing real good, you know. It was coming along real nice. Anyway, I think her lover got it into her head to get the business away from me, and said so. She made fun of me when I wanted to sleep with her.

Whenever I did come home, she was never there. Always had too much work. The restaurant business was her thing. I took care of the girls, and they missed me when I was out truckin. It was a treat for them when I came home. Now that I think about it, it's all probably because we got into bed together ALL IN INNOCENCE, you know . . . Then, 'cause my wife wasn't giving me any. The girls used to get into bed on Sundays with both of us, 'cept now, she was usually away. The girls loved their Daddy and I loved them. Don't know how it happened, but I used to get a hard-on and rub myself between their backsides and then it was over. We had a game. I said, 'Now your Daddy is gonna take you both out but first give him a liddle cuddle.' They knew what it meant. Sometimes I could just pick 'em up and squeeze 'em and just come by doin' that. Honest I didn't think I was doing no harm. My poor little girls . . . Don't know when I'll ever be allowed to see 'em again . . . [*breaks down*].

Psychologists treating incestuous families have observed how, in certain cases, the mother acts as a catalyst for the crime. In a passive way, she may silently conspire to get the children into bed with the father. According to the social worker in charge of the above case, the wife's 'hidden agenda' (lines of action she dared not consciously admit to herself) went something like this: 'Get my husband into trouble with the law – even if it means he molests the girls – and my lover and I will get the business and the girls.'

Manuel Sánchez claimed that his wife did not seem to

object to his having the girls in bed with him while she was out. She pretended she knew nothing of what was going on. Finally, she got the girls to confess and become irate, indignant and bent on vengeance. She used both her children and her husband to her own ends. As soon as the father was legally banned from entering the family house, she got her lover to move in. This proved especially painful and emasculating for Manuel Sánchez.

The above case illustrates how responsibility for incest may be in part attributable to *both parents*. However, in some cases the father is simply a psychopathic alcoholic who views the bodies of his wife and children as legitimate sexual property. He is also then a rapist who incidentally happens to be committing the crime of incest.

CASES OF MOTHER–SON INCEST

Sex between mother and son may be the least reported form of incest, but over the two-year period when I was completing my clinical internship as a student in California, out of a dozen women sex offenders registered at the clinic, I saw, in group therapy, one who had had incestuous relations with her pubescent son and another who had been an accomplice to her lover in sexually molesting her teenaged daughter. The theme of incest between mother and son was featured with notable subtlety in Louis Malle's film *Le Souffle au Coeur* (1971).

In *The Sex-Life Letters*, Greenwald and Greenwald (1974) present an allegedly true account by a 'Mrs J. P.' who is proud of her incestuous relations:

Sharing a bedroom with my two brothers, I took part in sex play with them from an early age. I was ten when I first experienced full intercourse with my eldest brother (then 13), and I subsequently became very active with my brothers and their friends, usually in group situations. At puberty I withdrew from this promiscuity, but continued and deepened my intimacy with my brothers.

The time came when we left home and went our separate ways (although I have retained a sexual relationship with them spasmodically), and I eventually met and married my husband. Our love life has been quite satisfactory, and we have a son of 12 and a little girl of five.

My husband is frequently away on business trips and it was during one of these business trips, a few weeks ago, that when looking in on the children last thing in the evening, I noticed my boy had almost lost his bed clothes. I went in to tuck him in – he was sound asleep – and found myself becoming aroused by the sight and feel of his passive naked body with his first soft down of pubic hair.

I was unable to resist kissing and then sucking his penis, and was rewarded by inducing a hard erection. I repeated this practice on several subsequent nights and brought him to a climax without awakening him.

On the last occasion my husband was away my boy awoke with a nightmare and to comfort him I took him into my bed. I was awakened later to find that he was against me rubbing his erect penis against my hips. I was able to manoeuvre myself, while feigning sleep, to enable him to enter my vagina from behind and achieve an ejaculation soon afterward. I now do not know whether to continue my secret relationship, or make open advances.

What is so wrong in complete family love? Incest is only a problem when pregnancies result, and I am safely on the Pill. As far as emotional problems are concerned, I can only cite my own case, where I feel sure I have a more richly satisfying sex life than the majority of 'morally perfect' women.

Greenwald and Greenwald replied to the above letter by pointing out that what the boy needs is a mother, not a mistress. Since, for many people, early recollections play a major role in an individual's sexual development, it is likely that a boy who had sex with his mother would end up with some kind of sexual handicap. Once again, it should be stressed that while this is a high probability it is not a total certainty. As we saw in the section above, some paedophilia victims report that they are undamaged by having sex with adults. This does not, however, mean that laws should change. Many, many children *are* hurt by adult molesters – far more than most people imagine.

CHILD MOLESTATION AND THE LAW

Practically all societies punish child molesters by sending them to prison or secure psychiatric institutions, some by even castrating or executing them. The child molester is usually so hated and despised that other prisoners serving life-sentences have been known to hold their own trials within the prison, even passing sentences of execution. Child molesters almost invariably require special protection while serving their sentences. Even mass murderers seem to feel superior to convicted paedophiles.

In California, 'Exciting the Lust of a Child Under Age Fourteen' (Penal Code 288) attracts a sentence of one year to life. The Mentally Disordered Sex Offenders Act (Penal Code 6316) formerly made it possible to send sex offenders to a psychiatric hospital for 'treatment' until the early 1980s, when a sadistic child sex murderer, released from a state hospital, 'proudly' and savagely killed a little girl.

The law in California specifically indicates that a child molester who is ten years older than a thirteen-year-old child and who 'copulates the mouth of that child shall be imprisoned for up to 15 years in the state prison'. Although women are rarely prosecuted for child molestation, they are subject to equal punishment. The law provides for a term of one year in the county jail for 'causing or contributing to the delinquency of a person under 18 years'. In addition, there are, among other similar provisions, several vagrancy laws which prevent strangers from loitering around schools.

In England, the punishments which apply to child molesters are as follows:

'Unlawful Sexual Intercourse with a Girl Under 16 Years' (Sexual Offences Act 1956, Section 6). Maximum penalty: two years' imprisonment. Only men or boys over fourteen may be convicted. Presumably, a fifteen-year-old boy could be given youth custody for having an affair with his fifteen-year-old girl friend. Lesbians cannot be convicted of having unlawful sexual intercourse with girls under sixteen.

'Unlawful Sexual Intercourse with a Girl Under 13 Years' (Sexual Offences Act 1956, Section 5). Maximum penalty: life imprisonment. A fourteen-year-old boy could be given youth custody for having sex with a twelve-year-old girl. Only males can be convicted.

Similarly, allowing premises to be used for sex with children can incur life imprisonment. A law dating from 1861 affords a seven-year sentence for 'stealing a child under the age of fourteen years'. However, any person can be punished for 'Indecency with Children Under 14' (Indecency With Children Act, 1960, Section 1(1)). Lesbian child molesters or women who make pornographic films using boys or girls under the age of fourteen could presumably be dealt with under this section.

PART FIVE

Gender Identity and Sexual Preference

23 TRANSVESTISM, TRANSSEXUALISM AND HERMAPHRODITISM

'The woman shall not wear anything which pertaineth unto a man, neither shall a man put on a woman's garment: for all that do so are abomination to the Lord thy God' – Deuteronomy 22:5

TRANSVESTISM

Charles d'Eon, that French spy of the eighteenth century, was so adept at cross-dressing that members of the London Stock Exchange placed bets on what his real sex would turn out to be at autopsy. Among some North American Indian tribes, the *berdache* were men who wore women's garments and behaved as though they were women; but the *berdache* were not necessarily homosexual, as the stereotype might suggest. The Sakpota, a group in Dahomey, used cross-dressing dancers to ward off evil spirits, and the Brazilian Yaruba encourage 'private' cross-dressing. Denis (1966) describes how a small Tahitian boy might decide that he is really a girl, wear skirts and let his hair grow without encountering either parental opposition or ostracism by public opinion:

... when they get older these men-women continue to be treated with amused tolerance. They are not particularly common. They dress and behave like women, and always do women's work such as washing, sewing and looking after babies. They are called *mahou*. The Tahitians made no extra fuss of an old man known as the Queen's *mahou*. He sported a white beard, wore a colourful frock, and paid attention to his hair. The venerable old gentleman was a completely accepted character on Papeete, far more than he would be in a so-called Western civilization.

The Western equivalent of the *mahou* is the transvestite (TV). **Transvestites** are people who habitually wear the clothing of the other sex. Most transvestites are heterosexual men, though some are homosexual men, and a few are lesbian women. Homosexual cross-dressers speak of 'going in drag'. It has become a relatively middle-class fad in many American cities for people to attend 'drag shows' where men put on female impersonation acts. Contrary to popular belief, these men are not necessarily transvestites. They may be heterosexual or homosexual men who perform professionally for pay and who enjoy the exhibitionism involved.

The performers are often remarkably gifted. Those who patronize one such of these establishments – for instance, the Queen Mary in Studio City, California, or Darcels in Portland, Oregon – are often unable to tell, at least in the soft theatre lighting, that the performers are men. Some of the performers are, however, transsexuals – men who have undergone a sex-change operation (see below). In a typical cabaret, the female inpersonators will mouth the words to songs by famous women singers. I have seen shows where the technique is perfected to the point where I have been convinced that the female impersonator on stage was the real performer. Comedians in drag can prove to be highly versatile at making fun of establishment values; bigoted anti-homosexual campaigners like Anita Bryant or the homophobic Californian Senator Briggs have been favourite targets for comic assault.

American intolerance of cross-dressing was originally

expressed by the Puritans, who invoked Deuteronomy 22:5: 'The woman shall not wear anything which pertaineth unto a man, nor shall a man put on a woman's garment.' Puritanical aversion to theatre was in part based on the use of cross-dressing where male actors played female roles. The Puritans would almost certainly have considered Japanese Noh and Kabuki theatre to be revolting since men traditionally played all parts. They would also reject Takarazuka theatre, in which all dancers and singers are women, even when male roles are depicted. Puritanical intolerance of 'fringe sexuality' is reflected by Section 887, subdivision 7, of the New York State Code of Criminal Procedure, which prohibits female impersonation, especially if it is used to defraud or solicit (Raymond, 1979).

Transvestism is largely determined by the extent to which an individual becomes sexually aroused by cross-dressing. The individual who becomes 'fetishistically' turned on by cross-dressing is likely to have a heterosexual orientation. Some heterosexual transvestites find the experience arousing enough to achieve orgasm. According to Diamond (1984), most homosexuals who cross-dress do so for bravado rather than for the erotic value, and also to attract other males. We have already seen how, like heterosexual men, they may perform for professional/financial purposes, but Warren (1974) notes that homosexual men in the gay community can be hostile towards men who wear female garments.

On a visit to San Francisco as a freshman college student, I was perplexed, when walking into a large hotel, to see people dressed in what turned out to be 'drag' fashion. The hotel was hosting an annual San Francisco function in which many homosexual men wear female garments. Many of the men wore the most lavish and apparently expensive ball gowns with long trains. They sported whips, false nails and eye-lashes, mascara, bright lipstick and blush. Other hotel guests could not help staring, which proved amusing to many of the 'drag queens', who were highly conscious of their own attire. Some even 'playfully' cracked whips at passers-by, passed provocative comments and were clearly having a whale of a time.

It should be stressed that going 'in drag' is viewed as a leisure activity. Most professional female impersonators disapprove of transvestites. As Newton (1972) explains:

> Female impersonators do not refer to themselves as transvestites. Sometimes in interviews one would reluctantly say 'well, I guess I'm sort of a transvestite,' but then he would quickly add, 'but I only do it for a living,' or 'this is my job.' To female impersonators, the real transvestites are the lone wolves whose individual and private experiments are described as 'freakish'. To them the transvestite is one who dresses as a woman for some 'perverted' sexual purpose.

Unlike Tahitians, Europeans and Americans refer children who cross-dress for 'expert' psychiatric attention. They are usually sent to centres which specialize in 'gender disorders'. The Gender Disorders Clinic at the University of California, Los Angeles, is one such centre. Cross-dressing behaviour is rare in young children, but, according to some observers, when it happens there is a strong indication that the child will become homosexual. Most parents loathe the idea that a child of theirs might turn out to be homosexual and subject the offspring concerned to quite intense psychotherapy to try to avert what may well prove inevitable.

Most cases of heterosexual transvestism first come to light among pubescent and adolescent males. However, some cases can occur as late as mid-life. Stoller (1979) believes that the transvestite typically puts women's clothing on as a matter of curiosity, and then, finding it erotically pleasing, decides he will repeat the behaviour. Three trends in male cross-dressing seem to emerge. First there are the men who are satisfied with a 'single garment or class of garments' as their fetish. In the second group are those who are content to dress up in full female regalia for a limited period of time – minutes or hours. Finally, there are the transvestites of the third group who are able to pass as women for prolonged periods. The latter type was portrayed in the film *Tootsie* (1983), in which Dustin Hoffman successfully and sensitively played the role of a 'woman' who becomes a national soap opera star without being detected until 'she' herself decides to come clean.

Although trousers have come to be accepted fashion for women in many societies, while men do not wear skirts (the Scots kilt is, within its own cultural context, emphatically a masculine garment), female transvestites are, according to Stoller (1979), virtually unheard of. Stoller, an experienced psychoanalyst who has researched sexual perversions for a number of years, records that he has encountered only two women who were sexually aroused by wearing men's garments, a third woman communicating her erotic interest in wearing men's clothing by letter. Furthermore, he claims to have been able to trace only one similar report in the research literature. And unlike men who find individual pieces of women's clothing, such as underwear, fetishistically exciting, those women transvestites did not find the garments themselves exciting, but were excited by wearing them. In contrast to many male transvestites, the women did not feel compelled to cross-dress, nor did they consider it their preferred form of sexual arousal or savour the texture and smell of men's clothing.

A CASE OF MALADJUSTED TRANSVESTISM

Most cases where transvestite disposition causes in individual to seek treatment occur among heterosexual men, often among those who are married. This particular fetish and ritualistic behaviour can produce anxiety and discontentment. Greenwald and Greenwald (1974) present the following account submitted by a tranvestite:

I am in my late 30s, married and have children, but at times have an overwhelming need to dress as a woman in every detail. I do this while alone and masturbate. Then I am disgusted with myself for a while but the need to be or resemble a woman always comes back. I suppose it all started in childhood when I tried on my sister's panties and gym slip. I had an erection and knew that lingerie was for me.

In the ensuing years before marriage, I overcame it by keeping occupied and dated lots of girls, but shortly after marriage I fell back into my old practice. This seemed to satisfy my sexual needs. Before we married, my wife was keen on relations with me, but the responsibilities of marriage have, I suppose, made me take life more seriously and now she no longer seems to want to have anything to do with me. The children were produced entirely out of wifely duty and she had an affair which she found very stimulating. The affair seemed to make the transvestism worse. A few years after this I dressed up in women's clothes and showed myself to my wife, thinking I was going mad. She offered to help, saying that it was all mind over matter. In desperation I recently got in touch with the Albany Trust and went for a short while to receive electrical treatment, shocks administered to me while looking at photographs of myself in female attire.

It was very embarrassing and I thought it had done the trick and threw away all my clothes. But several months later I bought new dresses and underthings and now permanently wear tights, panties and a girdle.

It's getting worse. I can understand that my wife cannot bear to have anything to do with 'deviations' as she calls them, but I am really beginning to feel that I want to dress as a woman all the time. I'd like her to come to me and humiliate me while dressed as a schoolgirl. Worse I would like a man friend.

Perhaps what I really need is a woman who would allow and even assist me in my practices because the sex act under these conditions would, I think, be very enjoyable.

In this example, the transvestite is having difficulty accepting his sexual desires. The case raises numerous questions. Of course, he could return to a quick course of limited behaviour therapy in which he would receive aversive stimulation, such as having to smell ammonia or being subjected to electric shock. It is, however, unlikely that, without a *comprehensive* therapeutic programme, he would achieve any permanent satisfaction. Furthermore, the case is probably more complex than it seems. Why did his wife seek the affair? Did it aggravate his tranvestism? Could both be convinced that consensual sex between adults, like cross-dressing, is not the most heinous of crimes – that it might be just another variation on the modern American sexual menu? Could this man learn to cross-dress in the presence of his wife, later discarding female attire in public?

A CASE OF LESBIAN CROSS-DRESSING

Greenwald and Greenwald (1974) also present the following account of lesbian cross-dressing in their anthology, *The Sex-Life Letters*:

So many men write in about getting sexually excited dressing in women's clothes – but what about girls dressing as men?

I am a lesbian and always wear trousers, as do most of us, but this is just comfortable and natural. However, on other occasions I go further and wear trousers that are very butch and put things down the front of them so that it looks as though I have a penis. This excites me terribly and very soon I have to masturbate.

I'm not sexually shy but have never told anyone about this and don't do it very often as I am happy with my girlfriend.

Freudians would probably accuse this woman of displaying 'classic penis envy'.

THEORIES OF TRANSVESTISM

Imagination is not lacking when it comes to inventing theories about human motivation. Once again, it cannot be overemphasized that there are no adequate accounts for why some people behave in this particular way: *no one really knows why certain individuals become transvestites.* Nevertheless, the theories postulated are sometimes bizarre in themselves, ranging from brain dysfunction, in particular cerebral centres (biological), to a desire to 'fuse with one's mother' (psychoanalysis), or the explanation that it is learned behaviour (behavioural psychology).

Theories on brain dysfunction were developed out of the observation that several transvestite patients who underwent lobectomies – the surgical removal of a portion of their brains – stopped having transvestite urges. Hunter, Logue and McMenemy (1963) noted how, when a thirty-nine-year-old man suffering from temporal lobe epilepsy and transvestism (thirty years of cross-dressing) had part of his frontal lobes removed, both the 'problems' were subdued. It should be stressed that major brain surgery is likely to 'cure' even the most vicious rapist. The research does not support any claims that transvestism is the result of brain disorder *per se*.

PSYCHOANALYTIC THEORY

The Oedipus complex and 'castration anxiety' are central to psychoanalytic explanations as to why some people become tranvestites. In terms of the Oedipus complex, little boys are supposed to have an unconscious desire to make love to their mothers. Most boys soon realize that they cannot gain sexual access to their mothers and are said to 'resolve' their Oedipal complexes by substituting the desire for mother with another more appropriate 'love object': in most cases, a girl friend or wife. What happens in the case of a transvestite is that the boy somehow realizes that he can have sexual relations with his mother's clothing, thereby obtaining vicarious and, initially, unpunished pleasure. The time usually comes, however, when the boy is caught and humiliated either by mother or some other female. This humiliation is thought to lead to 'castration anxiety' (Stoller, 1979).

'Castration anxiety' produces in the boy, according to Stoller, 'not just the fear of losing his genitals . . . but [also] the significance of his genitals in fixing him as a member of the sex to which he has long since committed himself in his core gender-identity'. The transvestite is afraid of women, who humiliate him. Therefore he hates and envies women. This leads him to seek revenge. Stoller puts it succinctly, 'The conflicts here are between the desire to harm females and fear of their strength, between wanting to have them (heterosexually) and wanting to be one of them (identification with aggressor), between preserving one's maleness, masculinity, and sexual potency and giving in to a woman's castrating attacks by becoming a woman.' The transvestite is said to be getting away with his 'triumphantly erect' penis, which is secretly stashed under women's garments. Thus, he passes as a woman while still holding on to his masculinity (his penis). Tollison and Adams (1979) encapsulate one psychodynamic view of tranvestism when they cite Sadger's (1921) scenario: 'When I put on my mother's dress I feel as if I were she herself, and so could arouse sexual feelings in myself and in my father, and possibly supplant her with him.'

The reader should bear in mind that many transvestites do not come from disturbed backgrounds. However, even though psychoanalytic theory is largely untestable and unprovable, it is worth noting that, in more than one case, transvestites have reported that they began cross-dressing after being sexually humiliated by women during childhood. As we shall see, the humiliation factor can also be accounted for by behavioural and learning theories.

BEHAVIOURAL THEORY

Tranvestism can be explained through straightforward conditioning. Tollison and Adams (1979), to illustrate how an association can be implicated in the genesis of crossdressing fetishes, present the case of a twenty-eight-year-old lawyer who referred himself for treatment for compulsive cross-dressing. A thorough sexual history of the patient revealed that he began cross-dressing aged fourteen years when an older female cousin came to stay with his family:

The patient remembers being sexually attracted to the cousin at the onset of her visit. During a particular family outing at a lake he accidentally viewed the cousin nude as she was changing into her swimsuit. The patient reported being highly aroused by this sight, but hurried back into the water to avoid being discovered. The patient reported fantasizing the sight of his nude cousin the remainder of the day and became increasingly aroused. Later the same day he took the girl's swimsuit from the clothesline and masturbated by rubbing his penis against the suit while fantasizing the woman.

For the next week or so the patient frequently fantasized the female cousin and attempted to repeat his voyeuristic experience by looking up her dress and peeping through the keyhole in her room. These efforts met with failure and frustration. Finally he slipped into her room to remove a pair of her soiled panties from the laundry room, and during the course of masturbation slipped the garment on. He then ejaculated by lying on his stomach and rubbing his penis against the garment and the bed.

The adolescent was finally caught with increasing amounts of his cousin's clothing. His mother prescribed a punishment which reinforced the entire pattern. She forced him to dress up as a woman and, together with the cousin, painted his face with make-up. After a while, his mother lost interest in the punishment and left the remaining duties to the cousin. The cousin made him put on a bra and noticed he had developed an erection under the dress. She teased him about it, and hit his erect penis with her hand. It all proved highly arousing to the young fellow. He masturbated to the memory while cross-dressed for years.

In behavioural terms, a chance encounter came to be *reinforced* by the mother's punishment. The reward or reinforcer for the sexual arousal was orgasm after repeatedly fantasizing the scene with his cousin. The first experience of seeing his naked cousin triggered the pattern. Then, seeing her panties stimulated the image of the naked cousin, who became the initial 'unconditioned stimulus' for his sexual arousal. The panties on the clothes-line served as the 'conditioned stimulus' – if he had not seen his cousin undressing, he would never have associated the panties on the line with sexual excitement. Additionally, his mother's punishment reinforced the association of sexual excitement with dressing as a woman. The patient subsequently maintained his fetish by masturbating to the cross-dressing scene.

Most behavioural psychologists would suggest that the above interpretation is incomplete, for the development of complex behaviour involves a complex interplay of many variables. In this case, inadequate social skills on the part of the patient and other environmental factors would probably also be significant. It should be stressed that the behaviourally orientated psychologist is generally more interested in *how* to modify maladaptive behaviour patterns, rather than in proffering complicated theories as to *why* the behaviour occurred. Simply gaining insight into the cause of a behaviour does not necessarily mean it can be changed.

TRANSSEXUALISM

While transvestites are content with dressing and perhaps passing as members of the other sex, they do not *become* the opposite sex. In contrast with transvestites, **transsexuals** do not remain content with temporary cross-dressing. Many transsexual personalities describe cross-dressing as a sort of band-aid – partial relief from the feeling of being imprisoned in a body in which nature has made an error. A male transsexual would claim that he has the *sex* of a man but the *gender* of a woman. He is said to be suffering from 'gender dysphoria'. Genuine male and female transsexuals yearn for a sex change, even if they must resort to drastic, often irreversible surgery under the plastic surgeon's knife. In one rather unusual case, a couple who had a child *both* seriously questioned their sexual identities: Eugene Brown had sex-change surgery to become Cathy Brown, and Christopher Brown thought of himself as a man although he remained 'legally' a woman (Diamond, 1984).

MALE TRANSSEXUALS

Male transsexuals are more numerous than female transsexuals. Primary male transsexuals may even manifest 'feminine' behaviour in early infancy, the boy behaving like a girl (Stoller, 1979) and even stating that he wishes he were one. Secondary male transsexuals develop urges to live as a woman when they grow older. Generally, as the transsexual matures, he will show no 'masculine' behaviour, despite the pressures of social disapproval at school. By adolescence, he may seek expert medical therapy, surgery to remove testes and penis, the construction of a vagina and the removal of excess body hair via electrolysis. Szasz (1980) cites this description of male-to-female surgery:

A perineal pocket for the neo-vaginal canal is then constructed by dissecting down into the perineum under the prostate and urethra and anterior to the rectum. The skin from the penis is inverted as one would turn a sock inside out and tucked down into the perineal pocket ... The urethra is shortened and implanted in a more natural location at the top of the vaginal opening ... We feel that this process creates realistic and functional external genitalia as well as a functioning vagina. In a minor third-stage operation in several patients we were able to use redundant tissue to construct a 'neo-clitoris'.

Prior to elective surgery, transsexuals may test themselves by trying to fit into the appropriate gender lifestyle. Male transsexuals have been known to enlist in the army, a traditionally 'tough male' haunt. They may *seem* to do well, others may perceive their behaviour as 'appropriate', but the transsexual remains unhappy. He then attempts to persuade everyone that the world is wrong, that he cannot live in the prison nature has proved. One of the first recorded male transsexuals was the Roman Emperor Heliogabalus (A.D. 218–22), who marched into Rome commanding that he be accorded the respect of an Empress. He also attempted auto-castration, allegedly in honour of a deity (Diamond, 1984).

The media sensationalized transsexualism in 1952–3, when an American army veteran made headlines after returning from a sex-change operation in Denmark. George Jorgensen returned as Christine Jorgensen after having his testicles and penis removed. Surgeons had created labia, a vagina and breasts. The result was a surge in demand for sex-change surgery. By the end of the 1970s, over 3,000 sex-change operations had been performed in the United States (Hilgard, Atkinson and Atkinson, 1979).

One 'famous' transsexual is Dr Renee Richards, who has appeared on nationwide television in the United States. Her case was controversial, not only because she made

public her post-operative psychological distress, but also
because she was, before treatment, an excellent male tennis
player. Dr Richards was eventually permitted to play
'women's tennis', but not without opposition from many
women tennis players, who thought that, having once been
a man, she would have an unfair advantage. Raymond's
(1979) ungenerous and sardonic remark that 'the public
recognition and success that it took Billie Jean King and
women's tennis years to get, Renee Richards has achieved
in one set. The new bumper stickers might well read 'it
takes castrated balls to play women's tennis', illustrating
the social stigmatization still encountered by many
transsexuals.

FEMALE TRANSSEXUALS

Despite the observation that millions of women now wear
'pants' or trousers, transsexualism occurs less frequently
among women. Female transsexuals are, like their male
counterparts, physiologically normal women who feel they
are really men misplaced in the body of a woman. Those
patients who receive sex-change operations typically
undergo radical bilateral mastectomy (breast removal),
hysterectomy (removal of the uterus), oophorectomy
(removal of the ovaries), and take supplemental testosterone, the male hormone which produces masculinization. In
some cases, the vagina can be closed, followed by phallo-
plasty – the construction of a penis by skin grafts. However,
such a 'penis' will seldom be properly functional.

THEORIES OF TRANSSEXUALISM

At birth and until they undergo sex-change surgery, transsexuals are physiologically normal. In men, the testes,
prostate and external genitalia function normally. Secondary sex characteristics develop normally at puberty, and

hormonal disturbances are not prominent. Why then, should some thousands of Americans and a proportionate number of Europeans elect to change their sex through drastic surgery? Once again, no one really knows, and once again, there are interesting theories. Most theorizing about the cause of transsexualism has been attempted by psychoanalysis.

PSYCHOANALYTICAL PERSPECTIVES

Stoller (1979) believes that the transsexual has developed what he calls a 'feminized phallus'. This is supposedly rooted in his grandmother's cold distant attitude towards his mother. Additionally, his grandfather is alleged to have encouraged masculine traits in the mother, Stoller believing that the transsexual's mother grows up 'as if she would become a female transsexual; she will only wear boys' clothes, plays only with boys as an equal, especially in athletics, wishes she were a boy and openly states that she would like a penis of her own'. In other words, she suffers from Freudian 'penis envy'. The mother then 'unconsciously' substitutes her son for the penis she never had. Mother and son form a 'symbiotic' relationship in which they fail to separate from each other.

Consequently, the son develops no masculine behaviour, the boy beginning to feel he is really a girl as a direct result of this 'symbiotic' relationship, even though he knows that, anatomically, he is a boy. His father is likely to be a weak, passive and therefore feminine man. Stoller suggests that the transsexual condition is the result of 'too much mother and too little father'. Furthermore, in the case of male transsexuals, mothers often became physically involved with their sons, sometimes sleeping in the same bed well into puberty. The parents are reported to have lived relatively celibate lives. In this way, the father poses no threat to the son, and there will be no Oedipal conflict for such a boy. This is because the boy will not, like 'normal' boys, want to 'possess' his mother sexually. Instead, he unconsciously desires to be like her, to fuse with her. Fusing with her avoids 'separation anxiety', a condition experienced in very early infancy. In short, the mother is responsible for her son's transsexual urges.

According to Stoller, parents are similarly responsible for the development of transsexual girls. Unlike the case with male transsexuals, neither parent here will have a 'gender disorder'. It is the mother who is initially responsible, because she was not a 'good mother' during the first few months of the girl's life, when she will supposedly have been withdrawn, depressed and paranoid. Instead of taking care of his suffering wife, the father then focuses attention on his daughter, including her in his masculine activities. As a result, she comes to over-identify with him and thereafter cannot reach her mother. In other words, the psychological mechanism is seen as the opposite of male transsexualism: male transsexuals are the product of 'smother love', female transsexuals the product of maternal neglect. Stoller considers female transsexualism to be psychologically similar to lesbianism, and it is worth noting that Raymond (1979) professes not to know 'any transsexually constructed feminists who do not also claim to be lesbians'.

LESBIAN-FEMINIST VIEWS ON TRANSSEXUALISM

Janice Raymond (1979) and Thomas Szasz (1980) both take firm stands against transsexual surgery. They refer to the new breed of helping professionals who are engaged in the highly lucrative business of sex-change surgery as 'transsexers'. Transsexers are the psychologists, psychiatrists, endocrinologists and plastic surgeons who help the transsexual to fulfil his or her transsexuality. Szasz believes that medical technology is responsible for the 'invention' of this new disease, primarily because the surgical techniques are available.

Szasz takes issue with Harry Benjamin, reputedly the 'father of transsexualism', who claims that the surgery is life-preserving, maintaining that transsexuals will invariably commit suicide without it. He likens his procedures to the administration of insulin in diabetes: both insulin and transsexual surgery are necessary to save lives. Szasz tartly notes that, while a diabetic will die of his disease without insulin, no one will die as a direct result of a disease invented by transsexer Harry Benjamin.

As Szasz observes, mental-health professionals are swift to punish or reward their patients. For example, people are given electro-shock therapy and drugs and made to spend prolonged periods in psychiatric wards. Women are rewarded with 'therapeutic abortions' if the expert deems her so mentally unstable as to be a suicide risk. As Szasz puts it, 'Since the discovery of transsexualism, psychiatrists have expanded the use of the risk [i.e. threat] of suicide, making it one of their criteria for granting transsexing as a life-saving procedure.' All too often, things go awry.

They did so in the case of one thirty-year-old female-to-male transsexual who elected, between 1970 and 1972, to undergo full transsexual surgery. The team who approved the surgery consisted of a psychologist, a psychiatrist, an endocrinologist, a social worker, a urologist and a gynaecologist. Radical surgery was approved once the team was totally convinced that, if not given the surgery, the patient would kill herself to escape profound 'gender dysphoria'. The patient understood that, while she would after surgery probably develop some male characteristics, such as facial hair, she would not be able to experience an erection with penetration in a heterosexual situation. Despite this, she went ahead with the operation.

The operation, however, did not allow the new 'man' the

possibility of fulfilling sexual relationships with heterosexual women. The women he dated were unaware that his sex was a new acquisition. As soon as they discovered he had once been a woman and could not function sexually in the way expected of a man, they rejected him. The result was massive depression. By 1976, the patient had attempted suicide for the third time. The rationale for the sex-change surgery in the first place was shown to be naïve and absurd, for had not the patient been given a sex change to prevent suicide attempts? Endocrinological and surgical techniques were evidently not sophisticated enough to transform the sex of a woman into that of a man.

But, so far as Szasz is concerned, even if the technology were sufficiently sophisticated to metamorphosize men into women and *vice versa*, he would still not approve. He does not see transsexualism as a disease, and asserts that 'surgical operations creating fake males and fake females are not treatments'. They are, rather, performed by people who do not 'think' and who are merely scrutinizing the nature of transsexualism. Sexologists 'are now busy attacking and defending sex-change operations' from a purely technical prospective. Unfortunately, Szasz does not elucidate what he means by the 'nature of transsexualism'. Instead, he attacks the transsexers as a new hybrid of an old farce. The old farce, founded on deception of the public by sex-change surgery on a person's body, was totally unnecessary research. Sex-change research is like doing fertility research on women who have undergone hysterectomy – a completely futile venture. On the other hand, while Szasz makes many valid objections to sex-change surgery, if therapists followed his advice merely to question the 'nature of' and 'reflect about what they and their patients are doing to one another', then potential help would elude the client.

Raymond's (1979) book, *The Transsexual Empire*, reflects a strong lesbian-feminist distaste for transsexualism. The lesbian-feminist movement regards both the pedlars of transsexual surgery and their respective patients as suspect. Those psychologists, urologists, gynaecologists, surgeons and psychiatrists who support sex-changing are sexist so far as this group is concerned. For example, a man who wants the mutilation must first demonstrate to the trans-sexers that he can pass as a woman. Passing as a woman means that he must be able to go about life – with penis and testicles still intact – in the style of a woman. This style is dictated by the doctors, usually male chauvinists, and implies stereotyped female behaviour: passivity, maternal-ism (as though men cannot be 'maternal'), assuming the supine position during intercourse with a real man, femi-nine body language and dress, and so on. The doctors and their transsexual patients are considered detestable, partly because they participate in and vicariously promote sexist attitudes about how women are supposed to be.

One of the stranger, not to say bizarre, variations in transsexualism is the man who becomes a 'lesbian feminist' after having had his penis and testicles removed. However, perhaps even more bizarre is Raymond's (1979) assertion that, 'Many women see the transsexual who claims to be a lesbian-feminist as the man who has paid the ultimate price of manhood in patriarchal society – giving up his balls.' Central to the lesbian feminism espoused by Raymond is a powerful distrust of anything male, even if it has been castrated. The transsexed lesbian feminist is distrusted because she can never really become a woman. Here is a 'Catch 22' situation, but loss of a penis does not mean the loss of an ability to penetrate women's sexuality. As Mary Daly (1983) says, their whole presence becomes a 'member' invading women's presence to each other and once more producing 'horizontal violence'. Transsexuals who become lesbian feminists are really part of a male conspiracy to 'colonize female bodies' and steal the 'feminist soul'. No lesbian-feminist transsexual can really dispose of hateful 'masculine behaviour'. According to Raymond, 'real women' who accept them into the lesbian-feminist fold are making a grave mistake.

The reason why they err is that transsexed men are merely eunuchs – castrated men who, by virtue of their sex, are nevertheless men and therefore detestable. And, of course, eunuchs were men whom other more dominant men had castrated to use as 'keepers of women'. Eunuchs kept women in their place, were safe with women because they were thought to have no sexual desires of their own, and often rose to hold positions of considerable power – traditionally, a masculine quality.

From this base, the male-conspiracy theory is taken into further lofty and absurd levels. The male-dominated medical profession is alleged to have treated such 'disorders' as feminism by intruding into female and feminist spaces and significant points in 'feminist time'. For instance, at the time when feminism first emerged, new medical specialities were invented to control it: gynaecology and obstetrics. Transsexual surgery came to be taken more seriously in the 1960s, about the same time as feminism was rooting itself more deeply. In keeping with conspiratorial theory, nothing is coincidental. Using a logic which may fairly be described as paranoid, Raymond writes, 'Finally the phenomenon of the transsexually constructed lesbian-feminist has occurred along with the 1970s movement of lesbian feminism.'

What is it that motivates this patriarchal plot? If we really wish to know, we must turn to mythology and archetypal urges. The plot portrays transsexuals as attempting to 'live out two basic myths: single parenthood (male mothering) and the making of women according to man's image'. In line with the conspiratorial theory, the doctors who fashion women out of male bodies are therefore playing at God. After all, in Greek mythology was not Athena derived from the male God Zeus' head, and, in Judaeo-Christian theology, was not Eve created by a patriarchal God out of Adam's ribs? Men who beg to become women are experiencing a type of 'womb envy', and the doctors who help them are self-serving louts who are fulfilling an essential male need to 'create their ultimate man-made woman'.

Even more fascinating is how the lesbian-feminist conspiratorial theory accounts for women who want to become men. Once again, everything depends on 'male-defined' realities – on 'men's terms'. Transsexualism is not a 'human' problem. It is a male problem, even though a quarter of all sex-change operations are women-to-men requests. Women who elect male-to-female reconstruction are being used by men for self-serving purposes: to reinforce patriarchy. The doctors who perform female-to-male reconstruction are furthermore accused of 'castrating' women to 'tame' the 'potentially deviant' among them. The theory states:

> Ultimately, female to male transsexuals are the 'final solution' of women perpetrated by the transsexual empire. Male to constructed female transsexuals attempt to neutralize women by making the biological woman unnecessary – by invading both the feminine and the feminist fronts. Female-to-constructed-male transsexuals neutralize themselves as biological women and also their potentially deviant power. This is merely the most extreme form of neutralization that is taking place also with unnecessary hysterectomies and with the movement toward androgyny. With both, the biological woman is not only neutralized but neuterized.

Raymond insists on referring to transsexuals by their original sexual status. In her eyes, such persons remain 'he', even though revised birth certificates, anatomy and the individual's 'personhood' all attest to the newly acquired sexual status. Sandy Stone, Renee Richards and Christy Barskey – all male-to-female transsexuals – become targets for her attack. Sandy Stone is attacked because she took too high a profile, and therefore too masculine a position, in a controversial 1977 dispute at the women-only Olivia Records Company. In Raymond's view, 'if Stone's commitment to and identification with women were genuinely woman-centred, he would have removed himself from Olivia and assumed some responsibility for the divisiveness' – this despite the fact that Stone demonstrated pro-social behaviour by organizing a women's sports team, co-ordinating a conference on violence and women, giving musical performances at all-women's centres and helping to staff a woman's centre. Christy Barskey is attacked because she, too, took a 'dominant' position, and therefore a 'bad male' one. Dr Renee Richards is attacked because she, too, was accorded a prominent position by the media.

Clearly, all this represents a new version of 'sexual apartheid', Raymond's attitudes suggesting **androphobia** – irrational fear of men. Her bizarre form of the condition manifests through her hatred of the few men who have had their bodies transsexed to approximate to those of a woman. All male attributes are bad. Even men who relinquish their testicles and penises are unacceptable. She acknowledges that, in the isolated rare instances where males are acceptable, they are only acceptable because they have embodied female attributes.

The above demonstrates **reverse sexism** (see page 37), a hatred of men and a blatant insensitivity to the suffering of those many thousands who experience 'gender dysphoria'. Paradoxically, it sounds remarkably similar to the hackneyed sexist attitudes of the male chauvinists themselves. Truly constructive arguments might concentrate on attacking a medical establishment which, in the United States, now charges anything up to $20,000 (over £14,000) for a sex-change operation. After all, sex-change surgery is probably motivated more by greed than by any elaborate male conspiracy.

HERMAPHRODITISM

The term **hermaphroditism** is derived from the Greek messenger god, Hermes, and Aphrodite, the goddess of love. Genuine hermaphroditism refers to a 'biological accident' in which an individual is born with the gonadal tissue (testes and ovaries) of both sexes. Hermaphrodites were formerly featured in fairground 'freak shows', where voyeuristic spectators would pay to see the 'half-man, half-woman'. The hermaphrodite is reported to be a 'true bisexual, born with one active ovary and one active testis and the ability, under certain circumstances, to impregnate themselves' (Durden-Smith and de Simone, 1983). However, Diamond (1984) asserts the self-impregnation of hermaphrodites to be a myth: 'they could not impregnate themselves even if they wanted to'.

When a human embryo is two or three months old, its sex can only be determined by examining the cell chromosomes. In other words, a two- or three-month-old male or female foetus looks indistinguishable. Both have tissues that will form into either testes or ovaries; both have a genital tubercle which will grow into either a penis or a clitoris. The course of development is determined by the function of the primitive sex gland or gonad. In a genetically male embryo (XY), this gland will become testes, while, in a genetically female embryo (XX), it will develop into ovaries. Once this process of sexual differentiation has occurred, the testes or ovaries then produce hormones – biochemicals which complete the growth process of internal reproductive organs and external genitals.

When the embryonic sex glands fail to secrete adequate quantities of male hormones (androgens) in a genetically male foetus (XY), then the newborn will arrive with female genitals even though it is *genetically* male. Female embryos (XX) do not, on the other hand, need female hormones (for example, oestrogen) to develop female sex characteristics; what they require instead is an *absence* of male hormones. When the hormonal balance is disturbed during pregnancy, the foetus may not complete male or female development and be born with undifferentiated genitals. For example, a girl may be born with a very large clitoris, a boy with a very small penis. Furthermore, the individual may be born with ovaries yet have a penis or be born with testicles yet have a vagina. Such individuals will qualify as true hermaphrodites.

True hermaphroditism is, however, extremely rare. One 'true' hermaphrodite who came to the attention of doctors at Stellenbosch University Hospital in South Africa was an eighteen-year-old Malawian, termed Mr Blackwell, who had been brought up as a boy but possessed both a penis and a small vagina. When he reached puberty, he developed shapely female breasts, but since Mr Blackwell wished to continue life as a male (not surprisingly, given the low status of women among many Southern African cultures), doctors performed a mastectomy to remove the breasts and also surgically closed up his vagina (Durden-Smith and de Simone, 1983).

Money and Erhard (1972) believe that the gender label given to a hermaphroditic infant at birth is probably more significant than hormones in the development of its sexual identity. This is supported by the example of a pair of genetically female (XX) twins who were born with 'ambiguous' genitalia as a result of having been exposed to excessive amounts of male hormone (androgens) as they developed as foetuses *in utero*. They were both born with ovaries because they were exposed to the male hormone only after fundamental female development had occurred. Surgery was performed to reduce the 'enlarged clitorides' of both females. One of the twins had developed 'feminized' genitals and was brought up as a girl. The other child had its genitals surgically reconstructed to appear like a penis and was reared as a boy even though, genetically, 'he' was a 'she'. In the event, both children were reported to have developed appropriate gender identities. The one who remained a girl grew up as somewhat 'tomboyish', but was otherwise a 'feminine' personality. The 'boy' was fully accepted by other boys and came to be romantically interested in girls.

Pseudo-hermaphroditism occurs with much greater frequency, at a rate of 1 in 100 or 1 in 200 in the population (Diamond, 1984). Pseudo-hermaphroditism refers to physical characteristics in which the individual differs from others in terms of his or her genetic make-up, endocrine system and anatomy. A majority of pseudo-hermaphrodites have a genetic condition: 'for example, the individual has an XXY chromosome set and the appropriate appearance of a feminized male, or an XO chromosome set and the appearance of a male' (Diamond, 1984). In most cases, pseudo-hermaphrodites do not suffer overt distress and are unaware of being different.

The case of Mrs Went in England represents an instance of pseudo-hermaphroditism. Mrs Went was born as a genetic male (XY) with testicular feminization syndrome. This meant that her body was insensitive to the male hormone, testosterone. While she had external female characteristics, she also possessed testes imbedded in her abdomen. Mrs Went was treated as a girl as she grew up and was not affected by the male hormones produced by her testes, the nature of her problem only coming to light when, at the age of twenty-three, she sought medical advice because she had not developed pubic hair or begun to menstruate. Smith and de Simone observe that whereas, under English law, Mrs Went was classed as a woman, under Scottish law she would be legally classified as a man – even though she looked and felt like a woman.

The conditions of both Mr Blackwell and Mrs Went were biologically induced. Short of invoking a religious interpretation, they essentially had no control over what was happening to their bodies. It is significant, however, that environmental contingencies should have been paramount in the development of their gender identities – to the extent where they chose to remain the gender in which they had been raised.

The same phenomenon has been demonstrated not only in cases of 'such biological error', but also in unfortunate cases of 'human error', as illustrated by the following story. When a pair of seven-month-old boy twins was sent for 'routine circumcision' in the United States during the early 1960s, the procedure ended in a bloody and messy tragedy when one of the boys had the end of his penis accidentally cut off. A team of medical experts from the Johns Hopkins Medical School, in consultation with the boys' parents, judged that the best thing would be for the mutilated child to undergo a sex-change operation. This meant his being submitted to the surgical removal of the remainder of his penis and also his external genitals, including his testes. A vagina was additionally constructed. At the onset of puberty, endocrinologists placed the boy on a regime of female sex hormones to facilitate the development of breasts and pubic hair. Fortunately, the story has a relatively happy ending. The eventual follow-up by Johns Hopkins University concluded that the child had adjusted very well to the decision to change his gender from male to female; the boy had allegedly grown up as a well-adjusted girl.

This case was hailed by some feminists as support for the idea that genes did not play such an important role as is usually assumed in establishing the gender in an individual. In other words, the hope was that males and females were essentially equal, because environmental contingencies influenced gender identity more strongly than did genetics.

Others, including Masters and Johnson, were said to be pleased with the result of the girl's social and psychological adjustment since it reinforced a social learning (environmental) basis for gender identity. It seemed as though 'nurture' was indeed stronger than 'nature'. However, despite the enthusiasm with which environmental factors were welcomed, it should be stressed that, if the 'boy' had not been given artificial female hormones, it is most unlikely that he could have developed into a well-adjusted woman. In the light of this, both nature (genetics/biology) and nurture (environment) play equally important roles in the development of gender – in other words, they affect each other on a constant basis.

The interplay of genes (nature) and how an individual is raised (nurture) is graphically illustrated within an extended family from the Dominican Republic. According to Durden-Smith and de Simone (1983), about 130 years ago a woman was born in that country who passed on a rather extraordinary genetic trait. The condition now affects thirty-eight individuals in twenty-three families based in three separate villages. All thirty-eight arrived in the world as 'girls', and were treated as girls – until they became 'boys' at puberty. The authors describe the case of Prudencio, who was called at birth Prudencia:

At around the age of twelve, his 'clitoris' grew into a penis and two hidden testicles descended into a scrotum formed by the lips of his 'vagina'. He became a male. 'He changed his clothes', says his father Gerineldo, 'which the neighbors just had to get used to. And he fell in love with a girl almost immediately.' Today Prudentio is in his early thirties. Like his brother Matilda, now Mateo, he is a brawny, elaborately muscled man. He is sexually potent and lives with his wife in the United States. Like seventeen of the eighteen children studied by a group headed by Cornell University's Julianne Imperato-McGinley – all of whom, she says, were raised unambiguously as girls – Prudentio seems to have had no problem in adjusting to the male gender, male sexual orientation and male roles. [The authors have changed the names of the individuals described to protect their privacy.]

The Dominican individuals differ from Mrs Went in that their bodies responded to the presence of male hormones at puberty. Mrs Went's response was limited as she did not experience 'masculinization'. Durden-Smith and de Simone attempt an explanation as to why the Dominican 'men' did not suffer 'the psychological breakdown that conventional wisdoms predict they should'. They propose several theories. First, that the children were really raised as boys and therefore developed the appropriate gender identities after transforming from 'girls' to 'boys'; but this seems unlikely in the light of eye-witness accounts. Secondly, there is the possibility that the children were raised 'with a good deal of confusion about what gender they were'; but this is ruled out since they did not as adults display any disturbance in their sexual identity. Finally, the authors advance their pet theory, namely, that the *brain is masculinized before birth by the presence of male hormones as the foetus grows*.

The concept of a 'masculinized brain' is a controversial one which has been used, without encountering much support, to explain why certain people become transvestites, transsexuals or homosexuals. Dörner (1981) in particular has advocated the idea that gender disorders may be the result of a 'masculinization' or 'feminization' of the brain during embryogensis – the development of the foetus in its mother's uterus. Dörner would say that gender identity disturbances result from an improper balance in male or female hormones while the baby is growing inside the mother. A genetically female child would thus develop a 'masculinized brain' if it were exposed to too much male hormone *in utero* and *vice versa* for a genetically male child which was exposed to too much female hormone.

24 HOMOSEXUALITY IN MEN AND WOMEN

'If a man also lie with a man, as he lieth with a woman, both of them have committed an abomination; they shall surely be put to death, their blood shall be upon them' – Leviticus 20:13

'Thou shall not lie with mankind, as with womankind; it is abomination' – Leviticus 18:22

'For this cause God gave them up unto vile affections: for even their women did change the natural use into that which is against nature: And likewise also the men, leaving the natural use of the woman, burned in their lust one toward another; men with men working that which is unseemly, and receiving in themselves that recompense of their error which was meet' – Romans 1:26–7

'Know ye not that the unrighteous shall not inherit the kingdom of God? Be not deceived: neither fornicators, nor idolators, nor adulterers, nor effeminate, nor abusers of themselves with mankind . . . Now the body is not for fornication, but for the Lord; and the Lord for the body' – Corinthians 6:9 and 13

GENERAL DESCRIPTION AND CHARACTERISTICS

Homo refers to the Greek root meaning 'sameness'. **Homosexuality** therefore refers to sexual behaviour between individuals of the same sex. The term does not convey any information about an individual's occupation, hobbies, state of health, manner of dress, credit rating, religion, mannerisms, marital status and so on. Women as well as men can be homosexual; female homosexuals are more frequently known as **lesbians**, in commemoration of when the Greek woman poet Sappho wrote about sexual passion between women on Lesbos, the island on which she lived and worked.

While homosexuality was for a long time considered, at

least in the United States and United Kingdom, to be a pernicious 'mental disease', or disorder, a dysfunction to be combatted by the 'new priests', the medical doctors, it has since 1978 been dropped from the American Psychiatric Association's approved list of psychiatric 'neuroses'. Homosexuality is now seen as an 'erotic preference' for partners of the same sex. Infrequent or occasional sexual activity between partners of the same sex does not *per se* constitute homosexuality; for someone to be labelled homosexual, they must *prefer* sexual activity with same-sex partners – even as heterosexuals must prefer sexual activity with other-sex partners. It needs to be pointed out that occasional heterosexual activity does occur among primary homosexuals, and occasional homosexual activity occurs among many parents who may be described as primary heterosexuals. For the concept of 'bisexuality', see the discussion below, page 308. For instance, 'homosexual activity may occur for a number of reasons: as a result of restricted choice of sexual partners; as a means of satisfying curiosity; as a religious ritual in some cultures; and as foreplay for arousal purposes in group sex; as well as in other more episodic ways' (Tollison and Adams, 1979).

Homosexuals constitute an oppressed minority. Although there are *per capita* more homosexuals than there are Jews, **homophobia** (an irrational fear and hatred of homosexuals) is probably as prevalent, though not as long-standing, as **Judaeophobia** (anti-semitism or an irrational fear and hatred of Jews). This was made overwhelmingly clear by the Germans prior to and during the Second World War, when both Jews and homosexuals were earmarked for concentration and extermination camps. While Jews wore yellow badges, male and female homosexuals wore pink badges, but both were otherwise accorded an equally low status. As we shall see, homosexuals have been attacked by the Church, in prisons, at school, in law, by politicians, on the street, by the police and, to some extent, in the media. In addition, we shall see that while homosexuality is a deviation from the statistical norm, it is no more 'bizarre' in its manifestations than heterosexuality, and is certainly not unusual. We include the topic in this book to show how it is that stereotypical reactions to and myths about homosexuality are themselves often deplorably bizarre. (It should be stressed that it is as difficult for a non-homosexual fully to appreciate the social stigmatization encountered by homosexuals, as it is difficult for the non-Jew to appreciate anti-semitism, the European-blooded South African, the plight of the black South African, the American who has no Indian ancestry, the degradation of the 'American Indian', and so on.

INCIDENCE

Kinsey, Pomeroy and Martin (1948) conducted the most extensive survey of sexual behaviour ever undertaken among Americans. In that survey, conducted almost forty years ago, when attitudes towards homosexuality were more oppressive, the figures presented for homosexuality probably underestimate the incidence as it is known to be today. In 1948, more homosexuals were 'in the closet' and the 'gay liberation' movement was not even thought of. It is highly probable that many of those interviewed by the Kinsey team evaded admitting to having had any homosexual encounters.

Nevertheless the survey found 37 per cent of the male population reporting at least one homosexual experience which resulted in orgasm, at some time between puberty and late life. A quarter of those interviewed claimed more than one homosexual experience between the ages of sixteen and fifty-five. Almost one fifth (18 per cent) claimed they had had the same number of homosexual contacts as they had heterosexual relations between the ages of sixteen and fifty-five. Four per cent were exclusively homosexual – that is, they had never had heterosexual contact after reaching puberty.

Kinsey *et al.* (1953) also came up with estimates for homosexual relations between women. About 28 per cent of women were estimated to have experienced some form of sexual encounter with one or more women by the time they had reached forty-five. Furthermore, between 13 and 20 per cent had achieved orgasm during such an encounter. One confirmed statistical difference between male and female homosexuals is that, on average, women have fewer sexual partners than men (Kenyon, 1968; Loney, 1973).

Homosexuality among men and women is confined to no specific category: it traverses all age groups, income levels, races, education levels, religious and cultural divisions, occupations and nationalities. It occurs in densely populated cities as well as in less populated urban areas. Furthermore, despite the American TV preacher Jimmy Swaggart's view, it occurs among other animals, including seagulls and pigeons.

HOMOSEXUAL LIFESTYLES AND MYTHS

It would be naïve to ignore the differences and similarities between heterosexual and homosexual lifestyles. Homosexuals may live lifestyles as varied as those of their heterosexual counterparts. Like heterosexuals, many may live as couples while being open to other relationships. Some homosexual men are excessively promiscuous – over 1,000 'contacts' in a year is not unknown.

Coleman (1972) terms the 'stereotypical' homosexual as the 'blatant homosexual'. This classification applies to the contrivedly 'effeminate' homosexual, to the 'tough butch' lesbian, and to *machismo* 'leather boys' who wear leather jackets, studs, and sport other sado-masochistic paraphernalia. This grouping would include other *avant-garde* styles. For example, on Gay Pride Day in the summer of 1980 in San Francisco, I saw two homosexual men brandishing long leather whips and dressed in the full black regalia of Catholic nuns talking to a perplexed and genuine Russian Orthodox priest.

Coleman also speaks of the 'desperate' male homosexual who frequents public toilets or tea-rooms. Although he claims that most of these men are unable to maintain long-term homosexual relationships, I came across at least two cases, referred for treatment by a probation department, where the individuals participated in anonymous public 'tea-room' sex yet had lived with another man in a committed relationship for several years prior to arrest. Furthermore, a great many men who indulge in 'tea-room' sex (fellatio, mutual masturbation, often without even seeing the other man's face) are married and, contrary to popular opinion, have fulfilling sex lives with their wives.

Another difference of homosexual from heterosexual men is that heterosexuals do not need to hide their 'heterosexuality', which is perceived by others as 'normal', Coleman identifying, by contrast, the secret homosexual man as someone who feels he needs to hide his homosexuality from family, friends and co-workers. Such individuals will not associate with the homosexual community, and no one would suspect their erotic preferences for other men; they are highly adept at covering up their true sexual identities. This type of lifestyle is the one most likely to produce immense anxiety. Some members of this group are secretive in relation to their families, but do associate with other homosexual men. For instance, a doctor told me he was 'quite happy about being gay, but I could *never, ever, ever* tell my folks. They are old and have been through too much in their lives.' He maintained a 'front', sharing an apartment with a woman, and his parents assumed she was his girlfriend. In reality, he spent most of his time at his male lover's home. Betty Berzon's (1979) sensitive article, entitled 'Telling the Family You're Gay', elucidates these problems and their solutions.

Another grouping involves the **situational homosexual** who participates in homosexual behaviour even though homosexuality is not his or her erotic preference. This type of behaviour may typically occur in same-sex boarding schools, prisons, psychiatric hospitals, or situations where individuals are isolated from the other sex. The phenomenon has, for example, been observed among miners in South Africa who are separated from their wives for months on end, and in China, where pre-marital sex is frowned upon.

Heterosexual male prisoners may rape other prisoners as a result of frustration, fear or a battle for dominance. In the true-story film, *The Executioner's Song* (1978), the murderer Gary Gilmore was shown willingly choosing to be America's first death-penality victim in ten years. He elected for death, partly because he preferred being dead to spending the rest of his life behind bars, where he would anally rape and be raped for the rest of his life. Gilmore was a heterosexual who claimed that at one moment 'I was being held down, and the next I was doing the holding down'.

The Russian psychiatrists Stern and Stern (1981) describe situational homosexuality in Soviet concentration camps:

> . . . one rarely meets 'real' homosexuals in the camps, men who were homosexuals before their imprisonment. I knew only one at camp ITK-12. On the other hand, homosexuality 'acquired' under constraint, the result of pure and simple rape, of a sordid system of slavery amongst prisoners – this sort of homosexuality

Gender Identity and Sexual Preference

was the fate of hundreds of prisoners: out of 1,500 prisoners at least 300 were homosexual, though not all would admit it.

Situational homosexuality also exists among heterosexual women (see above, 'Women Rapists', pages 157–64) in prisons or psychiatric units, and has even been known to occur in a women's sorority on a university campus in the United States. In this sorority, the women would initiate a 'sister' by stripping her and manipulating a broom handle into her vagina (Tollison and Adams, 1979). The difference between men' and women's camps in the Soviet Union is reported by one of the Sterns:

As far as I know, there is no caste system in the women's camps. Lesbianism is common and gives rise to the formation of groups which do not have the closed character of their male counterparts. There are the *zavoditeli*, the 'ring-leaders', the equivalent of the kingpins and active homosexuals in the men's camps, and the *skobniki*, the 'scrapers', who masturbate their companions. Most often, they make a career of it and earn considerable sums in that way. But, far from being an object of contempt, like the pederasts, they do not have to submit to the homosexual slavery of men's camps.

Homosexuality among the women of Britain's Holloway Prison is rampant. For many inmates, it is **situational**, in as much as one ex-prisoner observes (Cassidy and Stewart-Park, 1977):

A lot of women are looking for a mock cock while they're there. They may be basically straight women, or maybe they haven't discovered that side of themselves. There's a lot of role playing, probably a bit less last time I was in than the time before, but there was a lot of women really pretending to be men ... It's not a chivalrous thing to be a butch lesbian in Holloway, it's a way of getting your ironing done for you and getting kept in fags. It's quite a mercenary business if you want to handle it that way. Even I could be fooled sometimes with busts strapped back and sanitary towels made to look like a cock.

The next grouping encompasses **homosexual prostitu-tion**, which invariably occurs among men and is financially motivated. Runaway boys and otherwise destitute men find that they can hustle a lucrative living in this way. They may be observed by the dozen, 'hanging out' on Santa Monica Boulevard in Hollywood, California. A few blocks north, their female counterparts parade, looking for hetero-sexual trade on Sunset Boulevard. The incidence of lesbian prostitution is either non-existent, negligible or very much an underground phenomenon.

Finally, Coleman (1972) alludes to the **adjusted homo-sexual**, someone who has 'come out of the closet', who accepts his or her homosexuality and is not ashamed in the face of opposition from family or society. Members of this group are often connected with gay support networks, participate in political/therapeutic organizations to coun-teract the oppression of homosexuals, and live in commit-ted, monogamous relationships with a partner. The following case history illustrates one such relationship.

Russell and Albert had been lovers for a few years. They lived apart for six months, when Russell left their home town to study medicine in California. Albert joined Russell as soon as he had lined up a job as a free-lance photogra-pher for model agencies in California.

Russell was reared as a Seventh Day Adventist in a very conservative part of the country. He was a 'preacher' during adolescence. An only child, his family were both wealthy and supportive as he grew up. Unfortunately, he contracted polio as a child, and for a while wore a leg brace, but soon overcame the initial shame at being an 'odd man out' at school. Despite not being a great sportsman, he became very popular among his peers, had girl friends and dated regularly during high school. Russell first discov-ered that he was 'gay rather than straight' when he went on vacation to Spain with Albert.

'We were both about nineteen then. I was aware of a special feeling between us, but I never thought it would come to this ... The moment I knew I was in love with him? Well, if you really want to know, it was in the waves. Very romantic at sunset. Albert suddenly held me in his arms and kissed me as we were standing knee-deep in the surf. I felt an enormous sense of love, as though it were just right. It never felt that way with my girl friends, it just never did. I felt as though I were at home, finally at long last.'

Russell and Albert's relationship was not without its problems. Russell initially felt extremely guilty as a result of both religious and family pressures. He attempted to deny these feelings and the romantic vacation with Albert, hoping to sweep it all 'under the rug and lay it down to experience'. And so he tried dating women again, even going to bed with two, 'but it wasn't right. My heart lay with Albert, even though I knew it was going to be tough. I was in college at the time, majoring in pre-med subjects, and so I tried to ignore my true feelings – I had to get into med school, and that's no easy task.' Albert became extremely jealous when he visited Russell at his college dormitory and discovered him in bed with a woman. Albert told Russell to forget their entire relationship at that stage. This was the point when Russell knew he could not do so.

The two took an apartment off campus, and have lived together for the remainder of Russell's college career, Albert deciding to follow Russell to California when he got into medical school. Both believe that their relationship will last, are monogamous, and maintain that they are very much in love with each other. Neither 'looks' like the stereotypical homosexual, and the bigot who 'can always tell such things' would not be able to make a diagnosis by the way these men dress, speak or behave.

Albert's family initially totally rejected Russell and the

entire situation. They are Jewish and, while they at one time refused to allow Russell home for religious celebrations, have grown more tolerant of their son's choice. Russell says that his family is not pleased, but they never did make him an outcast, like so many others.

In *We're Here: Conversations with Lesbian Women*, Cassidy and Stewart-Park (1977) interviewed eleven lesbians, among them Pat Arrowsmith, who works for Amnesty International in London. Pat Arrowsmith is 'accomplished'; she studied at Ohio University, Liverpool University and Cambridge University. She was suspended from Cheltenham Ladies' College, and is known as an active member of the pacifist movement. Her activities caused her to spend time in prison between 1958 and 1974. On one occasion, she was force-fed after declaring a hunger strike for political reasons. She was placed in solitary confinement when she tried to form a prisoners' union. Part of the interview proceeds as follows:

Q. When were you first aware that you were a lesbian?

A. I went to a girls' boarding school and I was aware of being homosexual. I was very much in love with another woman, another girl, I mean. It never came to anything, I was very worried, you know. I hoped 'this is a phase that I will get out of'. I remember at Cheltenham, one of my schools, we had these sex talks telling you all about the facts of life, so they got out all these nice slides with all kinds of cocks and things on them. It was all quite interesting and we were invited at the end to ask any questions we wanted confidentially, of the person who was lecturing. We could be assured of a good hearing, we weren't to be afraid to ask anything, and I was very involved with my best friend. We weren't having an affair or anything, she sensed this and wasn't too happy about it, and I felt very guilty about this. It seemed to me quite unacceptable. Anyway, I was about seventeen or eighteen and I should have been getting interested in boys by then and this was a contemporary of mine, we were both in the same class.

Pat Arrowsmith goes on to describe the difficulties she experienced in forming her lesbian identity. She experienced unrequited love with a 'straight' woman, but eventually met Wendy, with whom she had lived for fourteen years. She considers her years with Wendy to be 'like any marriage'.

Well, I'd always seen it as something that would continue. We put our lives together in the way that people do when they marry, we never got down and swore fidelity to each other – that doesn't mean anything anyway. We regard our possessions in common, we do things together, we share a place, we both, I think, viewed this as something that would go on. That's all a marriage really does mean. Maybe it won't. But, I mean that anything can happen, as in any marriage . . . In my marriage, I've not stayed wholly faithful to Wendy or she to me – I think that one of the problems that can arise is that if you think one person is going to get hurt – or if you don't want it to end – or if you're afraid of jealousy, and you conceal what's going on – it removes an element of trust from your relationship inevitably – because you fall into the trap of dishonesty . . . I mean I only have one problem which most homosexuals have, and that's my parents, and that's mainly because they are so very old and they're invalids and very religious and my father's a clergyman . . .

WHAT KIND OF SEX DO HOMOSEXUALS HAVE?

Heterosexuals are often curious to know about 'how *they* do it'. Tollison and Adams (1979) put it succinctly when they state, 'There is no homosexual act that cannot be performed by a heterosexual couple. Any emergency room physician knows the frequency with which homosexuals and heterosexuals have foreign objects removed from their bowels which have somehow become lodged there.' The only difference is that heterosexuals can perform penis–vagina coitus. Male homosexuals as well as heterosexuals are known to indulge in anal intercourse, by using lubricants and through practice at relaxing the anal sphincter – 'the anus can readily admit an erect penis and even larger objects with little or no discomfort'.

Some heterosexual women who have experienced one or more homosexual encounters have claimed that their female sex partners were 'technically' more 'proficient' during intercourse than they had known male sex partners to be. A heterosexual women who had a sexual experience to the point of orgasm with a lesbian friend told me it was 'by far better with her than with any man . . . She just seemed to know what to do, how to touch me. And, you know, she was more gentle, less rushed. Even though I felt weird when she went down on me, after a while I let myself go, and even went down a little on her. All I can say is that it felt weird. I was a little stoned and we had some wine. She didn't seem to want to possess me like a man usually does, and took her time, and reassured me . . . If only most men were that good.' However, this particular woman claimed that she did not feel so 'emotionally satisfied' by lesbian experience. She loved the feeling of 'a man inside of me', which made her feel 'full, complete, better about myself, and I would radiate afterwards from inside'.

BISEXUALITY

One frequently asked question is, 'Can anyone really be bisexual?' The question is less easily answered than might be assumed. Bisexuality refers, in theory, to people who have both heterosexual and homosexual experiences. It is currently an 'intellectual/political' fad in some circles for people to engage in so-called 'AC-DC' behaviour (the term 'AC-DC' deriving from electricity in which current flow is described as being 'alternating' or 'direct', even though voltage, amperage and wattage are the same in both instances).

An active trade unionist told me she could no longer support a 'uni-directed sexual orientation'. 'It's no longer applicable,' she stated, 'because it is an outmoded capitalistic trait.' She explained her position: 'If you choose to be either straight or gay, you are limiting yourself. Sexuality has been ruled for too long by religious and patriarchal dogma, which dictates that you must have sex with this colour, religion or class and with that particular sex only. It is too limiting because it embraces rigid social structures, and how can I profess to challenge the current political order unless I practise what I preach?' When I asked her to think hypothetically about which sex she would choose 'if she had to', she finally said, 'Men. Yes, I would have to say men . . .'

Some claim that bisexuals are really homosexuals hiding behind a cloak of bisexuality. Tollison, Adams and Tollison (1979) shed some light on the issue via a penetrating experiment. Instead of simply asking people what their sexual preferences were, they obtained *actual sexual arousal patterns* by attaching experimental subjects to electrical equipment designed to measure levels of penile erection. The apparatus consisted of a 'penile plethysmograph' and a 'strain gauge' which was attached to each subject's penis. The subject is exposed to sexually explicit materials and levels of erection can be measured. The level of erection is expressed in percentages of 0 to 100. Subjects in such experiments are generally seated in the privacy of a 'sex booth', and communicate with the experimenter by way of intercom.

Thirty subjects participated in the experiment. They were divided into three groups consisting of, respectively, ten self-professed heterosexuals, ten homosexuals and ten bisexuals. All subjects were shown the following: (a) an explicit homosexual film depicting foreplay and oral-genital sex between two men; (b) an explicit heterosexual film depicting a man and a woman embracing and having sexual intercourse; (c) slides of nude male and female models; and (d) films of neutral stimuli composed of landscapes. Subjects were exposed to the neutral films while waiting for their erections to subside.

Experimental results revealed that the homosexuals and bisexuals both obtained high erection levels from the homosexual films and slides of nude men, whereas the heterosexuals were not aroused when they saw films and slides of a homosexual encounter or slides of nude men. In addition, subjects were asked to estimate their levels of erection. The homosexuals and heterosexuals were more accurate than bisexuals at predicting the direction of their erectile responses. In other words, if a heterosexual said he would be aroused by films and slides of sexual intercourse between a man and a woman or a slide of a nude woman, he was invariably correct. The same applied to homosexuals, who obtained erections from homosexual material but not from heterosexual material.

The bisexuals, on the other hand, claimed that they would be equally aroused by homosexual and heterosexual sexually explicit materials. They were wrong. *The pattern of sexual arousal among the 'bisexuals' was almost identical to that of the homosexuals.* Those subjects who claimed to be truly bisexual were not, in fact, physiologically aroused by heterosexual stimuli.

While these 'bisexuals' achieved no arousal from heterosexual films or slides, this does not deny that they have sex with both women and men. However, on the basis of this experiment, bisexual men appear to have an innate sexual preference for men rather than for women. The results of the experiment could indicate that bisexuality is something of a myth. It provides the type of experimental evidence which sceptics of bisexuality are looking out for. The fact that bisexuals are wrong when they claim they will be aroused by the nude women and scenes of male-female coitus may mean that they are in reality homosexuals who are unhappy with or resisting their sexual orientation.

A bisexual stance places the homosexual in a safer position, both socially and psychologically. He does not need to think of himself as 'abnormal' and avoids experiencing low self-esteem as a result of being labelled 'gay'. Instead, he may cultivate sexual experience with women and then state, 'I'm bisexual.'

It needs to be emphasized, however, that this experiment was based on a very small sample of subjects. If firm conclusions are to be drawn, the research needs to be replicated, using a larger number of subjects. It is also possible to conduct this kind of research with females by using a tampon-like device called a 'photo-plethysmograph', which measures the flow of blood to the vagina. The more blood, presumably, the more sexually aroused the woman (see Appendix, page 423).

THEORIES OF HOMOSEXUALITY: AN EXERCISE IN OPPRESSION

Partly as a result of lobbying by 'gay activists', homosexuality is no longer considered a disorder by the American Psychiatric Association. However, an individual is said to be 'ego-dystonic' about his or her sexual identity. This means that he or she has not adjusted to a particular orientation. In the light of this, the 'causes' for homosexuality should only be researched if homosexuality is proved to be an 'abnormal behaviour' (Davison, 1976). On the other hand, homosexuality is a 'deviation' from the 'statistical norm'. Like any minority, homosexuals have been scrutinized microscopically – without being fully understood. No one really knows why certain people become homosexual, even though many theorists *think* they can explain it.

Theories range from the sublime to the ridiculous, and include biochemical hypotheses, genetic predispositions and interuterine endocrinological distortions; psycho-analytical perversions, Oedipal eruptions, phallic fixations and 'autoerotic narcissistic' complications. Learning theory is invoked, smothering mothers are blamed and dictatorial fathers are denounced.

Most theories on the aetiology or causes of homosexuality imply that the behaviour is abnormal and therefore unde-sirable. The theories are, however, concerned with the behaviour of at least 12 million Americans, or 5 per cent of the US population (an underestimation of the true figures) who are or will become exclusively homosexual. Many of them not only openly state that they are 'gay', but are proud of it.

BIOLOGICAL FACTORS

Genetic explanations for homosexuality have been advanced, but studies of identical and fraternal twins have largely discounted them as artifactual. In other words, there is no evidence that homosexuality is 'inherited' any more than that it is a contagious disease.

Wakeling (1979) reviewed the literature on endocrinolog-ical differences between homosexual and heterosexual men. Some studies, using limited numbers of subjects, show higher levels of plasma oestradiol in homosexuals; others reveal no differences. Urine metabolites, androsterone and etiocholanolone have been shown to differ between homo-sexuals and heterosexuals in some cases. On the other hand, testosterone (male hormonal) levels do not differ between homosexuals and heterosexuals.

Female homosexuality has similarly been attributed to a so-called 'masculinized brain'. Durden-Smith and de

Simone (1983) interviewed Günter Dörner, who has been researching the biological basis for homosexuality for years. He explained:

Lesbians and female-to-male transsexuals seem to have abnormal levels, at least in part, of testosterone and estradiol (hormones). And if we give them estrogen, their lutenizing-hormone response is lower than that of heterosexual women, suggesting that their brains have been masculinized in some way. The cognitive patterns (the way they think) of their brain, too, may be somewhere intermediate between heterosexual men and heterosexual women. And their body build on the basis of certain measurements, may be closer to that of a man's. It is also possible that they age rather faster than normal women do – rather like men.

It has long been known that 'the mind can affect bodily functions'. For instance, stress can alter the normal level of certain hormones. Dörner misses the point that millions of homosexuals *and* heterosexuals are born with 'normal' hormonal levels. Furthermore, *both* heterosexuals and homosexuals may have 'abnormal' hormonal levels in later life. In other words, he neglects to consider the heterosexuals who have 'abnormal' hormonal levels yet do not become homosexual. The fact that Dörner's work is not substantiated scientifically is not the real issue here.

Most incredible is the fact that the search actually continues for a hormonal basis to explain homosexuality. It seems markedly similar to bio-racial theory, and not too different from the one the Nazis 'formulated' to explain the 'inferiority' of Jews, gipsies, blacks and other races. As neuro-scientists identify more and more neutro-transmitters, we know increasingly less about the function of the brain. Thus 'scientific' discussion of 'masculinized brains' in lesbians cannot be taken seriously. How would Dörner explain the non-stereotypical very 'feminine' lesbian anyway? Does he assume that all lesbians are 'butch'? Would he advocate a brain operation to 'cure' lesbians?

Based on his research at Humboldt University in East Germany, the answer to these questions would probably be yes. Durden-Smith and de Simone (1983) write:

> He quotes from a study in which male homosexuals obsessively attracted to children were 'cured' by an operation in their brain's *female* centre. And he himself performed a series of experiments that show, he firmly believes, that both male and female homosexuality are caused by the prenatal effect on the brain of either too little or too much of the male sex hormone – testosterone.

In fairness to Dörner, he does acknowledge that his work is controversial.

PSYCHOANALYTIC THEORY

Psychoanalytic approaches endorse a disease model. Tollison and Adams (1979) reviewed the literature from a psychoanalytic perspective, in which a majority of interpretations is focused on male homosexuals. In psychoanalytic or Freudian theory, the infant is seen as 'polymorphously perverse' – sexually directed to a variety of objects. Normal sexual development should end with the individual being attracted to an adult of the opposite sex. Homosexuals are not attracted to adults of the opposite sex. They are said to be fixated at an infantile stage of psychosexual development.

Homosexuals are viewed as being narcissistically stuck on their own genitalia. Therefore, they unconsciously choose a love object very much like themselves. Freud (1930) explained:

> In all cases we have examined we have established the fact that the future inverts, in the earliest years of their childhood, pass through a phase of very intense but short-lived fixation to a woman (usually their mother), and that, after leaving this behind,

they identify themselves with a woman and take themselves as their sexual objects. That is to say, they proceed from a narcissistic basis, and look for a young man who resembles themselves and whom they may love as their mother loved them.

In addition, male homosexuals are supposed to be highly preoccupied with and possessive of their penises. Discovery that girls do not have one simply confirms that the penis was castrated. If girls had their penises cut off, then the homosexual ensures that his organ is going to be protected by avoiding girls and women. Also, women are unconsciously viewed as lesser beings because of the loss of their penis.

In terms of the Oedipus complex, the homosexual is supposed to have experienced a 'castration anxiety' connected with incestuous feelings towards his mother, whose vagina he fears. These feelings are later transferred to other women. This castration anxiety is supposed to be connected with the fear that, because he unconsciously wanted to castrate his father, his father would mount a counter-offensive to castrate him first. The best defence is, therefore, to sexually avoid all women. In that way, he can keep his penis (Fenischel, 1945).

Psychoanalytic theories do not stop here. They also propose that the male homosexual unconsciously 'regresses' to an early psychosexual stage of development. For instance, all children are alleged to pass through the 'anal stage' of psychosexual development. Normally, they would leave this stage behind them as they mature. A homosexual is viewed as being immature, as being 'fixated' on his anal phase. Unable to resolve his Oedipus complex – his unconscious desire to have intercourse with his mother – the homosexual identifies with the mother. In this identification, he steps into her role, symbolically equating his anus with her vagina. In this event, he would become a 'passive' homosexual.

Male homosexuality has also been attributed to dominant 'seductive' mothers and to soft, passive, symbolically castrated fathers. The mother, being jealous of her son's possible associations with other women, creates in him an anxiety about sex with girls.

In a study by Wolff (1971), a large group of lesbians was compared with a large group of heterosexual women, both groups coming from similar social backgrounds. The lesbian experience was different in that their mothers were (allegedly) distant and uncaring; their fathers either unavailable or uncaring. The view is that the girl becomes lesbian because she is constantly seeking the love of her mother in other women. The lesbian is attempting to replace her mother's love by substituting other women. Since her father was unpleasant, she has never liked or trusted men.

SOCIAL LEARNING THEORY

Under this heading both homosexuality and heterosexuality are viewed as acquired or learned behaviours. To a large extent, learning involves the association of rewards (reinforcers) and certain behaviours, thoughts and images. Masturbation or romantic sexual encounters resulting in orgasm are rewarding. Early romantic homosexual encounters may be experienced as positive and as rewarding, making the individual more likely to repeat them both in masturbatory fantasy and/or in reality. Repetition strengthens the association. Coupled with a distaste for heterosexual activity, perhaps as a result of an unpleasant heterosexual encounter, the repetition in masturbatory fantasy of homosexual acts increases the likelihood that the individual will develop a preference for homosexuality. The role of unpleasant heterosexual experiences, or experiences which lead to a 'distrust' of the other sex, should be stressed. Once again, like anything else, social learning theory cannot fully account for the acquisition of a homosexual orientation.

THE CONTROVERSY OVER SEXUAL REORIENTATION THERAPY FOR HOMOSEXUALS

Sexual reorientation therapy is controversial on ethical grounds, and also because its effectiveness has not been established and because it may involve the administration of punishment in the form of electric shock, nausea-producing drugs or noxious odours. The following, from Bancroft (1974), exemplifies the types of treatment strategy employed in trying to get homosexual men to switch their sexual preference:

The deviant stimulus (e.g. slides of the deviant object) is presented to the subject and immediately followed by an unpleasant electric shock. This procedure is repeated many times. This is best exemplified in one of the methods of treatment of homosexuality reported by Feldman and MacCulloch. The patient watched a screen and at intervals a slide of an attractive male was displayed. In the last half second of the two-second period the subject received a shock. The slide and shock were terminated simultaneously. Approximately 24 such trials were involved in each session which lasted about 20 minutes.

Apomorphine to induce vomiting has also been used (McConaghy, 1970):

For the first treatment 1.5 mg of apomorphine were administered by sub-cutaneous injection, and after five minutes a slide of a nude or semi-nude male was projected on the wall of the room within the patient's vision. If the nausea produced was not sufficient, the dose was increased with subsequent injections of up to 6 mg. Severe nausea lasting about ten minutes without vomiting was considered a satisfactory response.

Other strategies involve 'covert sensitization', in which the patient is required to imagine unpleasant consequences following a homosexual encounter. He is taken on a guided fantasy in which extremely unpleasant events occur as a result of such an encounter. He might, for example, be required to imagine that he has to drink a soup composed of faeces, urine and vomit after having sex with a man. He may also be diagnosed as being afraid of women. In such cases, he will be given 'systematic desensitization' in which he imagines progressively 'threatening' heterosexual scenes while in a relaxed state. The relaxation is said to be 'incompatible' with his 'heterosexual anxiety'.

These treatments are conducted under the rubric of 'behaviour therapy', which does not mean that all behaviour therapists will advocate their use. Bancroft (1974), a 'pioneer' in the field, claims that he will employ such techniques for 'impeccable reasons' and only when the patient is convincing about his desire to 'rid himself' of homosexuality.

There is no question but that electric shocks and other aversive procedures will diminish practically any sexual arousal pattern. These procedures do not, however, necessarily encourage arousal in a heterosexual direction. Such **conditioning techniques** tend to be reminiscent of Anthony Burgess's novel, *A Clockwork Orange* (later a widely seen film), where the protagonist was conditioned out of his criminality, emerging as a nonentity, a depersonalized, broken man. But homosexuals are no longer people who are engaging in criminal behaviour. Among the questions raised by aversion treatments are: should we only treat illegal sexual behaviour, like child molestation and rape? Should we deny treatment to the homosexual who has unsuccessfully attempted therapy with a specialized 'gay therapist' designed to help him adjust to his homosexuality? Should we reserve such treatment for severe cases of childhood autism and rapists? And then, if we refuse available sexual reorientation treatment to any individual, are we not imposing our own values of 'right and wrong' on the individual concerned? Are we not discriminating against the patient's free will? The answers reside outside the scope of the present book, and are probably best answered, not by civil liberty groups, jurists and moralists, but ultimately by the patients themselves.

PROGRESS IN HOMOSEXUAL RIGHTS

Homosexuality is far more accepted today than it was in the days of Oscar Wilde. But homosexuals still face prejudice in the media, in prison, in religion, in law and in employment. For instance, the media will refer to 'homosexual murder' but never speak of a heterosexual murder. Formal religion does not sanction homosexuality. Homosexuals are not equal before the law – marriage between homosexuals is not recognized, even on a civil basis. This means that they cannot have foreign 'spouses' naturalized under immigration law. Over and above freedom from oppression, homosexuals seek equality with heterosexuals. Galloway (1983) presents the Charter for Gay Rights (Campaign for Homosexual Equality):

Charter for Gay Rights
Homosexual Equality demands the acknowledgement that homosexuality is a valid form of sexual expression, that lesbians and gay men have the right to lifestyles free from social and legal discrimination and that gay people make a contribution to society equal to that of heterosexuals.

This requires:

A. The elimination of sexism in all its forms;
B. The positive representation in education and the media of homosexuality and the lives of gay people;

C. The promotion of gay pride and of mutual support within the gay movement.

We demand:

1. The right to basic human freedoms of opinion of expression; of assembly; of movement; and of residence.
2. General equality in criminal law for gay people and heterosexuals, and equal application of the law.
3. That consensual sexual acts should not be the concern of criminal law. [This probably covers 'consenting' sexual intercourse with children, and may include 'men–boy' love].
4. The right to have, raise and care for children.
5. The securing of freedoms for lesbians and gay men from all forms of violence and intimidation; at work; at home; and on the streets.
6. The freedom from interference in our private lives.
7. The end of discriminatory harassment, questioning, arrest, detention or deportation of gay people.
8. The equal right of employment and the protection of that employment.
9. The equal access to all public services.
10. That gay people should receive equal treatment with heterosexuals in all respects of the civil law.

Despite the protestations of such religious fundamentalists as the Revs Jerry Fallwell and Swaggart in America, who, among other things, are – in Fallwell's own words – apt to 'tease' homosexuals, it should be stressed that some homosexuals, both male and female, have been 'married' in a religious context. These marriages are not generally rcognized in law; but they serve to 'dignify' homosexual love. Gerber (1982) described an instancé where two homosexual lovers, Jack McConnel and Michael Baker, wanted a 'legal' marriage. They arranged for Jack to change his name to Pat Lyn McConnel:

Michael went alone (permitted in Minnesota) to the licence bureau and obtained a marriage licence for Jack and 'Pat' to be married. On September 3, 1971, in a friend's apartment, a methodist minister solemnized their marriage as they said to each other:

'Touch me,' said McConnel, in his vows to his 29-year-old lover. 'I am your lover, brother, sister and friend.'

Said Baker: 'Hold me. I hold your spirit, emotion, reason and flesh.'

McConnel: 'Keep me. I hold you in joy, health, sickness, poverty, and wealth.'

Baker: 'I, Michael, take you, Jack.'

McConnel: 'I, Jack, take you, Michael.'

Baker: 'To be my wedded spouse.'

McConnel: 'To be my wedded spouse.'

Baker: 'To touch.'

McConnel: 'To hold.'

Baker: 'To keep.'

McConnel: 'Today.'

Baker: 'Tomorrow.'

McConnel: 'And yesterdays till death.'

Baker: 'As a sign of my love, with this ring, I marry you,' the lovers repeated to each other.

This may be the only same-sex couple to have accomplished a legal marriage in the United States. (SOURCE: *The Gay Crusaders*, by Kay Torbin and Randy Wicker.)

Religious acceptance of homosexuality manifests itself in several ways. For instance, there is a Roman Catholic gay organization which calls itself 'Dignity' and a gay synagogue in New York. Liberal gay Jews will recite the morning blessing in modified form: instead of saying, 'Blessed art Thou, Lord our God, who has made me a man [for men]', they recite the blessing for women, 'Blessed art Thou, Lord our God, who has made me according to Thy Will.' Further, the Union of American Hebrew Congregations, American Jewish Students Networks, Anti-Defamation League and other groups have adopted resolutions in support of gay rights (Brick, 1979).

Gay rights have been backed not only by the European Parliament, but *even* by the United States Supreme Court (*The Times*, 2 April 1985). The Supreme Court justices ruled that Texas A & M University had no right to ban a homosexual student group from visiting the university campus. The university was described as violating the human rights of homosexuals by refusing to recognize homosexuality officially. This was ruled as clearly unconstitutional. Reasons given by the university were that the Gay Student Service 'could lead to increased overt homosexual activity and resulting physical, psychological and disease ramifications'. The significant point here is that the highest court in the land supported homosexual rights at this point in time. It is highly unlikely that it would have upheld the gay activists' legal suit only a few years earlier. It is even less likely that a Gay Student Service would have had the courage at an earlier stage to organize in such a conservative state as Texas.

There is no question but that conditions have improved in most Western countries. For example, many large discotheques are exclusively gay or have a special 'gay night' once a week – an unthinkable concept not so long ago. Gay clubs are accepted in much the same way as white South Africans accept black soul music. Unlike the Soviet Union or Romania, where homosexuals regularly land in psychiatric hospitals to be treated for 'sluggish schizophrenia', or simply in prison camps, it is several years since homosexuality has been illegal in most European countries (except Ireland, Cyprus, and Spain). In post-revolutionary Iran, by contrast, homosexuals are routinely executed. Moreover, the method of execution changed when Iran began its long-drawn-out war with Iraq, homosexuals and other criminals being sentenced to die by having the blood drained out of their bodies. Ironically, the homosexual blood was acceptable for transfusion into the bodies of Islamic martyrs injured at the front.

Finally, the prominence of homosexuals in history needs to be noted. Homosexuality has *always* existed and was *not always* a criminal offence, although homosexuals, like witches and sorcerers, were at times mutilated or castrated, burned and tortured during the middle ages. 'Buggery' was made a criminal offence punishable by death in 1533 in England, even though 'other' homosexual acts remained legal. Boy prostitutes existed in Athens and Rome; the *pueri* were the Roman equivalents of 'renters' in Oscar Wilde's London (see 'Child Prostitution', pages 239–44). Attacks on homosexuality did surface occasionally. Male brothels in ancient Rome were discernible by the huge phalluses outside, a state of affairs which ended in A.D. 533 when the Roman Emperor Justinian legislated that homosexuals should suffer the death penalty.

Justinian blamed Jews, homosexuals and astrologers for the iniquity of the times and confiscated their property to increase his own wealth. Charlemagne (742–814) attacked homosexuality within the Church but made no change to existing laws. Edward II (1284–1327) was actively homosexual and made to suffer in a hideously appropriate way.

Among 'famous homosexuals' listed in Haeberle's *Sex Atlas* (1983) are the following:

Montezuma II (1480–1520): Aztec emperor
Henry III (1551–89): French king
James I (1566–1625): English king
Alexander von Humboldt (1769–1859): German naturalist and explorer
Hans Christian Andersen (1805–75): Danish writer
Nikolai Gogol (1809–52): Russian author
Walt Whitman (1819–92): American poet
Horatio Alger (1834–99): American clergyman and novelist
Camille Saint-Saëns (1835–1921): French composer
Peter Ilich Tchaikovsky (1840–93): Russian composer
Hector Macdonald (1835–1903): British general
Arthur Rimbaud (1854–91): French poet

André Gide (1869–1951): French writer
Marcel Proust (1871–1922): French novelist
W. Somerset Maugham (1874–1965): English writer
Gertrude Stein (1874–1946): American writer
John Maynard Keynes (1883–1946): English economist
Harold Nicolson (1886–1961): English diplomat
Federico García Lorca (1898–1936): Spanish poet
W. H. Auden (1907–73): Anglo-American poet

HOMOPHOBIA: THE FEAR AND HATRED OF HOMOSEXUALS

Homophobia refers to an intense fear and hatred of homosexuality. In 1969, a Harris opinion poll indicated that 63 per cent of Americans viewed homosexuality as harmful. Homosexuals have been discharged from the military, fired from their jobs, exposed and blackmailed on account of their sexual preferences. In the American military, both lesbians and gay men have been ousted or demoted from their ranks. Indeed, several servicemen filed lawsuits against the military during the 1970s and 1980s on the grounds of homophobia or sex-discrimination.

Homophobia, in the form of legal repression, exists not only in Islam, the Soviet bloc and many Third World countries, but is, as at 1983, still unlawful in the following American states: Montana; Nevada; Arizona; Utah; Kansas; Oklahoma; Louisiana; Arkansas; Missouri; Minnesota; Mississippi; Alabama; Georgia; Florida; North Carolina; South Carolina; Virginia; and Wisconsin (Kidron and Segal, 1984).

Homophobic practice is implied in England, where the heterosexual age of consent is sixteen, but remains twenty-one for consenting male homosexuals – as long as they are not in the army. Derogatory expressions like 'queer', 'faggot', 'poofta', 'queen', 'pansy', and 'homo' are analogous to racist insults like 'nigger', 'kyke', and 'honky'.

Homophobia in California was highlighted by the sad saga of State Senator John Briggs and Dan White. Briggs initiated Proposition 6, designed to oust all homosexual teachers, by referendum, from their jobs in the public school system. Fortunately, the people of that state voted against the measure; homosexual teachers were not prevented from teaching. One of Briggs's reasons for ejecting homosexual teachers was that he believed male homosexuals would molest boy students. He was tongue-tied when, in a television debate, Harvey Milk, a supervisor for San Francisco City Hall, informed him that a majority of child molesters were heterosexual men who sexually molested little girls. The following is an extract of an interview with Briggs in the *Los Angeles Times* (6 October 1978):

Interviewer: What has led to the ultimate destruction of civilization?

Briggs: What has? Oh, homosexuality (and) a permissive attitude.

Interviewer: You say that the free world is where this problem is, and in the Communist world they don't have this . . .

Briggs: Yes, because the government there believes that it is not healthy for the nation. But in this country, these people are protected by the Supreme Court . . .

Harvey Milk, as we said, was a supervisor on the San Francisco City Council. So was Dan White. White represented a conservative neighbourhood, and detested homosexuals and their 'carrying on'. Milk was a proud homosexual who told all gays to 'come out', to demand equality, to tell their parents, to lift the yoke of oppression off their backs. White hated the way homosexuals dressed, the way they behaved, the way they had 'taken over', 'demoralized' society. In short, he *hated* them as human beings and wanted to see something done about the 'homosexual problem'. Furthermore, *his* city had become a sort of Mecca for homosexuals, especially the Castro district.

White couldn't stand the liberal members on the City Council. He threw up his hands and, thoroughly disgusted and indignant, resigned. A few days later, he wanted his job back. Protocol required that the mayor put White's request to the board, which would vote on it. Everyone on the board had to approve if White was to get his job back.

The request was put before the board. Harvey Milk rejected it. Dan White, enraged, strutted along to San Francisco City Hall, which he entered through a window. He also took with him a handgun with *extra* ammunition. The ammunition found its way into the heads of both the mayor and Harvey Milk. Dan White was nevertheless not found guilty of first-degree murder. His defence attorneys pleaded the so-called 'twinkie defence', a defence in which it was asserted that, because White had eaten 'junk food' containing sugar, he was bound to lose his temper. White made an impassioned plea in court and the jury found him guilty of manslaughter. Homophobic White was released in 1984 after serving about five years in the state prison. A year later he killed himself.

THE LEGAL OPPRESSION OF HOMOSEXUALITY

Homosexuality is still not tolerated in most parts of the world. Homosexual acts between men are still punished in most Islamic countries. The Iranian régime, for instance, held public executions of homosexuals soon after the Ayatollah Khomeini came to power. In the Soviet Union, homosexuality is illegal and punishable by three to five years in a 'work camp'. Lesbianism, unlike male homosexuality, is not even acknowledged – the *Soviet Medical Encyclopaedia* simply states where the island of Lesbos is located. Homosexuality between men also remains a crime in

Mexico, Ireland, Cyprus, New Zealand and, technically, in some states of the United States.

In most European societies, both Eastern and Western, homosexuality has long since been decriminalized. The French government even moved to reduce the legal age of consent to fifteen years for both heterosexuals and homosexuals. The legal age of consent for male homosexuals is fifteen in Sweden, Denmark and Turkey; sixteen in Holland, Switzerland, Italy, Norway and Portugal; seventeen in Greece; eighteen in Austria, Belgium, Luxemburg, West Germany and Finland. The European Parliament even proposed that discrimination against homosexuals be removed from the workplace. While homosexuality is not considered a criminal activity in England, the government has been decidedly cautious about legitimizing it fully.

Like the Russians, the British do not acknowledge lesbianism. The House of Lords threw out a 1921 Bill aimed at making lesbianism a criminal activity. It considered that the idea of lesbianism would corrupt women who had never thought about it. Lesbianism was not seen as a serious moral problem because lesbians posed no threat to the all-male legislators. This raises the question of whether lesbians ever get into trouble with the law. The answer is: very infrequently. Less than ten such prosecutions occur in England annually.

One such case involved a teacher, Patricia Marshall, and a fifteen-year-old schoolgirl, who developed a 'crush' on each other. The girl's father at first welcomed the relationship, but after becoming suspicious of their closeness, 'bored a hole through his bedroom floor into his daughter's room below. Through it he saw them performing lesbian acts' (Crane 1982). The teacher and her student 'eloped' after being instructed never to see each other again. Caught soon after, Marshall was charged with abduction and 'indecent assault on a girl under 16', and sentenced to two years' probation because the judge felt she was going through an 'awkward period' in her life. Such 'light sentencing' would not have occurred had the teacher been a man.

Legal sanctions against male homosexuality are as enshrined and as ancient as anti-semitism. A fourteenth-century English law stated that 'those who have connection with Jews or Jewesses or are guilty of bestiality or sodomy shall be buried alive in the ground.' The death penalty for sodomy remained in full force right up to the nineteenth century. Between 1800 and 1835, more than eighty men were sentenced to death for homosexuality. As Crane (1982) points out, in 1806 more people were hanged for sodomy between consenting homosexuals than for murder. It was not until 1861 that executions of homosexuals were stopped in Britain and Ireland. Finally, in 1967, the Sexual Offences Act decriminalized active homosexuality between men so long as they conducted their sexual affairs in private and were over the age of twenty-one.

Not everyone approved of these measures. Lord Longford, who continues in the mid 1980s to fight for the parole of the sadistic 'Moors' killer, Myra Hindley – a woman who slowly tortured a child to death and tape-recorded sounds for subsequent sexual pleasure – said that the decriminalization of homosexuality was 'nauseating'. Lord Longford stated that, just because the government was decriminalizing homosexuality, it did not mean it was condoning it: 'We are doing no such thing . . . we condemn it as utterly wrongful,' he said.

Lord Longford was not mincing words: under English law, it remains an offence for sailors in the merchant marines to have sex with each other while serving on board ship.

Lesbians and heterosexuals are permitted to have sex at

the age of sixteen, but homosexual men must legally wait until they are twenty-one.

Homosexuality is illegal for both men and women who serve in the armed forces.

Only two homosexuals may congregate for the purposes of having sex, and they must do so in the privacy of their own home. It would therefore be illegal for three homosexual men to live together in the same home. This would make it no longer private. Since hotels are public places, homosexual men are not legally permitted to use hotel rooms for sexual purposes. However, several women could have group sex together in a hotel room, or in the privacy of their own home, without breaking the law.

SODOMY AND THE LAW

It will come as no surprise to find that, under strict Islamic law, sodomy, also known as anal sex, 'the infamous crime against nature', or bestiality, is punishable by death. However, it may come as a surprise to many readers that, *legally speaking*, Alex Comfort's (1972) sex manual *The Joy of Sex* incites people to break the law both in England and in many states of the United States. This is because the book describes the positive aspects of anal sex – insertion of the penis into the rectum of either a man or a woman. It is intuitively understandable that animals should be protected from sexual invasion, precisely because they cannot consent to sexual intercourse with a human being. However, in England and California, for instance, anal sex is totally illegal for everyone – *even between consenting married adults*. The relevant Californian codes read as follows:

California Penal Code 286 specifically affirms anal intercourse to be a major crime: '*Every person who is guilty of the infamous crime against nature, committed, with mankind, is punishable by imprisonment in the state prison not less than one year.*' Moreover, Penal Code 286.1 is aimed at anal rapists who can receive from five years to life. Code 287 states that, 'Any penetration, however slight, is sufficient to complete the crime against nature.'

Laws against sodomy have been traced to the Emperor Justinian (483–562), who believed the act to be the main cause of earthquakes. In English law, anal sex is called 'buggery', and has been prohibited since 1533 when Henry VIII reigned. Section 12 of the Sexual Offences Act (1956) states that it 'is a felony for a person to commit buggery with another person or with an animal', the maximum penalty being life imprisonment. If the other man consents to be buggered, and is over the age of sixteen, the sentence will be ten years. This law means that if either a man or woman engages in bestiality with a dog (and, as we have seen, several have admitted to such behaviour), he or she can be sent to prison for life. In fact, such a sentence is rarely imposed. One English court took the view that a man who sodomized a bitch was more deserving of sympathy than the animal. Furthermore, if a husband and wife admitted to having anal intercourse, in line with the suggestion made in some sex manuals, by way of variation, they could theoretically face a prison term. One sex researcher saw the irony in bestiality laws when he remarked that, 'If you butchered and ate your cow, no one would care. If you made love to your cow, you would be put in jail.'

Technically, hundreds of thousands of Californians and millions of American citizens, heterosexual and homosexual, are criminals because they indulge in genital stimulation, using mouth and tongue. In fact, a husband and wife can each receive a sentence from five years to life in the state prison for performing fellatio and/or cunnilingus together. Needless to say, the same penalties apply for lesbians and homosexual men. Oral sex is not, however, against the law in England.

PART SIX

More Sexual Deviations

'There are more things in heaven and earth, Horatio, than are dreamt of in your philosophy' – William Shakespeare, *Hamlet*, Act 1, Scene V

Introduction

This chapter introduces several types of sexual style, preference and variation. Reactions to the material are bound to vary among readers. The contents range from the more innocuous to the perverse and macabre. Some, like necrophilia, are disturbing, while others, like kleptolangia, are perhaps more benign and strange. The assortment includes sexual preferences, deviations and perversions, to demonstrate further the scope of bizarre sexual conduct among humans.

25 OTHER VARIETIES OF SEXUAL PREFERENCE

AUTO-EROTIC FATALITIES

Asphyxiophilia or **sexual asphyxia** is a solitary auto-erotic behaviour practised primarily by young men (Coe, 1974), but it has also been observed in young women and, on occasion, in older men (Hazelwood, Dietz and Burgess, 1981). The activity is intended to increase masturbatory pleasure, and usually takes the form of applying a ligature around the neck to impede the flow of oxygen to the brain. According to Resnick (1972), this results in 'relative hypoxia which heightens subjective sexual sensations'.

Some individuals use plastic bags to breathe in and out of in order to reduce their intake of oxygen. A few have been known to breathe lighter gas or a chemical aerosol. The use of amyl nitrate (a vasodilator), or 'poppers', as they are known in the subculture, has also been associated with auto-erotic practice. 'Poppers' are inhaled in vapour form and cause the arteries to expand, resulting in increased blood flow to the brain. However, the most usual method remains to simply use a noose. For instance, Hazelwood, Dietz and Burgess (1981) record how a twenty-eight-year-old telephone company employee died as a result of hanging himself with a hemp rope: 'The rope extended

from his neck to a tree limb approximately six feet over-
head. To the left front of the victim were four magazines
depicting nude females.'

Resnick (1972) describes this syndrome as 'erotized
repetitive hangings in which adolescent young men engage
in masturbation titrated to increasing self-manipulated
neck pressure', and estimates that 'at least 50 deaths
annually result from its practice' in the United States. Such
deaths may sometimes be confused with intentional suicide
or homicide, but the overwhelming majority of them occur
among young, white, middle-class, unmarried males who
do not intend to die as a result. Evidently, a reduction of
oxygen to the brain, when coupled with orgasm produced
by masturbating, heightens the 'pleasurable' sensations. In
his article entitled 'Erotized Repetitive Hangings: A Form
of Self-destructive Behaviour', Resnick suggests that 'unexpected death may result from unconsciousness due to
carotid sinus reflex and gradual asphyxia resulting from
complete body suspension'. Furthermore, he states, 'clini-
cians are alerted to question any unusual neck bruises on
their male patients'.

Masturbatory practices which lead to accidental death
do not always involve hanging or a reduction of oxygen
intake. A nineteen-year-old oriental man died while trying
to use an electric floor polisher to masturbate. Presumably
the young man used the vibrations of the polisher to excite
himself. Unfortunately, the polisher was improperly wired
to the ground wire and, when the youth touched the metal
radiator, the current passed through his body and killed
him. In another instance of accidental death caused by
auto-erotic activity, Hazelwood, Dietz and Burgess (1981)
recorded the following case:

A 23-year-old white female was found to have died as a result
of neck compression during dangerous auto-erotic activity. The

woman had used an extension cord to interconnect her ankles with her neck. She had used a slip knot as a self-rescue mechanism. Examination of the slip knot revealed that in tying it, the victim had inadvertently allowed her hair to become entangled in the knot, thereby preventing her from disengaging it.

In another incident, an eighteen-year-old youth was found dead inside a thirty-pound garbage can. His head protruded from the can, and he was in a foetal position. His wrists were secured together, and the mouth of the can was partially covered with chicken wire. The young man was so severely stuck inside the can that police had to use a chisel to cut him out. There was no evidence that drugs or alcohol were in his system, and his 'death was ruled to be the result of auto-erotic activity'. According to the authors, the victim's parents refused to believe that 'their son's death was sexually related'.

In the view of these authors, there is a strong sado-masochistic component to many cases of this kind. For instance, a search of a fifty-one-year-old male victim's home revealed pornographic photographs, '50 leather jackets, ropes, chains, handcuffs, leg irons, a penis vice, scrotum weights, electric shock devices, a variety of leather discipline masks and helmets'. The man also owned '107 pairs of leather gloves of which 29 were determined to have seminal stains inside, a mace with chain and spiked ball, canes, whips, and assorted padlocks'. When the man was found, he had been hanging from a tree suspended by a rope about his neck.

The precise reasons for these practices remain unknown.

NECROPHILIA

Necrophilia refers to a fetish in which the individual becomes sexually excited by corpses. The behaviour is extremely rare, and when it does come to light, invariably makes for newsworthy media coverage. The practice has been taboo for thousands of years, and Davis (1983) quotes Montaigne's description of Egyptian preventive measures against corpse defilement: 'Such frenzy . . . of the frantic Egyptian hot after the carcass of a dead woman he was embalming and shrouding: which gave rise to the law . . . that bodies of beautiful young women . . . should be kept three days before being put in the hands of the undertakers.'

There is a wide range of necrophilic behaviours. The necrophiliac may merely be content to masturbate while looking at a corpse, but the behaviour can go as far as having 'sexual intercourse' with the dead body. Some necrophiliacs, moreover, find pleasure in mutilating the dead bodies after 'sexual intercourse'. The most extreme cases involve killing a victim before sexually assaulting the body. For what they are worth, clinical assessments of necrophiliacs indicate that they are usually 'psychopathic personalities' (people who have no conscience) with 'paranoid', 'schizoid' and 'psychotic' features.

One of the more accomplished of recent necrophiliacs is Dennis Nilsen, a civil servant who, in 1983, admitted killing 'fifteen or sixteen' young homosexual men at his home in a North London suburb over a five-year period. Nilsen, a former policeman, would strangle his victims in their intoxicated sleep and then, after having intercrural sex (between the legs) and/or masturbating on the body, proceeded to boil the heads and carve the bodies into small pieces. Body parts were placed in plastic bags, down a manhole, under floorboards, burned in bonfires or buried in a near-by garden. The activity was only uncovered because Nilsen also attempted to use the plumbing system of the building where he was currently living to dispose of his victims. The plumbing failed and other tenants complained of a 'foul odour' emanating from the building.

Most, but not all, of Nilsen's victims were destitute young homosexuals. Nilsen showed *no remorse* at his trial, wore stylish clothes, and appeared to understand fully the charges against him. Numerous letters, poems and drawings about his practices show that Nilsen was 'artistic', 'sensitive' and aware of his 'evils'. He claimed that he had, by putting them out of their misery, performed a service to many of his victims.

Prior to cutting up a body, he would cover his own naked body with powder and, using mirrors, proceed to masturbate over the corpse. Aged thirty-seven at the time of his trial, Nilsen had originally developed his 'butchery skills' while in the British Army Catering Corps. He held a respectable job at the time of his arrest. After the trial, it was said that if his kitchen had been fitted with an efficient garbage disposal system, then the drains would never have blocked up ... Nilsen claimed that his passion for this behaviour was so compelling that he could have continued 'until I was sixty-five, when there would have been "thousands" of decimated bodies'.

Not surprisingly, psychiatric opinion on Nilsen differed. One expert witness gave evidence diagnosing him as a psychopath or anti-social personality in which grandiosity was a major feature. Another diagnosed him as 'Borderline False Self as if Pseudo-Normal Narcissistic Personality Disorder' (Masters, 1985).

Psychiatric diagnoses prove *especially* futile in attempting to portray the psychological nature of an individual such as Dennis Nilsen. Indeed, an analysis of Nilsen's handwriting, commissioned by Brian Masters, is perhaps about as, if not more, accurate than the psychiatric testimony presented at his trial. Extracts from the *Nilsen Papers*, written in prison by the mass murderer between February and December 1983, are included in Masters's (1985) thorough and disturbing account of the killer, his victims, and their disposal, all presented in a book aptly entitled *Killing for Company*. Perhaps the most accurate assessment of the killer comes from himself – clearly psychiatric commentary pales in the face of Nilsen's own accounts. One of the many typical accounts shows the cold, detached and clinical manner in which 'Des' (as he was known) Nilsen behaved after having strangled one of his victims, a stray Irish youth, the previous night:

I couldn't think what to do at all – at that stage. I was now feeling the full tired effects of the hangover. I pulled the bedclothes off the youth's body. I went to the wardrobe and took out some underwear and socks (still in their cellophane packets from Woolworth's). I dressed the youth in white Y-fronts, vest, and socks, and put back the bedclothes. I had a bath myself and got into bed with him. I held him close to me with my arms around him, and began to remove his pants and explore his body under the blankets. (I had an erection all the time.) When I tried to enter him my erection automatically subsided, I could feel that his body temperature was cooling. I got up and lifted him into my arms, laid him on the floor and covered him with an old curtain. I went back into bed and fell instantly asleep . . .

I heard somewhere that rigor mortis soon passes, so I could wait . . .

The next day he was still standing against the wall. I laid him on the floor and worked his limbs loose. I examined closely and systematically every part of him from his toes to his hair . . . I eased him into his new bed and covered him up. It was very cold under the floorboards. The cat got in there and I spent ten minutes coaxing her out. I replaced the boards and the carpet. I ripped up all his clothing and put it with his boots into the dustbin. A week later I wondered if his body had started to decompose. I disinterred him and pulled the dirt-stained youth onto the floor. His skin was very dirty. I stripped myself naked and carried him into the bathroom and washed the body. There was practically no discoloration and he was pale white. His limbs were more limp and relaxed than when I put him down. I got him out of the water. I carried the still wet youth into the room and laid him on the carpet. Under the orange side-lights his body aroused me sexually. I knelt over him and masturbated on to his bare stomach. Before I went to bed I suspended him by the ankles from the high wooden platform. He hung there all night, his fingers just touching the carpet. The next day, while he was still hanging upside down I stood beside him and masturbated again. I wiped him and took him down. I laid him on the kitchen floor and decided to cut him up, but I just couldn't do anything to spoil that marvellous body.

Nilsen burned the young Irishman, one of the first in a series, in a huge bonfire at the bottom of the garden at 195 Melrose Avenue, North London, on 11 August 1979. Nilsen was bent on making history, on making the most of every opportunity. His gross pathological insensitivity to others was demonstrated when he wrote that he suffered as much as the parents of a Canadian victim, a young man with whom he had spent less than a day, and fallen in love. Because he could not bear the idea of separating from the Canadian, who was due to leave for Canada within twenty-four hours, he strangled him and made 'love' to the dead body. Later, he wrote from prison that he should remain alive and not take the cowardly way out by committing suicide, and that he had ideas of becoming the son of the Canadian's parents. As he left for Her Majesty's Prison at Wormwood Scrubs, he attempted to remove tape from the window of the police van, so that photographers should get a good shot of him as he made his way to prison.

Over fifty years before Nilsen, the German necrophiliac, Peter Kürsten, had managed to evade capture for more than thirty years. Peter Kürsten competes with Nilsen in the annals of bizarre necrophilic feats *only* in terms of the number of sexually related murders he committed. Wilson and Pitman (1984) present his career as a sexual sadist who *combined* necrophilia with his killings. The authors also note that 'Hitler lost a talented lieutenant in Kürsten, one who might have outshone Eichmann or Heydrich in mass murder' when, having committed over forty killings, he was finally caught and sentenced to death by decapitation in 1931.

It is not unknown for persons with necrophilic tendencies to seek employment in morgues, funeral parlours and cemeteries. In the early 1980s, in California, an elderly woman was reported to have been caught attempting to have sexual relations with male corpses. It is, however, likely that sexually interfering with dead bodies is more of a man's domain.

Some individuals are simply content to pay prostitutes to lie as still as possible while they copulate, and prostitutes who cater to such preferences are skilled at making themselves up with wax powder to give the skin a pale look. Clients may also require the prostitute to wear a shroud and lie in a coffin. While Dennis Nilsen had this possibility open to him, he chose, instead, to indulge himself by making his fantasies real.

It has been suggested that men who purchase, and use, inflatable plastic or vinyl life-size dolls (see page 357, under the section on 'Pygmalionism') which are equipped with the necessary orifices for sexual intercourse, are manifesting a form of latent necrophilia. The dolls are motionless, do not respond and, essentially, represent dead women. But an individual can only be classified as necrophile-like if his primary sexual turn-on is through lifeless objects, whether these be real corpses or look-alike blow-up plastic dolls.

Another lurid and pathetic case of necrophilia in Britain involved a Methodist minister, the Rev. Emyr Owen, aged sixty-two, who was in March 1985 found guilty of molesting corpses. The minister was described as 'homosexual', and he confessed to mutilating corpses prepared for burial in the village church graveyard. He pleaded guilty on three counts of mutilating corpses and received a four-year prison sentence. It seems probable that, in the nine years he was a minister, he sexually abused many more than three dead bodies. Parishioners are most unlikely to suspect a man of God of being capable of such a perversion.

Mr Justice Evans, who presided over the trial, said: 'It was aggravated because you were trusted by the community by being the minister in charge of the church and entrusted by the deceaseds' families. You abused the trust of the living just as you dishonoured the dead. Your private homosexual practice became a private perversion. When you returned to the village for the first time, you were entrusted with dead bodies for burial. What you did is totally unacceptable in any civilized society' (*The Standard*, 26 March 1985). The judge may have been correct in his conclusion, except that, if the minister had been heterosexual, it is unlikely that he would have begun his summation with, 'your private heterosexual practice became a private perversion . . .'

It should also be pointed out that necrophilic rape occurred during the Second World War when Russian troops flung themselves on the still-warm corpses of vanquished German women (see 'Rape', page 176 above).

SEX AND THE TELEPHONE

Used and abused, the telephone is said to be the largest computer in the world. It connects hundreds of millions of people instantly at the 'push of a button'. Countless obscene calls are made locally, and even intercontinentally, and the vast majority are never traced. The obscene phone-caller is invariably a male, and the victim is as likely to be a woman he knows as one he has never seen in his life. The caller may simply breathe heavily down the line, or utter obscenities and sexually loaded suggestions to the woman on the other end. Some callers are juveniles seeking kicks, others become sexually aroused and take the whole thing seriously. The individual who derives sexual satisfaction out of calling a woman and uttering obscenities is, to put it mildly, usually somewhat maladjusted. Obscenities range from asking a woman if she wants to go to bed to more serious threats of rape.

The obscene phone-caller is similar to an exhibitionist in that he gains vicarious pleasure out of shocking, offending and outraging a woman, the objective being to obtain an emotional response out of the victim. The caller gains an artificial feeling of power, yet he is usually a coward. His behaviour is tantamount to symbolic rape, since he enters the woman's home without taking the risk of actually being there. He is safe unless he calls the same number repeatedly, in which case the telephone company can trace the number concerned. Since the problem is widespread, some people place special electronic safety systems on their telephone lines, which require a caller to dial in a special code before the number becomes obtainable.

An insidious variation in the use of telephones is the telephone trickster. Typically, the telephone trickster will attempt to seduce the woman he calls with 'sweet talk'. He manages to ingratiate himself using a fabricated story which the victim believes. He might, for instance, look up a Susan Ash in the telephone directory, then telephone her, saying he is a cousin of the Ashes from another city who said he should call since he has just moved. The two may arrange to meet for lunch at a designated restaurant, but the trickster merely goes to the restaurant and watches Susan Ash waste her time. Having 'tricked' her, he feels pathologically gratified.

Suicide prevention agencies have reported cases of the telephone masturbator (Bryant 1982). In these instances, the caller seeks a female therapist and concocts an elaborate crisis. He might, for example, tell the therapist that he is lonely and will commit suicide if he doesn't find a girl friend. The therapist enters into a crisis intervention strategy, oblivious of the fact that he is masturbating while talking to her. On discovering that the call is bogus, the therapist may feel used and exploited. She has been trapped in a 'Catch 22' situation. If she had slammed down the receiver, she could not have been certain that the caller was no genuine suicide risk; but if she continued the discussion, she was basically rewarding the caller's behaviour.

The telephone also lends itself to lighter, though still vicarious sexual excitement. Sexual entrepreneurs from Japan to the United States have capitalized on the 'market in obscene callers' by using the latest technology in telephone answering machines. The answering machines are capable of answering several hundred calls simultaneously and then playing back recorded messages to the callers. The pre-recorded messages are changed regularly, and range from descriptions of explicit sexual fantasies to the cries and moans of individuals reaching orgasm. The companies either ask the caller for a 'donation' to help continue the service, or come to a profit-sharing arrangement with the phone companies. Recently, in England, a group of school students found a public telephone booth which was broken. The phone was out of order in so far as it enabled the students to make intercontinental calls without charge. British Telecom reported that they had run up bills worth thousands of pounds to one of these 'sex numbers' in New York City. Some enterprising American prostitutes, exercising their constitutional rights, offer sexual experiences by telephone. Sex answer-services sometimes play pre-recorded messages, and, for a higher fee, will arrange personalized service. They also take all major credit cards.

Here are some examples of such advertisements, which are usually accompanied by a sexy snapshot portraying the theme of the particular service offered. These advertisements appeared in *Penthouse Variations* (December 1984):

The 144 pages of 'text' are filled with dozens of similar advertisements.

HYPNOPHILIA

Amanda was a forty-two-year-old divorced actress who sought therapy for both agoraphobia (an irrational fear of leaving her home) and sexual problems which considerably interfered with and disturbed her intimate relationships with men. The progress of therapy revealed an unusual condition. Amanda was especially sexually aroused by others who were *asleep*. She maintained that, when she was younger, she could seldom spend the entire night with a boyfriend because she would become even more aroused when he fell asleep.

Amanda revealed that, when she was a young child, her alcoholic father had sexually molested her: 'My father would fall asleep in the middle of a sentence. His body would become rigid and it was very difficult for my mother and I to get him into bed. Sometimes he would come home drunk and collapse asleep on top of me as I slept in my bed. My mother either thought nothing of his sleeping in my bed, or she simply didn't interfere [see the section on 'Incest', pages 255ff]. I felt both afraid and excited by my father. He used to touch my breasts and private parts and said that it was our little game, never to tell anyone or I would be severely punished by God.' Amanda stated that she would play make-believe games with her babysitter. These involved asking the baby-sitter to close her eyes and pretend she was asleep. Amanda would do the same and feel excited. She continued this behaviour until she was 'about twelve or thirteen, with my girl friend, when I slept over at her house'. When she was sixteen years old, she had a boyfriend who worked the night shift. He would fall asleep while necking in his car. Amanda claimed this was 'just the perfect deal'. However, she could never fall asleep if her boyfriend was sleeping because, 'I was just too excited. I would feel out of control if I did.' She claimed that she once had a boyfriend who 'went to sleep with a hard-on', and that this was 'incredible luck'. She admitted that her problem had caused difficulties in her marriage.

The patient also said that she had a phobia of anaesthesia, and this had caused her to have a panic attack before an operation. She attributed it to 'my father doing sexual stuff to me when I fell asleep as a child'. Amanda claimed that her father never actually penetrated her, but that he fell asleep on top of her, after 'playing around'. Her sexual fantasies invariably included a sleeping person. However, she said that she could only be aroused by a real living person; films of sleeping people did not excite her. Furthermore, she was 'excited by children, men and women, as long as they were sleeping'. The patient claimed that her attraction to sleeping people was 'more under control than it had been' because she was better at getting a good night's sleep 'without sleeping pills'.

In another case, an anaesthesiologist in California was in the habit of sexually interfering with female patients while they were under anaesthetic. The man was, as a result, incarcerated in a state psychiatric prison. He was in the process of intense litigation – against the staff at the hospital where he had worked. He was suing his fellow workers, doctors and nurses, for *not* having reported his illness sooner – despite the fact that, as a result of several lawsuits by angered former patients, the entire hospital had been forced to close down.

ACROTOMOPHILIA AND APOTEMNOPHILIA

Wallace *et al.* (1981) records how, in his later years, André Gide was reported to have been sexually excited by crippled, deformed children, 'in whom he recognized some aspect of himself'. Gide could possibly be described as having **acrotomophilic inclinations**, a term which indicates an erotic interest in people who have crippled limbs or are amputees. **Apotemnophilia**, on the other hand, refers to an extremely bizarre and rare erotic preference in which the individual is sexually excited by having his or her *own* limb amputated (Money, Jobaris and Furth, 1977). Money and his co-workers report two case histories in which patients requested limb amputation for sexual purposes. The causes of this type of sexual preference remain elusive. Interested readers can refer to the section on masochism (pages 130–1), where a masochistic doctor tells of his sexual fantasy involving amputation of his testicles.

ZOOPHILIA

Bestiality, bestiosexuality or **zoophilia** refers to sexual activity between humans and other animals. Sex with beasts has been condemned for thousands of years. In Leviticus, the prescribed punishment for a man or woman who 'lies with beast' was death. In the Middle Ages, in England, the animal victim was hanged alongside the human.

During the Nazi era, Hermann Göring engaged bulls to copulate cows for the entertainment of his guests, while, in an earlier age, Catherine the Great of Russia was said to have set up similarly stimulating displays outside her palace with stallions and fillies; but both these examples may be thought of as a type of voyeurism. In Balboa, Panama, it was popular in certain night clubs to feature donkeys copulating with women, to the delight of the audience, and generations of servicemen in the Middle and Far East have returned home with stories of similar spectacles. However, Nancy Friday's (1975) research led her to conclude that, 'I don't think there are many women who have actually been fucked by a bull or donkey, either – though it is supposed to be not entirely unknown at stag dinners.' Although zoophilia is not an especially popular sexual subject, there was sufficient public demand to support the making of a film, aptly titled *Animal Lovers*, in which a woman was shown having coitus with dogs, donkeys and pigs.

Despite the indiscretion of many a domesticated pet dog who embarrasses his owner by mounting the leg of a guest, the diagnosis of zoophilia is exclusive to humans. Sex objects range from insects to cattle – even to snakes! Zoophilic behaviour occurs in both men and women, and ranges from non-violent intercourse to the sadistic killing of animals for sexual gratification. For instance, Stolorow and Grand (1973) described the case of a twenty-five-year-old man who became sexually excited by squashing bugs. Tollison and Adams (1979) cited a report in which a small snake had to be surgically removed from a patient's bladder.

Perhaps the most classic image of sex between humans and animals is that of the mountain shepherd and his flock. The Italian film *Padre Padrone* depicted a lonely Sardinian shepherd who, as a very small boy, was made to spend long periods alone in the mountains tending his father's sheep. When he became an adolescent, the frustrated boy would tie up an animal's legs, insert his penis into her vagina and proceed to copulate.

The sadistic sex killer Peter Kürsten not only killed children and adult women for his sexual pleasures, but was reputed to have begun his career by masturbating dogs and mutilating sheep, pigs and goats for sexual kicks. He was aroused by the sight of an animal's blood.

The precise incidence of zoophilia is not known, but, in America, according to Kinsey *et al.* (1948 and 1953) about 8 per cent of men and 3 per cent of women admitted to sexual behaviour involving an animal. Most prosecutions occur in rural areas. Kinsey estimated that about 17 per cent of boys raised on farms experience orgasm as a result of direct contact with animals. Zoophilia can be relatively harmless. Contributors to *The Sex-Life Letters* (Greenwald and Greenwald, 1974) give the following examples, among others:

. . . I have a particular lady friend at the moment who practises zoophilia with her dog, a large mongrel. Often she strips naked while doing her housework and allows him to excite her from any position she happens to be in, sometimes making a paste of chocolate powder, sugar and milk and spreading it on her breasts for him to lick off . . .

My second experience came at the age of 18. I was a lorry driver, working for a small local firm, delivering corn, etc., to farms. Making a delivery one afternoon I could find no one at home, and therefore started to look into some of the outbuildings to find someone to sign my delivery sheet. Hearing sounds coming from the barn, I approached it and as I passed the window I saw the farmer's wife bending over some hay, doing her best to guide the penis of a large dog into her vagina. After entry was effected the dog worked away with gusto, to the obvious and extreme pleasure of the lady . . .

Sexual performances between women and animals are staged for money, and the perverse pleasure of a male audience. Stag films and hard-core pornography sporadically feature women in compromising situations with animals. For instance, in one pornographic magazine, a woman was shown having oral sex with a large German Shepherd – the dog was licking food off her vagina and she had her hand on its penis. Nancy Friday (1975) reproduces a woman's masochistic sexual fantasy in which she is made to have intercourse with a donkey:

. . . They must have played with the donkey's prick to make it stiff, as I feel the hard stiff shaft against my ass as they pull it towards me. I feel the long knob end against the lips of my cunt. It forces them apart and begins to enter my hole as the woman guides it up to me. I let out a cry of pain as it stretches the walls of my cunt. Inch by inch it slowly goes in and begins painfully moving up and back, in and out. The donkey's prick has been well greased, and after a few abrasive thrusts the fucking rhythm becomes easier. When they have about six inches of the donkey's prick up into me, they hold me still while the donkey pushes his massive prick up and down my cunt just like a piston: I wouldn't have believed it possible, but I am being fucked by a donkey!

While it is currently fashionable not to pass judgement about individual erotic preferences, it is safe to say that most people would view sex between a donkey and a human being as somewhat bizarre.

COPROPHAGIA, COPROPHILIA AND UROPHILIA

Coprophagia is the term given to those few individuals who are sexually gratified by consuming excrement – faeces and/or urine. Coprophagic themes have been depicted in pornographic films; for instance, a scene in *Pink Flamingoes*, starring an actor called Divine, showed Divine picking up a turd and eating it. **Coprophilia** does not involve actually eating excrement; it is a technical term used to describe a sexual practice in which the individual obtains sexual gratification out of playing with, masturbating into and/or smearing excrement. Both sexes have been clinically observed to indulge in scatological behaviour, in which the individual may be attracted to his or her own faeces, those of a partner or both. The incidence is unknown and, for obvious reasons, the practice is unhygienic.

Psychologists usually consider both coprophilia and coprophagia to be regressive behaviour as it is more common among young children, even though children probably do not derive any sexual pleasure as a direct result of smearing faeces. Scatological behaviours are more commonly seen in hospitalized, severely regressed psychotics. Practitioners who work with such severely disturbed patients are aware of the danger of hepatitis spreading between them. Adolf Hitler was thought to be among those distinguished practitioners of coprophilic sado-masochism. In current lingo, he might be described as enjoying a 'brown shower' – an activity in which one sexual partner defecates on the other, who is excited by the experience.

'Water sports or golden showers' are clinically known as **urophilia** – a sexual interest in urine. Havelock Ellis, who preceded Freud in pioneering the study of sexual behaviour, was allegedly aroused by the sight of women urinating. According to Wallace *et al.* (1981), when he was twelve years old, Ellis saw his mother squat and urinate on a side-path at the London Zoo. His sister told him that this meant that his mother was flirting with him. As an adult, he was excited by watching his lover, Françoise, urinating.

Martin Luther (1483–1546), father of Lutheranism and major protagonist of the Reformation, was interested in 'nocturnal pollutions' and other excretions to the point where he would wait a year before changing his bed linen. Luther would today be diagnosed by psychoanalysts as anally fixated; not only was he constipated and a sufferer from haemorrhoids, but, according to Wallace *et al.* (1981), he was known to cry out to the devil, 'I have shit in the pants, and you can hang them around your neck and wipe your mouth with it', and boasted he could 'drive away the evil spirit with a single fart'. 'He had an intimate relationship with his bowel movements, and regularly wrote home giving a score of his defecations.'

Several cases of urophilia or urolangia were described in a report submitted to *The Sex-Life Letters* (Greenwald and Greenwald, 1984) this one being among them:

. . . I could hear him straining and was wondering what he was trying to do. I soon found out. He was holding the bedclothes up with one hand and his penis in the other, and then I felt it. Hot urine on my belly, only a short burst, then he looked over me to see where it had gone. Satisfied with himself he gave me the full treatment. He directed his penis upward toward my breasts and proceeded to give sharp bursts of warm urine all down my body. I could feel it running down me. He then pulled my panties up and inserted his penis up the leg of my panties and started to masturbate on my wet belly. Simultaneously he played with my clitoris . . .

Coprophagia, coprophilia and urophilia may, as erotic preferences, be closely connected with sado-masochistic and 'regressive' behaviours, like klismaphilia, or the use of enemas, which we will next consider.

KLISMAPHILIA AND INFANTILISM

Klismaphilia refers to a condition in which people become sexually excited by receiving enemas. The behaviour occurs in both men and women; the precise incidence remains unknown. Denko (1976) described sixteen cases of klismaphilia where enemas were employed as an adjunct to or replacement for sexual intercourse. Most klismaphilics are ashamed of their behaviour and are secretive about it. They tend to indulge their pleasures in private, or ask someone else to administer the 'treatment' under pretext of being constipated. In addition, they are often thought to conceal the pleasure they receive from the nurse.

A small number of klismaphilics, however, learn to accept the practice without guilt and suffer no lowering of self-esteem. Others employ enemas as part of sado-masochistic rituals, transvestite or other atypical sexual 'expressions'. These practitioners seldom seek treatment since they have no wish to alter their behaviour.

In an earlier study, Denko (1973) presented two case histories. In one, an army officer developed klismaphilia as a result of childhood experiences in which his over-protective mother regularly gave him enemas, his father encouraging the practice. Further, 'despite obsessive thinking and phobias, this man's use of compulsive defences helped him to compartmentalize his abnormality and lead an externally normal life'. In the other case, a lawyer developed a love of enemas despite the fact that he had never experienced 'anal attentions' in childhood. This patient was described as intelligent and sensitive, but was somewhat psychopathic (guiltless).

The following klismaphilic preference was reported in Greenwald and Greenwald by a Mrs E. G.:

Since I was a girl of nine (I am now a widow of thirty-nine) I have held the view that an enema is a pleasurable experience. When I was a schoolgirl I spent a week in hospital after an operation. During that week I received several enemas. Although I felt embarrassed and humiliated, I actually enjoyed the experiences in a manner that is now difficult to recall precisely.

So lasting was the impression that I have never forgotten it and I have tried to relive it many times since. Between nine and nineteen I used to dwell on every detail and it was my principal fantasy when I masturbated. The mere sight of an enema syringe in a surgical store was enough to excite me.

I purchased a syringe when I was at college but self-administration was quite unsatisfactory. I had a girl friend who was a nurse and the first person to whom I confessed my unusual interests. When she offered to repeat the treatment, I accepted willingly and I found the experience very satisfying. After several occasions she proposed we switch roles so that I became the 'nurse'. I found this so satisfying that I surprised myself and began to wonder what was wrong with me.

This woman went on to describe how she enjoyed having a sexual partner inserting his finger into her anus, giving her 'playful spankings', and eventually giving her the 'full treatment'. She claims that she married a man who did not enjoy the enema experience. However, after his death, she managed to find a few lovers who were able to 'indulge my former pursuit'. She describes the situation: 'The same acute, mixed, bitter-sweet sensations are always there; being undressed, intimately examined, having my buttocks separated and my anus vaselined and finally being thoroughly syringed and masturbated simultaneously until I don't know which urge to obey first.'

Sexual infantilism is practised by some members of the sexual subculture, who as a rule employ a prostitute to give them 'baby treatment' for a sizeable fee. The practice typically involves placing the adult in nappies or diapers, the use of 'baby talk', and possibly the administration of spankings, or other humiliations. The adult may even soil himself in the presence of others, and then be 'cleaned up just like a baby'. Services for humiliation treatments abound in magazines like *Penthouse Variations*, a monthly publication. For instance, a 'MADAM X' offers the following advertisement:

> Painful
> Pleasures
> Await As
> I Bring
> You To Your Knees
> Call me
> If you
> Dare

The advertiser accepts major credit cards and the advertisement shows a photograph of a half-naked woman wearing provocative leather garments, draping a long whip over her shoulder. In another advertisement, cited by Davis (1983), a man advertised the following:

> White male seeks dominant mistress to serve as body servant and toilet slave. Crave humiliation, golden showers and oral toilet debasement. Phone 'Toilet Mouth' at . . . [*Fetish Times*, No. 14 (no date), personal columns]

PYROLANGIA

Pyrolangia refers to 'sexual arson' where the individual becomes sexually excited by setting fires. Most instances of arson are not, however, sexually motivated. Cox (1979) suggests that 'the arsonist may be diagnosed as subnormal, neurotic, psychotic or psychopathic'. Psychopathic arsonists, or those who suffer from a character disorder in which a 'normal' conscience is missing, are usually motivated by political or criminal vengeance, lovers' quarrels or to defraud insurance companies. This type of arson accounts for the majority of deliberately set fires. Psychotic arsonists – those who have 'lost touch with reality' and suffer severe thought disorders, are likely to act out their paranoid delusions. For example, several years ago I was travelling in the United States with a colleague on an interstate highway. As we passed a large crumbling and burned-out building, he casually said, 'A patient of Jane's [a student of his] did that. He thought that the staff there were out to get him, and told the court that Jesus instructed him to exorcize the devil out of the building. The number of crimes paranoid patients attribute to Jesus is alarming . . .' In another instance, an arsonist believed that the use of radiotherapy in the treatment of cancer functioned by 'burning out' the cancer. In his psychotic logic, he believed that by creating a really big blaze in his neighbourhood, he could eliminate all cancer cells, thereby protecting his children. In yet another case of psychotic arson, an arsonist burned down her lesbian lover's apartment, psychotically claiming that 'her clitoris [was] protruding from her ear' (Cox, 1979).

'Erotic arson', however, is rare, as we have said. It usually occurs in combination with other sexual psychopathologies. As Cox states, pyrolangia 'may be of overt sexual significance, and the patient will claim that he had his best ever orgasm as he watched the flames leaping up, or that his greatest moment of sexual excitement was when he was helping the fire service unsuccessfully to put out the fire which he had started'. This type of pyrolangia probably signifies an 'emotionally impotent' man – one who derives vicarious power out of creating a big blaze, something he secretly knows he has created.

It is perhaps not coincidental that, under English Common Law in the eighteenth century, men who murdered their masters – or ecclesiastical superiors – were executed by hanging, while women found guilty of murdering their husbands or master were burned alive. Ann Jones (1981) quotes William Blakestone's reasoning on the subject: 'as the natural modesty of the sex forbids exposing and publically mangling their bodies, their sentence . . . is to be drawn to the gallows, and there to be burned alive'. It should also be pointed out that, despite Blakestone's reasoning, the first thing to burn would be the woman's clothing, thereby exposing her naked, writhing body. It is more than likely that the man commissioned to set the women alight bathed himself in an ultimate Sadian sexual delight.

One of the twentieth century's most notorious sadistic killers, Peter Kürsten, derived further sexual excitement after savagely killing women and children by committing arson (see 'Sadistic Sex Murders' above, pages 102–9). He set fire to a barn, to two haystacks and a hayloft in 1904 – in addition to axe-murdering women, children and animals. Kürsten, who also happened to be a necrophiliac (see page 339), had orgasm when he returned to the graves of 'his' corpses when he set them on fire, after dowsing the decomposing bodies with petroleum.

A similar psychosexual configuration occurred with Denis Nilsen, the bizarre strangler of 'fifteen or sixteen' young men between 1981 and 1983 in the London suburbs of Cricklewood and Muswell Hill (see above, pages 336–9). After dissecting and sometimes boiling the bodily parts, Nilsen would take the remains to a special site where he would 'savour' the end results of his sexual accomplishments by making huge bonfires. He usually took his dog along for company.

PYGMALIONISM

Pygmalionism is an expression derived from the Greek myth in which a sculptor fell in love with his statue of a woman. In pygmalionism, there is a total or partial sexual fetish in which an inanimate (usually nude) statue or mannequin is the object of sexual gratification. The condition is seldom reported, unless, of course, the many brands of love doll available by mail-order and in sex boutiques are included under this heading (see 'Masturbation', page 81). Davis (1983) observed that, in pygmalionism, 'the sex object has the form of a being but the content of a thing. Pygmalionism and necrophilia, becoming sexually excited by corpses, are similar in that both objects are inanimate.'

Davis coined a neologism for necrophilia and pygmalionism: **reiphilia**. Reiphilia is, according to Davis, 'a general transformation perversion that involves sex with entities in the process of crossing the boundary between beings and things'. He goes on to quote Montaigne's description of a frenzied boy who 'defiled out of love the beautiful statue of Venus that Praxiteles had made'. It should be stressed that sexual excitement through inanimate objects is extremely rare.

EROTOMANIA: NYMPHOMANIA AND SATYRIASIS

People who suffer from an extremely rare condition in which they experience a state of continued, unabating and permanent sexual arousal are said to be **erotomaniacs**. In men, erotomania is called **satyriasis**, while in women it is referred to as **nymphomania**. Since frequencies of sexual intercourse between couples vary considerably, it is very difficult to diagnose and define either nymphomania or satyriasis. Both conditions tend to be confused with promiscuity.

For instance, according to Albert Gerber (1981) Brigitte Bardot 'boasted publicly that she had had more than 5,000 sexual partners'. Ms Bardot might have been exaggerating; if she was telling the truth, she would more likely be thought of as a promiscuous woman rather than a true nymphomaniac. Similarly, the fact that some heterosexual and homosexual swingers may have several hundred sexual contacts within a year does not mean that they are erotomaniacs. They are more probably promiscuous individuals who experience difficulty in forming intimate relationships with others, are afraid of commitment, subscribe to the erroneous belief that 'the more I sleep with, the more macho and loveable I am', or persons who simply enjoy a variety of different 'love objects'.

Genuine nymphomania or satyriasis may involve a psychological and/or physiological factors which contribute to an uncontrollable libido. The disorder may manifest itself among severely regressed psychotics, such as schizophrenics and manic-depressives in the manic phase of their illness. Sufferers may masturbate excessively, use obscene language and make sexual overtures to hospital staff or anyone who happens to be passing. In another form, a woman unable to achieve orgasm may seek out dozens of partners in the hope of finally finding the 'one and only' who will help her.

Satyriasis and nymphomania may also be viewed as obsessive-compulsive disorders, like compulsive hand-washing, in which the individual feels compelled to masturbate and/or have sexual intercourse with others. The behaviour can be so frequent that the individual actually loses weight. But satyriasis should not be confused with **priapism**, which is caused by a physical condition defined in the *Merck Manual* as 'a painful, persistent and abnormal penile erection, unaccompanied by sexual desire or excitation'.

In 1970, a Los Angeles woman suffering from nymphomania sued a cable-car company. She was awarded money by the court since she made the claim, presumably proven, that she developed excessive sexual urges after an accident involving a cable car and had subsequently engaged in intercourse with over a hundred men. The woman complained that she had lost several jobs as a result of her psychological/physiological injury. This case is not unbelievable, according to Tollison and Adams (1979), who cite a study in which it was shown that, if a part of the brain called the amygdala is damaged, the result may indeed be an unabating desire for sexual intercourse. Yet the case itself should be taken with a pinch of salt (bearing in mind the fact that American society is highly litigious).

According to Moore and May (1982), satyriasis or hypersexual symptoms can be 'associated with hormonal imbalances, drug abuse, temporal lobe epilepsy, tumours involving the limbic system, mania, schizophrenia, neuroses and personality disorders'. These authors also claim that many men who indulge in excessive sexual contacts with numerous women may, in fact, be trying to prove to themselves that they are not homosexuals. In this context, satyriasis could be seen as a defensive reaction. It becomes increasingly clear that erotomania is associated with a variety of conditions and that its cause is not fully understood.

FROTTAGE

Frottage occurs mainly among men (**frotteurs**) who become sexually excited by pressing their penises against the buttocks of fully clothed women. It is a relatively rare paraphilia which usually occurs in crowded situations, likely targets being women during the rush hour on crowded buses or subways. Because of the unavoidably close body contacts in such situations, the victim may often be unaware that a man is rubbing his penis against her bottom.

Allen (1979) described a case of combined frotteurism and quasi-exhibitionism. The patient, a twenty-five-year-old man, gained sexual excitement by rubbing his penis against women strangers in cinemas. He would keep his penis concealed under a coat, his victims being unaware of his manoeuvres. This patient had begun to masturbate after his mother withdrew an excessive love which she had shown him during childhood. The incidence of frotteurism is unknown, partly because it is seldom reported. Frotteurs are thought to suffer from impotence. Frotteurism should not be confused with the chauvinistic bottom pincher, whose victim is all too aware of his intentions.

BIGAMY

Gibbons are the only primates (other than humans) who have 'wives'. Chimpanzees, baboons, gorillas and other apes act out their sexual urges – provided they are 'dominant' members of their troupe – whenever any female is 'on heat'. Most humans are like the gibbon in respect of monogamy, and regulate themselves accordingly. In most Western countries, **bigamy** is a criminal offence, the term referring to the state of being married to more than one spouse. Bigamy is also known as **polygamy**. Polygamy is further divided into **polygyny** and **polyandry**. Polyandry occurs when a woman has more than one husband. Polygyny occurs when a man has more than one wife. Polygamy among certain groups, as, for instance, in Islam and in some primitive cultures, shares a similar disposition to that practised among the lower primates.

Ancient Jewish tradition permitted polygyny, it being a sign of wealth and higher status if a man could afford to buy more than one wife. Early Christian doctrine permitted only one spouse and frowned upon remarriage, even if the first spouse had died (Beserra, Jewel and Matthews, 1973). The crime of bigamy was considered an ecclesiastical one prior to 1603, when an appropriate statute was introduced in England under James I (Freeman, 1979). Statutes prohibiting bigamy and allocating specified punishments were carried to America by the Puritans.

In Islamic cultures, according to the Koran, a man may have up to four wives if he can afford them. The practice is also known as **tetragamy** and is quite common in, for instance, Saudi Arabia and among the Bedouin in the deserts of the Middle East and North Africa. Wealthy sheiks may choose to have concubines, women they purchase for sexual purposes, but do not actually marry them (see 'Sexual Slavery', page 23). Some Bantu groups of Southern Africa permit multiple marriage if the man can afford to pay *lobola* or enough cattle to the woman's father. The reverse applies in certain groups in India, where, although only one wife is 'taken', it is the bride's family who must pay an expensive dowry. A medical student who had recently returned from an exchange visit in India told me she was offered baby girls free of charge! Not only were the girls extra mouths to feed, but they were 'worthless commodities' – only sons bring in handsome dowries to their families. In his book *Hinduism*, Sen (1969) writes, 'Polygamy seems to be quite common, particularly in the *Mahabharata* [a Hindu epic], but curiously enough there is also one case of polyandry. Draupadi marries all five Pandava brothers.' Polyandry occurs much less frequently than polygyny, and has been observed on the Indian subcontinent along the Malabar Coast and in the foothills of the Himalayas.

Until 1890, when it was outlawed by the Church of Latter Day Saints, the Mormons of Utah practised a marginally less oppressive form of polygyny (Bryant, 1982). A Mormon man would only have sexual intercourse with a wife if she were not menstruating, lactating or pregnant, and then only if the wife invited him to do so. Her pretext for asking for sex would be for the sole purpose of procreation. Isolated bands of polygamous Mormons still practise their faith in the United States, and one such 'happy family' appeared on network television in 1983. The wives, children and 'impregnator' were all alike adamant that they should be allowed to practise polygamy without interference from the authorities.

One of the wives, an articulate lawyer, presented a compelling case in which she said there was no jealousy between the women. If the group attempted to marry 'legally' by obtaining marriage licences from the state, they could receive a fine of $5,000 or 'imprisonment in a county jail not exceeding one year or in the state prison not exceeding ten years' (California Penal Code, Sec. 283). According to Bryant (1982), 'there are an estimated 35,000 practising polygamists, or "pligs" as they are locally labelled, located in parts of Utah, Arizona, and Colorado, and in Mexico'. In both England and the United States, prosecution on polygamous charges is a great legal rarity (Freeman, 1979), but prosecutions are not entirely unknown. In 1983, a man was convicted of marrying dozens of women in the United States. He could not give his correct name as he had used hundreds of aliases. Nor could he remember all the names of the women he had married. But this was the case of a man, labelled by the press a 'foreigner', who only married women if they possessed a certain amount of money. In other words, he was a confidence trickster who invariably absconded with his latest wife's funds. He was eventually caught by one irate wife who tracked him down even as he was attempting to marry again.

Bryant (1982) mentions schizoid forms of bigamy known as the 'Pennypacker' syndrome, named appropriately after a theatrical comedy. In this case, a man secretly maintains two families, neither family knowing of the other's existence. Bryant writes, 'Truth is stranger than fiction, however, and only a few years ago, when a famous American multi-millionaire died, it was revealed that he had maintained two families in two different communities. Litigation concerning the distribution of the estate was heated and protracted.'

KLEPTOLANGIA

Kleptolangia refers to sexual excitement derived from stealing an object. The motivation is usually based on danger – symbolic of the forbidden. I have heard of burglars who have been psychologically assessed to show what some psychologists call an 'internalized sexual psychopathology' and who have been reported to ejaculate at the point of escaping the premises they are in the process of robbing.

Some sex offenders specialized in the theft of undergarments and lingerie. The victim may be known to the thief, but is usually a stranger. In Philip Roth's novel *Portnoy's Complaint* (1969), the central character steals his sister's brassières and masturbates while dangling them in the bathroom. Such behaviour is generally innocuous, represents guilt over sexual matters and is more likely to occur in early adolescence. Kleptolangia is not, however, always innocuous. It is often a precursor in the sexual genesis of rapists (see page 148ff). Indeed, a proportion of rapists are also charged with theft in addition to the sexual crime.

The behaviour may also occur among some child molesters who will steal the underwear of potential victims. Stealing undergarments is a way for the perpetrator to become anonymously intimate with another person. Often, the kleptolangic will sniff and/or use the stolen garment, soiled or unsoiled, as a masturbatory aid.

PARAPLEGAPHILIA

The sexual preference in which paraplegics or paralysed, handicapped persons are the object of an individual's sexual desires is known as **paraplegaphilia**. Persons who prefer a type of sexual partner who is physically handicapped may suffer from low self-esteem. They tend to feel in control of the sexual situation – for obvious reasons. A twenty-four-year-old woman told me that she liked people in wheelchairs because she felt more powerful. The incidence of this sexual preference remains unknown.

It should be stressed that the fact that an individual is married to, or has, a partially or fully handicapped sexual partner does not necessarily imply a 'sexual deviation'. Many such relationships are rewarding, fulfilling and mature. Contrary to popular myth, the sensual lifestyle of many handicapped persons is rich and full.

GERONTOPHILIA

A sexual preference for a much older partner, **gerontophilia**, occurs in both sexes. For instance, a twenty-year-old may seek sexual relations with an eighty-year-old. There is a far greater social stigma attached to older women having affairs with younger men.

In this regard, in early 1984, the *Star* (Johannesburg)

reported that a Danish sexologist suggested that 'male prostitutes be brought into Danish old age homes to help old ladies with their sexual needs'. The sexologist, Professor Sten Hegeler, said that women prostitutes were already servicing elderly males. In other words, he felt there should be *equality* between the sexes so far as prostitution is concerned. The subject of geriatric sex has been taboo for far too long and, because of this, the elderly are discriminated against. To quote the *Star*'s Foreign News Service in an aptly titled article 'To Keep the Home Fires Burning': 'Professor Hegeler thinks a part-solution to youth unemployment would be for suitable young men to be employed to work at old age homes to keep the elderly women happy' – Scandinavian liberalism and humanity at its best.

MYSOPHILIA

Gerber (1982) describes **mysophilia** as a dependency on something soiled or filthy, 'such as sweaty underwear or used menstrual pads'. The section on 'Coprophilia' (page 350 above) contains a description of how Martin Luther (1483–1546) 'frequently waited more than a year to change his bed sheets, permitting them to become saturated with the smell of sweat, and after his marriage he often touched "specific parts" of his wife's body while being tempted by the devil' (Wallace *et al.*, 1981).

SEXUAL VAMPIRISM: SEX AND BLOOD

Sexual vampirism has been observed only on *rare* occasions. The term refers to a desire to take blood from a victim – though not in quite the same manner as Count Dracula. Once, when visiting a psychiatric hospital in a Third World country, I observed a psychiatric interview of a nineteen-year-old man who had been admitted for observation after being charged with breaking and entering and child molestation. As the interview progressed, so the sordid and tragic details emerged.

The young man had broken into a boarding school during the night and kidnapped an eight-year-old-boy. The assailant was equipped with an iron rod and 'medical supplies' which included a hypodermic syringe. The victim was 'kept quiet' simply by being knocked unconscious. 'I just hit him a little bit, just enough to keep him quiet. Then I took him down to a playing field. I wanted to give him a blood-test. And that was what the syringe was for,' the offender said nonchalantly. Then, he continued, 'I didn't mean to harm him. I just want to forget about the whole thing and get out of here as soon as possible.' As the interview proceeded, it emerged that the young man had not actually had the gall to draw blood out of his victim, but he did admit to having become sexually excited by the fantasy of doing so.

Fortunately, cases of sexual vampirism are rare. When they do occur, they may confidently be considered as acting out by severely disturbed persons. Sexual vampirism is associated with a combination of psychiatric diagnoses, such as schizophrenia, anti-social personality disorders, sexual sadism and dissociations.

The connection between blood and sex is not, however, always associated only with severe psychiatric conditions. One bizarre advertisement, which was placed in a Danish sex and singles magazine, stated that the advertiser would pay women for their used tampons. He did not say how he became sexually excited by the tampons, or in what way he would put them to use.

In another instance, a German woman from Munich described a procedure which some readers may find sexually sordid. She said that her lover would cut his chest and abdomen with a razor blade, making only shallow incisions. The couple then proceeded to have sexual intercourse while smearing his blood over both their bodies. The woman had initially found the practice 'abominable', but later came to enjoy her lover's unusual, masochistic and perverse sexual preference.

EROTIC PIERCING

Buhrich (1983) made a study of the sexual practice of erotic piercing, associated with homosexuality, sado-masochism, bondage fetishism, and tattooing, based on six women and 154 men who advertised in the dalliance columns of an American publication dedicated to those with an interest in the erotic piercing of genitals. His conclusions stressed a connection between erotic piercing and homosexuality.

In the summer of 1981, I saw a young man on Castro Street, a predominantly homosexual area of San Francisco, who had rings passed through both nipples. Gold chains were attached to these rings, and the chains were attached to another ring which was passed through an area of skin just below the navel. The sequence of chains was then attached to another chain, by which another man, dressed in leather, led him around.

In the sado-masochistic *Story of O*, Réage (1970) describes how the central character, O, has a ring pierced through her labia. This enables her to be led around by a dominant man, Sir Stephen. 'Penis ornamentation' usually consists of passing studs through the glans of the penis. This is usually done for masochistic reasons, but, in Japan, the insertion of a pearl under the skin of the penis is performed for reasons which are not masochistic. The *yakuza*, or Japanese underworld, do this to 'give superior sexual satisfaction to the woman and so enable the *yakuza* to maintain a hold on the prostitutes they pimp for; supposedly the pearl-penis provides more sexual gratification than that of any customer' (Diamond, 1984).

FETISHISM

Strictly speaking, a **fetish** is said to occur when an individual is sexually aroused only by specific objects and is generally unable to achieve sexual satisfaction without their presence. A 'normal' fetishist may be aroused by a specific part of the body, like legs, buttocks or breasts. Some individuals are *only* attracted to certain skin complexions, nose shapes, ankle width, body types and so on. Fetishism covers a broad range of behaviours. It exists on a continuum, between what are perfectly usual and general sexual triggers and responses and what are highly esoteric and personal sources of stimuli, and therefore represents an area in which it is impossible to say what is truly 'abnormal' or 'normal'.

Fetishism only becomes a problem when it limits the scope of an individual's sexuality or interferes with the liberty of another. For example, if a man can respond only to women who wear a certain type of rubber lingerie during intercourse, he automatically eliminates numerous potential relationships from his life. Similarly, a woman who finds only 'powerful' men who drive motor-cycles sexually appealing is missing out on many potentially fulfilling relationships.

The *American Heritage Dictionary* defines a fetish as 'an object believed to have magical power' or 'an object of obsessive attention or reverence'. Some fetishists accord a 'sexual magic', as it were, to underwear, silk and leather apparel, and the huge market for items made out of special materials is well attested in pornography magazines. Other popular 'fetish objects' are hair, high-heeled boots, furs, and feet. Leather fetishists may often be found in the sado-masochistic subculture for 'Sado-Masochism' (see page 109 above), the wearing of leather among machismo male homosexuals, for instance, being an affirmation of their virility which binds them to the group.

Severe problems can arise when a fetish is compounded with a panoply of other sexual 'perversions', as in the case of a fifteen-year-old marginally retarded youth who was attracted to little girls of three or four years. Not only did he molest them sexually (for 'Paedophilia', see page 217) but was, in particular, attracted to those with long straight blonde hair. Brown or black hair held no 'interest' for him. The attraction was so strong that he had forcefully 'stolen' the hair of certain girls (see 'Kleptolangia', page 363 above) by cutting some off with a pair of scissors. He had hoaxed one girl into believing that he was 'playing hairdresser', much to the chagrin of her parents, which led to the circumstances being investigated by the police. When they interviewed numerous children in the neighbourhood, the 'scandal' broke loose. (The boy may, in part, have been conditioned into finding hair arousing: initially, the mere sight of a little girl with blonde hair arousing him until, after a short period, he became aroused by the hair alone.)

GERBILLOPHILIA

A most strange and unusual sexual behaviour has recently (1985) surfaced in the United States. The bizarre practice, labelled **gerbillophilia**, involves the insertion of a *living* gerbille into the rectum. Gerbilles are small rodents which usually live in desert areas. They do not have sharp claws and in the normal way are regarded as making excellent children's pets.

An abuser inserts a large funnel into his rectum and allows one of the little animals to creep inside. The funnel is then removed, and as the gerbille crawls and struggles against suffocating, toxic gas in the bowels, it provides, practitioners claim, sexual 'pleasure' – if, indeed, that is the appropriate term. The dead animal is excreted in the normal eliminative process.

The phenomenon first came to light in a Texas town where the demand for gerbilles, according to the press, exceeded the supply. In addition, doctors at one hospital were perplexed by repetitive gastro-intestinal infections in one of their patients. On being questioned further, he admitted to the practice of inserting gerbilles into his rectum for purposes of sexual arousal.

PART SEVEN
In Search of Ultimate Orgasm

Introduction

> 'By happy alchemy of mind
> They turn to pleasure all they find.'
> – Matthew Green, *The Spleen* (1737)

Human fascination with mystery, magic and alchemy is as ancient as the human obsession with the 'higher powers' of the sex drive. The spiritual alchemists, those charismatic purveyors of faith – gurus, shamans, priests and medicine men – many of whom traded on deep human insecurity, eagerly tapped what they knew to be a highly lucrative market in the need to explain the unexplainable.

Some made fantastic claims about a miraculous 'immaculate conception', or evil spirits who sexually molest unsuspecting pious men and women during the night. Others added new ideas about the power of sexual energy to witchcraft, voodoo and mythology. Others spoke of attaining spiritual enlightenment or *nirvana* through prolonged sex rites. Many offered membership in sexual utopias – clubs in which new sexual promiscuities could be tested.

While the more 'primitive' experts sold magical cures for impotence, or potions to enchant lovers, their colleagues of today sell anything from spiritual enlightenment through sex, to books on 'rediscovered' parts of the female anatomy which can allegedly lead to super-orgasm.

If aphrodisiacs worked, they did so more out of powerful beliefs than anything else. The 'faith traders' used a combination of charisma, insight and an understanding of human weaknesses to manipulate large groups of needy people. Faith triumphed over the need for proof.

So long as I believe that a certain herb will make me sexually more potent, then I may very well become more potent. So long as I believe the guru's claim that incessant sex without orgasm will get me to God, to *nirvana*, then I may very well become 'enlightened'. If I have faith in a persuasive leader who offers me membership in a sexual utopia, I may very well find myself in my utopia. Since I, myself, do not know the secrets of life, and long to have faith and ultimate security, I may well believe that Jesus's mother Mary was 'impregnated' by God and that, as such, God manifested perfectly in man to die for my sins.

My soul needs mythology to explain the unexplainable. I am afraid of the dark, and so I grope for anything remotely resembling light. I need to belong, to find my roots, to feel connected with and loved by an impersonal cosmos. And so I search out the magic of the world and believe those who seem to know.

This section is concerned with sexual superstitions, the search for ultimate orgasm and God, narcissism, the paranormal, sexual utopias and some of the many avenues along that search. I have selected those areas which I felt were most representative of the ways in which people have searched for pleasure and magical answers to life. Let us never forget that sex, like oxygen, fuels the continuation of life.

26 GOD, SEX, SUPERSTITIONS AND SEXUAL UTOPIAS

APHRODISIACS AND SEX DRUGS

The term **aphrodisiac** originates in Greek mythology. Aphrodite, Goddess of Love, was created out of sea-foam when the God Chronos murdered and castrated his own father, afterwards throwing the mutilated genitals into the ocean. An aphrodisiac is a potion or drug alleged to stimulate the libido or sex drive in both men and women. **Anaphrodisiacs** are substances, alcohol among them, which reduce libido when consumed in excess.

The desire for aphrodisiacs is ancient and almost universal. In spite of the magical thinking, hope, wishing and incantations, true aphrodisiacs do not exist. When aphrodisiacs seem to exert an effect, it is more a function of a powerful belief than of any inherent sex ingredient. For example, according to Reay Tannahill (1980), who gives a brief survey of the history of aphrodisiacs, the Chinese believed that what they called 'bald chicken drug', blended plants such as *Polygala japonica, Cuscuta japonica*, and *Boschniakia glabra*, would enhance sexual potency. The legend behind the power of this drug concerns an official who, as a result of using it regularly, was said to have so much sexual staying power and desire that not only did he father three sons after the age of seventy but his wife was unable to sit or lie down as a result of his sexual demands. When the official discarded the drug in the barnyard, a cock swallowed it. The cock then mounted the first hen in sight and spent several days performing *coitus noninterruptus*. The frantic cock pecked at the hen's head until the hen became bald – hence the name given the drug.

The Indian *Kama Sutra* lists numerous tonics, herbs and preparations to 'attract others to yourself' and 'subjugate the hearts of others'. One method advocated is that a man should anoint his *lingam* (penis) with a mixture of white thorn apple, the long pepper, the black pepper and honey, so as to 'subjugate' a woman during intercourse. Since such a preparation would most likely irritate and burn both the penis and vaginal membranes, it is not clear how it would facilitate the subjugation of woman. The *Kama Sutra* also suggests grinding up the remains of a kite (a bird of prey), which must have died 'a natural death', with cowage and honey. Other potions recommended are ointments composed of burned camel bones, orris root and mango combined with honey, which, when 'anointed' on the penis, will drive a woman to ecstatic heights.

Many aphrodisiacs were, in their invention, based on symbolism and sympathetic action. For example, thousands of rhinoceroses and deer were, and still are, slaughtered for their horns, simply because they resemble the erect phallus, and the rhinoceros population in Africa is actually so seriously endangered that several wealthy Texans have established farms to breed the animals in the United States. Slices of rhinoceros horn are currently on sale as aphrodisiacs in Hong Kong. Since onions look like ovaries, they were recommended in ancient Greek civilization as potent cures for frigidity in women. Olives were consumed because they are similarly shaped to testes. Oysters get their reputation for having aphrodisiac properties because their shells resemble vaginal labia. Peppers produce a 'hot' sensation when they come into contact with mucous membranes in the mouth or vagina, and cooked okra is supposed to resemble vaginal lubrication.

Spanish fly is one of the well-known aphrodisiacs. This potion is made from ground-up dried corpses of *Cantharis* beetles and acts as a strong inflammatory agent which will irritate the gastro-intestinal tract and excretory system. It is thought that the origin of the belief in it as an aphrodisiac lies in farmers observing cattle eating the beetles and then behaving as if on heat. In human males, the drug does cause erection, but the erection is painful and is a reflex action caused by inflammation of the urinary tract. In fact, a dosage strong enough to have an effect on male or female genitalia may also be strong enough to cause acute or even fatal kidney damage. Spanish fly is therefore a dangerous substance and it is doubtful whether advertisers in pornographic magazines ever actually mail the 'real thing' to their customers.

Another alleged aphrodisiac is **mandrake root**, which contains the drugs atropine and scopolamine. Paradoxically, these can in actuality produce depressed respiration and confusion. In Genesis, Leah and Jacob were said to have used the root as a sexual aid but, as Diamond (1984) points out, 'Jacob and Leah may have slept together, but perhaps that was all they did.' Diamond tested the aphrodisiac **yohimbine**, which comes from the bark of the yohimbe tree, found in the Cameroons. It was tested in both animals and humans, but despite drug company claims that it facilitates erection when combined with testosterone, Diamond was unable to confirm the product as a true aphrodisiac. Other myths about aphrodisiacs include the belief that consuming eryngo roots, asparagus, eels or ginseng, among a wide assortment of obscure minerals, plants and animals, will increase libido.

Alcohol is known to reduce inhibition in general and, when taken in moderate doses, facilitates a reduction in sexual inhibition. However, as a result of its depressive effect on the central nervous system, it also often impairs erectile ability. **Marijuana**, or **cannabis**, can relax some people, but is also a drug which tends to reduce sexual interest in others. In fact, the sustained use of marijuana (once a day for two months) reduces both sexual activity and the production of sperm in males, since it reduces the output of the male hormone, androgen. In women it does, however, seem to correlate with a higher probability of orgasm, though we do not know what effects it can have on the developing foetus.

Methaqualone (Mandrax, Quaaludes or Ludes as the pills are also called) is a hypnotic drug believed by some to produce incredible ultimate orgasms. They claim it has the effect of producing subjective euphoria – a form of excited hypnosis. Though particularly popular in the United States, the drug is extremely dangerous because the user can overdose on a few tablets. For good reason, it is banned in both Britain and North America. It seems surprising that the drug should be thought of as a sex drug. Users can seldom remember what actually happened when they were stoned on it.

Several pornographic magazines advertise 'sex pills', 'sex creams' and 'sex vitamins', all being uniquely developed by famous scientists and sexologists. The advertising industry added insult to injury when, during the early 1980s, passengers on New York City subways were confronted with an advertisement directed at black males. The aphrodisiac? Vitamins *boosted with zinc*, an ingredient essential to the ultimate function of a healthy prostate gland. This formula is, by way of implication, supposed to make the black American male (for some reason it was not aimed at white men) more virile.

More powerful than mere vitamins is the drug **amyl nitrate**, which is normally used in cardiology for patients suffering from a lack of oxygen supply to the heart (angina pain). The drug is a vasodilator, meaning it acts rapidly to dilate blood vessels throughout the body. Subjective effects include light-headedness and rapid pulse rate. The drug is usually legitimately administered by placing a small tablet under the tongue. On the black market, however, the drug is made available in liquid form. Abusers inhale the vapour to experience a short-lived 'high' consisting of total numbness, rapid heart rate and momentary blissfulness. It is a drug which seems to have emerged in the gay community, although it is also popular among heterosexuals. Recently, amyl nitrate 'poppers' or 'locker room' has been used to enhance orgasm. The user sniffs the vapour at the point of 'orgasmic inevitability', a physiological stage of already heightened arousal and rapid pulse. The consequent orgasm has been called 'ultimate', 'indescribable' and 'cosmic'. It must be stressed that this practice is extremely dangerous and can result in fatal cardiac arrest or heart attack among other unwanted side-effects.

Less dangerous, but perhaps equally strange, is the use of **pheromones**, chemical scents which are supposed to attract women in the same way as apes are attracted to each other. One trademarked after-shave, Androstat, is alleged by its manufacturers to contain these hormones, which are either synthesized chemically or derived from animal glands. For example, musk oil, extracted from the almost extinct Tibetan musk ox for sale at over £2,500 a pound, is thought to have aphrodisiac properties. In another example, the Ethiopians are said to torture the civet cat, a small burrowing animal which secretes a substance near its testes when made afraid or angry. This substance is used in perfumes, which are claimed to be sexually alluring in human beings (Diamond, 1984).

There is, however, *no hard evidence* to show that women are irresistibly attracted by the 'smell' of sex hormones in the same way as animals. On the other hand, one study did show that women were more inclined to seat themselves on cinema seats previously sprayed with pheromones than on unsprayed seats (Cook and Wilson, 1979).

Last but not least, we come to **cocaine**, an illegal 'recreational drug' which has turned out to be an exceedingly prevalent fad of the 1980s. The drug has associations with Freud, who conducted some of the original research into its effects. Freud initially thought that the drug was a panacea or cure-all covering everything from depression to fatigue, and his main interest was in its medicinal properties as an anaesthetic. He never referred to it as an aphrodisiac. [Cocaine may, in fact, act as an aphrodisiac for some people, but only because, at a cost of about £70 a gram (more than gold), it is associated with power and prestige, regarded in many cultures as sexual turn-ons.]

The drug is commonly 'snorted' as a white crystalline powder into the nose, though it can also be smoked in its 'free-base' form, or injected. Users claim that it produces an unsurpassed feeling of clarity and well-being. Cocaine is similar to amphetamines in that it may prolong erection, but this sometimes leads to 'priapism' or prolonged painful erection. The paradox with cocaine intoxication is that, while it may enable both men and women to have lengthy sexual intercourse, it can also leave them unable to reach orgasm. Cocaine can also be placed directly on the clitoris and this, some women claim, results in heightened sexual arousal; but this seems hard to explain when the drug is known to act as a local anaesthetic. Americans are estimated to spend £26 billion on the drug annually, and millions are dependent on it, sometimes to the point of becoming psychotic.

There are scientists who continue to strike out in hot pursuit of love chemicals and who refer to mysterious neurotransmitters secreted in the right hemisphere of the brain. They suggest that certain foods, like chocolate and carbohydrates, act as the building blocks from which the love chemicals are made by the body. A diagnosis called 'hysteroid dysphoria' was even invented to describe the depression experienced when people fall out of love. Wollman and Lotner (1983) spoke, in their book called *Eating Your Way to a Better Sex Life*, of 'sexual nutrition'. It stands to reason that healthy bodies will facilitate healthy sex. There is, however, no causal relationship between super-nutrition and super-sex.

THE SENSATIONALIZATION OF THE VAGINA: THE 'DISCOVERY' OF THE G-SPOT

As we have seen, the narcissistic search for ultimate sexual pleasure is not something new to the twentieth or Freudian century. For many decades, Westerners have been 'rediscovering' the sexual knowledge of 'mysterious' ancient Eastern and Middle Eastern civilizations and, unsurprisingly, the penis and female genitalia have been explored with microscopic precision. These organs have been represented in art throughout the ages, and described in literature, including the Bible, and early 'sex manuals' such as the *Kama Sutra*.

The genitalia, and the paroxysms of pleasure which they can produce, were, and still are, the object of obsessive and often excessive fascination. Nevertheless, orgasm in women has not traditionally been an important topic, despite the fact that humans rank among the few species where females can experience multiple orgasms. (Female chimpanzees have been observed to have multiple orgasms when stimulated with a vibrator in laboratory conditions.)

As far back as the Greek physician, Galen of Pergamon (A.D. 129–99), semen was confused with vaginal secretions. Thomas Szasz (1980) quotes Galen's 'treatment' of 'hysteria' in the woman, a 'treatment' in which the doctor masturbated the patient by massaging her genitals:

Following the warmth of the remedies and arising from the touch of the genital required by the treatment, there followed twitchings accompanied at the same time by pain and pleasure after which she emitted turbid and abundant sperm [i.e. genital secretions]. From that time on she was freed of all the evil she felt.

Indeed, Galen preceded the modern sex-therapy shamans, Masters and Johnson, by 1,750 years when he observed and recorded 'live orgasm' by women. Yet in his description of female orgasm it seems from this statement at least, that he was unaware of the fundamental differences between the seminal fluid of the man's ejaculate and the woman's vaginal secretions. Even so, he was one of the first to appreciate the importance of the female orgasm, and his treatment prescription had overtones (almost Freudian) which reflected the idea that women are sexually repressed and therefore emotionally weaker. In our present century, once the notion that women could and indeed should be orgasmic became more generally acceptable, the search for the ultimate female orgasm was on in no uncertain terms. It was in 1950 that a German physician, Ernst Grafenberg, claimed to have discovered a supposedly new erotic zone in the vagina.

This 'new zone' was termed the **Grafenberg spot** *or* **G-spot** by American sex researchers Whipple and Perry. The spot itself is supposedly located on 'the anterior wall of the vagina along the course of the urethra'. When stimulated, it is said to cause 'gushes' of 'fluids', not 'urinary in character' and with no 'lubricating significance'. In other words, when the G-spot is adequately stimulated a woman can, by using her fingers, 'ejaculate'.

One researcher at the American Psychological Association Convention in 1982 remarked that heterosexual couples would begin to ask each other, 'Did you spurt yet?' in response to this new discovery. The audience for the paper packed the hall, the new discovery having caused quite a stir in America where, as one journalist put it, 'They hype almost anything, so why should a part of the vagina, hitherto ignored, not be hyped, especially if it's got to do with improving orgasm in women!' Despite the excitement caused by the publication of the book on the G-spot and innumerable articles on the subject, most women remain unable to find their G-spots or 'ejaculate' special fluids while in the throes of ultimate orgasm. The entire concept of the G-spot has, like many another topic in sexuality, been sensationalized to the point of earning itself a reputation (along with Spanish fly) in the annals of sexual mythology.

It can only be hoped that women do not suffer needless performance anxiety after reading about the wonders of this newly discovered part of their anatomy, the so-called G-spot, and then, having failed to locate it, worry that they are 'abnormal' and not 'performing' to the required standard. Happily, most of the women I have spoken to on the subject seem to take the G-spot with a pinch of salt.

IMMACULATE CONCEPTION AND DISCARNATE SPIRITS

Extraordinary, unusual and mystical beliefs about sex continue to be pervasive. For instance, several hundred million believing Christians believe in parthenogenesis, immaculate conception, or automatic conception. In essence, they believe that Jesus's mother, Mary, was fertilized by a divine spirit, the Holy Ghost. Mary had not needed to have sexual intercourse to become pregnant.

Jesus himself is thought to be immortal because his father, God, had no knowledge of death. The ultimate human being, Jesus, was produced out of the ultimate sexual encounter – union between Mary and God. The entire story can only be explained in terms of a religious miracle.

The belief in the ability of spirit beings to visit humans for sexual purposes was especially prevalent during the Middle Ages when monks thought that an evil spirit could sexually molest the living in their sleep. This evil spirit was known as a **succubus** if it tried to seduce a man, or as an **incubus** if it tried to molest a woman. Monks attributed their wet dreams or nocturnal emissions to the visitation of an evil spirit. Women who had sexual dreams blamed the experience on these supernatural phenomena and would pray for them to go away.

PSYCHIC PHENOMENA AND SEX

The term 'psychic phenomena' refers to those human experiences which are paranormal or inexplicable in scientific terms. In the jargon of parapsychology, the ability to move objects without touching them is known as **psychokinesis**; the ability to know that an aeroplane will crash on a particular date in the future is called **precognition**; the ability to communicate thought is called **telepathy**; and the ability to 'leave' one's body and travel about merely by thinking of the place one wants to be is called **astral travel**.

Astral travel infers that people can consciously leave their bodies while deeply relaxed or asleep. Typically, the astral traveller is aware of himself falling asleep. He experiences what is usually described as a humming sound and 'vibrations' as he watches his body fall asleep. He can then leave his body through his stomach or head and float around the room. Once in the 'astral body' the person is said to have 360° vision and to be able to go anywhere in the world or universe merely by thinking about a destination. Some astral travellers even claim that they have been to the moon. Why, then, should not such astral travellers meet each other for the purpose of having 'astral sexual intercourse'? Robert Monroe (1973) in his book, *Journeys Out of the Body*, claims that it happens. He even founded an institute on the East Coast of the United States to train others in the practice of out-of-the-body experience.

'Astral sex' is among the myriad of fascinating and sometimes unbelievable experiences recounted by Monroe. The astral traveller is able to leave his or her body to have 'sex' with other travellers or even with departed souls who have no body to return to. When two astral travellers meet for the purpose of a sexual encounter, the orgasm they enjoy is described as a powerful and pleasurable 'electric charge'. All they have to do to 'ground' the positive male charge with the negative female charge is touch each other. The 'astral orgasm' is then experienced as a powerful 'electric' pulse throughout the entire astral body. Many people claim that they can 'leave their bodies' at will, and serious scientific research into establishing the credibility of astral travel was conducted during the 1970s by the psychologist, Charles Tart, at the University of California.

The equally fascinating and inexplicable phenomenon of **telekinesis** has even been implicated in a 1974 paternity suit in Sweden when the Israeli psychic, Uri Geller, was sued for allegedly bending the metallic contraceptive IUD of an unsuspecting woman. The woman claimed that Geller was liable to child support because she became pregnant after he, using his telekinetic powers, bent her IUD and made it ineffective – *even though he had never had any physical contact with it.*

MYSTICAL ENLIGHTENMENT (NIRVANA) AND SEX

Almost all religious movements have something to say about the role of sexuality in spiritual enlightenment. Most religious doctrines simply regulate sexual expression: sex should only take place between married men and women, at certain times; or, among some fundamentalists, only for the purpose of procreation. However, various mystical branches of religion have long recognized the 'divinity', 'creativity', or 'Godliness' inherent in the pleasures of sexual intercourse.

There are many paths towards spiritual enlightenment or that state of absolute awareness beyond the limitations of space and time achieved by such masters as the Buddha or Jesus. Most routes to enlightenment require total abstinence from the pleasures of everyday life, usually advocating celibacy and poverty, a complete detachment from sensory experience and, often, complete devotion to a guru who will encourage the devotee to follow the correct path. However, not all journeys towards enlightenment follow a path of denial. There are, indeed, a few which advocate indulgence and excess.

THE INDIAN TANTRIC CULT

One deviation from the usual paths of spiritual liberation is the Indian **Tantric Yoga** cult. Rawson (1973) suggests that Tantra probably originates in Buddhist traditions. Tantra stands on its own in that it champions non-orgasmic sexual intercourse as the royal road to spiritual liberation, enlightenment and bliss. Its mysticism advocates the worship of the female sexual or creative energy (*sakti*) together with male sexual energy. It emphasizes the female or *kundulini* 'energy' located at the base of the spine.

As in other forms of yoga, there are six points of psychic power known as *chakras* which are believed to run along the spinal column or *sushunna*. The *kundulini* energy is symbolized by a serpent, and is said to be waiting dormant at the base of the spine or root *chakra*. The energy is waiting to surge up through all the *chakras*, and when it reaches the highest centre or *sahasrara*, liberation and freedom from the senses or endless cycle of reincarnations is achieved. The *sahasrara* is situated at the top of the skull and is symbolized by the lotus flower.

The *kundulini* is stimulated by yoga exercises, many of which require a specialized form of sexual intercourse between a man and woman. Great caution is taken by male and female devotees *not to reach orgasm*. Adherents practise slow coitus for hours on end while meditating on magical diagrams, or *yantras*, and reciting sacred words, or *mantras*. It is said that enlightenment comes to few devotees, but that when it does come, the person concerned is endowed with supernatural powers and spiritual transcendence.

Well-known Tantric temples in India include the Black Pagoda and Sun Temple at Konarak. Rawson (1973) describes the Tantric saint as being

so happy as to seem crazy; his eyes roll, reddened with wine. He sits on silk cushions surrounded by works of art, eating hot pork cooked with chillies. At his left sits a girl skilled in the arts of love, with whom he drinks and repeatedly has ecstatic sexual intercourse; he continually makes music with his vina [a stringed instrument], and sings poems; all of which he weaves together into rituals.

THE RAJNEESH CULT: THE ORANGE PEOPLE AND TANTRIC SEX

Tantra and variations on Tantric themes are practised by tens of thousands of 'spiritual seekers' in the West, and among those who have embarked on indulgence as the road to spiritual liberation are the followers of the Indian guru, Bhagwan Shree Rajneesh (1979). His followers are known as the Orange People because they used to wear orange robes, now plum-coloured. The cult is famous in the United States, not only because of its sexual activities, but because it moved its unusual headquarters from India to take over the town of Antelope (renamed Rajneeshpuram) in Oregon.

Like other Eastern gurus, Bhagwan Shree Rajneesh proposes the concept of the 'dissolution of the ego' as the key towards becoming spiritually enlightened. This means that people have to face the ugliness of desire within themselves. They must confront their fears, jealousies, sexual possessiveness, 'money-madness' and 'power addiction' if they are to gain ultimate release from earthly existence, but since this book is concerned primarily with bizarre sex practices, it will only focus on the sexual or Tantric aspects of the Rajneesh philosophy.

Bhagwan Shree Rajneesh uses paradox – and a good deal of jargon – to put his 'message' across. In his own words, 'Tantra is not indulgence at all.' Repressed sexuality causes people to 'go mad'; 'sex energy is life energy'. To get closer to God, people should explore their sexuality without fear.

This is why the cult's devotees have participated in orgies and aggressive group sex, sometimes to the point of breaking one another's bones. In Bhagwan's view, the 'whole world is sex-obsessed', and if this obsession could only disappear, people would no longer be money-mad. And it is, of course, being money-mad that causes misery. (Not surprisingly, only those who are spiritually enlightened can afford to indulge in materialism, precisely because they are detached from the world. Rajneesh owned a fleet of Rolls-Royce cars and amassed millions.) The Orange People believe that sex will bring them closer to divinity, towards God. Bhagwan says, 'Sex is one of those activities given by nature and God in which you are thrown again and again to the present moment. Ordinarily you are never in the present – except when you are making love, and then too for a few seconds only.' By making love for hours on end in the Tantric tradition, awareness will expand and become complete: 'Man is half, woman is half'; the object is to unite the two through prolonged sexual intercourse, to raise the *kundulini* at the base of the spine and enter the blissful state of total awareness. One difference between the Rajneesh philosophy and original Tantric approaches to enlightenment is that Rajneesh approves of orgasm during intercourse while more traditional adherents believe that orgasm should be avoided and the 'energy' channelled to the higher brain centres.

Ma Satya Bharti (1983), a devotee of Bhagwan Shree Rajneesh (who gave her that name) wrote a book called *The Ultimate Risk* in which she recounted the stories of several other Westerners who went to the Rajneesh Ashram in the Indian town of Poona in search of spiritual enlightenment. One woman, Priya, was told by Bhagwan to take the Tantra group exercises. She had attended lectures in which Bhagwan advocated sex and explained the differences between auto-eroticism, homosexuality and heterosexuality. Out of these, heterosexuality was the best way to reach God, because 'only when you have bridged your sex energy with the opposite polarity (after having had lots of *guided* sexual intercourse) is there an integration in you and you begin to grow towards *brahnacharya*, celibacy'. In other words, devotees should indulge sexually in order to *become truly celibate*. Once in that state, the guru said, successful devotees would be able to 'live in a constant state of orgasm, a constant state of ecstasy'. According to Bhagwan, homosexuality is 'not considered harmful, it is not a sin, there is nothing wrong in it, but it is not helpful either. You have to go beyond.'

He prescribed specific exercises to raise sexual energy, and Priya was instructed to 'go to the toilet and shower with 49 other naked people prancing around'. People were blindfolded and had sex with each other. To activate the *kundulini* sexual energy at the base of the spine, devotees placed their fingers on their genitals and focused on feeling the female sexual energy as it rose up through the navel *chakra*, the heart *chakra*, the throat *chakra*, the third-eye *chakra* and finally to the top of the head, or crown *chakra*. They massaged each other sexually. Every now and then, the exercises would grow too threatening for someone – usually a woman – and, as Priya did, she would break down and sob as her devoted allegiance to her guru Bhagwan was put to the test.

Bhagwan Shree Rajneesh (1979) endorses the Tantric idea that love is 'the greatest phenomenon on earth' and that the 'greatest experience of humanity is orgasm'. Orgasm takes the man and the woman into momentary oblivion, far outside their egos, and they disappear, an experience the French call *la petite mort*. The objective is the dissolution of the ego – ceasing to be attached to being in the world. Enlightenment is, in part, living in this state of private awareness perpetually. In the view of the guru, female energy is located in the right hemisphere of the brain and is not rational, rational thought being an obstacle to enlightenment. The fact that women are less rational means that they lose their minds less frequently, do not commit suicide as often as men and kill far fewer people than men do during war. As the guru puts it:

The feminine mind is more joyous because it is more poetic, more aesthetic, more intuitive. But if you are not attached to any part and you are just a witness, then your joy is utter, ultimate. This joy we have called 'anand' – bliss. To know and witness this is to become one, absolutely one; then the woman and the man in you disappear completely, then you are lost in oneness. Then orgasmicness is your moment-to-moment existence. And in that state, sex disappears automatically – because there is no need. When a person lives orgasmically 24 hours a day, what is the need?

The Rajneesh foundation has centres in many European and North American cities. It attracted the attention of the media in North America when its followers took over the town of Antelope in Oregon. Devotees found stray hitch-hikers on American highways, brought them to Antelope and had them registered as voters. In this way the cult managed to gain political control over the town. The guru himself could be seen, very infrequently, waving to his devotees from the back of one of his Rolls-Royces.

According to William Scobie of the *Observer* (29 September 1985) several of the guru's followers ganged up against him, stole $55 million of the cult's money, then fled to Germany. Ma Sheela, chief secretary and leader of the insurrection against the Bhagwan, is also alleged to have poisoned the water supply of The Dalles, Oregon, an action which caused over 600 residents to become ill. The Bhagwan claims that Sheela and her gang tried to poison the state's District Attorney, Michael Sullivan, who almost died of poisoning in 1983. Sheela denied the allegations, claiming the guru to be a fraud. Sheela, who used to be Bhagwan's lover, subsequently lived in Germany with her new lover, but was later arrested and has now been extradited to the United States, where she faces 600 counts of attempted murder.

Towards the end of 1985 the guru had replaced his top devotees with wealthy Southern Californian Hollywood supporters. He lived in a state of perpetual fear, surrounded by armed guards, and had a helicopter flying above his car to protect his life. Bhagwan was finally arrested when he attempted to flee the United States on a private jet. He was thrown into jail and finally agreed to leave the country for less hostile climes in India. The guru is currently contemplating relocation to an island in the South Pacific.

THE MOVEMENT OF SPIRITUAL INNER AWARENESS AND SEX

The **Movement of Spiritual Inner Awareness** (MSIA) was founded by an American called John Roger. MSIA is included here because, like the Rajneesh group, it represents one of many Westernized versions of Eastern spiritual traditions. While concepts such as *karma*, reincarnation, and enlightenment are incorporated into the MSIA 'package' the emphasis is profoundly American in that it focuses on 'practical spirituality'. In other words, 'becoming spiritual' does not, from the MSIA perspective, require endless hours of meditation in a Zen Buddhist monastery. (Americans, of course, appreciate instant reward. They do not, as a people, like delaying gratification – even in the realms of 'spiritual enlightenment'. For this reason, instant enlightenment packages, those which do not advocate self-denial and are not too difficult, are popular.) The MSIA approach requires no stoic self-denial, sexual abstinence, fasting or vows of poverty. Instead, it embraces health, wealth, and sexual fulfilment as part of 'spirituality'. While MSIA members do not seem to indulge in the sexual extremities of the Rajneesh cult, John Roger is an advocate of some rather unusual notions about the role of sex in spiritual growth.

The claim of John Roger might well be that, as a guru, Bagwan practises 'spiritual deceit', his yoga being 'concerned with the lower centres of the body' (the genital *chakras*), and that, because of the emphasis, his spiritual followers will fail to become enlightened and will have to reincarnate back on to the 'earth plane' after they die. By contrast MSIA teachings are concerned only with the higher 'spiritual centres of the body' – the third-eye *chakra*, the throat *chakra* and the top of the head or crown *chakra* (supposedly fully developed in the Buddha and Jesus).

Seekers are instructed to concentrate on focusing themselves on their 'higher selves', that intuitive knowing or 'God' part of themselves that can see the 'God' within others. Sexuality is a part of nature, therefore a part of God.

In the words of Roger (1977), sexuality is beyond morality – there is no 'good or bad' – and everything is a question of 'frequencies'. Women have a 'greater negative polarity' or 'sexual frequency', and men have 'greater positive polarity'. Sexual intercourse is described as an 'electro-chemical-magnetic charge that takes place between the man and the woman'. Roger claims that men 'release their negativity through the normal process of energy exchange with a woman' (one way of saying sexual intercourse) and women release negativity when they have their periods. He also says that, if men 'block the flow' of sexual or 'creative' energy, they will probably develop prostate trouble and 'problems related to the genital area'. Anger, guilt and a desire for revenge contribute to such blocks of sexual energy, which can also lead to excess weight around the buttocks, abdomen and hip areas. (Such assertions are made without any concrete evidence to support them.)

It therefore comes as no surprise to find Roger suggesting that celibacy leads to psychiatric illness. A 'block' in a creative sexual energy, 'stirred' by 'Spirit', causes 'sexual drives . . . [to] reflex back up into the stomach and intestinal areas and then up into the shoulder, neck, and facial areas'. Acne may occur, and the neck may slip out of alignment. Roger claims that women manifest their sexual blocks by suffering menstrual cramps and exploding 'for no apparent reason' during their periods.

So-called sexual deviations – sadism, voyeurism, masochism, lesbianism, homosexuality, hermaphroditism, child molestation and tranvestism – are not 'spiritually' wrong for Roger, who asserts that, 'Spiritually, there is no morality in these areas.' But spiritual liberation requires that 'you must always be judicious about your activities – always'. Accordingly the soul knows no morality.

It may be illuminating to quote some of Roger's MSIA jargon. He writes, for example, that promiscuity is no help to those who want to become spiritually liberated:

> The action of the conjugal relationship is a very rapid way to mix the frequencies of your beingness with those of your partner ... If you engage in a relationship with someone who is also having sexual relations with others, you will receive not only his frequency but the frequencies and emotions of those with whom he has exchanged energies. You become a 'garbage collector', and that can be hell.

People should not deride prostitutes, because they may be 'finishing up some *karmic* situation' from a past life. In line with Eastern belief, judging a prostitute could lead to being born into similar circumstances in a future life. Prostitutes themselves have absorbed so many sexual 'frequencies' in to their bodies that they no longer have a clear image of who they really are.

Homosexuality is also explained in terms of *karma*. It, too, is neither right nor wrong. Homosexuals are viewed as fighting against their *karma* – the result of actions in present and prior lives. Once the homosexual accepts the *karmic* situation, his problems will disappear. The homosexual man simply has more 'feminine energy' in his 'lower self'. The lesbian simply has more 'masculinity' in her 'lower self'.

Masturbation is alleged to cause 'thought forms' to extend out of a person's body. This implies that sensitive 'psychic' or clairvoyant people are then able to see the person's aura (the etheric field around the body), which will contain representations of what the person has been thinking. These sexual 'thought forms' are said to be caused by the persistent fantasizing about particular sexual scenes. For this reason, sensitive persons will recognize someone as a 'local stud' or say, 'He thinks he's really a lady's man.'

PAGANISM, WITCHCRAFT AND SEX

Beliefs about the supernatural and sex abound in hundreds of societies, and it would be impossible to deal with them all in the present book. It should, however, be worth considering a few examples.

According to Reay Tannahill, Northern Buddhism, as followed in Tsinhai, China, differs from Tantric Buddhism in drastic ways. Sex is not, in this tradition, seen as a healthy path to enlightenment. Rather is it enshrouded in shame and guilt – to the point where menstrual blood and childbirth are often associated with spiritual doom. The sect believes in heaven and hell, but, unlike the Christian conception of hell, believes there are about 84,000 hells into which the sinner can be sent, depending on transgression during life. A woman who has the audacity to die during childbirth can expect to go to the 'blood hell' reserved especially for mothers who die at such a time. There she can expect to eat clotted blood and amniotic fluid until she is able to reincarnate back on to the earth plane, where she will have to face the bad *karma* caused by having died in childbirth.

The Mbom of the Cameroon believe that only women can be witches, the source of a witch's power lying in her vaginal secretions and pelvic cavity. By contrast, a man's magical powers are located in his head.

In New Guinea, the Kiwai-Papua consider the vagina to be the origin of all witchcraft and refer to the female genitalia as being as 'dangerous as an open grave'. But even though the vagina can be this dangerous, its powers can also be harnessed for good. When a member of the

Kawai-Papua goes hunting, his wife lies naked with her legs spread apart near the door through which he departed, in this way magically attracting the game.

Among the Maori of New Zealand, the vagina is called *Te whare ao aitu*, which means 'the house of the dead'. This is in line with their mythology, in which the hero of creation was strangled by a vagina when he sought the answer to immortality.

The magic of female sexual powers associated with 'voodoo' is practised by the *Umbanda* cult of Latin America and the Caribbean. The cult attracts both the poor and affluent, who believe that a female medium can lift spells, contact the dead and exorcize bad luck. Typically, the medium goes into a trance in which she speaks in tongues. Often her voice will change into that of a man, said to be the voice of the male spirit literally residing within her. The spirit will then instruct the client on the right course of action. One ethnologist described an instance in which a man sought the help of such a medium after consistent bad luck in business. The client's troubles, according to the medium's inner male spirit (*marimbondo*), were caused by a scorned fiancée who had paid an evil spirit to bring him bad luck in business and ruin his sexual prowess. The solution to the problem lay in sending the client and all the men present to 'have a pee'. After a few months, the client reported that his business was doing much better and that he had regained his lost sexual skills.

ASTROLOGY AND SEX

There is, of course, no acceptable scientific basis for astrology, which means that there is no reasonable logical basis for astrologers' claims concerning the individual's astrological sign and his or her personality characteristics. Nevertheless, millions of people, in search of meaning, and sometimes in reaction to scientific materialism, continue to believe in astrology. Astrology is not only used to describe personality characteristics, but it is thought by many to be a reliable way of predicting and controlling the future. Its uses can include help in choosing a spouse or business partner and 'explaining' both positive and negative events in the believer's life as well as in the lives of loved ones.

In parts of India, marriages are still arranged by a *gataka* or marriage broker, who uses the stars to organize the most harmonious marriage between a young girl, usually prepubescent, and an older man of the same sub-caste. The use of a marriage broker can be considered so important that the bride's father will go into debt to pay for the service.

In the West, the equivalent of millions of pounds and US dollars are spent each year by clients turning to astrologers to calculate intricate astrological charts so that they can use them to gain a 'better understanding' of themselves, make important business decisions or get married – purely on the basis of what the stars say. Judith Bennett's (1981) book, *Sex Signs*, is highly symptomatic of the narcissistic age in which we live. It is entirely devoted to the emotional and sexual qualities governed by each of the twelve signs of the Zodiac, Bennett describing it as 'a breakthrough book, a dramatic, unique marriage of astrology, psychology, and female sexuality. It goes directly to the point most relevant to today's woman: how can she develop awareness of herself, become attuned to the universal planetary rhythms that affect her, and obtain a key to her own love and power.' In addition to being bizarre, Bennett's 'psycho-astrological' theories are actually rather humorous.

The following summaries provide examples of a few 'sexual characteristics' of each sign as these are described in *Sex Signs*:

1. **Aries women** (born 21 March to 20 April) are said to be 'magnetic', have a 'high libido', require a man who is completely sure of his masculinity, likely to dabble 'in early

sexual experiments' and, when 'blocked', liable to be 'horny, bitchy, impatient, angry and finally ill'. The Aries woman is inclined to fall in love with ease, enjoy long drawn out sex and, according to Bennett, 'seems to prefer a man who finishes the sex act with hard thrusting'. Among her fantasies, the Aries woman is supposed to love power and, of all things, exhibitionism. Thus, Bennett writes, 'She often visualizes herself wearing a black garter belt, stockings, and boots, carrying a whip, and acting out a scenario of sexual domination in front of a frenzied audience.' Furthermore, Aries women are said to love homosexual and group sex fantasies, and to enjoy masturbating.

2. The **Taurus woman** (born 21 April to 20 May) is supposed to 'require monogamy in marriage' because she is especially prone to jealousy. Her 'appearance is very female, and she learns to walk with the bearing of a princess'. In intercourse, she is liable to want slow seduction coupled with romance, 'total involvement of the emotions and the mind, building to a slow, natural orgasm . . . orgasm in which the body shakes and continues periodic spasms for a long time', and to experience a 'complete feeling of release with a soothing and analgesic effect on the entire body'. [At this point, it seems pertinent to ask whether most women, regardless of their 'birth sign' or sexual orientation, do not desire these sorts of sensation during intercourse.] The Taurus woman also likes to be 'dominated by a man who is all man'. She loves oral sex, and one of her favourite sexual positions is *soixante-neuf*. Showing no regard for all those born under the sign of Taurus, Bennett writes that, 'In extreme cases, the Taurus Woman can be a devotee of coprophilia, an attraction to filth and excrement. In these encounters, she becomes aroused by rubbing her body with it, and some urinate on their partners as part of foreplay.' It goes without saying that no study to test whether there are more coprophiliacs born under the sign of Taurus is cited to back up this most incredible claim.

3. The **Gemini woman** (born between 21 May and 20 June) is said to be likely to have a 'complex' love life. She can also 'function well in the good old American tradition of sexual quickies'. She likes getting two men for the price of one, is 'mysteriously' sexy, and is more interested in IQ than in genitals. Bennett claims that Gemini women are more likely to become brutalized in relationships, develop a neurotic sex

drive, and enjoy 'dirty talk' during sexual intercourse. Also, 'when she puts her hands in his [her lover's] pocket, she wants more than to feel his genitals; she wants attention, security, companionship'. As a child, she is curious about the events 'behind her parents' closed bedroom door' [Bennett neglecting to ask what children are not interested in a forbidden place]. In sexual intercourse, the Gemini teases, has explosive and verbal orgasms, cools her passions quickly, needs affection and only requires one episode of intercourse. She is also capable of assuming the dominatrix role of S-and-M mistress because of an innate cruelty – according to *Sex Signs*.

4. The **Cancer woman** (born between 21 June and 20 July) is said to have hormones which 'awaken early', and to be, believe it or not, more likely to masturbate, pursue a secret extra-marital affair, and slower to reach sexual arousal than her sisters born under other signs. During intercourse, she is initially reluctant, requires 'a great deal of dermatological stimulation', dislikes quick penetration, does not go for elaborate sexual positions, loves embellished sexual fantasies, and needs more lubrication than women born under other signs. She is capable of 'intense orgasms', but is more likely to be 'frigid'. Bennett also seems to think that the Cancer woman is more apt to have sexual rape fantasies than other women.

5. **Leo women** (born between 21 July and 21 August) are amorous and fiery. They are more romantic, stylish, formal and gossipy. Leo women are said to be *femmes fatales* who use men to massage their egos. The Leo woman needs 'her man' to tell her consistently that she is the greatest, that he will love her for ever, finds her the most intelligent woman he ever encountered and so on. In sexual intercourse, she plays the game designed to boost her ego, is sensuous and inclined to watch herself making love. She, too, 'may be orgasmic but remains untouched on deep emotional levels'. Leo women need ambitious, rich and considerate men who are well-mannered, uncritical and, well, essentially perfect.

6. The **Virgo woman** (born between 22 August and 22 September) is categorically described as 'repressed' and one who will attract 'losers'. She also learns how to become technically proficient at sex, will not hesitate to visit 'dirty clubs', and is very capable of playing out her husband's whore fantasies. She is 'endlessly interested in her own sexual responses' and

may embark on a 'sexual binge' involving dildos, benwa balls [masturbatory aids], peacock feathers, egg-shaped vibrators and acrobatic sexual positions – all in the cause of overcoming her 'repressed' nature. Ironically, she doesn't like 'messy sex', but may like 'oral sex', and needs an experienced lover who can be her teacher in the sexual arts. However, she does have a 'kinky' side, one in which she might enjoy sporting spiked heels and leather gear and all while brandishing a cat-o'nine-tails.

7. **Libra women** (born between 23 September and 22 October) are inclined to marry early and to require especially understanding men. Unfortunately, judging by what *Sex Signs* says about her sexuality, the female Libra does not emerge as being especially sexy, since she is more inclined to fall in and out with 'the idea of love' rather than in love itself. Libra is disparagingly portrayed as someone who uses 'feminine wiles' to get what she wants.

8. The **Scorpio woman** (born between 23 October and 22 November) is obsessed with power and 'uses sex to obtain it'. She is 'mystical', hungers for male bodies, enjoys sniffing, stroking and tracing, is extremely intense and vindictive. In sexual intercourse, she is initially reluctant, but becomes totally involved, lubricates suddenly, and, believe it or not, also has intense orgasms. She likes lovers who grunt, breathe heavily, use obscene words, use hard pelvic thrusts so that the penis touches her cervix, and is multi-orgasmic. She also likes a man with a dash of 'sadism', 'sensitivity', lots of sex appeal, and 'total sexual expertise'. She supposedly enjoys sex in exotic places [the text being written as though others do not]. Bennett states the following of Scorpio women: 'I suspect that a Scorpio is responsible for that ingenious recent invention, the flexible shower-hose with power nozzle. How else could a woman masturbate to her heart's content in the bathtub?' [Were shower-hoses, one is tempted to inquire, therefore developed merely for the sexual arousal of women?]

9. The **Sagittarius woman** (born between 23 November and 20 December), in Bennett's words 'loves orgies' because, 'Group sex is a powerful aphrodisiac to her, and she barely comprehends the meaning of jealousy or shame.' She likes 'firm, strong, powerful intercourse'. This woman is made for making love all night long, until she is totally spent and exhausted. Multiple orgasms are her cup of tea, which is why she loves

orgies, because when one partner is finished through exhaustion, another can continue. Once she is finally satiated, she feels warm, at peace, and at one 'with the universe'. Furthermore, 'she loves any kind of intercourse – anal, oral, and vaginal'. The Sagittarian woman is inclined to keep a supply of amyl nitrate (see 'Aphrodisiacs', page 374) to help with reviving a 'spent' lover. One of the most bizarre ideas demonstrating that the author of *Sex Signs* has an obscure imagination in drawing conclusions is the 'logic' she uses to explain how Sagittarian women may become 'aficionado[s] of anal sex and vaginal sex from behind'. Incredibly, Bennett assumes that because Sagittarian women love animals, 'dogs and horses especially', this love 'leads her to sexual fantasies that may in fact stem from her childhood experiments'.

10. The **Capricorn woman** (born between 21 December and 19 January) is supposed not to 'relish complicated sexual moves'. Typically, she will have had at least one crush 'on a female upper-class member or a teacher, but she is probably too embarrassed to talk about it'. She is prone to being attracted to boys at an early age. She is then liable to be attracted to older and financially secure men, to fail in marriage, be a devoted lover and love order, while 'her lover may quickly find himself under her as she rides him to happy oblivion'. She likes the '69' position because she doesn't favour one-sided activity. Her preferences are mutually pleasurable oral sex, 'wild bronco ride of woman on top', and she will shout, scream and 'scratch with abandon' as she reaches climax. Capricorn women have a secret desire to be 'subjugated sexually', but do not usually like S & M.

11. The **Aquarian woman** (born between 20 January and 18 February) is prone to both experimentation and tradition. Bennett says she is the kind of woman who would employ 'the missionary position during a video playback of *2001*. For her, the brain is the most important sexual organ.' Poor Aquarius. She can be 'downright unappealing', at times aloof, and afraid of being sexually vulnerable. In this sexual astrology, Aquarian woman are seen as 'early bloomers' who are turned on by the *idea* of sex rather than by sex itself. They are likely to have had numerous sexual relationships prior to marriage (as do not many women born under other constellations?) and to go in for extramarital sex. Another 'profound' statement of Bennett's on the Aquarian female is that, 'Things seem to

happen to her, including divorce' – allegedly because she does not seem to be in control of her life.

12. Finally, but not least, Bennett describes the **Pisces woman** (born 19 February to 20 March) as having difficulty with sex because, during childhood, her 'mother appears untouchable, so the daughter finds it difficult to participate in deep sexual intimacy'. During adulthood, she replays these problems from childhood, is fickle, marries young, marries frequently, and 'resembles the sleeping Snow White'. If inexperienced, she is like a 'delicate flower', but if she is 'mature' the Piscean woman can be 'sensitive, sensuous, and unusually creative' as a lover. She is also thought to have strong masochistic tendencies, to be one who can ascend the greatest 'spiritual heights' or fall 'down into the depths of sado-masochism, exploitation, drugs, or total self-denial'. The Piscean woman is also supposed to be a good subject for 'astral sex' and prefers her male lover to thrust gently, one of her fantasies being 'playing a whore' when in love. Bennett advises the Piscean woman to use Tantra (see pages 385ff above) in her crusade for spiritual enlightenment.

RADICAL COMMUNITIES AND SEX

THE ONEIDA COMMUNITY

Spouse-sharing is not simply a late-twentieth-century fad, and people were questioning conventional socio-sexual morality long before the so-called 'sexual revolution' of the 1960s. One man who taxed authoritarian attitudes towards sex and marriage in nineteenth-century New England was John Humphrey Noyes, a graduate of a theological seminary who attended the Yale Divinity School. His place in the history of American sexual morality is enshrined for ever as he founded what amounted to the first 'free-love' commune, the **Oneida community**, in the mid-nineteenth century at Oneida, New York. The history of Noyes and the Oneida community is extensively and superbly described by Gay Talese (1980) in *Thy Neighbour's Wife*.

Noyes believed that monogamy was equivalent to spiritual illness, that married women were being used as machines to produce children, and that 'Complex Marriage' and eugenics (selectively breeding the perfect human specimens) would enhance the spiritual growth of any community. Inhabitants of the Oneida community, which was organized very much like a modern kibbutz with its own communal industry and child-rearing programme, participated in the system of 'Complex Marriage' in which men and women were free to have sex with whomever they chose. Members were discouraged from forming selfish attachments with each other, Noyes's ultimate aim being to have **omnigamy**, a concept whereby all adults could and should have heterosexual intercourse with each other. All those within the community were essentially married to each other (except that homosexuality was not on Noyes's religious agenda). Noyes believed that feeling shameful about the sex organs was to be scornful of the very God who created them. He therefore approved of regular love-making, and differed profoundly from his ecclesiastical contemporaries in appreciating the fact that women could and should enjoy orgasmic sex.

Yet how could women enjoy sexual intercourse without becoming pregnant and producing too many children for the community to support? The solution was simple: birth control was practised without unpleasant condoms or spermicides. The men learned *karezza*, or the art of prolonged sexual intercourse without ejaculation. The practice helped women to get more pleasure out of sex while reducing the risk of falling pregnant. In any event, pregnancy would reduce the availability of sexually active women in the Oneida community.

What about desired pregnancies? Since Noyes was viewed as messianic by his followers, they allowed him to choose who would breed with or from whom. Noyes selected those couples which he thought would produce the best children. And no one seemed to mind. After all, Oneida's tin-spoon factory was highly lucrative. Everyone received complete medical and dental care, new clothing, and excellent food which was eaten in a central dining rooms. The main mansion sported croquet and baseball facilities, and was even fitted with a Turkish bath. Those who enjoyed boating could sail on Oneida's lake. Oneida was everyone's utopia.

What happened when people formed romantic attachments? The 'problem' of 'unnatural' possessiveness was dealt with by exploiting group power. For example, when it was noted that little girls had formed attachments to particular dolls, supposed to be held in common, all the children were assembled in front of adults who indoctrinated them in the virtues of sharing and not being possessive. The children were then asked to vote whether, as the adults suggested, there should be a 'doll burning' bonfire. The boys did not like dolls, and were quick to vote in favour of the motion. The girls then rapidly gave way to group pressure and the disrobed dolls met a fiery end. Dolls, according to Noyes, ran counter to the commandment, 'Thou shalt not make a graven image . . .' Adults were chastened in public for forming 'committed' sexual attachments with each other. Like any modern encounter-group 'facilitator', Noyes knew that humiliation in public was a powerful way to manipulate and control any group – no matter how large.

Community children were sent to the Oneida school, and some were accepted by Ivy League universities; some became professionals and returned to the community. The Oneida children must rank among the first, and perhaps only, white Americans to receive **practical sex education**. On Noyes's word, adolescents deemed mature enough by him would receive sex lessons from 'selected' adults. Older experienced women would get into bed with teenage boys and teach them the facts of life. Noyes himself and chosen cohorts would 'teach' young virgins about sex after indoctrinating them with ideals of non-possessiveness. The philosophy demanded consistent increase of love, and sexual love was definitely seen as its expression. Oneidans did not own their bodies, nor could they own the body of another, as happened in outside 'barbarian' marriage. According to Noyes, only God had that right.

Those who converted to Oneida were expected not only to give their absolute allegiance to Noyes but also to donate their worldly possessions to the community. In due course, the community started new businesses and became wealthy and influential. Noyes was politically astute enough to abolish the policy of 'Complex Marriage' and pending charges of bigamy against the group were dropped. At the same time as championing women's rights within the Oneida community, Noyes was a total dictator. When other men disapproved of his decision to appoint his son Theodore – who had formed illicit, exclusive love attachments and squandered a personal legacy in New York City – to be his successor, they were punished. Their punishment: they were no longer permitted to be 'first husbands' to virgins awaiting their deflowering. Noyes was unjust when it suited him.

His faults aside, Noyes certainly deserves acclaim as a social innovator, albeit an eccentric one, who questioned the socio-sexual puritanical climate of nineteenth-century America. Instead of merely thinking about social change, he offered a practical alternative. In many ways, Noyes was way ahead of his times, but it was not long before Anthony Comstock – the notoriously sadistic, moralizing anti-obscenity crusader – organized public opinion against the Oneida community. Noyes left the community to live in Canada, but it continued to flourish after abandoning its policy of selective breeding and omnigamous marriage. It is both ironic and a strong sign in favour of 'natural' pair-bonding (seen in species as diverse as birds and humans) that, after the departure of Oneida's guru, the unmarried women became less willing to bed down with any man than they once had been. Indeed, they changed their attitudes in preference of marriage to a single man. In *Thy Neighbour's Wife*, Talese (1980) writes that, after Noyes left Oneida, the

> ... unmarried women and children, and many nubile virgins too, were now less eager to offer up their bodies in the blithe spirit of free love when they no longer felt the pervasive presence of freedom and love extending through the community. Many women abstained from sex during this time, to the chagrin of the men, while other women began to insist on something more than just bodily pleasure and praise from the men they favoured – they wanted to be possessed, and to possess in turn, and to extract from the objects of their affection the promise of eventual marriage.

The community's spirit of socio-sexual communism began to fall apart. The young started to acquire private possessions and become romantically involved with each other. Mothers began to assert their rights over what happened to their children. By 1879, Noyes had publicly renounced 'Complex Marriage', but he stated that he had no regrets about the past. The descendants of Oneida 'degenerated' into monogamous couples and those who remained there became wealthy owners of stock in the Oneida company, which grew into a $100 million company during the 1970s.

SANDSTONE RETREAT: A SEXUAL UTOPIA OF THE 1970S?

The **Sandstone Retreat** was one of many American experiments in the therapeutic human potential movement which explored 'inner space' and concepts like 'free love'. It focused on revaluation of contemporary values in the hope of achieving not only sexual *nirvana* but, like Oneida, a better world. Sandstone was conceived by a middle-class American couple, John and Barbara Williamson, who had begun to adventure into 'alternative lifestyles' at their home in the opulent *nouveau riche* Los Angeles suburb of Woodland Hills in the late 1960s.

The Williamsons questioned what they viewed as the limiting, smug and unhealthy sexual values most people cling to. They believed in open marriage and 'free love'. Invitations were issued to parties at their home in which nudity was encouraged, possessiveness and jealousy discouraged, and a willingness to participate in 'self-discovery' required.

John Williamson realized that fulfilling his vision of a **love community** on a grander scale would require more adequate facilities and much more of his time. And so, in 1968, he found a site high up in Topanga Canyon – a beautiful, rocky, and rustic canyon in the Santa Monica Mountains north of Los Angeles. He sold his electronics company and used the proceeds to buy the property. It was named Sandstone and came to feature a heated swimming pool, a ranch house, sundecks, lawn and fishpond. The rooms inside the house were nicely decorated but sex-centred – there were mattresses and fireplaces. People were allowed one free visit, but the annual membership fee was $240. The rules required people to come as a couple, to ensure a balanced ratio of men to women. Drugs, children and 'people into bad trips' were forbidden.

During the 1970s, many Californians were open to the idea of the exploration of 'inner space'. Encounter groups, sensitivity training, primal therapy, EST, Carlos Casteneda and Esalen topped the list. It seemed only logical, amid the anti-intellectual climate of the period, that people would choose 'body over mind'. At Sandstone, guests and visitors could walk around in the nude. They could participate in group sex if they chose to. The atmosphere was free.

Newcomers quickly learned the group rules by observing the behaviour of more experienced guests. Most reported initially feeling shy, some were excited and others were repulsed and thought of the decline of Imperial Rome. However, as time went by, most guests became desensitized to nudity and open sex. In keeping with the 'humanism' of the time, no one was directly forced to have sex with anyone. Gay Talese, who spent time at Sandstone, described what visitors to the downstairs 'ballroom' would see:

After descending the red-carpeted staircase, the visitors entered the semi-darkness of a large room where, reclining on the cushioned floor, bathed in the orange glow from the fireplace, they saw shadowed faces and interlocking limbs, rounded breasts and reaching fingers, moving buttocks, glistening backs, shoulders, nipples, navels, long blonde hair spread across pillows, thick dark arms holding soft white hips, a woman's head hovering over an erect penis. Sighs, cries of ecstasy could be heard, the slap and suction of copulating flesh, laughter, murmuring, music from the stereo, cracking black burning wood.

The 'Sandstone Experience', where strangers met for the purpose of group-copulation, to stretch their 'value systems' to the limit and to 'expand sexual awareness' resulted in both emotional benefits and costs. We will look at the benefits first.

Those with low self-esteem and poor self-confidence in approaching the other sex, were able to observe how more confident members of their own sex would make appropriate sexual overtures to the other sex. This served as a form of **vicarious learning** and enabled those with poor self-confidence to see how high-self-esteem people deal with rejection – by *not* taking the rejection personally and simply moving on to the next opportunity.

Women who were reared to be reticent and non-assertive were encouraged to make open sexual advances to men whom they found sexually attractive. Women could become sexually active rather than remain sexually passive.

Guests were encouraged to accept sexuality as normal and healthy. Stereotypes about age and what constitutes physical attractiveness were worked through. Performance anxiety was worked through and, according to Alex Comfort (1973), 'fat men and women scored as often as thin ones, and newcomers could see this'.

Some visitors may have benefited from having sexual intercourse *in front of* others. Traditional attitudes towards sex emphasize sex in privacy, and this was a symptom of general 'uptightness' about sexual intercourse. By having sex in the open, some individuals overcame self-defeating beliefs about sex – such as 'sex is dirty', 'I must perform and have an orgasm every time', 'My partner must always have an orgasm to ensure that I'm sexually proficient,' and so on.

Finally, many people confronted the confusion of love with sex. Having sex with someone does not necessarily mean that you are in love with them – even though warm feelings are exchanged. Some guests reported feeling *closer* to their spouse even after watching him or her having sexual intercourse with someone else. Comfort (1973) writes: 'In shared openness, as opposed to closed swinging, which is anxiety-promoting, at least until the couple has compared notes after, both sexes found that the sight of a lover relating sexually to someone else – often while still holding their regular partner's hand – was moving, exciting and finally immensely releasing. There was nothing to be afraid of.' He goes on to say that many couples often felt closer to each other, 'because of a feeling that the parts of their personhood which they felt had been taken had been returned as loving gifts'.

Against all this optimism, however, it is important to describe the emotional costs of the 'Sandstone Experience'. Among the lists of potential costs and outright harm were the following.

The break-up of marriages and families as a result of jealousy and/or one partner falling blindly 'in love' with someone else. Statistics on the number of guests harmed by Sandstone are unavailable, but, as a trainee in clinical psychology in the Los Angeles area during the late 1970s and early 1980s, I came across two seasoned psychologists who had treated more than one 'damaged' couple earlier involved with Sandstone. It is, of course, impossible to claim that Sandstone ever caused divorces and emotional suffering, but it was certainly connected with some degree of unhappiness and confusion.

Another potential problem was that of some guests developing an emotional and social dependence on Sandstone. This is a danger which persists in almost all organized groups, religions and cults; the victims are known as 'growth group junkies'. Finally, group sex is conducive to the rapid spread of venereal disease. At a time when sexually transmitted disease can be fatal when it takes the form of Acquired Immune Deficiency Syndrome (AIDS), groups like Sandstone are hardly likely to be as popular as they once were.

While Sandstone might be seen at best as nothing short of a symptom of bored opulence, and at worst as a legitimized, self-indulged orgy in an age of unbridled selfhood, it and its offshoots are here to stay. By the mid-1970s, Sandstone had been sold by the Williamsons to a social worker called Paul Paige, who saw the financial potential in Sandstone as a business. Paige organized Gestalt therapy sessions, Rolfing, bioenergetics, weekend retreats at $250 a head and, in keeping with the American position that everything should be converted to profit, turned it into yet another 'emotional growth' enterprise.

APPENDIX

Psychological and Medical Treatments for Sexual Deviations

Introduction

This Appendix is included for those readers interested in psychological and medical treatment of sexual 'deviations'. It is, however, by no means a complete guide to the numerous psychological and medical methods, effectual and ineffectual, currently in use for this purpose. Those described are simply 'techniques' used within a variety of therapeutic disciplines. It should be stressed that this in no way claims to be a text on psychotherapy or 'how to treat' sexual deviation. [The interested reader should refer to the superb text on general psychotherapy, by Arnold A. Lazarus, *The Practice of Multimodal Therapy* (1981); and for treatment of sexual disorders in particular, to Tollison and Adams, *Sexual Disorders; Treatment, Theory and Research* (1979).]

According to Herinck (1980), there are over 250 different therapy systems currently in use. Americans can avail themselves of such illustrious-sounding therapies as 'bioplasmic therapy', 'Senoi Dream Group therapy', 'hypno-introspection', 'neutrotone therapy', 'mandala therapy', 'Tibetan psychic healing', 'primal therapy' and 'rebirthing', among others. No doubt there are certain zealous or unscrupulous practitioners of 'fringe' therapy systems who do attempt 'treatment' of major sexual 'deviations' without a full knowledge or competence in the area. In other words, while a 'faith healer' may often have highly salubrious effects on many distressed persons, he is seldom qualified, both in scientific skill and 'artistic' ability, adequately to treat sexual 'deviations'. Simply seeing any lay or unqualified therapist can be ineffectual at best, and at worst outright dangerous: it would be like seeking the assistance of an aviation mechanic for treatment of a malignant tumour. Referrals to a specialist are best made through recognized university departments of clinical psychology, departments of psychiatry and recognized psychological and medical associations (Tollison and Adams, 1979).

1 ASSESSMENT OF SEXUAL BEHAVIOUR

A thorough assessment of the individual's 'sexual style' is vital to any subsequent modification of a so-called deviant or unwanted pattern of sexual arousal. Assessment of a sexual problem should involve a thorough psychological and medical investigation. Psychological assessments usually involve an extensive interview, a thorough investigation of the client's life history, and a complete sexual history. This may also involve psychological testing and the **physiological measurement** of the individual's sexual arousal to a series of sexually explicit materials. Medical assessments range from a detailed dietary history to any physical illness which may have an effect on sexual behaviour, as, for instance, in the case of diabetic disorders or the prescription or non-prescription of certain drugs. Once again, these considerations lie outside the scope of this book. Since this is not a text on the treatment of sexual deviations, the discussion is limited to the physiological measurement of human sexual arousal.

Physiological measurement involves both genital and non-genital measures. For instance, non-genital measures include heart rate, respiration, electrical conductivity across the skin (perspiration), blood pressure and dilation of the pupils. Genital measures include penile erection in the human male and genital vaso-congestion (blood flow to the vaginal walls) in women.

Tollison and Adams (1979) reviewed the experimental literature on non-genital measures as indicators of sexual arousal, and found, essentially, that non-genital measures do not provide reliable, valid or accurate data, primarily because humans respond physiologically – in terms of heart rate, blood pressure, galvanic skin response (electrical conductivity during skin perspiration) and pupil dilation – to non-sexual states. In other words, increases in these measures also occur, for instance, when watching a horror movie, hearing a loud sound or becoming sexually aroused when watching sexually explicit films. The same principles are employed in lie detection tests with equal unreliability. For example, a person undergoing a lie detection test could, by biting his or her inner mouth, completely alter the result of the lie detection test. It is for such reason that lie detection tests are inadmissible in most courts of law.

Is there, then, a reliable, valid and objective form of sexual truth detection? The answer is affirmative for psychological assessment purposes, but largely negative for legal purposes. Nevertheless, it is safe to say that, in the human male, it is unlikely that his penis will 'lie' when he is exposed to sexually explicit materials (during the waking state). It is also highly probable that measurement of pelvic vaso-congestion in the human female is the most reliable way to measure her direct sexual arousal.

There are more data on the *actual* arousal in the human male than in the human female. This is partly because of the social stigma attached to experimenting sexually with women, partly because many more men are sex offenders, and partly because it is for technical reasons somewhat easier accurately to measure an erection in a man than blood flow in the genital region of women.

It should also be stressed that patients in physiological assessment are presented with adequate informed consent forms. The clinician should answer all the client's questions, get written consent and fully debrief the client afterwards. (This practice is well established in the United States, but, in Great Britain, doctors are not compelled to 'debrief' patients because there is no Freedom of Information Act. This is perhaps why malpractice suits are seldom successful in the United Kingdom, where no patient can see his or her own medical file if the doctor withholds permission.)

MEASURING SEXUAL AROUSAL IN MEN

Penile erection can be measured in two ways: by measuring (a) **the volume** or (b) **the circumference** of the penis. During erection, the volume of blood in the penis increases. Changes in the actual volume of the penis can be measured by a device which measures displaced air in a glass cylinder.

Although it is not so sensitive to minor changes in erection, a device called a 'strain gauge', which measures penile circumference, is less expensive, easier to fit and more long-lasting than the glass cylinder. The strain gauge is, essentially, a hollow rubber band filled with mercury. It is fitted mid-shaft over the penis in the privacy of a 'sex booth', then wired to an electronic machine which, after calibration, will enable the clinician to observe objectively changes between 0 to 100 per cent in the client's erection. The booth is designed so that sexually explicit materials can then be presented to the client and any erectile responses be measured directly. Sexually explicit materials include audiotaped sexual 'stories' which are played to the individual over headphones, slides of sexually explicit materials (which are projected either from within the booth itself or through a frosted-glass panel) or videotapes of sexually explicit films.

Sexually explicit materials available include a diverse range of themes, both normal and deviant. They include both 'consenting' and 'non-consenting' themes in several contexts: homosexual, heterosexual, paedophilic, exhibitionistic and voyeuristic. For instance, a heterosexual rapist would be exposed to a sequence of audiotapes and videotapes. At first he might be played a pre-recorded story depicting a 'normal' heterosexual interaction. He would subsequently be played a pre-recorded story depicting a typical rape sequence. For example, he might at first listen to the following script while his erectile response is measured:

MUTUALLY CONSENTING SEQUENCE
You are returning from an evening out with a woman whom you find sexually attractive. She invited you in to her home for coffee. You accept, and in fact are titillated by the prospect of being able to get to know her better.

She has lovely eyes, just the colour you like, and is proportioned perfectly. If you like large-breasted women, she will have large breasts. Let your imagination create exactly the circumstances you like best.

You are both sitting on the sofa and begin to hold hands. You look into her eyes and she into yours. Soon your mouths are pressed together. You feel a rush, her breath is getting deeper, and both your hearts begin to race. You remove her blouse and she unbuttons your shirt. You can feel yourselves perspiring as you both become sexually excited. You know she wants you and you begin to feel her breasts. As the foreplay proceeds, you touch her warm moist vagina, and she caresses your now erect, throbbing penis. You are aroused by the way in which she moves, smells and sounds. She asks you to make love to her and you know that she really wants you.

You both move into the bedroom.

Soon you are both naked and under the sheets. You feel her breasts, her erect nipples, and her warm, moist vagina wants your throbbing, erect penis.

This scenario is an example of one of the many 'mutually consenting' adult heterosexual vignettes available. Some

depict oral-genital sexual encounters, others further variations, but the theme remains unchanged. The tester wants
to see how the individual, in this case a rapist, is responding
to mutually consenting sexual interactions. This facilitates
a comparison with other sex scenes so that patterns of an
individual's sexual 'style' can be studied. The rapist, or the
man accused of rape, will, for example, also be exposed to
audiotapes and/or videotapes of 'typical' rape stories. If the
individual has been accused or found guilty of raping a
woman, he will be exposed to rape sequences in which the
victim is a woman. However, if his target was an adult
man, he will be exposed to rape sequences involving men.
His erectile responses can also be investigated if the target
is a child, and so on.

A TYPICAL HETEROSEXUAL RAPE SEQUENCE

You are frustrated, you are angry with the world and you feel as
though life hasn't treated you fairly. [This is a typical emotion in
pre-rape states.] You plan to get some pussy, to steal a bit. You
may or may not be married – in any event, you are not interested
this time in someone you know.

You go out in the streets. You watch many attractive women
passing by. You hate a certain part of them, but you don't know
exactly what it is that makes you so angry. You plan an attack.

You have been watching an attractive woman shopping. You
follow her to her apartment and wait. You check to see that she
lives alone. Being clever at these things, you manage to break into
her apartment. You put a stocking over your head to prevent
detection.

She is in the shower. You lie in wait, perhaps going through the
drawers in her bedroom. As she emerges from the shower she
screams. You say, 'Shut up, bitch.' You love the fear on her face.
The expression makes you feel powerful. You are going to show
this bitch that you're the boss, you're in control. You show her
your knife, just to scare her more. 'Shut up, bitch, or else you'll
be shut up for a long time.' She goes silent. You tell her that so
long as she remains silent and does exactly as you say she'll
survive, you tell her, 'I'm going to rape you.' You're lucky that

you don't have to bother with tearing off her clothes. All you have to do is get her dressing-gown off and she's yours.

You grab hold of her. She resists a little. Just as you thought, you can't trust bitches, and so you decide to teach her a little lesson. You slap her around a little, then say, 'I could kill you.' Who does she think she is, anyway? She lies still and you take her to her bedroom and rip off the gown. You see her crying. This excites you. Her sweet body is all yours, for the taking. You get a hard-on and rape her, just fuck her until you come. It's over in seconds.

A TYPICAL EXHIBITIONIST SEQUENCE
You are excited by the idea of scaring a strange woman. You feel the urge coming on and you decide to visit a nearby university campus or park. Somewhere where you can escape from quickly.

Soon you are there. You get a hard-on just at the thought. You want to see the expression of fear on the woman's face. It gives you pleasure. You find an open window and secretly watch a woman as she goes about her business. You begin to take out your penis. You may or may not be masturbating, but in any event you are excited, delighted at the prospect of being seen. You have been there for quite some time. Suddenly, she sees you and gives a cry, 'Pervert!' You run away, satisfied with your accomplishment.

In the case of child molestation (see 'Paedophilia', page 217), the clinician will want to ascertain whether the paedophile is aroused to adults and children or to children only, and, most importantly, whether he is motivated by violence. All these factors are highly relevant in writing more than adequate psychological reports which may be presented in court. Although interviewing the individual and administering psychological tests are an essential component of psychological report writing, they are not sufficient when dealing with sex-offender cases. The physiological assessment of sexual arousal is an essential ingredient when formulating a psychological report on a defendant or inmate. Individual liberty is at stake. Cursory psychiatric interviews and a few psychological tests make for incomplete, often incompetent, assessment of the individual's sexual 'lifestyle'.

One frequently asked question is, 'What about "normal" men? Are they not excited by rape, slides of nude children, and other "deviant" behaviours?' The answer is yes – but *not to the same extent*. Further, normal males show lower levels of erection to deviant materials than do sex offenders. Normal males, for instance, show sexual arousal to slides of nude minors, but are more responsive to ones of adults, and usually do not react with any significance to non-consenting situations. Most paedophiles are non-violent and will not be aroused by violence to children; but they will not generally be sexually aroused by adults. In addition, when asked to try and suppress arousal to deviant materials, the sex offender is less able to do so than the normal subject. Many sex offenders will say that they did not respond to a deviant stimulus. Some might even believe that they rarely became aroused and are amazed when presented with the 'hard facts' of their sexual arousal patterns.

FAKING

Sex offenders are less able to 'fake' if they are indeed listening to the tape or looking at the slides or TV monitor in the sex booth. In order to check, a TV camera can be mounted in the sex booth which enables the operator outside to view the client's face – to check whether his eyes are open, whether he has taken the headphones off, and so forth. Furthermore, the audiotapes can be mixed with random bleep sounds. The individual presses a button every time one of these bleep sounds is heard, satisfying the operator that he is, indeed, paying attention. Such measures, while perhaps seemingly invasive, are necessary in psychiatric prisons where inmates will literally do anything to fake good responses in the hope of obtaining favourable reports from the hospital's 'sex laboratory', thereby getting out sooner.

Another frequently asked question is, 'What do you make of the non-responders, those who do not respond to any of the sexually explicit materials?' Indeed, this can be a problem. Non-response may result from numerous factors, which range from physiological impotence to cultural injunctions against sex and outright faking. Physiological reasons may involve something like diabetes or drugs for hypertension, in which case the individual is sometimes unable to achieve an erection. Cultural factors may involve religions where sexuality is denied, as happened, for instance, with a teacher in a Catholic school who was accused of sexually molesting eleven- and twelve-year-old boys. He said he had not done so and 'would never do such a thing. I'm planning to become a priest anyway.' The evidence in court was overwhelmingly against him, despite three lie detection companies he hired to bolster his case (obliging him to mortgage his home to raise the money). Even so, he did not respond to any of the slides, audiotapes or videotapes. He had become totally petrified and shocked at having to expose his private sex life to forensic psychologists. In other words, he became afraid, and fear is an antidote to any erection. Furthermore, the teacher claimed he had never had an erection in his life. 'I go to mass every morning. I'm a good Catholic.' It becomes increasingly clear that, while physiological assessment of sexual behaviour is best obtained by changes in the individual's erection, no utterly foolproof method exists.

In another case of 'attempted' faking, a man aged approximately forty was accused of having molested his ten-year-old daughter. He used to take care of the girl every second weekend after obtaining a divorce from his wife. When the man was referred for pre-trial psychological assessment, he maintained that he would not become aroused to any sexual stimulus, whatever it was. He was, after all, 'a pornographer myself. I doubt that you'll have anything that will turn me on.' True to his word, he responded to nothing. He was exposed to an entire battery of psychophysiological sex-testing: to slides of boys and girls aged between three and eighteen, adult men and women, audiotapes depicting sexual encounters with 'compliant' and 'non-compliant' children, and rapes of adult men and women. Finally, as a last resort, he was exposed to videotapes, which are usually only used when the individual has not responded to the 'less powerful' stimuli of slides and audiotapes. He did not respond to these either – until he saw a scene in which two adult women inserted a vibrator into the vagina of a girl of about nine or ten years. His erection, which had until then stayed below the 10 per cent mark and therefore been clinically meaningless, literally shot up to over 90 per cent full erection. Confronted with this information, he realized that he had a socio-sexual predilection in which he found young girls sexually exciting. He also admitted to having faked earlier by suppressing his arousal to the other stimuli, and to have had other sexual encounters with young girls. He was specifically attracted to 'hairless vaginas'.

MEASURING SEXUAL AROUSAL IN WOMEN

As we have said, it is possible objectively to measure physiological arousal in women. The process of sexual arousal is, from a physiological perspective, similar between the sexes, and studies show that women do respond to erotica. One difference between men and women may be that men respond more to visual stimuli, women more to verbal stimuli (Eysenck and Wilson, 1981).

Physiological arousal in women is measured by objectively observing increases in vaginal blood flow. Like men, blood flow to the genitalia is directly associated with sexual arousal. Other emotional states, like anger, fear, and anxiety, inhibit blood flow to the genitalia in both men and women.

There are two main ways in which pelvic blood flow can be monitored. First, it can be measured by observing a rise in temperature. Thermisters (electronic thermometers) attached to a diaphragm ring accomplish this easily. The only problem is that fitting individual diaphragms for varying sizes of female genitalia is an inconvenient process. A second, more elegant method, derives from photoplethysmography.

Photoplethysmography uses light to measure blood flow to the vaginal area. Essentially, a photoplethysmograph is a transparent tampon-like device, constructed out of glass or a hard plastic, which is inserted into the vagina. A light source is located at one end of the 'tampon' and a photoelectric cell is situated at the other. Light is directed towards the vaginal wall and the photoelectric cell detects the amount of reflected light. The more sexually aroused the woman, the greater the blood flow in her vagina; which results in darker vaginal walls that will reflect less light. This can be measured by electronic equipment outside the sex booth.

The number of physiological studies on sexual arousal in men far exceeds the number conducted on women, and while it has been shown that women respond to erotica in much the same way as men, I do not know of any studies which measure sexual responses in women to so-called 'deviant' stimuli. While there is no urgent need for continued microscopic study of human sexual behaviour, it would prove interesting to find out more about sexual arousal in women. In many ways, such a study could prove politically awkward. For instance, while erection levels in response to videotapes of enacted rape have been measured in 'normal' males, there are, to my knowledge, no reports on sexual arousal to rape in 'normal' women. (A graduate student at one American university told me she had not been allowed to conduct such a study by the university's 'protection of human subjects committee' – the same committee which had previously permitted her to conduct the same study using male subjects.)

---

2 TECHNIQUES IN THE MODIFICATION OF SEXUAL BEHAVIOUR

INTRODUCTION

There is a variety of techniques available to modify sexual behaviour, methods ranging from long-term 'talk-therapies', like psychoanalysis, to much shorter courses of behaviour therapy. There is no evidence to say that, just because it takes thirty years to acquire an unwanted behaviour, it will take a long time to eliminate it and replace it with another more desirable. This is true not only of smoking, phobic states, shyness, depression and a host of other conditions, but also for the spectra of sexual problems ranging from anorgasmia to the deviations. This section presents several, but by no means all, of the methods used in behaviour therapy (a term first used in the 1950s by the celebrated psychologist, Arnold A. Lazarus) and medicine.

BEHAVIOUR THERAPY

On its own, behaviour therapy is not a complete therapy. Like psychoanalysis, it can be limited, rigid and hackneyed. However, the light has finally begun to shine through the dark clouds of psychotherapeutic fanaticism. Orthodox

psychoanalysis and pure behaviour therapy are giving way
to the 'psychotherapeutic reformation' currently under way
in the United States. (More complete, thorough and effective therapy is set out in Arnold Lazarus's 'technically
eclectic' **multimodal therapy**, and members of the clinical
divisions of the American Psychological Association voted
the multimodal approach to psychotherapy the most influential approach to psychotherapy.)

Behaviour therapy implies a sort of 'behavioural engin-
eering', in which both animal and human behaviour
is 'shaped', 'extinguished', 'controlled', 'increased',
'decreased' and otherwise **manipulated** or **modified**.
Modification of behaviour is, in part, achieved by a complex series of manipulated rewards and punishments. (The
interested reader should refer to **operant** and **classical
conditioning** and **social learning theory** in Wilson and
O'Leary's (1980) *Principles of Behaviour Therapy* for a thorough explanation of the rationale and various mechanisms
involved.)

Behaviour therapy still arouses heated academic, social
and ethical debate, the term having become a sort of
'emotional trigger word'. I recall how, as an undergraduate
majoring in psychology, I was revolted by the idea of
complicated animal experiments, the results of which were
applied to human beings. How, I asked, could anyone
compare rats and pigeons with intricate, complex, 'spiritual' beings like *Homo sapiens*? It seemed ridiculous, downright arrogant, a sign of the alienating technocracy in which
we had come to live. Indeed, I thought behaviour therapy
synonymous with a new technocratic religion, and my
feelings were further confirmed when I saw the film *A
Clockwork Orange* based on Anthony Burgess's novel. In this
futuristic film, the central character, a rapist, was 'treated'
by electrical aversion therapy – under the auspices of the

state. The 'treatment' literally *shocked the rapist out of his system*.

This was proof enough for my sophomoric mind that we were headed for 'downbeat' times in America, at least so far as psychology was concerned. Further, my college, Reed College, hosted a debate on behaviour modification in 1974. Both B. F. Skinner, a pioneer in behaviour modification, and Thomas Szasz attended the conference, and neither would look at the other during lunch. The entire subject seethed; it was enshrouded in hatred, mystery and bigoted opinion.

So heated are these debates, that some practitioners who condone ECT (electroconvulsive therapy – passing an electrical current through the brain to induce convulsion; a 'recognized' but poorly understood medical treatment for depression) reject aversive techniques to modify the 'inappropriate' sexual behaviour of sex offenders (Tollison and Adams, 1979).

I certainly would never have imagined myself using **aversive** techniques (punishment) to 'modify' the behaviour of rapists, paedophiles, exhibitionists or other criminal sex offenders, only a few years later. Yet, in the event, there I was, treating these offenders, with their 'informed consent', using aversive techniques in addition to comprehensive multimodal therapy (in-depth assessment, individual therapy, group therapy and an array of psychological procedures). Furthermore, I would certainly never have believed that I would one day consider some of the aversive techniques as ultimately compassionate and effective.

Aversion therapy is usually called into service when sexual behaviour is actively undesirable. The undesirable behaviour (such as rape, child molestation or exhibitionism) is also usually pleasurable or self-rewarding, often resulting in orgasm. Therefore the behaviour maintains or nourishes itself.

Aversive techniques *aim to have the individual identify unpleasant, punishing experiences as a consequence of a specific 'undesirable' behaviour*. The rationale is that this will result in a reduction of the unwanted behaviour. For instance, if an alcoholic is put on antabuse medication, every time an alcoholic beverage is consumed, he or she will experience extreme aversive nausea. Drinking alcohol then becomes associated with vomiting and unpleasantness. Consequently, he or she will drink less while on antabuse. If a paedophile imagines his hands developing suppurating sores each time he touches a child's body, he may come to associate touching children with a horrible outcome.

When using aversive techniques to modify unwanted sexual behaviour, it is essential that new more pro-social behaviours are substituted in their place. It is futile simply to eradicate particular sexual behaviours without also encouraging legal, mutually consenting ones. Therefore, in *addition* to aversive conditioning, the client is placed in 'social skills' training groups, 'assertiveness' training groups and sex education classes, and is monitored over a long period of time. The following sections describe the range of aversive procedures: olfactory aversion; chemical aversion; electrical aversion; shame aversion; assisted covert sensitization; masturbatory satiation; and aversion relief.

OLFACTORY AVERSION

Olfactory aversion uses 'bad smells' as the unpleasant stimulus. Patients are required to smell valeric acid or ammonia (smelling salts) while exposed to the deviant sex stimulus. For instance, a paedophile would be required to look at slides of nude children, which are especially exciting to him. He then *self-administers* the valeric acid or ammonia when he becomes aroused. A rapist would, for instance, be required to do the same thing while watching videotapes of rape scenes. If the patient is a homosexual rapist, he is shown slides or videotapes depicting male rape; if he is a heterosexual rapist, the victim will be a woman; a flasher would be played audiotapes depicting an arousing exhibitionistic sequence, and so on. Since sexual arousal is so specific to each individual, the patient is often requested to write out his own fantasies, which are then recorded by a technician and played back to him over headphones. The therapist or technician is able to monitor the patient's erection on a plethysmograph while the patient sits in the privacy of the sex booth.

As soon as the patient starts to develop an erection – and this can occur quite rapidly if the deviant stimulus is especially exciting to him – he is encouraged (over the intercom headphones) to sniff the ammonia or valeric acid from a vial he holds in his hands. Since obnoxious odours are aversive and incompatible with sexual arousal, the erection subsides. Sexual excitement in response to deviant materials and fantasy becomes associated with an unpleasant experience. Furthermore, the patient is encouraged to carry a vial of smelling salts around with him *outside* the treatment situation. He can effectively use the ammonia whenever he feels the urge to act out deviantly. A number of flashers and paedophiles have claimed that this is an effective form of prevention. (Carrying around a vial of smelling salts often provides a 'sense of security' for those patients who are 'placebo responders' – 'magical thinkers' who believe that having a vial of ammonia in the pocket acts as a sort of charm protecting them from ugly urges liable to cost a prison term.)

The advantage with ammonia as opposed to valeric acid is that it is not corrosive, will not stain and can be purchased from any pharmacist. However, ammonia has less aversive an odour than valeric acid, which is more foul, acrid and rancid. In a typical treatment using olfactory aversion, the patient enters the private sex booth, closes the door and slips on a sterile strain gauge over his penis. This enables the operator outside the booth to observe changes in his erective response on the plethysmograph. Prior to exposure to slides, audiotapes and videotapes, the erection is at 0 per cent. As soon as the patient starts to become aroused (above 30 per cent erection) in response to the 'deviant' stimulus, he is instructed to self-administer whiffs of ammonia or valeric acid. The erection subsides while the patient is still being exposed to deviant sexually explicit materials.

It is worth noting that, long before the advent of formal behaviour therapy, Mexican Indians used 'olfactory aversion' on their daughters. Mothers would hold their daughters' heads over pots of hot chile spice if they felt the daughter was being sexually attracted by a boy. The vapours would cause the girls' eyes to smart and weep – they were painful and caused irritation of the mucous membranes. The girl would thus come to connect boys with pain.

CHEMICAL AVERSION

In chemical aversion, the aversive stimulus is the administration of an emetic (nausea-producing) drug while being exposed to the deviant sex stimulus. For instance, an exhibitionist might be encouraged to 'flash' his penis just as nausea comes on. Cross-dressers *who want to change their cross-dressing behaviour* will be encouraged to cross-dress at the onset of nausea.

Problems with administering emetic drugs involve individual differences. Some people respond rapidly to a set dosage while others do not seem to respond as quickly. Furthermore, some patients experience extremely unpleasant side-effects as a result of emetic drugs. This treatment is not used frequently, and I am not aware of many practitioners who advocate its use.

ELECTRICAL AVERSION AND AVERSION RELIEF

Electrical aversion became popular when Feldman and MacCulloch (1971) reported 'treating' homosexuals, at their own request, with electric shock. The Feldman and MacCulloch report has probably incensed more people, lay and professional, homosexual and heterosexual, than any other behaviour modification technique to date.

Since homosexuality is no longer regarded as a 'mental disease' by the American Psychiatric Association, it is unlikely that many practitioners actually use it to 'cure' homosexuality – even when the homosexual asks for it. When homosexuals do ask for sexual reorientation treatment, they are said to be 'ego-dystonic' and may then be referred to a therapist who is sensitive to social adjustment problems faced by the homosexual. Electrical aversion therapy is more appropriately used as part of a *voluntary* programme in the treatment of rapists, paedophiles, exhibitionists and other sex offenders. Interestingly, in the case of paedophiles who want to switch their sexual preferences to adult men, *behaviour therapy is used actively to encourage adult homosexuality*.

In electrical aversion therapy, the patient is asked to select a level of shock which he finds most unpleasant. The shock intensity will never exceed that level. The patient is then exposed to the deviant stimulus, in the case of a paedophile, for example, a slide of a naked child. He is told to look at the deviant slide for a short time and that he can switch off the slide when he no longer experiences it as sexually exciting. Slight electric shock is administered to his forearm as soon as he becomes aroused. If he does not switch the slide off, the intensity of shock is increased. As soon as the slide is switched off, the shock is stopped and a slide of an attractive adult (male in the case of a homosexual, female in the case of a heterosexual) is presented. The patient experiences **aversion relief**, that is to say, he learns to associate an appropriate legal sexual stimulus (an adult) with relief of punishment.

In an interesting and innovative trial, Forgione (1976) got paedophiles to act out their child-molesting behaviour with life-sized mannequins of children. Photographs of this behaviour were taken, and the paedophiles were subject to electric shock while viewing the photographs. Evidently, the procedure was effective in reducing paedophilic tendencies.

ASSISTED COVERT SENSITIZATION

Covert sensitization employs imagination and imagery as the aversive stimulus. It is considered a more benign form of aversive conditioning than other approaches. (The procedure works best with those who are able to use their imagery – to use their 'mind's eye' in which they picture themselves in the situations described to them.) During assisted covert sensitization, the patient provides the therapist with deviant sexual fantasies that have a *modus operandi* specific to his deviant behaviour. The therapist then constructs a fantasy in which the patient imagines himself in a relaxed state, with eyes closed, becoming sexually aroused by engaging in deviant behaviour. Instead of ending with satisfaction, the fantasy involves aversive experiences, from which the patient can escape if he ceases the deviant behaviour. The technique is probably more effective with voyeurs, exhibitionists, paedophiles and those who indulge in anonymous sex in public restrooms. The technique also lends itself to the use of olfactory aversion. A typical sequence in the treatment of a paedophile would proceed as follows:

 AROUSAL PHASE
Allow yourself to relax, feel the muscles of your body relaxing [sometimes a relaxation procedure is used when the patient is

—

anxious or new to treatment]. You are in a playground where there are lots of sexy children, very sexy kids. You have become friendly with some of these children who love to take your dog out for walks. As you say, you like six- to-eight-year-olds, boys and girls. Allow yourself to imagine the most recent experience you told me about. Recall the playground. You can see the children playing. See how you become friendly with that nine-year-old boy and his seven-year-old sister.

You have befriended them, even fallen in love with them, as you say. You love their undeveloped bodies. The skin is so soft, they are so innocent, look up to you, make you feel important. Imagine little Dianne and John. See their faces, as you invite them into your house to give them some ice-cream and let them play with your dog.

You have arranged a 'little game' with them, the same one you do usually. And they have promised to keep it a secret so long as you give them the goodies and let them play with your dog. You love it when they take off their clothes and allow you to give them a bath. You become extremely excited when you see the small hairless penis and vagina. The kids let you touch them there. It feels so good as you caress them.

AVERSIVE PHASE
All of a sudden the door of the bathroom flies open. (Start sniffing ammonia.) It is the police. They are taking photographs of you and the children. It's proof and you're caught redhanded. The children begin to cry and they *vomit* all over you because they feel that they are guilty of getting you into trouble. (See the vomit.) Their lives are ruined now. They will have to give evidence in court against you. You can see the vomit. The police scream that you'll be beaten up in prison and that some judges are sentencing child molesters to thirty-year terms, going for every count under the law. You feel disgusted with yourself. You have brought suffering to innocent children and their families through your own selfishness. Your hands have broken out in disgusting sores. Observe these sores. They are the result of your having touched these children.

AVERSION RELIEF PHASE
You manage to escape from the situation by jumping out of the window. Now you run outside into the darkness. You feel relief at being away from that horrible situation you created. You tell

yourself that you'll never try that again and that you're going to try to learn how to overcome your fear of having a sexual relationship with an adult.

These 'treatments' are often powerful emotional experiences for patients. They are designed to be.

One of the advantages of assisted covert sensitization is that it can be tailored to the needs of the individual. For instance, a fifteen-year-old boy with a lower than normal IQ who molested little girls would 'play doctor' with three- and four-year-olds in his neighbourhood. In the process, he would tie them up and insert objects into their anuses and vaginas. The boy 'respected' characters from the science-fiction film *Star Wars*, but was not at all afraid of, for instance, 'police images'. When, in his imagination, he experienced the disapproval of several of his heroes, his mother reported that his nagging to be allowed to babysit stopped altogether for six months – while he was in treatment. (His overall treatment was, in fact, more complex and comprehensive than twice-weekly sessions of assisted covert sensitization.)

An added advantage of this procedure is that it is less impersonal than most other behaviour therapy techniques. It requires that the patient trust the therapist, and often requires a good deal of therapeutic innovativeness and creativity. The procedure can be used by itself or in the course of a therapy session.

SHAME AVERSION

In shame aversion, the patient is required to engage in sexually deviant behaviour *in front of* several observers. The shame of embarrassment is the aversive stimulus. An exhibitionist might, for example, be allowed to flash at women accomplices. Normally, women are shocked when they see his exposed penis. Instead, this time, the accomplices ridicule his behaviour. He cannot escape from the situation. If he does make an attempt, he can only enter the next room, where more accomplices wait to ridicule him.

At present, as with other behavioural procedures, the long-term effectiveness of shame aversion remains unknown. The technique has been applied to frotteurs, tranvestites, voyeurs, paedophiles (using mannequins), and exhibitionists (Serber, 1970).

MASTURBATORY SATIATION

In **masturbatory satiation**, the patient is required to masturbate to orgasm – in the privacy of the sex booth – to non-deviant fantasy, or to one in which the theme and content is legal. An operator monitors the procedure from outside the sex booth over an intercom. Once this is accomplished, the patient is required to try and masturbate while *verbalizing out loud* to his 'deviant' fantasy. He experiences the deviant fantasy as aversive, the rationale being that he will associate his deviant fantasy with displeasure. In other words, he will no longer find rape, child molestation or whatever other deviant fantasy may be involved, a sexual turn-on. At the same time, he learns that non-deviant, 'socially appropriate' fantasies can be rewarding.

A corollary of masturbatory satiation is **verbal satiation**, which involves endless repetition of the deviant fantasy *ad nauseam*, with masturbation. The patient is required to repeat his deviant rape, child molestation or other deviant fantasy non-stop until the mere thought of the fantasy is repulsive to him, the idea being that too much of anything is inherently aversive.

NON-AVERSIVE BEHAVIOURAL TECHNIQUES: PRO-SOCIAL SEXUAL SKILLS

Behavioural techniques are not confined to aversive procedures. Patients are also taught to modify their sexual fantasies. Many rapists, for instance, report redundant exclusive masturbatory fantasies which have always centred around non-consenting themes. Many paedophiles report never having had a sexual fantasy featuring an adult, let alone one of having sexual intercourse with one.

Learning to become aroused by non-deviant, mutually consenting sexual fantasies is like learning to swim for the first time – it is more difficult for an adult. Once the new skill is learned, it becomes entrenched, something not easily unlearned. In the same vein, the old maladaptive sexual behaviour is not forgotten. This means that many sex offenders should be assessed over long periods to ensure that the original maladaptive sexual behaviour is not reactivated. Some psychologists look upon sex offenders as 'junkies' who are addicted to a certain sexual style: the patient is viewed as a 'recovered' sex offender.

Marquis (1970) coined the term **orgasmic reconditioning** to describe a procedure in which patients shift their masturbatory fantasies from deviant to non-deviant content at the point of orgasmic inevitability. Over time, the deviant fantasy is shifted increasingly towards the non-deviant fantasy. The patient recites his fantasy out loud in the privacy of the sex booth. In some sophisticated sexual behaviour laboratories, one technician can monitor up to six patients at a time by constantly switching the intercom among booths. It is necessary to monitor the patients to ensure that they are following the treatment strategy.

One of the benefits of this type of treatment is that patients learn that socially appropriate sexual fantasies can be rewarding – often for the first time in their lives. Several patients are delighted to discover that they can be aroused by sexual behaviour which will not get them into trouble. In addition, some patients are encouraged to masturbate while being exposed to explicit non-deviant stimuli (video-tapes, slides, magazines) as homework assignments.

SEXUAL SURROGATES

When, through fear or inadequate social skills, a patient does not have access to a sex partner, sexual surrogates are often used as an adjunct to therapy in helping the patient to learn 'appropriate sexual skills'. Sexual surrogates, although paid, are not 'prostitutes' who solicit on street corners. In fact, they deeply resent any insinuation that there is a connection between the two professions. Substitute sex partners, or 'teachers', come from all segments of the population; some are even housewives who earn a little extra money with the approval of their husbands.

They are usually employed to help sexual dysfunctions, like premature ejaculation, impotence, and retarded ejaculation, in heterosexual men. However, they are also effective in the education of certain sex offenders, particularly paedophiles. Paedophiles may, for instance, realize that they can do the impossible and have meaningful, pleasurable sexual intercourse with adult women, often for the first time. (It is highly unlikely that surrogates can be effective in the treatment of 'recovered rapists'.)

The practice of using surrogates has, however, been condemned as highly controversial, socially undesirable and suspect. Szasz (1980), for instance, attacks Masters and Johnson's practice of 'paying women to have intercourse with men'. He points out that sexual surrogacy is potentially illegal and states that there is a similarity between 'old-fashioned prostitution and new-fashioned sex therapy'. And he is quite right. There is no denying the similarity. On the other hand, sexual surrogates are not prostitutes in the colloquial sense of the term.

They are not authentic prostitutes because they are in the United States certified by an organized association of sexual surrogates. 'Qualified' sexual surrogates are trained to be 'sensitive' to the sexual and emotional needs of their 'clients'. Unlike 'street prostitutes', they are allegedly trained in sex education, an area in which many clients are clearly deficient. In addition, they are trained in massage, many clients being unaware of their senses and experiencing performance anxiety, a phobia of adult women in general and/or their genitalia in particular. Surrogates gently expose their clients to sensuality and sexuality in a non-threatening, secure environment. A typical treatment might involve ten sessions, starting with touching hands while fully clothed and ending, at the final session, with sustained intercourse.

The advantages of employing sexual surrogates as an adjunct to therapy far outweigh the disadvantages. The disadvantages are largely based on ethical considerations, money being exchanged for sex lessons. The essential advantage of sexual surrogates or surrogate wives, as they have been inappropriately labelled, is that the 'service' encourages the client actively to change his behaviour. A positive change in behaviour should lead to improved self-esteem; the client starts to see and think about himself as being competent sexually.

While the vast majority of sexual surrogates are women who service men, there have been reports of sexual surrogates for homosexual men.

MEDICAL TREATMENTS

Sexual disorders have been treated by traditional medical methods since the seventeenth century. Medicine has almost always reflected the *zeitgeist*. For instance, doctors had 'legitimate' methods to 'treat' masturbation during eras when the behaviour was thought to be caused by the devil. Even the renowned Henry Maudsley, a British psychiatrist, disapproved of masturbation in the late nineteenth century. He thought it contributed to insanity. And in late nineteenth-century America, The American Institute for the Insane advocated castration for masturbators.

Currently, some sex offenders are treated using similar archaic medical methods. The severity of medical treatments varies among countries. Rapists and paedophiles, for instance, have been subject to castration, psychosurgery (cutting out parts from the brain), anti-psychotic drugs (neuroleptics), and anti-sex-drive drugs. Civil liberties groups, surgeons, psychiatrists, judges, juries and sometimes the patients themselves are involved in decisions to use medical treatments. Often the patient has little choice, since his freedom can depend on his compliance in giving an 'informed consent' for treatment.

CASTRATION AND CHEMICAL CASTRATION

In 1983, a South Carolina judge sentenced three rapists guilty of a particularly horrific incident to choose between either thirty years in prison or castration. Castration or testalectomy is a radical and irreversible surgical removal of the testes. The practice was first recorded by Farel in 1892 (Crawford, 1981). Once the testes are removed, there is a dramatic reduction in the male sex hormone, testosterone. Libido or sexual desire decreases in response to this absence of male hormone.

Castration was used in ancient civilizations to subdue male animals and to provide eunuchs to protect women owned by royalty in societies as distant as Turkey and China. Side-effects may involve hot flushes, breast growth, sweating, loss of body hair and general malaise. The major side-effect desired in the case of rapists is an absence of libido.

Some European countries, most notably Denmark, legislated that dangerous sex offenders could 'voluntarily' submit to castration as a form of treatment. Sturup (1972) claims that the treatment is effective. Of a total of 3,186 castrated sex offenders in six European countries, only sixty-nine or 2.5 per cent reoffended after treatment. Freeman (1979) writes that of 900 castrated Danish men between 1929 and 1959, only ten reoffended after surgery.

Yet, despite such glowing reports, castration is beset with problems. The sex offenders can purchase hormonal replacement drugs, either legimately or on the black market, to regain their sexual prowess. In addition, a small amount of male hormone (androgens) is produced in the adrenal gland which is not removed in castration. This means that, in some cases, even though the man has no testicles, he will still maintain a certain amount of 'sex drive'.

Crawford (1981) points out that castration of paedophiles is unwarranted because it can produce an even lower self-esteem; sometimes low enough to contribute to suicide. Understandably, however, many victims, their families and a misinformed public are likely to approve of such a solution. Despite public approval of the death penalty, floggings, castration and other radical measures, the practice of castration can hardly be viewed as appropriate in 'civilized' countries. It is not appropriate, in my view, even in those Islamic countries where amputation is standard punishment. Freeman reports that flogging is still in use as retribution for sexual offences on the Isle of Man (in the British Isles), and prophesies that 'the time will come when hormonal and surgical "treatment", if not other forms described above, will also be removed from the battery of the prison medical officer'.

DRUGS

Another dimension to this radical sphere of treatment is the use of drugs to curtail the sex drive. It has long been known that psychotics treated with phenothiazines (for example, Thioridazine, Thorazine, Stelazine) experience a drastic reduction in sex drive because they cause a reduction in testosterone plasma levels. Thus, despite side-effects which include nausea, diarrhoea and Parkinsonian tremors, sex offenders are sometimes treated with such agents. Critics suggest that the sex offender is 'chemically straitjacketed'. Proponents applaud the 'chemical straitjacketing' of 'filthy felons', rapists and child molesters.

Depo-Provera (medroxyprogesterone acetate), which can be used as a birth control pill in women, has also been used to treat outpatient rapists. The drug causes a decrease in testosterone in the male. Money (1970) gave a report of eight sex offenders being successfully treated with Depo-Provera. In other words, they no longer showed any signs of deviant sexuality. In the United States, drug trials in the treatment of sex offenders are stringently controlled. For example, state hospitals usually require the permission of the director of a state mental health department before proceeding with treatment. One compulsive, habitual rapist begged for Depo-Provera: 'I'd rather have small balls and live on the outside than have big balls and end up in San Quentin.' He was refused treatment on political grounds – because a chief in the distant state capital was afraid of upsetting certain pressure groups. In all probability, this man will serve his term in a state psychiatric prison and end up being released – to rape again.

In one ironic twist of fate, a judge in the Mid-West sentenced the heir of a major pharmaceutical company to present himself for 'chemical castration' for the repeated rape of his fourteen-year-old step-daughter from the time she was seven years old. The irony was that the heir's great-grandfather had started the company 118 years before, and the drug used (Depo-Provera) to 'chemically castrate' him was made by this same company. The heir was also given five years' probation and sentenced to spend a year in the local county jail (*The Argus*, 31 January 1984).

Another promising anti-libidinal drug is **cyproterone acetate** (Androcur). This drug blocks the receptor sites which respond to testosterone. The drug has not yet been passed by the United States Food and Drug Administration and was not, at the time of writing, available in the United States.

PSYCHOSURGERY

Psychosurgery in the treatment of sex offenders involves destroying certain parts of the brain to produce a 'change' in behaviour. In the film, *One Flew Over the Cuckoo's Nest*, Jack Nicholson acted the part of a convict in a state psychiatric hospital who undergoes irreversible psycho-surgery and essentially ends as a vegetable. The practice is fraught with controversy because, for ethical and legal reasons, incarcerated offenders cannot be assumed to give a proper informed consent to the operation. Fortunately, psychosurgery as a legitimate treatment is on the wane in most civilized countries. In a sense, cutting away a part of a person's brain is like cutting a piece of life out of him and is tantamount to a partial death penality. In other words, it kills much of the person's identity while keeping his body alive.

References

Abel, G., Levis. D., and Clancy, J. 'Aversion Therapy Applied to Taped Sequences of Deviant Behaviour in Exhibitionists and Other Sexual Deviations: A Preliminary Report', in *Journal of Behavior Therapy and Experimental Psychiatry*, 1970, Vol. 1, pp. 56–60.

Abel, G., Blanchard, E., Barlow, D., and Movissakalian, M., 'Identifying Specific Erotic Cues in Sexual Deviations by Audiotaped Descriptions', in *Journal of Applied Behavior Analysis*, 1975, Vol. 8, pp. 247–60.

Abel, G. G., Barlow, D. H., Blanchard, E. B., and Guild, D., 'The Components of Rapists' Sexual Arousal', in *Archives of General Psychiatry*, 1977, No. 34, pp. 895–903.

Abelson, J. H., 'Apprenticeship in Prostitution', in *Social Problems*, 1974, 12, pp. 287–97.

Ackerman, D. L., *The Only Guide You'll Ever Need to Marry Money*, Simon & Schuster, New York, 1982.

Ackroyd, P., *Dressing Up*, Thames & Hudson, London 1979.

Allen, C., *A Textbook of Psychosexual Disorders*, Oxford University Press, 1969.

Allen, C., *The Sexual Perversions and Abnormalities*, Greenwood Press, Westport, Conn. 1979. (Originally published by Oxford University Press, 1940.)

American Psychiatric Association, *Diagnostic and Statistical Manual of Mental Disorders* (third edition), American Psychiatric Association, Washington, DC, 1978.

Amnesty International, British Section, *Prisoners of Conscience in the USSR*, Quartermaine House, Sunbury, Middlesex, 1975.

Amnesty International, *Evidence of Torture: Studies by the Amnesty International Danish Medical Group*, Amnesty International Publications, London, 1977.

Amnesty International, *Torture in Greece*, Amnesty International Publications, London, 1977.

Amnesty International, *Political Imprisonment in South Africa*, Amnesty International Publications, London, 1978.

Amnesty International, *Law and Human Rights in the Islamic Republic of Iran: A Report Covering Events within the Seven Month Period Following the Revolution of February 1979*, Amnesty International Publications, London, 1980.

Amnesty International, *Amnesty International Report, 1984*, Amnesty International Publications, London, 1984.

Amnesty International, British Section, *Religious Intolerance*: Paper prepared for the UN Special Rapporteur on Religious Intolerance and Discrimination on Grounds of Religion or Belief, Amnesty International, London, (n.d.).

Bagley, C., 'Incest Behaviour and Incest Taboo', in *Social Problems*, 16, 1968.

Bancroft, J., *Deviant Sexual Behaviour: Modification and Assessment*, Clarendon Press, Oxford, 1974.

Baker, D., Telfer, M.A., and Richardson, C. E., 'Chromosome Errors in Men with Anti-social Behaviour', in *Journal of the American Medical Association*, 214, 1970.

Bandura, A., *Social Learning Theory*, Prentice Hall, Englewood Cliffs, NJ, 1977.

Barbach, L., and Levine, L., *Shared Intimacies*, Corgi Books, London, 1981.

Barry, K., *Female Sexual Slavery*, Avon Books, New York, 1979.

Bauer, B. A., *Woman and Love*, Vols. 1 and 2, Liveright Publishing, New York, 1971.

Bennett, J., *Sex Signs*, Pan Books, London, 1981.

Berben, P., *Dachau 1933–1945*, The Norfolk Press, London, 1975.

Berg, A., *The Sadist*, Medical Press of New York, New York, 1954.

Berkow, R. (ed.-in-chief), *The Merck Manual*, Vol. 1, Merck, Sharp and Dohme Laboratories, Rakway, NJ, 1982.

Bernard, J., *The Future of Marriage*, Yale University Press, 1982.

Berne, E., *Sex in Human Loving*, Pocket Books, New York, 1971.

Berzon, B., *Positively Gay*, Mediamix Associates, Los Angeles, 1979.

Beserra, S. S., Jewel, N. M., and Matthews, M. W., *Sex Code of California*, Public Education and Research Committee of California, Berkeley, 1973.

Bharti, Ma Satya, *The Ultimate Risk: Encountering Bhagwan Shree Rajneesh*, Rajneesh Foundation, London, 1983.

Bieber, I., 'Homosexuality: The Ethical Challenge', *Journal of Consulting and Clinical Psychology*, 1976, 44, pp. 163–6.

Billingham, N., 'In Prison', in B. Galloway (ed.), *Prejudice and Pride: Discrimination against Gay People in Modern Britain*, Routledge & Kegan Paul, London, 1983.

Bord, J., and Bord, C., *Earth Rites*, Granada, London, 1983.

Boring, E. G., Langfeld, H. S., and Weld, H. P., *Foundations of Psychology*, John Wiley, New York, 1948.

Bowlby, J., *Attachment and Loss*, Penguin Books, Harmondsworth, Middlesex. 1971.

Boyd, D., *Swami*, Rider, London, 1976.

Brecher, E. M., *Treatment Programs for Sex Offenders*, Government Printing Office, US Department of Justice, Washington, DC, 1978.

Brick, B. L., 'Judaism in the Gay Community', in B. Berzon (ed.), *Positively Gay*, Mediamix Associates, Los Angeles, 1979.

Brown, R. S., and Courtis, R. W., 'The Castration Alternative', in *Canadian Journal of Criminology*, 1977, Vol. 19 (2), pp. 157–69.

Brownmiller, S., *Against Our Will: Men, Women and Rape*, Simon & Schuster, New York, 1975.

Bryant, C., *Sexual Deviancy and Social Proscription*, Human Sciences Press, New York, 1982.

Buhrich, N., 'The Association of Erotic Piercing with Homosexuality, Sadomasochism, Bondage, Fetishism, and Tattoos', in *Archives of Sexual Behaviour* (St Vincent's Hospital, Darlinghurst, Australia), 1983, Vol. 12(2), pp. 167–71.

Burg, B. R., 'The Sick and the Dead: The Development of Psychological Theory on Necrophilia from Krafft-Ebing to the Present', in *Journal of the History of the Behavioral Sciences*, 1982, Vol. 18 (3), pp. 242–54.

Burgess, A. W., Groth, A. N., and McCausland, M. P., 'Child Sex Initiation Rings', in *American Journal of Orthopsychiatry*, 1981, Vol. 51 (1), pp. 110–19.

Burns, R., 'The Fight for Equality', in B. Galloway (ed.), *Prejudice and Pride: Discrimination against Gay People in Modern Britain*, Routledge & Kegan Paul, London, 1983.

Calef, V., and Weinshel, E. M., 'On Certain Neurotic Equivalents of Necrophilia', in *International Journal of Psycho-Analysis*, 1972, Vol. 53 (1), pp. 67–75.

Carrera, M., *Sex: The Facts, The Acts and Your Feelings*, Sphere Books, London, 1981.

Cassidy, J., and Stewart-Park, A., *We're Here: Conversations with Lesbian Women*, Quartet Books, London, 1977.

Cautela, J. R., and Wisocki, P. A., 'Covert Sensitization for the Treatment of Sexual Deviations', in *Psychological Record*, 1971, Vol. 21 (1), pp. 37–48.

Cavenar, J. O., Spaulding, J. G., and Butts, N. T., 'Autofellatio: A Power and Dependency Conflict', in *Journal of Nervous and Mental Disease*, 1977, Vol. 165 (5), pp. 356–60.

Chesler, P., *Women and Madness*, Avon Books, New York, 1973.

Chesler, P., *About Men*, The Women's Press, London, 1978.

Christodorescu, D., 'Female Transsexualism', in *Psychiatria Clinica*, 1971, Vol. 4 (1), pp. 40–5.

Coe, J. I., 'Sexual Asphyxias', in *Life-Threatening Behavior*, 1974, Vol. 4 (3), pp. 171–5.

Cohen, M. L., Seghorn, J., and Calnas, W., 'Sociometric Study of the Sex Offender', *Journal of Abnormal Psychology*, 1969, 74, pp. 249–55.

Cohen, M. L., Garofalo, R., Boucher, R., and Seghorn, T., 'The Psychology of Rapists', in *Seminars in Psychiatry*, 1971, 3, pp. 307–27.

Coleman, J. C., *Abnormal Psychology and Modern Life*, Scott, Foreman, New York, 1972.

Comfort, A., *Sexual Behaviour in Society*, Gerald Duckworth, London, 1950.

Comfort, A., *The Joy of Sex*, revised edition. Quartet Books, London, 1974a.

Comfort, A., *More Joy of Sex*, revised edition, Quartet Books, London, 1974b.

Cook, M., and Howells, K. (eds.), *Adult Sexual Interest in Children*, Academic Press, London, 1981.

Cook, M., and Wilson, G. (eds.), *Love and Attraction*, Pergamon Press, Oxford, 1979.

Cooper, A. L., Ismail, A. A., Phanjoo. A. L., and Love, D. L., 'Antiandrogen (cyproterone acetate) Therapy in Deviant Hypersexuality', in *British Journal of Psychiatry*, 1972, Vol. 120, p. 554.

Cooper, A. J., 'A Placebo-controlled Trial of the Antiandrogen Cyproterone Acetate in Deviant Hypersexuality', in *Comprehensive Psychiatry*, 1981, Vol. 22 (5), pp. 458–65.

Coopersmith, S., *The Antecedents of Self Esteem*, W. H. Freeman, San Francisco. 1967.

Cox, M., in Rosen., I. (ed.), *Sexual Deviation*, Oxford University Press, 1979.

Crane, P., *Gays and the Law*, Pluto Press, London, 1982.

Crawford, D., 'Treatment Approaches with Paedophilia', in M. Cook and K. Howells (eds.), *Adult Sexual Interest in Children*, Academic Press, London, 1981.

Daly, M., 'At Work', in B. Galloway (ed.), *Prejudice and Pride: Discrimination against Gay People in Modern Britain*, Routledge & Kegan Paul, London, 1983.

Danto, B. M., 'Violent Sex and Suicide', in *Mental Health and Society*, 1978, Vol. 5 (1–2), pp. 1–13.

Davis, M. S., *Smut*, University of Chicago Press, 1983.

Davison, G. C., 'Elimination of Sadistic Fantasies by a Client-controlled Counter-conditioning Technique: A Case Study', in *Journal of Abnormal Psychology*, 1974, 73, pp. 84–90.

Davison, G. C., 'Homosexuality: The Ethical Challenge', in *Journal of Consulting and Clinical Psychology*, 1976, 44, pp. 157–62.

Denis, A., *Taboo*, W. H. Allen, London, 1966.

Denko, J. D., 'Klismaphilia: Enema as a Sexual Preference', in *American Journal of Psychotherapy*, 1973, Vol. 27 (2), pp. 232–50.

Denko, J. D., 'Klismaphilia: Amplification of the Erotic Enema Deviance', in *American Journal of Psychotherapy*, 1976, Vol. 30 (2), pp. 236–55.

de Riencourt, A., *Sex and Power in History*, Dell Publishing, New York, 1974.

Diagram Group, *Sex: A User's Manual*, G. P. Putnam's Sons, New York, 1981.

Diamond, H., *Sexwatching*, Macdonald, London, 1984.

Dickson, A., *A Woman in Your Own Right*, Quartet Books, London, 1982.

Dietz, P. E., and Evans, B., 'Pornographic Imagery and Prevalence of Paraphilia', in *American Journal of Psychiatry*, 1982, Vol. 139 (11), pp. 1493–5.

Dobson, M., 'At School', in B. Galloway (ed.), *Prejudice and Pride:*

Discrimination against Gay People in Modern Britain, Routledge & Kegan Paul, London, 1983.

Dodson, B., *Liberating Masturbation*, Bodysex Designs, New York, 1974.

Dörner, G., 'The Differentiation of Neuroendocrine System and Fundamental Processes of Life', in *Folia Endocrinol, jap*, 1981, 57, pp. 298–304.

Drury, J., *Don Juan, Mescalito and Modern Magic*, Arkana, London, 1985.

Duquesne, T., and Reeves, J., *A Handbook of Psychoactive Medicines*, Quartet Books, London, 1982.

Durden-Smith, J., and de Simone, D., *Sex and the Brain*, Warner Books, New York, 1983.

Durrell, A., 'At Home', in B. Galloway (ed.), *Prejudice and Pride: Discrimination against Gay People in Modern Britain*, Routledge & Kegan Paul, London, 1983.

Dworkin, A., *Our Blood*, The Women's Press, London, 1976.

Dworkin, A., *Pornography*, The Women's Press, London, 1981.

East, W. N., 'Sexual Offenders', in *Journal of Nervous and Mental Disorders*, 1946, 103, pp. 626–66.

Ellis, A., 'The Effectiveness of Psychotherapy with Individuals Who Have Severe Homosexual Problems', in *Journal of Consulting Psychiatry*, 1958, 20, pp. 191–5.

Ellis, A., and Sagarin, E., *Nymphomania: A Study of the Oversexed Woman*, Guilbert Press, New York, 1964.

Epstein, A. W., 'Relationship of Fetishism and Transvestism to Brain and Particularly to Temporal Lobe Dysfunction', in *Journal of Nervous and Mental Disease*, 1961, 133, pp. 247–53.

Eskapa, R. D., 'Differences in Attributional Style, Multidimensional Locus of Control, and Self-esteem in Paedophiles and non-Paedophiles', Doctoral Dissertation, California School of Professional Psychology, Los Angeles, 1983.

Eskapa, S., *Woman Versus Woman*, William Heinemann, London, 1984.

Evans, M. (ed.), *The Woman Question*, Fontana Paperbacks, London, 1982.

Everaerd, W., 'A Case of Apotemnophilia: A Handicap as Sexual Preference', in *American Journal of Psychotherapy*, 1982, Vol. 37 (2), pp. 285–93.

Eysenck, H. J., *Sex and Personality*, Abacus, London, 1978.

Eysenck, H. J., and Wilson, G., *The Psychology of Sex*, New English Library, London, 1981.

Faderman, L., *Surpassing the Love of Men*, William Morrow, New York, 1981.

Fehlinger, H., *Sexual Life of Primitive Peoples*, London, 1921.

Feldman, M. P., and MacCulloch, M. J., 'The Application of Anticipatory Avoidance Learning to the Treatment of Homosexuality. I. Theory, Technique and Preliminary Results', in *Behavior Research and Therapy*, 1965, 2, p. 165.

Feldman, M. P., 'Aversion Therapy for Sexual Deviations: A Critical Review', in *Psychological Bulletin*, 1966, 65, pp. 65–79.

Feldman, M., MacCulloch, M. J., Mellor, U., and Pinschoff, J., 'The Application of Anticipatory Avoidance Learning to the Treatment of Homosexuality: The Sexual Orientation Method', in *Behavior Research and Therapy*, 1966, 4, pp. 289–99.

Feldman, M. P., and MacCulloch, M. J., *Homosexual Behaviour: Therapy and Assessment*, Pergamon Press, Oxford, 1971.

Fenelon, F., *The Musicians of Auschwitz*, Michael Joseph, London, 1977.

Fenischel, O., *The Psychoanalytic Theory of Neurosis*, W. W. Norton, New York, 1945.

Fisher, H. E., *The Sex Contract*, Granada, London, 1982.

Ford, C. S., and Beach, F. A., *Patterns of Sexual Behavior*, Harper & Row, New York, 1951.

Forel, A., *The Sexual Question*, Rebman, London, 1908.

Forgione, A. G., 'The Use of Mannequins in the Behavioral Assessment of Child Molesters: Two Case Reports', *Behavior Therapy*, 1976, 7, pp. 678–85.

Foucault, M., *The History of Sexuality*, Penguin Books, Harmondsworth, Middlesex, 1981.

Frankl, V. E., *Man's Search for Meaning*, Hodder & Stoughton, London, 1959.

Freedman, A., 'Psychoanalytic Study of an Unusual Perversion', in *Journal of the American Psychoanalytic Association*, 1978, Vol. 26 (4), pp. 749–77.

Freeman, M., 'The Law and Sexual Deviation', in I. Rosen (ed.), *Sexual Deviation*, Oxford University Press, 1979.

Freud, S., *Civilization and Its Discontents*, Hogarth Press, London, 1969. (First published in English, 1930.)

Freud, S., *Three Essays on the Theory of Sexuality*, Penguin Books, Harmondsworth, Middlesex, 1983. (First published in English, 1955.)

Freund, K., 'Diagnosing Homo- or Heterosexuality and Erotic Age-preference by Means of a Psychophysiological Test', in *Behavior Research and Therapy*, 1967, 5, pp. 209–28.

Freund, K., Sedlacek, F., and Knob, K., 'A Single Transducer for Mechanical Plethysmography of the Male Genitalia', in *Journal of the Experimental Analysis of Behavior*, 1970, 8, pp. 169–70.

Freund, K., 'Erotic Preferences in Paedophiles', in *Behavior Research and Therapy*, 1973, 5, pp. 339–48.

Freund, K., Langevin, R., Cibiri, S., and Zajac, Y., 'Heterosexual Aversion in Homosexual Males', in *British Journal of Psychiatry*, 1973, 122, pp. 163–9.

Freytag, F. F., 'Hypnotherapeutic Explorations of Early Enema Experience', in *American Journal of Clinical Hypnosis*, 1971, Vol. 14 (1), pp. 24–31.

Friday, N., *Forbidden Flowers*, Pocket Books, New York, 1975.

Friday, N., *Men in Love*, Hutchinson, London, 1980.

Friday, N., *My Secret Garden*, Virago: Quartet Books, London, 1975.

Friedan, B., *The Feminine Mystique*, Dell Publishing, New York, 1963.

Friedlander, A. H., *Out of the Whirlwind*, Schocken Books, New York, 1976.

Gagne, P., 'Treatment of Sex Offenders with Medroxyprogesterone Acetate', in *American Journal of Psychiatry*, 1981, Vol. 138 (5), pp. 644–6.

Gagnon, J. H., 'Female Child Victims of Sex Offenses', in *Social Problems*, 1965, pp. 176–92.

Gagnon, J. H., and Simon, W., 'Sexual Deviance in Contemporary America', in *Annals of the American Academy of Political and Social Science*, 1968, 376, pp. 106–22.

Gagnon, J. H., and Simon, W., *Sexual Conduct: The Social Resources of Human Sexuality*, Aldine, Chicago, 1973.

Galloway, B. (ed.), *Prejudice and Pride: Discrimination against Gay People in Modern Britain*, Routledge & Kegan Paul, London, 1983.

Galloway, B., 'The Police and the Courts', in B. Galloway (ed.), *Prejudice and Pride: Discrimination against Gay People in Modern Britain*, Routledge & Kegan Paul, London, 1983.

Gardner, D., *Survive: Don't be a Victim*, Warner Books, New York, 1982.

Gathorne-Hardy, J., *Love, Sex, Marriage and Divorce*, Jonathan Cape, London, 1981.

Gebhard, P. H., Gagnon, J. H., Pomeroy, W. B., and Christenson, C. V., *Sex Offenders: An Analysis of Types*, Hayes & Row, New York, 1965.

Geen, R. G., and Pigg, R., 'Acquisition of an Aggressive Response and Its Generalization to Verbal Behavior', in *Journal of Personality and Social Psychology*, 1970, 15, pp. 165–70.

Geer, J. H., Morokoff, P., and Greenwood, P., 'Sexual Arousal in Women: The Development of a Measurement Device for Vaginal Blood Flow', in *Archives of Sexual Behavior*, 1974, 3, pp. 359–66.

Gerber, A. B., *The Book of Sex Lists*, W. H. Allen, London, 1982.

Gibbens, T. C. N., *Child Victims of Sex Offences*, Institute for the Study and Treatment of Delinquency, London, 1963.

Gibson, E., and Klein, S., *Murder 1957–1968*, Home Office Research Studies No. 3, HMSO, London, 1969.

Gilbert, A. N., 'The Africaine Courts-martial: A Study of Buggery and the Royal Navy', in *Journal of Homosexuality*, 1974, Vol. 1 (1), pp. 111–22.

Goldstein, M. J., and Kant, H. S., *Pornography and Sexual Deviance*, University of California Press, 1973.

Green, G., 'The Church', in B. Galloway (ed.), *Prejudice and Pride: Discrimination against Gay People in Modern Britain*, Routledge & Kegan Paul, London, 1983.

Greenberg, H. R., Blank, H. R., and Greenson, D. P., 'The Jelly Baby', in *Psychiatric Quarterly*, 1968, 42 (2), pp. 211–16.

Greenwald, H., and Greenwald, R., *The Sex-Life Letters*, Granada, London, 1974.

Greer, G., *The Female Eunuch*, MacGibbon & Kee, London, 1970.

Greer, G., *Sex and Destiny*, Secker & Warburg, London, 1984.

Griffin, S., *Pornography and Silence*, The Women's Press, London, 1981.

Groth, A. N., and Burgess, A. W., 'Rape: A Sexual Deviation', in *American Journal of Orthopsychiatry*, 1977, Vol. 47 (3), pp. 400–406.

Groth, A. N., *Men who Rape: The Psychology of the Offender*, Plenum Press, New York, 1979.

Haddon, C., *The Limits of Sex*, Michael Joseph, London, 1982.

Haeberle, E. J., *The Sex Atlas*, Sheldon Press, London, 1983.

Hall, C. S., *A Primer of Freudian Psychology*, New American Library, New York, 1954.

Hamparian, D. M., Schuster, R., Dinitz, S., and Conrad, J., *The Violent Few*, Lexington Books, Lexington, Mass., 1978.

Harford, B., and Hopkins, S. (eds.), *Greenham Common: Women at the Wire*, The Women's Press, London, 1984.

Harris, A., and Peacock, S., *Sexual Exercises for Women*, Quartet Books, London, 1985.

Hatfield, T., *Sandstone Experience*, Signet Books, New York, 1976.

Hauck, P., *Jealousy*, Sheldon Press, London, 1981.

Hazelwood, R. R., Deitz, P. E., and Burgess, A. W., 'The Investigation of Autoerotic Fatalities', in *Journal of Police Science and Administration*, 1981, Vol. 9 (4), pp. 404–11.

Heimel, C., *Sex Tips for Girls*, Simon & Schuster, New York, 1983.

Hendrickson, R., *The Literary Life and Other Curiosities*, Penguin Books, Harmondsworth, Middlesex, 1982.

Herinck, R. (ed.), *The Psychotherapy Handbook*, New American Library, New York, 1980.

Hilgard, E. R., Atkinson, R. L., and Atkinson, R. C., *Introduction to Psychology*, Harcourt, Brace, Jovanovich, New York, 1979.

Hite, S., *The Hite Report*, Dell Publishing, New York, 1981.

Hoon, P. W., Wincze, J. P., and Hoon, E. F., 'Physiological Assessment of Sexual Arousal in Women', in *Psychophysiology*, 1976, 13, pp. 196–204.

Howard League for Penal Reform, *Unlawful Sex*, Waterlow Publishers, London, 1985.

Howells, K., 'Some Meanings of Children for Paedophiles', in M. Cook and G. D. Wilson (eds.), *Love and Attraction, an International Conference*, Pergamon Press, Oxford, 1979.

Howes, K., 'The Media', in B. Galloway (ed.), *Prejudice and Pride: Discrimination against Gay People in Modern Britain*, Routledge & Kegan Paul, London, 1983.

Humphreys, R. A. L., *Tearoom Trade: Impersonal Sex in Public Places*, Duckworth, London, 1970.

Hunt, M. M., *Sexual Behavior in the 1970s*, Playboy Press, Chicago, 1974.

Hunter, R., Logue V., and McMenemy, W. H., 'Temporal Lobe Epilepsy Supervening on Longstanding Transvestism and Fetishism', in *Epilepsia*, 1963, 4, pp. 60–65.

Hymowitz, C., and Weissman, H., *A History of Women in America*, Bantam Books, New York, 1981.

Ibrahim, A. I., 'Deviant Sexual Behavior in Men's Prisons', in *Crime and Delinquency*, 1974, Vol. 20 (1), pp. 38–44.

'J', *The Sensuous Woman*, Granada, London, 1973.

Jackson, B. T., 'A Case of Voyeurism Treated by Counterconditioning', in *Behavior Research and Therapy*, 1969, 7 (1), pp. 133–4.

James, W., and Kedgley, S. J., *The Mistress*, Abelard-Schuman, London, 1973.

Janssen-Jurreit, *Sexism*, Farrar, Strauss & Giroux, New York, 1982.

Johnston, J., 'The Myth of the Myth of the Vaginal Orgasm', in M. Evans, *The Woman Question*, Fontana Books, London, 1982.

Jones, A., *Women Who Kill*, Fawcett Colombine, New York, 1981.

Kahn, S., and Davis, J., *Sexual Preferences: The Kahn Report*, W. H. Allen, London, 1982.

Kant, H. S., 'Exposure to Pornography and Sexual Behavior in Deviant and Normal Groups', in *Corrective Psychiatry and Journal of Social Therapy*, 1971, Vol. 17 (2), pp. 5–17.

Kelly, B., 'On Woman/Girl Love, or Lesbians Do "Do it"', in *Gay Community News*, Boston, 3 March 1979.

Kenyon, F. E., 'Studies in Female Homosexuality: Social and Psychiatric Aspects', in *British Journal of Psychiatry*, 1968, 114, pp. 1337–50.

Kidron, M., and Segal, R., *The New State of the World Atlas*, Pan Books, London, 1984.

Kiley, D., *The Peter Pan Syndrome*, Dodd, Mead, New York, 1983.

Kinsey, A. C., Pomeroy, W. B., Martin, C. E., and Gebhard, P. H., *Sexual Behavior in the Human Female*, W. B. Saunders, Philadelphia, 1953.

Kinsey, A. C., Pomeroy, W. B., and Martin, C. E., *Sexual Behavior in the Human Male*, W. B. Saunders, Philadelphia, 1948.

Kirtner, E. W. (ed.), *War Crimes Trials*, Vol. IV: The Hadamar Trial, William Hodge, London, 1949.

Kitzinger, S., *Women as Mothers*, Fontana Books, London, 1978.

Koplin (?), *George Washington Law Review*, May 1977, pp. 848–50.

Kraemer, W., *Forbidden Love, The Normal and Abnormal Love of Children*, Sheldon Press, London, 1976.

Krafft-Ebing, R. von., *Psychopathia Sexualis*, Rebman, New York, 1912.

Kupfermann, J., *The MsTaken Body*, Robson Books, London, 1979.

Kutchinski, B., 'The Effect of Easy Availability of Pornography on the Incidence of Sex Crimes: The Danish Experience', in *Journal of Social Issues*, 1973, 29, pp. 163–81.

Labelle, A., 'All Holes Barred', *Forum*, July 1986.

Laffin, J., *The Dagger of Islam*, Sphere Books, London, 1979.

Langfeldt, T., 'Sexual Development in Children', in M. Cook and K. Howells (eds.), *Adult Sexual Interest in Children*, Academic Press, London, 1981.

Lapierre, D., *The City of Joy*, Doubleday and Company, New York, 1985.

Lasch, C., *The Minimal Self*, Picador, London, 1984.

Laws, D. R., and Pawlowski, A. V., 'A Multi-purpose Biofeedback Device for Penile Plethysmography', in *Journal of Behavior Therapy and Experimental Psychiatry*, 1973, Vol. 4 (4), pp. 339–41.

Laws, D. R., Keyer, J., and Holman, M. L., 'Reduction in Sadistic Arousal by Olfactory Aversion: A Case Study', in *Behavior Therapy*, 1978, 16, pp. 281–5.

Lazarus, A. A., *Multimodal Behavior Therapy*, Singer, New York, 1976.

Lazarus, A. A., *The Practice of Multimodal Therapy*, McGraw-Hill, New York, 1981.

Leech, K., *Youthquake*, Sheldon Press, London, 1973.

Leeds Revolutionary Feminist Group, 'Political Lesbianism: The Case against Heterosexuality', in M. Evans (ed.), *The Woman Question*, Fontana Books, London, 1982.

Legman, G., *Rationale of the Dirty Joke*, Jonathan Cape, London, 1969.

Lewis, R. H., *The Browser's Guide to Erotica*, Panther Books, London, 1983.

Lihn, H., 'Sexual Masochism: A Case Report', in *International Journal of Psycho-Analysis*, 1971, Vol. 52 (4), pp. 469–78.

Lindholm, C., *Generosity and Jealousy*, Columbia University Press, 1982.

London, L. S., and Caprio, F. S., *Sexual Deviations*, Linacre Press, Washington, DC, 1950.

Loney, F., 'Family Dynamics in Homosexual Women', in *Archives of Sexual Behavior*, 2, 1973.

Longmore, L., *The Dispossessed*, Jonathan Cape, London, 1959.

Lorand, S. (ed.), *The Yearbook of Psychoanalysis*, Imago Publishing, London, 1946.

Lovey, K., *On Aggression*, Harcourt Brace and World, New York, 1966.

Lowery, S. A., and Wetli, C. V., 'Sexual Asphyxia: A Neglected Area of Study', in *Deviant Behavior*, 1982, Vol. 4 (1), pp. 19–39.

Lowse, A. L., *Homosexuals in History*, Weidenfeld & Nicolson, London, 1977.

'M', *The Sensuous Man*, Dell Publishing, New York, 1984.

McBain, E., *Hail to the Chief*, Random House, New York, 1973.

McCary, J. L., *Human Sexuality*, D. Van Nostrand, New York, 1973.

McCarty, D., 'Women Who Rape,' unpublished paper, Albany, New York, 1981.

McConaghy, N., 'Penile Response Conditioning and Its Relationship to Aversion Therapy in Homosexuals', in *Behavior Therapy*, 1970, 1, pp. 213–21.

MacDonald, J., *Rape Offenders and their Victims*, Charles Thomas, Springfield, Ill., 1971.

Maddox, B., *Married and Gay*, Harcourt, Brace, Jovanovich, New York, 1982.

Maletzky, B. M., '"Assisted" Covert Sensitization in the Treatment of Exhibitionism', in *Journal of Consulting and Clinical Psychology*, 1971, 42, pp. 34–40.

Marcus, M., *Taste for Pain*, Souvenir Press, London, 1981.

Marquis, J. N., 'Orgasmic Reconditioning: Changing Sexual Choice through Controlling Masturbatory Fantasies', in *Journal of Behavior Therapy and Experimental Psychiatry*, 1970, 1, pp. 263–71.

Marshall, D. A., and Suggs, R. C., *Human Sexual Behavior*, Basic Books, New York, 1971.

Marshall, J., 'The Medical Profession', in B. Galloway (ed.), *Prejudice and Pride: Discrimination against Gay People in Modern Britain*, Routledge & Kegan Paul, London, 1972.

Martin, D., and Lyon, P., *Lesbian Women*, Bantam Books, London, 1972.

Masters, B., *Killing for Company*, Jonathan Cape, London, 1985.

Masters, W. H., and Johnson, V. E., *Human Sexual Response*, Little, Brown, Boston, 1966.

Masters, W. H., and Johnson, V. E., *Human Sexual Inadequacy*, Little, Brown, Boston, 1970.

Mead, M., *Culture and Commitment*, Bodley Head, London, 1970.

Meldrum, J., 'On the Streets', in B. Galloway (ed.), *Prejudice and Pride: Discrimination against Gay People in Modern Britain*, Routledge & Kegan Paul, London, 1983.

Milgram, S., *Obedience to Authority: An Experimental View*, Harper & Row, New York, 1974.

Money, J., and Brennan, J. G., 'Sexual Dimorphism in the Psychology of Female Transsexuals', in *Journal of Nervous and Mental Disease*, 1968, 147, pp. 487–99.

Money, J., and Primrose, C., 'Sexual Dimorphism and Dissociation in the Psychology of Male Transsexuals', in *Journals of Nervous and Mental Disease*, 1968, 147, pp. 472–86.

Money, J., 'Use of an Androgen-depleting Hormone in the Treatment of Male Sex Offenders', in *Journal of Sex Research*, 1970, 6, pp. 165–72.

Money, J., 'Prefatory Remarks on Outcome of Sex Reassignment in 24 Cases of Transsexualism', in *Archives of Sexual Behavior*, 1971, Vol. 1 (2), pp. 163–5.

Money, J., and Erhard, A., *A Man and Woman, Boy and Girl*, Johns Hopkins University Press, 1972.

Money, J., 'Human Behavior Cytogenics: Review of Psychopathology in Three Syndromes – 47,XXY; 47,XYY; and 45,X', in *Journal of Sex Research*, 1975, 11, pp. 181–200.

Money, J., Jobaris, R., and Furth, G., 'Apotemnophilia: Two Cases of Self-demand Amputation as a Paraphilia', in *Journal of Sex Research*, 1977, Vol. 13 (2), pp. 115–25.

Monroe, R. A., *Journeys Out of the Body*, Anchor/Doubleday, New York, 1973.

Moore, S. L., and May, M., 'Satyriasis from a Contemporary Perspective: A Review of Male Hypersexuality', in *Hillside Journal of Clinical Psychiatry*, 1982, Vol. 4 (1), pp. 83–93.

Morris, D., *The Naked Ape*, Jonathan Cape, London, 1967.

Morris, D., *Manwatching*, Triad/Panther Books, London, 1977.

Mostyn, F. E., *Marriage and the Law*, Oyez Publishing, London, 1976.

Murray, F. S., and Beran, L. C., 'A Survey of Nuisance Telephone Calls Received by Males and Females', in *Psychological Record*, 1968, Vol. 18 (1), pp. 107–9.

Newman, Graeme, 'World Violence', an unpublished study, 1980, cited in D. McCarty, 'Women Who Rape', unpublished paper, Albany, New York, 1981.

Newman, L. E., and Stoller, R. J., 'Spider Symbolism and Bisexuality', in *Journal of the American Psychoanalytic Association*, 1969, Vol. 17 (3), pp. 862–72.

Newman, L. E., and Stoller, R. J., 'The Oedipal Situation in Male Transsexualism', in *British Journal of Medical Psychology*, 1971, Vol. 44 (4), pp. 295–303.

Newton, E., *Mother Camp: Female Impersonators in America*, Prentice-Hall, Englewood Cliffs, NJ, 1972.

Nicholson, J., *Men and Women*, Oxford University Press, 1984.

O'Carroll, T., *Paedophilia: The Radical Case*, Peter Owen, London, 1980.

O'Neil, N., *The Marriage Premise*, Bantam Books, New York, 1978.

O'Neil, N., and O'Neil, T., *Open Marriage*, Evans Books, New York, 1972.

Ornstein, H. A., *Cruelty and Kindness*, Prentice-Hall, Englewood Cliffs, NJ, 1976.

Panton, J. H., 'Personality Differences Appearing between Rapists of Adults, Rapists of Children and Non-violent Sexual Molesters of Female Children', in *Research Communications in Psychology, Psychiatry and Behavior*, 1978, Vol. 3 (4), pp. 385–93.

Parker, C., *How to Avoid Sex*, New English Library, London, 1982.

Penney, A., *How to Make Love to a Man*, Clarkson Potter Publishers, New York, 1981.

Phillips, A., and Rakusen, J., (eds.), *Our Bodies, Ourselves*, Penguin Books, Harmondsworth, Middlesex, 1984. (Originally published by the Boston Women's Health Collective, 1971.)

Phythian, B. A., *Concise Dictionary of English Slang and Colloquialisms*, Hodder & Stoughton, London, 1982.

Pickles, S., *Queens*, Quartet Books, London, 1984.

Quinsey, V. L., and Carrigan, W. F., 'Penile Responses to Visual Stimuli: Instructional Control with and without Auditory Sexual Fantasy Correlates', in *Criminal Justice and Behavior*, 1978, Vol. 5 (4), pp. 333–42.

Rachman, S. J., and Philips, C., *Psychology and Medicine*, Pelican Books, Harmondsworth, Middlesex, 1978.

Rada, R. T. (ed.), *Clinical Aspects of the Rapist*, Grove & Stratton, New York, 1978.

Rada, R. T., Laws, D. R., and Kellner, R., 'Plasma Testosterone Levels in the Rapist', *Psychosomatic Medicine*, 38, 1967.

Rajneesh, B. S., *The Tantra Vision*, Vols. 1 and 2, Rajneesh Foundation, Poona, India, 1979.

Randell, J., 'Indications for Sex Reassignment Surgery', in *Archives of Sexual Behavior*, 1971, Vol. 1 (2) pp. 153–61.

Raskin, D.E., and Sullivan, K. E., 'Erotomania', in *American Journal of Psychiatry*, 1974, Vol. 131 (9), pp. 1033–5.

Rawson, P., *Tantra*, Thames & Hudson, London, 1973.

Raymond, J. G., *The Transsexual Empire*, Beacon Press, Boston, 1979.

Réage, P., *Story of O*, Olympia Press, London, 1970 (fine trade edition).

Rechy, J., *City of Night*, Granada, London, 1965.

Reitz, W. E., and Keil, W. E., 'Behavioral Treatment of an Exhibitionist', in *Journal of Behavior Therapy and Experimental Psychiatry*, 1971, Vol. 2 (1), pp. 67–9.

Resnik, H. L., 'Eroticized Repetitive Hangings: A Form of Self-destructive Behavior', in *American Journal of Psychotherapy*, 1972, Vol. 26 (1), pp. 4–21.

Reuben, D., *How to Get More out of Sex*, W. H. Allen, London, 1976.

Revitch, E., and Weiss, R. G., 'The Paedophilic Offender', in *Diseases of the Nervous System*, 23, 1962.

Rieber, I., and Sigusch, V., 'Psychosurgery on Sex Offenders and Sexual "Deviants" in West Germany', in *Archives of Sexual Behavior*, 1979, Vol. 8 (6), pp. 523–7.

Roberts, J. M., *The Pelican History of the World*, Pelican Books, Harmondsworth, Middlesex, 1980.

Robertson, M., and Amnesty International, *Torture in the Eighties*, Amnesty International Publications, London, 1984.

Robinson, P. A., *The Sexual Radicals*, Granada, London, 1972.

Roger, J., *Sex, Spirit and You*, Baraka Books, New York, 1977.

Rosen, I. (ed.), *Sexual Deviation*, Oxford University Press, 1979.

Rosen, R. C., and Kopel, S. A., 'Penile Plethysmography and Biofeedback in the Treatment of a Transvestite-exhibitionist', in *Journal of Consulting and Clinical Psychology*, 1977, Vol. 45 (5), pp. 908–16.

Rosen, R. C., and Kopel, S. A., 'Role of Penile Tumescence Measurement in the Behavioral Treatment of Sexual Deviation: Issues of Validity', in *Journal of Consulting and Clinical Psychology*, 1978, Vol. 16 (6), 1519–21.

Rossi, A. S. (ed.), *The Feminist Papers*, Bantam Books, New York, 1974.

Rossman, P., *Sexual Experiences between Men and Boys*, Maurice Temple Smith, London, 1985.

Rowbotham, S., *Woman's Consciousness, Man's World*, Penguin Books, Harmondsworth, Middlesex, 1973.

Russell, Lord of Liverpool, *The Scourge of the Swastika*, Cassell, London, 1954.

Rycroft, C., *A Critical Dictionary of Psychoanalysis*, Penguin Books, Harmondsworth, Middlesex, 1972.

Sadger, J., *Sie liehre von geschlechtsverirrungen*, Brezona, Vienna, 1921.

Safran, C., 'Plain Talk about the New Approach to Sexual Pleasure', in *Redbook*, March 1976.

Saghir, M. T., and Robins, E., 'Homosexuality: 1. Sexual Behavior of the Female Homosexual', in *Archives of General Psychiatry*, 1969, Vol. 20 (2), pp. 192–201.

Schmidt, G., and Schorsch, E., 'Psychosurgery of Sexually Deviant Patients: Review and Analysis of New Empirical Findings', in *Archives of Sexual Behavior*, 1981, Vol. 10 (3), pp. 301–23.

Schneir, M. (ed.), *Feminism*, Vintage Books, New York. 1972.

Schoenfeld, E., *Jealousy*, Pinnacle Books, New York, 1979.

Schoettle, U. C., 'Treatment of the Child Pornography Patient', in *American Journal of Psychiatry*, 1980, Vol. 137 (9), pp. 1109–10.

Scobie, A., and Taylor, A. J., 'Perversions Ancient and Modern: 1. Agalmatophilia, the Statue Syndrome', in *Journal of the History of the Behavioral Sciences*, 1975, Vol. 11 (1), pp. 49–54.

Selkin, J., 'Rape', in *Psychology Today*, January 1975.

Sen, K. M., *Hinduism*, Penguin Books, Harmondsworth, Middlesex, 1969.

Serber, M., 'Shame Aversion Therapy', *Journal of Behavior Therapy and Experimental Psychiatry*, 1970, 1, pp. 213–15.

Shapiro, L., 'Of Human Bondage', in *Time Out*, 24–30 January 1985.

Sheehy, G., *Passages*, E. P. Dutton, New York, 1976.

Shephard, M., *Beyond Sex Therapy*, Penthouse Press, New York, 1975.

Sherwin, R. V., 'Sodomy', in R. Slovenko (ed.), *Sexual Behavior and the Law*, Springfield, Ill., 1965.

Silber, S. J., *The Male*, Charles Scribner's Sons, New York, 1981.

Simpson, M., and Schill, T., 'Patrons of Massage Parlors: Some Facts and Figures', *Archives of Sexual Behavior*, 6 (6), November 1977.

Skinner, B. F., *Science and Human Behavior*, Macmillan, New York, 1953.

Smith, S. R., 'Voyeurism: A Review of the Literature', in *Archives of Sexual Behavior*, 1976, Vol. 5 (6), pp. 585–609.

Socarides, C. W., 'Sexual Perversion and the Fear of Engulfment', in *International Journal of Psychoanalytic Psychotherapy*, 1973, Vol. 2 (4), pp. 432–48.

Socarides, C. W., 'The Psychoanalytic Theory of Homosexuality: with Special Reference to Therapy', in I. Rosen (ed.), *Sexual Deviation*, Oxford University Press, 1979.

Solanas, V., *SCUM Manifesto*, The Matriarchy Study Group, London, 1983.

Statutes of the Republic of South Africa – Criminal Law and Procedure: Immorality Act, No. 23 of 1957, Amended, 1967, 1969. Group Areas Act, No. 36 of 1966, Amended, 1969, 1972, 1974, 1975, 1977, 1978, 1979, 1982.

Steinem, G., *Outrageous Acts and Everyday Rebellions*, New American Library, New York, 1983.

Steinmetz, S., 'The Battered Husbands', *in Time*, March 1978.

Stern, M., and Stern, A., *Sex in the Soviet Union*, W. H. Allen, London, 1981.

Stoller, R. J., 'A Contribution to the Study of Gender Identity', in *International Journal of Psychoanalysis*, 1964, 45, pp. 220–26.

Stoller, R. J., 'Passing in the Continuum of Gender Identity', in J. Marmer (ed.), *Sexual Inversion: The Multiple Roots of Homosexuality*, Basic Books, New York, 1965.

Stoller, R. J., 'Transvestites' Women', in *American Journal of Psychiatry*, 1967, 124, pp. 333–9.

Stoller, R. J., 'The Term "Transvestism"', in *Archives of General Psychiatry*, 1971, 24, pp. 230–7.

Stoller, R. J., 'The Gender Disorders', in I. Rosen (ed.), *Sexual Deviation*, Oxford University Press, 1979.

Stoller, R. J., 'Erotic Vomiting', in *Archives of Sexual Behavior*, 1982, Vol. 11 (4), pp. 361–5.

Stolorow, R. D., and Grand, H. T., 'A Partial Analysis of a Perversion Involving Bugs', in *International Journal of Psychoanalysis*, 1973, Vol. 54 (3), pp. 349–50.

Stone, L., *The Family, Sex and Marriage in England 1500–1800*, Penguin Books, Harmondsworth, Middlesex, 1979.

Storr, A., *Sexual Deviation*, Penguin Books, Harmondsworth, Middlesex, 1977.

Sturup, G. K., 'Treatment of Sexual Offenders in Herstedvester, Denmark: The Rapists', in *Acta Psychiatrica Scandinavica*, 1968, 44 (suppl. 204), pp. 1–62.

Sturup, G. K., 'Castration: The Total Treatment', in H. L. Resnik and M. E. Wolfgang (eds.), *Sexual Behaviors: Social, Clinical, and Legal Aspects*, Little, Brown, Boston, Mass., 1972.

Stutley, J., and Stutley, M., *A Dictionary of Hinduism*, Routledge & Kegan Paul, London, 1977.

Swanson, D. W., 'Adult Sexual Abuse of Children: The Man and Circumstances', in *Diseases of the Nervous System*, 1968, 29 (10), pp. 677–83.

Szasz, T., *Sex: Facts, Frauds and Follies*, Basil Blackwell, Oxford, 1980.

Szasz, T., *Sex by Prescription*, Anchor Press, New York, 1980.

Talese, G., *Thy Neighbour's Wife*, William Collins, London, 1980.

Tannahill, R., *Sex in History*, Hamish Hamilton, London, 1980.

Tanner, L. B. (ed.), *Voices from Women's Liberation*, New American Library, New York, 1970.

Taylor, G. R., *Sex in History*, Thames & Hudson, London, 1953.

Tollison, C. D., and Adams, H. E., *Sexual Disorders*, Gardner Press, New York, 1979.

Tollison, C. D., Adams, H. E., and Tollison, J. W., 'Physiological Measurement of Sexual Arousal in Homosexual, Bisexual and Heterosexual Males', unpublished MS., University of Georgia, cited in *supra*.

Toner, J. D., *The Facts of Rape*, Arrow Books, London, 1977.

Unwin, J. D., *Sex and Culture*, Oxford University Press, 1934.

Van Putten, T., and Fawzy, F. I., 'Sex Conversion Surgery in a Man with Severe Gender Dysphoria: A Tragic Outcome', in *Archives of General Psychiatry*, 1976, Vol. 33 (6), pp. 751–3.

Vial, G., *Matters of Fact and Fiction*, Granada, London, 1977.

Vilar, E., *The Polygamous Sex*, W. H. Allen, London, 1976.

Vogt, J. H., 'Five Cases of Transsexualism in Females', in *Acta Psychiatrica Scandinavica*, Vol. 44 (1), pp. 62–88.

Wagner, M. K., 'A Case of Public Masturbation Treated by Operant Conditioning', in *Journal of Child Psychology and Psychiatry and Allied Disciplines*, 1968, Vol. 9 (1), pp. 61–5.

Wakeling, A., 'A General Psychiatric Approach to Sexual Deviation', in I. Rosen (ed.), *Sexual Deviation*, Oxford University Press, 1979.

Walker, K. (ed.), Burton, Sir Richard, and Arbuthnot, F. F. (trans.), *The Kama Sutra of Vatsyayana*, Kimber Pocket Editions, London, 1963.

Wallace, I., Wallace, A., Wallechinsky, D., and Wallace, S., *The Intimate Sex Lives of Famous People*, Arrow Books, London, 1981.

Walmsley, R., and White, K., *Sexual Offences: Consent and Sentencing*, Home Office Research Studies No. 54, HMSO, London, 1979.

Walton, A. H. (ed.), *The Perfumed Garden*, Granada, London, 1982.

Warner, N., 'Parliament and the Law', in B. Galloway (ed.), *Prejudice and Pride: Discrimination against Gay People in Modern Britain*, Routledge & Kegan Paul, London, 1983.

Warren, C. A., *Identity and Community in the Gay World*, John Wiley, New York, 1974.

Watts, A., *Myth and Ritual in Christianity*, Thames & Hudson, London, 1954.

Weil, S., *The Need for Roots*, Harper & Row, New York, 1971.

Weiss, P., 'Porn Martyr', in *Forum*, 1984.

West, D. J., 'Adult Sexual Interest in Children: Implications for Social Control', in M. Cook and K. Howells (eds.), *Adult Sexual Interest in Children*, Academic Press, London, 1981.

White, M. J., 'The Statue Syndrome: Perversion? Fantasy? Anecdote?', in *Journal of Sex Research*, 1978, Vol. 14 (4), pp. 246–9.

Whiteley, S., *Dealing with Deviants*, Hogarth Press, London, 1972.

Williams, L. N., 'Buggery – Maximum Punishment Varying with Specified Facts – Whether Each Maximum Implies a Distinct Offence (Great Britain)', in *Criminal Law Review*, 1984, pp. 366–7.

Wilson, C., *Order of Assassins: The Psychology of Murder*, Rupert Hart-Davis, London, 1972.

Wilson, C., *The Occult*, Granada, London, 1975.

Wilson, C., and Pitman, P., *Encyclopaedia of Murder*, Pan Books, London, 1984.

Wilson, E., *What Is To Be Done about Violence Against Women?*, Penguin Books, Harmondsworth, Middlesex, 1983.

Wilson, G., *Love and Instinct*, Maurice Temple Smith, London, 1981.

Wise, T. N., 'Urethral Manipulation: An Unusual Paraphilia', in *Journal of Sex and Marital Therapy*, 1982, Vol. 8 (3), pp. 222–7.

Wolfe, L., *The Cosmo Report*, Corgi Books, London, 1982.

Wolff, C., *Love between Women*, Harper & Row, New York, 1971.

Wollman, L., and Lottner, L., *Eating Your Way to a Better Sex Life: The Complete Guide to Sexual Nutrition*, Pinnacle Books, New York, 1983.

Young, P. T., *Motivation and Emotion*, John Wiley, New York, 1961.

Zavitzianos, G., 'Fetishism and Exhibitionism in the Female and Their Relationship to Psychopathy and Kleptomania', in *International Journal of Psycho-Analysis*, 1971, Vol. 52 (3), pp. 297–305.

Zechnich, R., 'Exhibitionism: Genesis, Dynamics and Treatment', in *Psychiatric Quarterly*, 1971, Vol. 45 (1), pp. 70–75.

Index